"Evangelicalism is said to be in the midst of an identity crisis. If so, it would be hard to imagine a more inspiring or compelling remedy than that offered by Garth M. Rosell in *The Surprising Work of God*. Well-chosen quotations from the writings, speeches, and personal correspondence of Ockenga, Graham, and others reflect Rosell's extensive research and engage the reader with their brilliance, spiritual insight, and enduring relevance. Rosell's convincing admiration for his subjects is balanced, however, by many salutary reminders of how the heroes of his story, like their modern successors, struggled to live up to their convictions. Indeed, if modern evangelicalism is to resolve its identity crisis, it needs to recapture the vibrant and holistic faith of its founding fathers and, wherever possible, go beyond them not by undermining their vision of civility, social transformation, and cultural engagement but by attempting more faithfully to fulfill it."

—**Gordon P. Hugenberger**, senior minister, Park Street Church, Boston

"Garth Rosell has made one of the most significant contributions to the history of American twentieth-century evangelicalism. Not only does he bring to this project his gifts as a noted historian but he also brings the text to life with insights gleaned from his personal friendships and working relationships with Harold John Ockenga and Billy Graham. This is must reading for anyone who wants to know more about the phenomenon of contemporary American evangelicalism. And it is a fascinating and insightful read for those of us who call ourselves evangelicals and want to know more about the individuals and events that have shaped who we are during the past half century."

—**John A. Huffman**, pastor, St. Andrew's Presbyterian Church, Newport Beach, California; chairman of the board, Christianity Today International

"As I neared the end of this book, I contacted our seminary students and told them that this is a must read. Much more than a history of the evangelical movement in the mid-twentieth century, Garth Rosell's *The Surprising Work of God* is a compelling charge for today's Christian leaders. Presented as the story of two friends, Harold John Ockenga and Billy Graham, this carefully detailed narrative (don't miss the footnotes!) tells of what happens when a rising generation commits to believe with biblical conviction and to move forward with courage. As I turned each page, I began to believe anew in how the sovereign work of God will once more surprise us as we, the people of God, set our agenda on building bridges, not walls, for his glory. It was a new day for Ockenga, Graham, and their band of brothers as they believed that nothing would be impossible through God. This book will leave you in that same realm of expectations for our generation."

—**Barry Corey**, president, Biola University

"The American evangelical movement today owes its strong cultural presence and evangelistic vigor to a generation of men and women who are in danger of being forgotten. Garth Rosell offers us a family album filled with both panoramic views of a growing movement and intimate snapshots of those who rode the crest of the wave of revival that was about to break on mid-century America. It's an exciting story, and as the son of one of those early revivalists, Rosell is just the person to tell it."

—**Jennifer Trafton**, managing editor, *Christian History & Biography*

THE
SURPRISING
WORK OF GOD

Harold John Ockenga, Billy Graham,
and the Rebirth of Evangelicalism

****

GARTH M. ROSELL

B

Baker Academic

a division of Baker Publishing Group
Grand Rapids, Michigan

Published by Baker Academic
a division of Baker Publishing Group
P.O. Box 6287, Grand Rapids, MI 49516-6287
www.bakeracademic.com

Printed in the United States of America

Library of Congress Cataloging-in-Publication Data
Rosell, Garth.
    The surprising work of God : Harold John Ockenga, Billy Graham, and the rebirth of Evangelicalism / Garth M. Rosell.
        p.   cm.
    Includes bibliographical references and index.
    ISBN 978-0-8010-3570-8 (pbk.)
    1. Ockenga, Harold John, 1905– 2. Graham, Billy, 1918– 3. Evangelicalism—United States—History. I. Title.
BX7260.O3R67 2008
277.3′0825—dc22   2008005063

For Janie
my dearest friend

CONTENTS

ILLUSTRATIONS

PREFACE

This book is the fulfillment of an old promise—one that I made to Audrey Williamson Ockenga not long after her husband's death in 1985.[1] Having decided to donate Harold John Ockenga's papers to Gordon-Conwell Theological Seminary, where he had served as president for nearly a decade, Audrey asked if I would be willing to use the papers to tell the story of the mid-twentieth century rebirth of evangelicalism and the role her husband had played in helping give the movement its shape and direction.[2]

Those who were privileged to know Ockenga's charming wife will understand why I so readily agreed to her request.[3] But I also had reasons of my own for accepting the assignment. Early in 1978, President Ockenga had written to invite me to come to Gordon-Conwell Theological Seminary to serve as academic dean and professor of church history.[4] What initially drew

1. Harold John Ockenga was born July 6, 1905, and died February 8, 1985. He is buried in the Hamilton Cemetery on Bay Road in Hamilton, Massachusetts, across from the historic First Congregational Church of Hamilton (originally the Third Parish of Ipswich).

2. The Harold John Ockenga Papers are currently housed at the Ockenga Institute on the campus of Gordon-Conwell Theological Seminary in South Hamilton, Massachusetts, and consist of several thousand books and more than one hundred archival boxes of sermons, letters, notes, articles, institutional records, various collected materials, artifacts, and personal memorabilia. Ockenga was president of Gordon-Conwell Theological Seminary from its founding in 1969 until his retirement in 1979. See Garth M. Rosell, "America's Hour Has Struck," *Christian History & Biography*, Fall 2006, 12–19; Garth M. Rosell, "A Godly Heritage," *Contact*, Winter 2007, 26–29; Garth M. Rosell, ed., *The Vision Continues: Centennial Papers of Gordon-Conwell Theological Seminary* (South Hamilton, MA: GCTS, 1992).

3. Audrey Williamson Ockenga was born June 30, 1909, and died March 24, 1988, almost three years after her husband. She is buried near him in the Hamilton Cemetery. Her children had the words from Proverbs 31:26 inscribed on the memorial stone: "She openeth her mouth with wisdom, and in her tongue is the law of kindness."

4. Harold John Ockenga to Garth M. Rosell, March 22, 1978, and Rosell to Ockenga, March 30, 1978, Rosell Papers.

me to accept his invitation, and what has kept me at the seminary ever since, was the remarkable vision of spiritual, cultural, and institutional renewal that not only gave birth to Gordon-Conwell and scores of other evangelical institutions but also helped to transform much of the religious landscape in America and throughout the world. At the core of that vision was a single, powerful idea: that all of creation belongs to God. "There is not a square inch in the whole domain of our human existence," to borrow the stirring words with which Abraham Kuyper concluded his inaugural address at the Free University of Amsterdam, "over which Christ, who is Sovereign over *all,* does not cry: 'Mine!'"[5]

Speaking at the National Association of Evangelicals Constitutional Convention in 1943, Harold John Ockenga voiced similar convictions.[6] "I believe," declared the pastor of Boston's Park Street Church, "that the United States of America has been assigned a destiny comparable to that of ancient Israel." Yet, he lamented, America "is passing through a crisis which is enmeshing western civilization. Confusion exists on every hand. We are living in a very difficult and bewildering time." The "kingdom of hell," with its "indifference to God," rampant "secularism," and preoccupation with fleshly interests, is "at hand."

"The hour has arrived," Ockenga argued, "when the people of this nation must 'think deeply or be damned.' We must examine our direction, our condition and our destiny. We must recognize that we are standing at the crossroads and that there are only two ways that lie open before us. One is the road of the rescue of western civilization by a re-emphasis on and revival of evangelical Christianity. The other is a return to the Dark Ages of heathendom which powerful force is emerging in every phase of world life today." There is "a 'now or never' urgency in this matter. The time to strike is here. The iron is hot. The door is open. The need is great." Indeed, the world is waiting "for the clear cut, definite, sane and progressive leadership which can inaugurate a new era for Christian influence and effectiveness."[7]

For many of the weary warriors of the bitter fundamentalist-modernist battles, into which so many Christians had been drawn during the 1920s and 1930s, Ockenga's challenge must have come as a breath of fresh air.[8] Rather

5. Abraham Kuyper, "Sphere Sovereignty," in *Abraham Kuyper: A Centennial Reader*, ed. James D. Bratt (Grand Rapids: Eerdmans, 1998), 488.

6. Ockenga's presidential address was delivered to the 148 delegates who had assembled at the LaSalle Hotel in Chicago on the morning of May 4, 1943. For the early development of the NAE, see Arthur H. Matthews, *Standing Up, Standing Together: The Emergence of the National Association of Evangelicals* (Carol Stream, IL: National Association of Evangelicals, 1992).

7. Quotations are taken from Harold John Ockenga, "Christ for America," *United Evangelical Action,* May 4, 1943, 3–4, 6. A manuscript version of this address can be found in the Ockenga Papers.

8. For a discussion of the fundamentalist-modernist controversy, see George M. Marsden, *Fundamentalism and American Culture: The Shaping of Twentieth-Century Evangelicalism, 1870–1925* (New York: Oxford University Press, 1980).

than a continuation of the strategy of withdrawal, here was a challenge to reclaim the culture and its institutions. Instead of retreat, here was a call to advance the gospel throughout the world. In place of discouragement and fear, here was new hope for spiritual power and refreshment. Rather than endless argumentation, division, and fragmentation, here at last was the possibility of united evangelical action.[9] Harold John Ockenga's stirring address, so enthusiastically received by most of the delegates, became a kind of manifesto for the resurgent evangelicalism that came to dominate mid-twentieth-century America. Rooted in the rich soil of America's Great Awakening, this "New Evangelicalism," as Ockenga was to label the movement by the late 1940s, sought to join together Christians of many denominations to reclaim every segment of God's creation.[10] United by a shared theological focus (the cross), a shared authority (the Bible), a shared experience (conversion), a shared mission (worldwide evangelization), and a shared vision (the spiritual renewal of the church and society), the burgeoning evangelical movement set out to recapture the culture for Christ.[11]

Centers of learning had to be reengaged. "We have a need of new life from Christ in our nation," Ockenga was convinced, and "that need first of all is intellectual." Unless "the Church can produce some thinkers who will lead us in positive channels our spiral of degradation will continue downward." Furthermore, he continued, "there is great need in the field of statesmanship." Where were the political leaders "in high places of our nation," he asked, with "a knowledge of and regard for the principles of the Word of God?" The need was "even more evident in the business world," he continued, where models of Christian integrity had become a rarity. Most of all, he concluded,

9. See my introduction to essays by Mark Noll, Timothy Smith, and Bruce Shelley in Garth M. Rosell, ed., *The Evangelical Landscape: Essays on the American Evangelical Tradition* (Grand Rapids: Baker Academic, 1996) for an earlier version of the argument.

10. Harold John Ockenga, "The New Evangelicalism," *Park Street Spire*, February 1958, 2–7. The terms, "new evangelicalism" or "neo-evangelicalism" were coined by Ockenga in the late 1940s and used widely for a decade or so. By the late 1950s, however, Ockenga, Edward John Carnell, and a number of other "new evangelical" leaders increasingly replaced the new terminology with designations such as "evangelicalism," "biblical Christianity," or "historic orthodoxy." See, for example, Carnell to Ockenga, December 4, 1958, Ockenga Papers.

11. For an excellent introduction to the evangelical movement, see Douglas A. Sweeney, *The American Evangelical Story: A History of the Movement* (Grand Rapids: Baker Academic, 2005); and David W. Bebbington and Mark A. Noll, gen. eds., A History of Evangelicalism: People, Movements and Ideas in the English-Speaking World, a series of five major studies published by InterVarsity. For a listing of the broad range of published studies on evangelicalism, three bibliographies are especially helpful: Norris A. Magnuson and William G. Travis, *American Evangelicalism: An Annotated Bibliography* (West Cornwall, CT: Locust Hill, 1990); Edith L. Blumhofer and Joel A. Carpenter, *Twentieth-Century Evangelicalism: A Guide to the Sources* (New York: Garland, 1990); and Robert D. Shuster, James Stambaugh, and Ferne Weimer, *Researching Modern Evangelicalism* (New York: Greenwood, 1990). See also the bibliographical essay by Leonard I. Sweet in Sweet, ed., *The Evangelical Tradition in America* (Macon, GA: Mercer University Press, 1997), 1–86.

there must be a new power in personal life. Unless this message of salvation which we hold to be the cardinal center of our Christian faith really does save individuals from sin, from sinful habits, from dishonesty, impurity and avarice, unless it keeps them in the midst of temptation, what good is it? Christians today are altogether too much like the pagan and heathen world both in actions and in life.[12]

What the church needs most at the present time and in the future, he argued, "is *saints*, great Christians—Christ-loving men and women." Salvation would be found neither in "a new economic-social order" nor a "political new deal" but rather in "Bible Christianity, with Christ as the leader and eternity in view."[13]

After years of discouragement, an increasing number of Christians seemed eager to heed Ockenga's call and to embrace his vision. Indeed, as the movement grew, spurred in large measure by the powerful youth movements of the 1930s and 1940s and the great citywide crusades that marked the 1950s, the burgeoning evangelical movement became increasingly global in its vision and practice. Two centuries of exceptional missionary expansion coupled with the impact of two world wars had helped reawaken the American church to its larger global responsibilities.[14] "Over the past century," Philip Jenkins argues, "the center of gravity in the Christian world has shifted inexorably southward, to Africa, Asia, and Latin America."[15] The same movement toward the Global South, as those regions have come to be called, can be charted within the evangelical movement itself.[16]

While the reality of this massive shift has only begun to dawn on many within the American church, its roots can be seen at least as far back as the founding of the church at Pentecost, and its missionary expressions can be found in virtually every era of Christian history. Consequently, it should come as no surprise that at the very heart of the evangelical awakening of the mid-twentieth century was a passion for worldwide evangelization. From their earliest years, in fact, youth movements such as Youth for Christ, Pentecostal outpourings such as those that occurred at Azusa Street in 1906, and ecumenical organizations such as the National Association of Evangelicals (NAE) were

12. Ockenga, "Christ for America."
13. Ibid.
14. "One of the most striking facts of our time," wrote Kenneth Scott Latourette, "is the global extension of Christianity." See Latourette, *The Emergence of a World Christian Community* (New Haven: Yale University Press, 1949), iii.
15. Philip Jenkins, *The Next Christendom: The Coming of Global Christianity* (New York: Oxford University Press, 2002), 2. See also Todd M. Johnson and Sun Young Chung, "Tracking Global Christianity's Statistical Centre of Gravity, AD 33–AD 2100," *International Review of Mission* 93, no. 369 (April 2004): 166–81; and "Describing the Worldwide Christian Phenomenon," *International Bulletin of Missionary Research* 2 (April 2005): 80–84.
16. See Donald M. Lewis, ed., *Christianity Reborn: The Global Expansion of Evangelicalism in the Twentieth Century* (Grand Rapids: Eerdmans, 2004).

global in their aspirations and vision.[17] Indeed, it was not by chance that Beatenberg (Switzerland) was selected as the geographical site for the most significant mid-century gathering of evangelical youth leaders, the Youth for Christ Congress for World Evangelization held in August of 1948. As a result of these and subsequent efforts, millions of Christians within America and throughout the world were drawn into evangelicalism's burgeoning ranks and shaped by the vision that Ockenga had so forcefully proclaimed at the National Association of Evangelicals Constitutional Convention in 1943.

Most of the events and personalities of the 1940s and 1950s are now forgotten. My own recollections would have remained equally vague, I suspect, were it not for the fact that I grew up in the home of one of the movement's most prominent leaders. Among my earliest childhood memories were the occasions when I joined with thousands of others to hear my father, "Merv" Rosell, preach or went with my parents or with friends to hear Jimmie Johnson, Billy Graham, Bob Pierce, Torrey Johnson, Jack Wyrtzen, Charles E. Fuller, J. Stratton Shufelt, Grady Wilson, Percy Crawford, Jack Shuler, Amy Lee Stockton, Oswald Smith, T. W. Wilson, and a host of others proclaim the gospel through preaching and music to the burgeoning crowds that gathered to hear them.

Since my father spoke of them so often, many of these evangelists (along with the team of musicians who often traveled with them) seemed almost like part of our extended family. Some even visited our home to enjoy good conversation, eat some of my mother's wonderful cooking, or sign her tablecloth. They told wonderful stories; wrote beautiful letters to one another; published books and articles; played pranks; gave each other nicknames (on occasion, for example, Billy Graham called my father "Spike"); looked after those in need; laughed, wept, and prayed together; and loved God with all their heart, soul, mind, and strength.

I loved being around them. I loved hearing them preach. I loved having my father tell me stories about them. But most of all, I remember the sense of absolute wonder and awe that would suddenly come over my father when his comments would turn, as they invariably did, to a discussion of the surprising work of God in their midst. And I remember the terrible urgency to preach the gospel that seemed to grip my father and all of his preacher friends. Like Jonathan Edwards before them, they were absolutely amazed that God had

17. See, for example, Cecil M. Robeck Jr., *The Azusa Street Mission and Revival: The Birth of the Global Pentecostal Movement* (Nashville: Thomas Nelson, 2006); *Youth for Christ* magazine, special revival issue, October 1950; Mel Larson, *Young Man on Fire: The Story of Torrey Johnson and Youth for Christ* (Chicago: Youth Publications, 1945); Bruce L. Shelley, "The Rise of Evangelical Youth Movements," *Fides et Historia*, January 1986, 47–63; Vinson Synan, *Century of the Holy Spirit: 100 Years of Pentecostal and Charismatic Renewal, 1901–2001* (Nashville: Thomas Nelson, 2001); and Karla D. Poewe, ed., *Charismatic Christianity as a Global Culture* (Columbia: University of South Carolina Press, 1994).

chosen them. They were thrilled to be a part of it all, of course, but they were absolutely certain that they had not caused it, and they all knew in their heart of hearts that if they dared to take even the smallest measure of credit from that which belonged solely to the sovereign Lord of the universe, "their lips would turn to clay," as they often phrased it.

It is the story of those remarkable individuals and those amazing years that I have sought to tell in the following pages. The participants were far from perfect, of course, and what began here in America with such promise in the 1930s, 1940s, and 1950s was all too quickly overrun by angry divisions and personal animosities. Yet there is still much to learn, as my father often remarked, from an era that was so profoundly marked by "the pure and holy presence and power of God" and so deeply touched by "the white heat of revival."

The surprising work of God, of course, has not ceased. While the flame of revival may have become more difficult to find in all the familiar places, it appears to be burning with white heat once again among the diverse peoples of the Global South.[18] Perhaps we simply need to look for it with fresh eyes in some less familiar places.

---

18. Philip Jenkins, *The New Faces of Christianity: Believing the Bible in the Global South* (New York: Oxford University Press, 2006).

1

THE SURPRISING WORK OF GOD

On a crisp New England morning, hundreds of friends and family gathered at the First Congregational Church in Hamilton to bid farewell to Harold John Ockenga.[1] There to deliver the eulogy was an old friend. "He was a giant among giants," reflected Billy Graham. "Nobody outside of my family influenced me more than he did. I never made a major decision without first calling and asking his advice and counsel. I thank God for his friendship and for his life."[2]

The friendship between Ockenga and Graham is of more than passing significance for the study of contemporary evangelicalism.[3] For thirty-five years, from

1. Harold John Ockenga died of cancer on February 8, 1985, at the age of seventy-nine. The funeral service was held at 11:00 a.m. on Monday, February 11, 1985, at the Hamilton Congregational Church near the home in which Ockenga died. The service was presided over by Paul Toms, pastor of Park Street Church in Boston, and Harold Bussell, pastor of the Hamilton Congregational Church. See Randy Frame, "Modern Evangelicalism Mourns the Loss of One of Its Founding Fathers," *Christianity Today*, March 15, 1985, 34–36. Memorial services were also held at Park Street Church and in the chapel of Gordon-Conwell Theological Seminary.

2. Billy Graham, "Harold John Ockenga: A Man Who Walked with God," *Christianity Today*, March 15, 1985, 35.

3. Of the scores of books about Billy Graham's life and work, two deserve special mention: *Just as I Am: The Autobiography of Billy Graham* (San Francisco: HarperSanFrancisco, 1997); and William Martin, *A Prophet with Honor: The Billy Graham Story* (New York: William Morrow, 1991). For Harold John Ockenga, see Harold Lindsell, *Park Street Prophet: A Life of Harold Ockenga* (Wheaton:

Harold John Ockenga and Billy Graham
(courtesy of Gordon-Conwell Libraries)

the Boston Revival of 1950 to Ockenga's death in 1985, these two men—perhaps more than any others—embodied, symbolized, and guided a burgeoning and increasingly worldwide evangelical movement. By mid-century, Harold John Ockenga was widely known as "Mr. Evangelical," and during the 1950s and 1960s, as historian George Marsden suggests, the broadest and perhaps most universally accepted definition of an evangelical was simply "anyone who likes Billy Graham."[4]

The distinctive shape and direction of contemporary evangelicalism owes more than a little to the unique blending of geographical regions, theological perspectives, collegial networks, personal styles, and ministerial experiences of these two remarkable individuals. Born and raised in Chicago, educated in the Midwest and Northeast, and based for most of his professional life in New England, Ockenga became the embodiment of what the old Puritans would have called the "learned pastor."[5] Born in Charlotte, educated in the South and Midwest, and based for most of his professional life in the mountains of North Carolina, Graham came to embody not only the gracious piety of Southern evangelicalism but also the revival fervor and fresh enthusiasm of the great youth movements of the 1930s and 1940s.[6]

Van Kampen, 1951) and John M. Adams, "The Making of a Neo-Evangelical Statesman: The Case of Harold John Ockenga" (PhD diss., Baylor University, 1994).

4. George M. Marsden, *Understanding Fundamentalism and Evangelicalism* (Grand Rapids: Eerdmans, 1991), 6.

5. Born July 6, 1905, Harold John Ockenga was the only son of Herman and Angie Ockenga. Herman Ockenga, who was not a professing Christian during Harold Ockenga's early years, worked for the Chicago Transit Authority and was a sometime grocer. Harold's mother, a devout Methodist, had him baptized in the nearby Austin Presbyterian Church. She and the children often attended the Olivet Methodist Church, on Chicago's west side, where, at the age of eleven, Harold John became a member. Converted in 1916 at an old-fashioned Methodist campground in Des Plaines, Illinois, he went on to pursue academic degrees and/or studies at Taylor University (1923–27), Princeton Theological Seminary (1927–29), Westminster Theological Seminary (1929–30), and the University of Pittsburgh (completing the MA degree in 1934 and the PhD degree in 1939).

6. Born November 7, 1918, William Franklin Graham Jr., known in the early years as "Billy Frank" and later as "Billy," was the oldest of William Franklin and Morrow Coffey Graham's four children. His parents belonged to the Associate Reformed Presbyterian Church in Charlotte, where he was baptized, and they ran a successful four hundred–acre dairy farm. Converted in September of 1934 at

The combination of these two much older religious cultures, forged in the fires of the powerful spiritual awakening that swept across America and around the world during the mid-twentieth century, helped give shape and substance to a movement that many contemporary Christians identify as "evangelicalism." It is this story, pictured in microcosm by the friendship between Harold John Ockenga and Billy Graham, that this book attempts to tell. Linking the steepled church with the revival tent, the aroma of candles with the smell of sawdust, the passion for personal holiness with the love of truth, the quest for purity with the yearning for unity, the comfort of structure with the fresh winds of the Spirit, the majestic organ with the singing saxophone, the three-piece suit with the blue denim jacket, and the first-world with the Global South, the contemporary evangelical movement, as Alister McGrath suggested more than a decade ago, "seems set to continue its upswing into the next millennium."[7]

Understanding the Evangelical Movement

Before we can begin this story, however, we need to take a moment to look back to the beginnings of the movement.[8] There is a sense in which all genuine followers of Jesus Christ—from every corner of the earth and throughout every era of Christian history—can appropriately call themselves "evangelical." After all, the term is taken directly from the Bible. The Greek noun *euangelion* simply means "good news," "glad tidings," or "gospel," and the Greek verb *euangelizesthai* is usually translated "to announce good news" or "to proclaim the gospel."[9] All true followers of Jesus Christ—whose lives have been claimed by the sovereign God, whose sins have been forgiven through the atoning work of Jesus Christ, whose behavior is being transformed by the power of the Holy Spirit, and whose deepest desire is to proclaim in word and deed the good news that "God was in Christ reconciling the world unto

a Mordechai Fowler Ham evangelistic crusade, Graham attended Bob Jones College, the Florida Bible Institute, and Wheaton College. Although he pastored a Baptist church in Western Springs, Graham became increasingly involved with Youth for Christ and eventually agreed to serve on its staff.

7. Alister McGrath, *Evangelicalism and the Future of Christianity* (Downers Grove, IL: InterVarsity, 1995), 10–11. While admitting that there is "evidence of weakness and complacency within [evangelicalism's] substantial ranks," McGrath predicted that "the future of Christianity seems to belong to the movement" (10–11). See also Christian Smith, *American Evangelicalism: Embattled and Thriving* (Chicago: University of Chicago Press, 1998).

8. See Douglas A. Sweeney, *The American Evangelical Story: A History of the Movement* (Grand Rapids: Baker Academic, 2005); Mark A. Noll, *The Rise of Evangelicalism: The Age of Edwards, Whitefield and the Wesleys* (Downers Grove, IL: InterVarsity, 2003); Marsden, *Understanding Fundamentalism and Evangelicalism*; and Randall Balmer, *Blessed Assurance: A History of Evangelicalism in America* (Boston: Beacon, 1999).

9. For a discussion of these terms and their use in Scripture and the early church, see Michael Green, *Evangelism in the Early Church* (Grand Rapids: Eerdmans, 1970), 48–77.

Himself"—can rightly call themselves a "gospel woman," a "born-again man," or an "evangelical Christian."

But not everyone who might properly lay claim to the term *evangelical* has done so. Of the approximately six and a half billion people alive in the world today, slightly more than two billion identify themselves as Christians. Of those two billion Christians, according to some estimates, at least two hundred fifty million can properly be identified as evangelical.[10] The total number may be significantly higher, however, since many Pentecostals, charismatics, and neocharismatics also claim to be evangelical.[11] Whatever figures are used, there is little question that evangelicals make up a substantial and rapidly increasing percentage of world Christianity.[12]

What seems equally clear to those who study global trends is the fact that a growing number of evangelicals now live outside the Western world. "Recent decades have shown the beginning of a major shift in the Christian center of gravity," observed Winston Crawley.

> It is not yet complete and may not be so for many more decades—but it is well under way and appears irreversible. The heartland of Christianity, located in Europe for more than a millennium (with North America recently added), seems sure in the 21st century to be found in what we have called the Third World (or Two-Thirds World). On the most superficial level, numbers themselves reflect the change: the majority of Christians now live outside Europe and North America."[13]

While most historians trace the origins of the modern evangelical movement to sources in either Europe or North America, it should come as no surprise

10. Figures are taken from David B. Barrett, Todd M. Johnson, and Peter Crossing, eds., "Missiometrics 2005: A Global Survey of World Mission," *International Bulletin of Missionary Research* 29, no. 1 (January 2005): 27–30. See also David B. Barrett, George T. Kurian, and Todd M. Johnson, *World Christian Encyclopedia* (New York: Oxford University Press, 2001); and David B. Barrett and Todd M. Johnson, *World Christian Trends* (Pasadena: William Carey Library, 2001).

11. Mark Noll argues: "In the same historical perspective, modern-day Pentecostals must be considered part of the broader evangelical family since they are descended from nineteenth-century leaders who emphasized holiness and the work of the Holy Spirit, and who were themselves decisively shaped by the teaching of several important leaders of the eighteenth-century revivals, especially John and Charles Wesley," *The Rise of Evangelicalism*, 18.

12. I am grateful to Todd M. Johnson, director of the Center for the Study of Global Christianity at Gordon-Conwell Theological Seminary and one of the principal authors of the *World Christian Encyclopedia*, for alerting me to some of these important trends.

13. Winston Crawley, *World Christianity: 1970–2000* (Pasadena: William Carey Library, 2001), 48–49. Crawley estimated in 2000 that 59 percent of Christians lived in Latin America, Africa, Asia, and Oceania (up from only 43.1 percent in 1970). This shift is documented and mapped in Todd M. Johnson and Sun Young Chung, "Tracking Global Christianity's Statistical Centre of Gravity, AD 33–AD 2100," *International Review of Mission* 93, no. 369 (April 2004): 166–81. For similar arguments, see Philip Jenkins, *The Next Christendom: The Coming of Global Christianity* (New York: Oxford University Press, 2002); and Gerald H. Anderson and Thomas F. Stansky, eds., *Mission Trends*, no. 3, *Third World Theologies* (New York: Paulist Press, 1976).

that the movement would spread so quickly to other parts of the world. One of the most distinctive features of evangelicalism has been its passion for world evangelization, the missionary mandate to spread the gospel to each individual and every culture around the globe.[14] So successful were evangelicals' efforts, in fact, that the geographical center of world Christianity has moved from Europe to Africa, and the profile of a typical evangelical Christian now reflects cultures, languages, and patterns of behavior that are largely unknown in the West.[15] It would seem safe to assume, if these trends continue, that the future character and direction of the evangelical movement will be determined largely by the younger churches in what Philip Jenkins calls the Global South.[16] The days of Western hegemony seem to be over. "If I were to buy stock in global Christianity," historian Martin Marty once said, "I would buy it in Pentecostalism."[17]

Although it is difficult to predict with any certainty the future direction of evangelicalism, it is possible to discover a great deal about its past. While the beginnings of the modern evangelical movement can be elusive, most historians now agree that its origins can be found in the great religious revivals that swept across England, Scotland, Ireland, Wales, and, most especially, the American colonies during the eighteenth century.[18] This "series of revivals," historian Mark Noll argues, "marked the origin of a distinctly evangelical history."[19] Known as the Great Awakening in America and the Evangelical Revival in Britain, the work of George Whitefield, John and Charles Wesley, William and Gilbert Tennent, Samuel Davies, Jonathan Edwards, and a host

14. See Andrew F. Walls, *The Missionary Movement in Christian History* (Maryknoll, NY: Orbis, 1996); Timothy C. Tennent, *Christianity at the Religious Roundtable* (Grand Rapids: Baker Academic, 2002); Lamin Sanneh, *Whose Religion Is Christianity? The Gospel Beyond the West* (Grand Rapids: Eerdmans, 2003); Stephen Neill, *A History of Christian Missions*, 2nd ed. (New York: Penguin, 1991); Dana L. Robert, *American Women in Mission* (Macon, GA: Mercer University Press, 1996); Kenneth Scott Latourette, *A History of the Expansion of Christianity*, 7 vols. (Grand Rapids: Zondervan, 1970); and Patrick Johnstone and Jason Mandryk, eds., *Operation World: When We Pray God Works* (Waynesboro, GA: Paternoster USA, 2001).

15. For a discussion of the worldwide growth of evangelical Christianity, see Donald M. Lewis, ed., *Christianity Reborn: The Global Expansion of Evangelicalism in the Twentieth Century* (Grand Rapids: Eerdmans, 2004).

16. Philip Jenkins, *The New Faces of Christianity: Believing the Bible in the Global South* (New York: Oxford University Press, 2006).

17. Quoted in Laurie Goodstein, "More Religion, but Not the Old-Time Kind," *New York Times*, January 9, 2005, sec. 4, pp. 1, 4.

18. For a helpful discussion of origins, see Leonard I. Sweet's bibliographical essay in Sweet, ed., *The Evangelical Tradition in America* (Macon, GA: Mercer University Press, 1997), 1–86; Richard F. Lovelace, *The American Pietism of Cotton Mather: Origins of American Evangelicalism* (Grand Rapids: Christian University Press, 1979); and Noll, *The Rise of Evangelicalism*. Of course, there are some who would argue that the beginnings of modern evangelicalism should primarily be identified with the sixteenth-century Protestant reformers.

19. Noll, *The Rise of Evangelicalism*, 18–19.

of others provided the rich soil in which the new movement could begin to grow.[20]

To understand evangelicalism, therefore, one must first understand the religious revivals in which the movement was born and from which it continues to draw its primary nourishment.[21] Simply stated, when the revival fires have burned most brightly, the evangelical movement has tended to be the strongest and most unified.[22] When religious revivals have waned, evangelicals have tended to become fractious and fragmented. The historical connections between the two, to paraphrase Len Sweet's delightful line, make it as impossible to distinguish evangelicalism from the American revival tradition as it would be "to unscramble a mixed omelette."[23]

The Great Awakening of the Eighteenth Century

"There has been near unanimity across the theological spectrum," Roger Finke and Rodney Stark note, "that something extraordinary happened" in the American colonies during the 1730s and early 1740s.[24] Labeled the Great Awakening by most historians, these were the revivals that helped to launch the modern evangelical movement.[25] We see these beginnings most clearly in

20. David Bebbington, *Evangelicalism in Modern Britain: A History from the 1730s to the 1980s* (Grand Rapids: Baker Academic, 1992); Sweeney, *The American Evangelical Story*; W. R. Ward, *The Protestant Evangelical Awakening* (Cambridge: Cambridge University Press, 1996); and D. G. Hart, ed., *Reckoning With the Past: Historical Essays on American Evangelicalism* (Grand Rapids: Baker Academic, 1995).

21. A religious revival, as I am using the term, is a renewal of spiritual vitality sent to a local church as a gift from the sovereign and merciful God and always producing in the believing community a deeper love for God, a more faithful obedience to God's Word, and a more active concern for one's neighbor. When there is a general sweep of revival across traditional boundaries (denominational, regional, class, etc.) and multiple churches, I generally prefer to use the term "awakening." For information on religious revivals and awakenings, see Richard Owen Roberts, *Revival Literature: An Annotated Bibliography with Biographical and Historical Notices* (Wheaton: Richard Owen Roberts, 1987); Earle E. Cairns, *An Endless Line of Splendor: Revivals and Their Leaders from the Great Awakening to the Present* (Wheaton: Tyndale, 1986); Bernard A. Weisberger, *They Gathered at the River: The Story of the Great Revivalists and Their Impact on Religion in America* (Chicago: Quadrangle, 1966); and Keith J. Hardman, *Seasons of Refreshing: Evangelism and Revivals in America* (Grand Rapids: Baker Books, 1994).

22. Robert Finke and Rodney Stark have noted the continuing debate among historians and social scientists as to "the causes of these awakenings," *The Churching of America, 1776–1990* (New Brunswick, NJ: Rutgers University Press, 1992), 87.

23. See Sweet, *The Evangelical Tradition in America*, 1. Reflecting on historian William G. McLoughlin's famous comment that the "story of American Evangelicalism is the story of America itself in the years 1800 to 1900," Sweet argued that "it would be as difficult to unscramble a mixed omelette as to separate Evangelicalism from nineteenth-century American culture."

24. Finke and Stark, *The Churching of America*, 87.

25. Not all historians, of course, have been comfortable with the term "Great Awakening." See Jon Butler, *Awash in a Sea of Faith: Christianizing the American People* (Cambridge, MA: Harvard

the "debates" between Jonathan Edwards[26] and Charles Chauncy[27] over the nature of the revivals that were breaking out in towns and villages throughout the Massachusetts Bay Colony.[28] Like many New England pastors, Chauncy had watched the spread of religious revivals with both fascination and growing alarm. Soon convinced that this new wave of "enthusiasm" would do significant damage to the more orderly and reasonable style of congregational life that he clearly preferred, the pastor of Boston's First Church set out on a tour of New England to observe firsthand what was taking place. Far from allaying his fears, his travels prompted him to write a lengthy treatise titled *Seasonable Thoughts on the State of Religion in New England*. Documenting what he believed to be the "many and great Mistakes" of the revivals, *Seasonable Thoughts* established Chauncy as the leader of the Old Lights, an emerging anti-revival party within New England congregationalism, and it provided the movement with its "first comprehensive statement of the new American rationalism."[29]

The Emergence of New Light Evangelicalism

While admitting that some "errors" had accompanied the revivals, Jonathan Edwards was convinced that "the surprising work of God" in Northampton,

---

University Press, 1990) for an alternative view. For a discussion of the Great Awakening, see Joseph Tracy, *The Great Awakening* (Edinburgh: Banner of Truth, 1997); Charles H. Maxson, *The Great Awakening in the Middle Colonies* (Chicago: University of Chicago Press, 1920); Edwin Scott Gaustad, *The Great Awakening in New England* (New York: Harper & Brothers, 1957); Wesley M. Gewehr, *The Great Awakening in Virginia* (Durham, NC: Duke University Press, 1930); and J. J. Bumsted, ed., *The Great Awakening* (Waltham, MA: Blaisdell, 1970).

26. Jonathan Edwards (1703–58) was pastor of the Congregational Church in Northampton, Massachusetts. See George M. Marsden, *Jonathan Edwards: A Life* (New Haven: Yale University Press, 2003); and Iain H. Murray, *Jonathan Edwards: A New Biography* (Edinburgh: Banner of Truth, 1987). The best collection of Edwards' writings can be found in the multivolume *Works of Jonathan Edwards* currently being produced by Yale University Press. See esp. C. C. Goen, ed., *The Great Awakening*, vol. 4 of *The Works of Jonathan Edwards* (New Haven: Yale University Press, 1972). Professor Goen's extended introduction to this volume (pp. 1–95) is one of the best introductions to Jonathan Edwards available in print.

27. Charles Chauncy (1705–87) was pastor of the First Church in Boston. See Charles H. Lippy, *Seasonable Revolutionary: The Mind of Charles Chauncy* (Princeton, NJ: Princeton University Press, 1972).

28. This was not a debate in the classic sense. Rather, what we have are a series of written documents describing the position taken by each man in response to the religious revivals that had broken out in many locations throughout New England. The documents to which I refer are Edwards's *Distinguishing Marks* (1741); Chauncy's *Enthusiasm Described and Caution'd Against* (1742); Edwards's *Thoughts on the Revival of Religion* (1742); and Chauncy's *Seasonable Thoughts on the State of Religion in New England* (1743). These documents can be found in convenient (albeit abbreviated) form in Alan Heimert and Perry Miller, eds., *The Great Awakening: Documents Illustrating the Crisis and Its Consequences* (Indianapolis: Bobbs-Merrill, 1967), 204–304.

29. Heimert and Miller, *The Great Awakening*, 292.

where he was serving as pastor of the Congregational Church, and throughout the American colonies was fundamentally genuine.[30] In his *Some Thoughts Concerning the Present Revival of Religion in New-England*, Edwards criticized those who used as their primary authority something other than the Holy Scriptures. "The error of those who have had ill thoughts of the great religious operation on the minds of men, that has been carried on of late in New England (so far as the ground of such an error has been in the understanding, and not in the disposition), seems fundamentally to lie in three things: *first*, in judging of this work a priori; *secondly*, in not taking the Holy Scriptures as an whole rule whereby to judge of such operations; *thirdly*, in not justly separating and distinguishing the good from the bad."[31]

Edwards had taken up this final "error," as he phrased it, in his 1741 commencement address at Yale College. Using as his scriptural text the instructions in 1 John 4:1 ("Beloved, believe not every spirit, but try the spirits whether they are of God; because many false prophets are gone out into the world" KJV), Edwards argued that even during the apostolic age, an era of Christian history that was marked by "the greatest outpouring of the Spirit of God that ever was," the "counterfeits did also then abound." Because "the Devil" has always been "abundant in mimicking both the ordinary and extraordinary influences of the Spirit of God" it was "necessary that the church of Christ should be furnished with some certain rules, and distinguishing and clear marks by which she might proceed safely in judging of spirits, and distinguish the true from the false, without danger of being imposed upon." Consequently, the "Apostle here, of set purpose, undertakes to supply the church of God with such marks of the true Spirit as may be plain and safe, and surely distinguishing, and well accommodated to use and practice."[32]

Taking his cue from the text, Edwards then listed nine "negative signs," or "evidences," that might actually occur during the revivals but did not of themselves either validate or invalidate the revivals as a genuine work of God: (1) that the revival is carried on in a way that is "unusual or extraordinary"; (2) that the revival produces unusual "effects" on the body (i.e., "tears, trembling, groans, loud outcries, agonies of body or the failing of bodily strength"); (3) that the revival "produces a great deal of noise about religion"; (4) that the revival creates "many impressions" on the participants' "imaginations"; (5) that "means are made use of in producing" the revival (i.e. godly example, the use of reason, the preaching of God's Word, observation of others who have been awakened, including one's spouse, etc.); (6) that "many that seem to be the

30. See Jonathan Edwards, *A Faithful Narrative of the Surprising Work of God in the Conversion of Many Hundred Souls in Northampton*, in Goen, *The Great Awakening*, 128–211.

31. Jonathan Edwards, *Some Thoughts Concerning the Present Revival of Religion in New-England*, in Goen, *The Great Awakening*, 293.

32. Jonathan Edwards, *The Distinguishing Marks of a Work of the Spirit of God*, in Goen, *The Great Awakening*, 226. The full text is found on pages 226–88.

subjects" of the revival "are guilty of great imprudences and irregularities in their conduct"; (7) that "some delusions of Satan" are "intermixed with the work"; (8) that some who "were thought to be wrought upon, fall away into gross errors or scandalous practices"; and (9) that the revival "seems to be promoted by ministers insisting very much on the terrors of God's holy law, and that with a great deal of pathos and earnestness."[33]

After listing the "negative signs," Edwards turned his attention to the five "sure, distinguishing, Scripture evidences and marks of a work of the Spirit of God, by which we may proceed in judging of any operation we find in ourselves, or see among people, without danger of being misled"—namely, we know that a revival is genuine when it (1) "operates after such a manner, as to raise their esteem of that Jesus that was born of the Virgin, and was crucified without the gates of Jerusalem; and seems more to confirm and establish their minds in the truth of what the Gospel declares to us of his being the Son of God, and the Saviour of men"; (2) lessens "the lust of the flesh, and the lust of the eyes, and the pride of life" and promotes an "earnest seeking" for "the kingdom of God and his righteousness"; (3) produces "a greater regard to the Holy Scriptures"; (4) leads "persons to truth, convincing them of those things that are true"; and (5) produces "a spirit of love to God and man."[34]

Edwards's powerful defense of the revivals soon established him as the de facto leader and most powerful apologist of the New Light party, the ardently pro-revival wing of colonial congregationalism. While the theological contours of both Old Light rationalism and New Light evangelicalism were only beginning to take shape, one can hear in the debates between Charles Chauncy and Jonathan Edwards the early thunder of a gathering storm.[35]

What Do Evangelicals Believe?

The distinguishing marks of the New Light evangelicals, as reflected in the writings of Edwards and many of his contemporaries, became the core beliefs that have characterized and sustained the evangelical movement from its beginnings to the present day. Listings of these core beliefs can be found in many sources. Alister McGrath, for example, offers "a cluster of six controlling convictions": (1) "The Supreme authority of Scripture as a source of knowledge of God and a guide to Christian living"; (2) "The majesty of Jesus Christ, both as incarnate God and Lord and as the Savior of sinful humanity"; (3) "The Lordship of the Holy Spirit"; (4) "The need for personal conversion";

---

33. Ibid., 226–88.

34. Ibid.

35. Joseph Haroutunian, *Piety Versus Moralism: The Passing of the New England Theology* (New York: Harper & Row, 1970); and Frank Hugh Foster, *A Genetic History of the New England Theology* (Chicago: University of Chicago Press, 1907).

(5) "The priority of evangelism for both individual Christians and the church as a whole"; and (6) "The importance of the Christian community for spiritual nourishment, fellowship and growth."[36] Randall Balmer, while noting the problems inherent in such generalizations, offers three: (1) "the centrality of conversion"; (2) "the quest for an affective piety"; and (3) "a suspicion of wealth, worldliness, and ecclesiastical pretension."[37]

Perhaps the best known listing comes from David Bebbington, who suggests in his influential study of *Evangelicalism in Modern Britain* that there are

> four qualities that have been the special marks of Evangelical religion: *conversionism*, the belief that lives need to be changed; *activism*, the expression of the gospel in effort; *biblicism*, a particular regard for the Bible; and what may be called *crucicentrism*, a stress on the sacrifice of Christ on the cross. Together they form a quadrilateral of priorities that is the basis of Evangelicalism.[38]

The major priorities in Bebbington's quadrilateral, rooted in his study of British evangelicalism, are remarkably similar to those found among America's New Light evangelicals. At the center is the cross, reflecting evangelicalism's deep and continuing conviction that "God so loved the world that he gave his one and only Son, that whoever believes in him shall not perish but have eternal life" (John 3:16 NIV). Around the cross, and flowing out from the historic teachings associated with it, are four additional convictions that more than any others have characterized the evangelical movement throughout its history: (1) a shared authority (the Bible); (2) a shared experience (conversion); (3) a shared mission (worldwide evangelization); and (4) a shared vision (the spiritual renewal of church and society).[39]

Taken together, these five distinguishing marks have provided the theological and practical glue that has held the constantly shifting coalition called evangelicalism together for nearly three centuries through many toils and snares and across many social, geographical, and political boundaries. These emphases did not originate, of course, with the New Lights. Although American Evangelicalism, as an identifiable historical movement, was born in the revivals of the Great Awakening, its core values were a legacy from many centuries of Christian history. From Continental Pietism, the powerful seventeenth- and eighteenth-century renewal movement led by Philip Jacob Spener and August Francke, evangelicals drew a passion for missionary outreach, a new emphasis

36. McGrath, *Evangelicalism and the Future of Christianity*, 55–56.
37. Randall Balmer, *Encyclopedia of Evangelicalism*, rev. and exp. ed. (Waco: Baylor University Press, 2004), 245.
38. Bebbington, *Evangelicalism in Modern Britain*, 2–3.
39. For an earlier listing of these core beliefs, see Garth M. Rosell, "Charles G. Finney: His Place in the Stream of American Evangelicalism," in Sweet, *The Evangelical Tradition in America*, 132.

on holy living, and an active concern for one's neighbor.[40] From Count Zinzendorf and the Moravians they learned the centrality of Christian community, the importance of missions, and a passion for Christian unity.[41] From Protestant reformers including Martin Luther, Ulrich Zwingli, John Calvin, and Menno Simons, they inherited a love for the Bible, a renewed understanding of the doctrine of justification by grace through faith, a new boldness in reforming the church and preaching the Word, and a fresh understanding of God's majesty and sovereign power.[42] From the great martyr tradition of the Christian church they drew an understanding of the enormous cost of discipleship and the confidence that, by God's grace, it was possible to endure suffering.[43] From contemporaries in the British Isles such as John and Charles Wesley, George Whitefield, and Howel Harris, America's eighteenth-century evangelicals drew a passion for righteousness, a love for social justice, some practical principles for making disciples, and a fervent yearning for genuine spiritual awakening.[44] From America's African American congregations—what has often been called "the invisible church"—they came to learn a love for the Bible, a new power in preaching, a fresh spontaneity in worship, a renewed concern for the practical needs of the community, and a willingness to take a stand against injustice.[45]

40. See Carter Lindberg, ed., *The Pietist Theologians* (Oxford: Blackwell, 2005); Lovelace, *The American Pietism of Cotton Mather*; F. Ernest Stoeffler, *The Rise of Evangelical Pietism* (Leiden: Brill, 1971); Philip Jacob Spener, *Pia Desideria* (Philadelphia: Fortress, 1964); K. James Stein, *Philipp Jacob Spener: Pietist Patriarch* (Chicago: Covenant, 1982); Gary R. Sattler, *God's Glory, Neighbor's Good* (Chicago: Covenant, 1982); Dale W. Brown, *Understanding Pietism* (Nappanee, IN: Evangel, 1996); and Peter Erb, *Johann Arndt: True Christianity* (New York: Paulist Press, 1979).

41. See A. J. Lewis, *Zinzendorf the Ecumenical Pioneer: A Study in the Moravian Contribution to Christian Mission and Unity* (Philadelphia: Westminster, 1962); J. Taylor Hamilton and Kenneth G. Hamilton, *History of the Moravian Church* (Bethlehem, PA: Moravian Church of America, 1967); Ward, *The Protestant Evangelical Awakening*; and Katherine M. Faull, *Moravian Women's Memoirs* (Syracuse: Syracuse University Press, 1997).

42. Alister E. McGrath, *Reformation Thought: An Introduction*, 3rd ed. (Oxford: Blackwell, 1999); Timothy George, *Theology of the Reformers* (Nashville: Broadman, 1988); and Denis R. Janz, ed., *A Reformation Reader: Primary Texts with Introductions* (Minneapolis: Fortress, 1999).

43. Few evangelical homes were without some version of either *Foxe's Book of Martyrs* or *The Martyrs Mirror*. See Stephen R. Cattley, ed., *The Acts and Monuments of John Foxe*, 8 vols. (London: Seeley and Burnside, 1841); Thieleman J. van Braght, *The Bloody Theater or Martyrs Mirror* (Scottdale, PA: Herald, 1950); and Herbert B. Workman, *Persecution in the Early Church* (London: Charles Kelly, 1906).

44. See D. Michael Henderson, *John Wesley's Class Meetings: A Model for Making Disciples* (Nappanee, IN: Francis Asbury, 1997); Henry D. Rack, *Reasonable Enthusiast: John Wesley and the Rise of Methodism* (London: Epworth, 1989); Leon O. Hynson, *To Reform a Nation* (Grand Rapids: Francis Asbury, 1984); Geoffrey F. Nuttall, *Howel Harris, 1714–1773: The Last Enthusiast* (Cardiff: University of Wales Press, 1965); Arnold Dallimore, *George Whitefield*, 2 vols. (Edinburgh: Banner of Truth, 1970); Harry S. Stout, *The Divine Dramatist* (Grand Rapids: Eerdmans, 1991); Frank Lambert, *Pedlar in Divinity* (Princeton, NJ: Princeton University Press, 1993); Leigh E. Schmidt, *Holy Fairs: Scotland and the Making of American Revivalism* (Grand Rapids: Eerdmans, 2001); and George Clarkson, *George Whitefield and Welsh Calvinistic Methodism* (Lewiston, NY: Mellen, 1996).

45. While its influence was less obvious in the eighteenth century, the black church had an enormous and growing impact on the evangelical movement throughout the nineteenth and twentieth

The Puritan Heritage

All of these movements—and others that might be listed as well—helped shape and deepen American evangelicalism's self understanding. Among its many predecessors, however, none left a deeper impact than the heritage of the English and American Puritans.[46] As historian Sydney E. Ahlstrom suggests in *A Religious History of the American People*, "Puritanism provided the moral and religious background of fully 75 percent of the people who declared their independence in 1776."[47]

Puritanism first emerged in mid-sixteenth century England, only a generation or so after Henry VIII's break with Roman Catholicism in 1534.[48] Considered by many to represent a second wave of the English Reformation, the movement drew into its ranks many of those who believed that the work of reform had not yet been completed.[49] Convinced that the Church of England needed further purification, these early Puritans provided their evangelical offspring with a set of basic convictions that sustained the movement throughout the next three centuries.

In 1629 John Winthrop, a graduate of Trinity College (Cambridge) and a practicing lawyer, began to develop plans for what was to become the Massachusetts Bay Colony.[50] By August 26, 1629, he and eleven others had signed

---

centuries—especially with the explosive growth of Pentecostalism following the Azusa Street revivals in 1906. See E. Franklin Frazier, *The Negro Church in America* (New York: Schocken Books, 1966), and C. Eric Lincoln, *The Black Church Since Frazier* (New York: Schocken Books, 1974); Albert J. Raboteau, *Slave Religion* (New York: Oxford University Press, 1980); Andrew Billingsley, *Mighty Like a River: The Black Church and Social Reform* (New York: Oxford University Press, 1999); Cheryl J. Sanders, *Saints in Exile: The Holiness-Pentecostal Experience in African American Religion and Culture* (New York: Oxford University Press, 1999); Timothy E. Fulop and Albert J. Raboteau, *African-American Religion* (New York: Routledge, 1996); and Henry H. Mitchell, *Black Preaching* (Philadelphia: Lippincott, 1970).

46. On the Puritan movement, see Leland Ryken, *Worldly Saints: The Puritans as They Really Were* (Grand Rapids: Zondervan, 1990); Francis J. Bremer, *The Puritan Experiment: New England Society from Bradford to Edwards* (Hanover, NH: The University Press of New England, 1995); Perry Miller and Thomas H. Johnson, *The Puritans: A Sourcebook of Their Writings* (Mineola, NY: Dover, 2001); Alan Heimert and Andrew Delbanco, eds., *The Puritans in America* (Cambridge, MA: Harvard University Press, 1985); and Robert P. Martin, *A Guide to the Puritans* (Edinburgh: Banner of Truth, 1997).

47. Sydney E. Ahlstrom, *A Religious History of the American People* (New Haven: Yale University Press, 1972), 124.

48. Alec Ryrie, *The Gospel and Henry VIII: Evangelicals in the Early English Reformation* (Cambridge: Cambridge University Press, 2003); A. G. Dickens, *The English Reformation* (Philadelphia: Penn State University Press, 1994); John N. King, ed., *Voices of the English Reformation* (Philadelphia: University of Pennsylvania Press, 2004); and A. G. Dickens and John Tonkin, *The Reformation in Historical Thought* (Oxford: Blackwell, 1985).

49. Alan Simpson, *Puritanism in Old and New England* (Chicago: University of Chicago Press, 1955). Simpson argued that Puritans were united by two central convictions: the importance of conversion and a basic dissatisfaction with the ecclesiastical status quo.

50. For a biography of Winthrop, see Francis J. Bremer, *John Winthrop: America's Forgotten Founding Father* (New York: Oxford University Press, 2003).

an agreement to emigrate to the New World, provided that the charter of the colony could be legally transplanted. This being assured, in early April of 1630, a fleet of four ships embarked for America. Others would soon follow. After a brief stay in Salem, they settled on a peninsula dominated by three prominent hills and known to the locals as *Shawmut*. They named their new village Boston.[51] In his famous sermon "A Model of Christian Charity," John Winthrop challenged his fellow pilgrims to help in the construction of a model Christian community, a biblical commonwealth, a place where conformity to the teachings of the Bible would be clearly visible. The only way

> to provide for our posterity, is to follow the counsel of Micah, to do justly, to love mercy, to walk humbly with our God. For this end, we must be knit together in this work as one man. We must entertain each other in brotherly affection, we must be willing to abridge ourselves of our superfluities, for the supply of others' necessities. We must uphold a familiar commerce together in all meekness, gentleness, patience, and liberality. We must delight in each other, make others' conditions our own, rejoice together, mourn together, labor and suffer together, always having before our eyes our commission and community in the work, our community as members of the same body.

If we do so, Winthrop continued, "we shall find that the God of Israel is among us, when ten of us shall be able to resist a thousand of our enemies; when he shall make us a praise and glory that men shall say of succeeding plantations, 'the Lord make it like that of New England.' For we must consider that we shall be as a city upon a hill. The eyes of all people are upon us, so that if we shall deal falsely with our God in this work we have undertaken, and so cause him to withdraw his present help from us, we shall be made a story and a by-word through the world." Therefore, Winthrop concluded, "let us choose life, that we and our seed may live by obeying his voice and cleaving to him, for he is our life and our prosperity."[52]

Convinced that they were the "New Israel," these Bay Colony Puritans were certain that God had sent them on an "errand into the wilderness," to build in the New World exactly the kind of community—that city upon a hill—that various constraints had not allowed them to build in the Old World.[53] Their ultimate hope as passionate reformers was the creation of such a compelling Christian community in Boston that "our dear Mother," as Winthrop referred

51. See Perry Miller, *The New England Mind* (Cambridge: Belknap, 1983); Conrad Cherry, ed., *God's New Israel: Religious Interpretations of American Destiny* (Englewood Cliffs, NJ: Prentice-Hall, 1971); and Samuel Eliot Morison, *Builders of the Bay Colony* (Boston: Northeastern University Press, 1981).

52. A brief portion of this famous sermon can be found on a plaque near the steps of Boston's State House. The quotation in this text, put into modern English by the editors, is from Heimert and Delbanco, *The Puritans in America*, 91–92.

53. See Perry Miller, *Errand into the Wilderness* (Cambridge, MA: Harvard University Press, 1975).

to the Church of England, would see the error of her ways and Anglicans would joyously follow the pattern set down by their American brothers and sisters. Unlike the separatist Puritans (Pilgrims) who had settled in Plymouth in 1620 and Salem in 1626, the nonseparating Massachusetts Bay Colony Puritans had not yet given up on the Church of England.[54]

With this reformist vision in mind, the Bay Colony Puritans began in 1630 to build their model community. Patterned largely on Calvin's Geneva,[55] they sought to construct a fully integrated society with the church at the very center and with every other segment of community life, from education and work to politics and law, directly related to it. As a result of this Puritan model, historian Sidney Mead says, America can be called "the nation with the soul of a church."[56]

As one might expect, the church they sought to build reflected their strong interest in ecclesiastical reform. Standing in the tradition of the Magisterial Reformation, they were sure that church and state must work closely together. Puritans were followers of John Calvin, so Puritan theology was intended to follow his teaching. Iconoclastic by conviction, they were convinced that their meetinghouses must remain plain and unadorned. As practitioners of the Psalm tradition in worship, they wanted their worship services to remain free of hymns and instrumentation. As people of the book, they centered their gatherings on reading, praying, teaching, and preaching the Bible.

Given the importance they placed on the experience of religious conversion, it should not be a surprise to discover that the Puritans made "new birth" a major requirement for church membership.[57] While all were expected to attend public worship, only those who could provide a credible account of God's saving work in their lives could become members of the church. Church members were also required to sign their names to the church covenant, lead morally upright lives, be sound in their theology, and be willing to place themselves under the discipline of the church. These additional requirements were all matters that potential members could control. What they could not produce through their own efforts was the experience of conversion. While they might prepare themselves for its arrival, most

54. For more information on the Plymouth Plantation, see Samuel Eliot Morison, ed., *Of Plymouth Plantation, 1620–1647*, by William Bradford (New York: Knopf, 1993); Dwight B. Heath, ed., *Mourt's Relation: A Journal of the Pilgrims at Plymouth* (Bedford, MA: Applewood, 1963); Edward Winslow, *Good Newes from New England* (New Bedford, MA: Applewood, n.d.); Sydney V. James Jr., ed., *Three Visitors to Early Plymouth* (Bedford, MA: Applewood, 1997). All of these are eyewitness accounts of the colony's first years.

55. See William Monter, *Calvin's Geneva* (New York: Wiley, 1967).

56. Sidney E. Mead, *The Nation with the Soul of a Church* (Macon, GA: Mercer University Press, 1985).

57. For the Puritan understanding of church life and conversion, see Edmund S. Morgan, *Visible Saints: The History of a Puritan Idea* (Ithaca, NY: Cornell University Press, 1965); and Geoffrey F. Nuttall, *Visible Saints: The Congregational Way, 1640–1660* (Oxford: Blackwell, 1957).

were convinced in their hearts that only the sovereign God could bring it about.[58]

Throughout the early years of the Massachusetts Bay Colony, conversion remained the primary requirement for church membership.[59] Church membership, in turn, was the primary requirement for full participation in the society. In political life, only regenerate church members could vote and hold political office. Furthermore, as the "New Israel," the Bay Colony Puritans tended to take their legal structures and laws directly from the Old Testament. In the worship of God, only the Psalms could be sung. Work was to be done for the glory of God and to serve the common good. In raising their families, the Bible was to be their ultimate guide.[60]

The Puritan Practice of Piety

Undergirding the Puritan vision—the call of God to construct a Christian society—was the Puritans' daily disciplined practice of piety.[61] While Sunday worship was clearly the focal center of the week, the Puritans understood that their faith was to be lived out throughout the week. In the home or on the job, daily life was filled with conversations about spiritual matters, Bible studies and prayer meetings, seminars and lectureships, and seasons of fasting and prayer. Family prayers, each morning and evening, and times of private devotion throughout the day were all part of a familiar rhythm of worship leading to the great services of public worship on Sunday.[62]

Even the educational institutions established by the Puritans, from the elementary and grammar schools in the local communities to the establishment

58. See Norman Pettit, *The Heart Prepared: Grace and Conversion in Puritan Spiritual Life* (Middletown, CT: Wesleyan University Press, 1989).

59. Gradually, the central importance of conversion was eroded by practical pastoral concerns. See Robert G. Pope, *Half-Way Covenant: Church Membership in Puritan New England* (Eugene, OR: Wipf & Stock, 2002); and Williston Walker, *The Creeds and Platforms of Congregationalism* (New York: Pilgrim, 1991).

60. For Puritan preaching, see Harry S. Stout, *The New England Soul: Preaching and Religious Culture in Colonial New England* (New York: Oxford University Press, 1986); for Puritan ecclesiology, see Paul Chang-Ha Lim, *In Pursuit of Purity, Unity, and Liberty: Richard Baxter's Puritan Ecclesiology in Its Seventeenth-Century Context* (Leiden and Boston: Brill, 2004); for the Puritan understanding of law, see Edgar J. McManus, *Law and Liberty in Early New England* (Amherst: University of Massachusetts Press, 1993); for the Puritan family, see Edmund S. Morgan, *The Puritan Family* (New York: Harper Torchbooks, 1965); for Puritans and education, see Samuel Eliot Morison, *The Intellectual Life of Colonial New England* (Ithaca, NY: Cornell University Press, 1956); for the Puritan crafts, see Carl Bridenbaugh, *The Colonial Craftsman* (Chicago: University of Chicago Press, 1964); for the Puritan merchant, see Bernard Bailyn, *The New England Merchants in the Seventeenth Century* (New York: Harper, 1964).

61. See Charles E. Hambrick-Stowe, *The Practice of Piety: Puritan Devotional Disciplines in Seventeenth-Century New England* (Chapel Hill: University of North Carolina Press, 1982).

62. For a description of public worship in the Puritan communities, see Horton Davies, *The Worship of the American Puritans* (Morgan, PA: Soli Deo Gloria, 1999).

of Harvard College in 1636, were intended to contribute to a life of informed piety. "Let every student be plainly instructed and earnestly pressed," as *New England's First Fruits* (1643) described the early rules and precepts that were observed at Harvard College, "to consider well the main end of his life and studies is, *to know God and Jesus Christ which is eternal life*, John 17:3, and therefore to lay *Christ* in the bottom, as the only foundation of all sound knowledge and Learning."[63]

John Eliot, the great Puritan linguist, pastor, and missionary, after describing in some detail the heavy demands of a life of true piety, told his listeners: "Let no man say ''Tis impossible to live at this rate.'"[64] After all, he continued, we all know of those who in fact have done so—"though, alas! 'tis to be lamented that the distractions of the world, in too many professors, do becloud the beauty of an heavenly conversation." Then concluding his sermon, Eliot voiced some unforgettable sentiments: "Our employment lies in heaven. In the morning, if we ask, 'Where am I to be to day?' our souls must answer, 'In heaven.' In the evening, if we ask, 'Where have I been to-day?' our souls may answer, 'In heaven.' If thou art a believer, thou art no stranger to heaven while thou livest; and when thou diest, heaven will be no strange place to thee; no, thou hast been there a thousand times before."[65]

As the decades passed, however, it became increasingly apparent that the old Puritan vision was beginning to fade. New interests and preoccupations emerged to replace many of the old commitments and practices. Bitter battles, from the antinomian controversy in the 1630s to the Salem witch trials in the 1690s, had divided neighborhoods and fragmented communities.[66] New policies, from the Half-Way Covenant to the lowering of the bar on the sacrament of holy communion,[67] challenged the central role that conversion had traditionally played as a requirement for church membership. Furthermore, increasing affluence and social stability as the Puritan communities matured seemed to make dependence on God less attractive to some and less necessary to others.

---

63. *New England's First Fruits* (London: R. O. and G. D. for Henry Overton, 1643), app. D in Samuel Eliot Morison, *The Founding of Harvard College* (Cambridge, MA: Harvard University Press, 1995), 432.

64. John Eliot (1604–90) was teacher of the church in Roxbury, a position he held until his death. He prepared a catechism and a grammar in the Algonkian language and translated the entire Bible as well as the Westminster Larger Catechism into that tongue. Called the Apostle to the Indians, he was largely responsible for the conversion and discipleship of some 3,600 Native Americans. See Ola Winslow, *John Eliot: "Apostle to the Indians"* (Boston: Houghton Mifflin, 1968).

65. From a sermon by John Eliot (recorded by Cotton Mather). Hambrick-Stowe, *The Practice of Piety*, xv–xvi.

66. See David D. Hall, ed., *The Antinomian Controversy, 1636–1638: A Documentary History* (Durham, NC: Duke University Press, 1990); David D. Hall, ed., *Witch-Hunting in Seventeenth-Century New England: A Documentary History, 1638–1693* (Boston: Northeastern University Press, 1999); and *Records of Salem Witchcraft, Copied from Original Documents* (Roxbury, MA: W. Elliot Woodward, 1864).

67. Pope, *Half-Way Covenant*.

Whatever the reasons, the original dream of constructing a biblical city on a hill seemed less urgent in the early eighteenth century than it had in the early seventeenth century when the ships had first arrived. Sermons urging individual and corporate repentance were preached.[68] Special days of fasting and prayer encouraging renewed commitment were called. Yet the dreams of spiritual renewal and reform cherished in many a Puritan heart seemed increasingly out of reach. "Pointing to the lives of their parents," Harry Stout notes, preachers continually reminded their hearers "how far short of that pattern the children had fallen."[69]

The Great Awakening in Northampton

It was into this slough of despond, as John Bunyan might have called it, that the fresh winds of revival began to blow. Exactly a century after the founding of the Massachusetts Bay Colony, scores of villages throughout New England and beyond were touched by the surprising work of God.[70] One of the towns most profoundly affected was Northampton. Although it had experienced "five harvests," as Solomon Stoddard, the town's second pastor, had described those seasons of spiritual refreshment between 1680 and 1719, by the time of Stoddard's death in 1729 most of the town's inhabitants seemed "insensible of the things of religion, and engaged in other cares and pursuits."[71]

"Just after my grandfather's death," as Jonathan Edwards, the town's third pastor, tells the story,

> it seemed to be a time of extraordinary dullness in religion: licentiousness for some years greatly prevailed among the youth of the town; they were many of them very much addicted to night-walking, and frequenting the tavern, and lewd practices, wherein some, by their example exceedingly corrupted others. It was their manner very frequently to get together in conventions of both sexes, for mirth and jollity, which they called frolics; and they would often spend the greater part of the night in them, without regard to any order in the families they belonged to: and indeed family government did too much fail in the town.

68. See Sacvan Bercovitch, *The American Jeremiad* (Madison: University of Wisconsin Press, 1991).

69. Stout, *The New England Soul*, 75.

70. The revivals of what came to be known as the Great Awakening actually began in the Middle Colonies under Dutch Reformed pastor Theodore Frelinghuysen. Soon, they were also being experienced in New England and throughout the South. See Tracy, *The Great Awakening*; Maxson, *The Great Awakening in the Middle Colonies*; and Gaustad, *The Great Awakening in New England*.

71. Solomon Stoddard (1643–1729) was pastor of the Congregational Church in Northampton from 1672 until his death in 1729. His grandson, Jonathan Edwards, joined him in 1727 as associate pastor. When Stoddard died, Edwards took over his duties as the primary pastor of the congregation. The story is taken from Edwards, *Faithful Narrative*, 97–212. The "five harvests" took place in 1680, 1684, 1697, 1713, and 1719.

It was become very customary with many of our young people, to be indecent in their carriage at meeting, which doubtless would not have prevailed to such a degree, had it not been that my grandfather, through his great age (though he retained his powers surprisingly to the last) was not so able to observe them.[72]

Furthermore, Edwards continued,

there had also long prevailed in the town a spirit of contention between two parties, into which they had for many years been divided, by which was maintained a jealousy one of the other, and they were prepared to oppose one another in all public affairs. But in two or three years after Mr. Stoddard's death, there began to be a sensible amendment of these evils; the young people shewed more of a disposition to hearken to counsel, and by degrees left off their frolicking, and grew observably more decent in their attendance on the public worship, and there were more that manifested a religious concern than there used to be.[73]

A series of events, including three unusual deaths and several remarkable conversions, seemed to create more of a religious concern in people's minds. In particular, Edwards writes,

I was surprised with the relation of a young woman, who had been one of the greatest company-keepers in the whole town. When she came to me, I had never heard that she was become in any wise serious, but by the conversation I then had with her, it appeared to me that what she gave an account of was a glorious work of God's infinite power and sovereign grace; and that God had given her a new heart, truly broken and sanctified. I could not then doubt of it, and have seen much in my acquaintance with her since to confirm it.[74]

News of her conversion

seemed to be almost like a flash of lightning, upon the hearts of young people all over the town, and upon many others. Those persons amongst us who used to be farthest from seriousness, and that I most feared would make an ill improvement of it, seemed greatly to be awakened with it; many went to talk with her, concerning what she had met with; and what appeared in her seemed to be the satisfaction of all that did so. . . .

This work of God, as it was carried on, and the number of true saints multiplied, soon made a glorious alteration in the town; so that in the spring and summer following, *anno* 1735, the town seemed to be full of the presence of God: it never was so full of love, nor so full of joy; and yet so full of distress, as it was then. There were remarkable tokens of God's presence in almost every house. It was a time of joy in families on the account of salvation's being brought

72. Ibid., 146.
73. Ibid.
74. Ibid., 149.

unto them; parents rejoicing over their children as newborn, and husbands over their wives, and wives over their husbands.[75]

As a result of the Northampton revival, according to the *Faithful Narrative*, some three hundred fifty were "savingly wrought upon"; the congregation became "alive in God's service"; the Sabbath was "a delight"; the singing of the Psalms was "greatly enlivened"; and the young people of the town began to spend their time "in talking of the excellency and dying love of Jesus Christ, the gloriousness of the way of salvation, the wonderful, free, and sovereign grace of God, his glorious work in the conversion of a soul, the truth and certainty of the great things of God's Word, the sweetness of the views of his perfections, etc." Further, those who had been formerly converted "were greatly enlivened and renewed with fresh and extraordinary incomes of the Spirit of God"; those who had been uncertain about their salvation "had now their doubts removed by a more satisfying experience, and more clear discoveries of God's love"; those who visited town "had their consciences smitten and awakened"; and the inhabitants of other towns, upon hearing of what God had done in Northampton, were "seized with deep concern about the things of religion."[76]

Five Distinguishing Marks

Woven into the fabric of Edwards' *Faithful Narrative* are the five distinctive threads of historic evangelicalism: the centrality of Christ's atoning work on the cross, the essential experience of religious conversion, the foundational authority of the Bible, the importance of spreading the gospel, and the possibility of individual and corporate renewal. Forged in the revival fires of the Great Awakening, these distinguishing marks remained at the center of the movement for more than three centuries.

The experience of Northampton was but a microcosm of what began to happen in hundreds of towns throughout all thirteen colonies. Spread by the powerful preaching of George Whitefield—the "grand itinerant"—and by scores of other preachers throughout the American colonies, the Great Awakening produced perhaps as many as fifty thousand new converts; revitalized old congregations; spurred the establishment of colleges such as Brown, Princeton, and Rutgers; and brought new hope to those for whom the old Puritan vision had begun to fade.[77]

75. Ibid., 149, 151.
76. Ibid., 151–52.
77. For the remarkable ministry of George Whitefield, see John Gillies, *Memoirs of Rev. George Whitefield* (Middletown, CT: Hunt & Noyes, 1838); Joseph Belcher, *George Whitefield: A Biography* (New York: American Tract Society, 1857); Richard Owen Roberts, *Whitefield in Print* (Wheaton: Richard Owen Roberts, 1988); *George Whitefield's Journals* (Edinburgh: Banner of Truth, 1998); and *Letters of George Whitefield: For the Period 1734–1742* (Edinburgh: Banner of Truth, 1976).

Harold John Ockenga and Billy Graham

Nearly two centuries later, as Harold John Ockenga looked out on the enormous crowd that had assembled at Boston's Mechanics Hall, he became convinced that events akin to America's Great Awakening had returned to New England. "I believe that 1950 will go down into history," he later reflected, "as the year of heaven-sent revival." "God is moving as He has not moved in America at least for four decades and as He has not moved in New England for two centuries."[78] "Voices of despair" had long been saying that it is "too late for revival," that "apostasy will grow worse and worse."[79] The Scriptures assure us, however, that "times of refreshing" will come—and now, at long last, "America's hour has struck." Nothing in the past two hundred years "can compare with what our eyes have seen and what our ears have heard and our hands have handled in the last three months in the cities of New England."[80]

As a student of history, Ockenga was aware of the many revivals that had taken place throughout New England over the previous two centuries.[81] George Whitefield, Charles Finney, Lyman Beecher, Nathaniel Taylor, Dwight Moody, J. Wilbur Chapman, Billy Sunday, "Gipsy" Smith, and a host of others had labored with considerable success in the New England vineyard between 1750 and 1950.[82] Furthermore, since its founding in 1809, Park Street Church had not only hosted many of these "seasons of refreshing" but had also opened its pulpit to virtually every major evangelist from Finney to Sunday. New England in general and Park Street Church in particular were no strangers to spiritual awakening.[83] While deeply grateful for these earlier revivals, Ockenga

78. Harold John Ockenga, "Is America's Revival Breaking?" *United Evangelical Action*, July 1, 1950, 3–4, 8, 13–15.

79. Harold John Ockenga, "The Hope for a Revival," *Bulletin of the National Association of Evangelicals for United Action* 1, no. 2 (September 1, 1942): 1.

80. Ockenga, "Is America's Revival Breaking?" 3.

81. Ockenga's personal library, now housed in the Ockenga Institute at Gordon-Conwell Theological Seminary, includes scores of titles relating to the history of revival. Numerous references to the New England revivals and those who led them can also be found throughout the nearly three thousand manuscript sermons that are part of the Ockenga Papers.

82. See Martin Moore, *Boston Revival, 1842* (Boston: John Putnam, 1842); Benjamin W. Williams, *The Old South Chapel Prayer Meeting: Its Origin and History; with Interesting Narratives, and Instances of Remarkable Conversions in Answer to Prayer* (Boston: Tilton, 1859); Garth M. Rosell and Richard A. G. Dupuis, eds., *The Memoirs of Charles G. Finney: The Complete Restored Text* (Grand Rapids: Zondervan, 1989); H. M. Grout, ed., *The Gospel Invitation: Sermons Related to the Boston Revival of 1877* (Boston: Lockwood, Brooks and Co., 1877); Arcturus Z. Conrad, ed., *Boston's Awakening* (Boston: The King's Business, 1909); and Kathryn T. Long, *The Revival of 1857–58: Interpreting an American Religious Awakening* (New York: Oxford University Press, 1998).

83. For accounts of Park Street Church revivals in 1823 (Beecher/Taylor), 1826–27 (Dwight), 1831–32 (Finney), 1840 (Kirk), 1857 (Finney), 1877 (Moody), 1909 (Chapman/Alexander), and 1917 (Sunday), see H. Crosby Englizian, *Brimstone Corner: Park Street Church, Boston* (Chicago: Moody, 1968).

Billy Graham's 1950 meetings at Mechanics Hall in Boston (taken from *Revival in Our Time: The Story of the Billy Graham Evangelistic Campaigns* [Wheaton: Van Kampen, 1950])

had become convinced that the Boston Revival of 1950, and the subsequent series of New England revivals that it spawned, marked the beginning of an even greater outpouring of God's Spirit upon America. You no longer "have to wait [un]til next year," Ockenga proclaimed. "You don't have to wait ten years. You don't have to pray anymore, 'Lord, send a revival.' The revival is here! . . . revival is the solution to all our problems."[84]

The revival Harold John Ockenga is referring to broke out in the early hours of 1950. Encouraged by Allan Emery Jr., a leader in Boston's business community and a member of Park Street Church, Ockenga invited a thirty-one-year-old preacher named Billy Graham to speak at a New Year's Eve youth rally in Boston's six-thousand-seat Mechanics Hall and remain as the speaker for an eight-day evangelistic series to be held early in January of 1950 at Park Street Church.[85] The New Year's Eve service at Mechanics Hall came as a complete surprise. The six thousand who jammed the hall, along with the hundreds of people who were turned away, suddenly made the event front page news. "Evangelist Graham Draws 6000 from 'Eve' Celebration," proclaimed the *Boston Sunday Herald*, where "evangelist Billy Graham told Boston's biggest New Year's Eve party last night that 'the Devil can be run out of Boston.'"[86] The *Boston Post*, in its Sunday edition, carried a full report

84. Harold John Ockenga, "Boston Stirred by Revival," *United Evangelical Action*, January 15, 1950, 2, 15; and Ockenga, "Is America's Revival Breaking?" 3, 13–15.

85. Lawrence Dame, "Billy Graham Rally Tomorrow," *Boston Herald*, December 31, 1949.

86. W. E. Playfair, "Evangelist Graham Draws 6000 from 'Eve' Celebration," *Boston Sunday Herald*, January 1, 1950, and "May Never See the Year 2000," *Boston Post*, January 6, 1950, 1.

of the four-hour meeting along with a detailed description of the service, a listing of its major participants, and a dramatic picture of the crowd that had filled Mechanics Hall to overflowing.[87]

At the close of the service, Ockenga rose to announce to the crowd the arrival of the New Year. Having witnessed the remarkable events of the evening, he also told the audience that they were part of something much larger than a single service. Indeed, they were standing at a crucial "turning point" in Christian history. "We not only stand at mid-century on the threshold of the New Year," he argued, "but at the beginning of a new era in the history of mankind." In the face of enormous national and international problems, "millions of Americans believe an old-fashioned spiritual revival could preserve our God-given freedoms and way of life." There are indications "from coast to coast that America is on the verge of such an awakening." America must therefore fall upon its knees in repentance and prayer. What we are now experiencing here in Boston, Ockenga concluded, is nothing short of the kind of "surprising work of God" that came to New England two centuries ago under the ministry of Jonathan Edwards.[88]

The Forging of a Friendship

By linking Billy Graham with Jonathan Edwards, Ockenga was also declaring that the glorious new era of spiritual revival on which he believed they were embarking would be characterized by the same old-fashioned truths that had given evangelicalism its character and vitality in the past. The Boston Revival not only provided the context in which a deep and lasting friendship could be forged between Ockenga and Graham but it also marked the beginning of a powerful new coalition of movements, geographical regions, and networks of friends that would reshape the religious landscape in America and throughout the world.

But we are getting ahead of our story. Before we can bring these streams together we must first visit the headwaters.

87. *Boston Post*, January 1, 1950, 15.
88. Ibid.

2

✳✳✳✳✳✳✳✳✳✳✳✳✳✳✳✳✳✳✳✳✳✳✳✳✳✳✳✳✳✳✳✳✳✳✳✳✳✳✳

THE LONE WOLF

Few would have imagined in the summer of 1905 that the son born to Herman and Angie Ockenga would grow up to be a giant among giants. Harold John's rather frail body, which seemed to make him particularly susceptible to injury and illness, often prevented him from participating in neighborhood activities near the family's west Chicago home.[1] These times of forced idleness, however, proved to be a blessing in disguise—for they provided regular opportunity for quiet reflection and critical analysis. Harold John loved to think. From his earliest years, he found solace in the life of the mind.

His father, Herman, worked for the Chicago Rapid Transit Company.[2] He was also an active member of the Kiwanis Club of Austin, the region of Chicago where the family lived, and he served for a time as an officer of that organization.[3] Although he had only limited formal education, Herman was an avid reader and helped introduce his children to the world of books. He and his wife also sought to instill in their family the values of thrift and good, hard work.[4] While the family was far from wealthy, they were comfortable

1. By his teen years, Harold John had overcome his physical difficulties and had become an advocate for strenuous exercise and good health. See Ockenga to Virginia Ray, August 4, 1930, Ockenga Papers.

2. See Herman Ockenga to Harold John Ockenga, January 28, 1931, Ockenga Papers.

3. The Kiwanis Club of Austin met each Thursday at noon at the Austin YMCA. Herman Ockenga is listed on its letterhead as secretary. See Herman Ockenga to Harold John Ockenga, September 11, October 4, and November 27, 1930, Ockenga Papers.

4. By the age of nine, Harold John Ockenga had secured his first job delivering orders for a local grocery store from 8:00 a.m. until 9:00 p.m. each Saturday. He subsequently worked as a butcher and a "train caller" for the Chicago Rapid Transit Company.

by the standards of that day. The Ockengas' modest two-story, wood-framed home on North Long Avenue was more than adequate for the needs of the growing family.

Harold's mother, Angie, was an ardent Methodist. Determined to raise her children in the Christian faith, she regularly took Harold and his sisters with her to worship, Sunday school, and prayer meetings at the Austin Presbyterian Church and the Olivet Methodist Episcopal Church. Like Susanna Wesley before her, Angie Ockenga sought to pass on to her children her own deep love for God, his Word, and the beauty of his creation.[5] She became for Harold and his sisters not only the center of family life but also the dominant force in their spiritual development.[6] The priorities of her life, as she expressed them in one of her letters to Harold, were to "attend strictly to duty," to "take all disappointments graciously," to attend worship and prayer meetings regularly, and to "try and live [a] more holy [life]."[7]

Conversion

Encouraged by his mother's example, Harold John became an active and enthusiastic member of the Olivet Methodist Episcopal Church.[8] Attending a variety of services each Sunday—including the class meeting, Sunday school, worship, the Junior Epworth League, a Bible study, and Young People's Society—he immersed himself in the life of the church. Inspired by the preaching of his pastor, Dr. Ladd-Thomas, he even began to consider the possibility of someday becoming a preacher himself. Such a choice still seemed unlikely, however, since Harold knew that it would mean the abandonment of his childhood dream of becoming a famous trial lawyer.[9]

It was during the summer of 1916, at the age of eleven, that Harold went with the other members of his Sunday school class to an old-fashioned Methodist camp meeting in Des Plaines, Illinois. There, with tears in his eyes, he and several other members of the class knelt at the altar at the close of the

5. On Susanna Wesley's remarkable life and work, see Charles Wallace Jr., ed., *Susanna Wesley: The Complete Writings* (New York: Oxford University Press, 1997).

6. The importance of Angie Ockenga's love and encouragement, her wisdom and guidance, and her deep personal piety can be seen in her letters to her son. See, for example, the twenty-six letters from Angie Ockenga to Harold John Ockenga, written between September 19, 1930, and March 4, 1931, Ockenga Papers. Throughout these letters, she gives her son advice on a range of topics from marriage to denominational affiliation, offers him financial help, and repeatedly tells him how proud she is of him and the hard work he is doing.

7. Angie Ockenga to Harold John Ockenga, January 2, 1931, Ockenga Papers.

8. Harold was baptized as an infant at the Austin Presbyterian Church. At the age of eleven, he joined the Olivet Methodist Episcopal Church. See Harold Lindsell, *Park Street Prophet: A Life of Harold John Ockenga* (Wheaton: Van Kampen, 1951), 12–13.

9. Lindsell, *Park Street Prophet*, 18–19.

service to give their lives to Christ. "There is no doubt," he later told the three hundred friends who had gathered at the Austin Methodist Episcopal Church to hear his first sermon, "that I was saved from my sins at that time. . . . I had often wondered why I could not just live a good life and do good deeds and be saved." Then the answer came. "It is not by works" that anyone "can receive salvation from his sins." Rather, "it is by the grace of God."[10]

Despite his experience at Des Plaines, Harold John continued to struggle spiritually. "I walked out of that meeting as a person living the regenerate life," he later testified, "but what did it mean to me? I had been moved in soul and had hungered to eat of the bread of life; I had knelt at the altar and along with many others my hunger was appeased." Yet he continued "groping in the darkness for the light."[11] Sensing his turmoil, Alice Pfafman, the superintendent of young people's work at Austin Methodist Episcopal Church, invited Harold to join some of the other young people from the church in attending a conference sponsored by Knox College. At the closing session, on the morning of December 31, 1922, as seventeen-year-old Harold John would later write, "I heard a man deliver an address from the Old Testament which changed my life." After describing the atoning work of Christ on the cross, the preacher challenged each of us to "pour out our lives" as an act of worship to God.[12]

Following the service, Harold and his friends gathered "in an upper room in the Galesburg Hotel." It was there, as the group knelt together in prayer, that his life was, he believed, quite literally transformed. On "the last day of the year 1922," he later wrote, God gave me "a sense of peace and of contentment and of joy" that was truly "wonderful." "We took the afternoon train to Chicago and arrived in time to attend a New Year's Eve Service. During that service," he concluded, "I made my first public testimony as a Christian."[13]

In his various accounts of these events at Galesburg, what Harold describes is actually a series of three distinct yet interrelated experiences of God's grace. The first, which he came to speak of as his "reclaiming" by God, was an assurance of salvation. Sensing that he had "strayed far from God" following his conversion at the Des Plaines campground, he found himself increasingly

10. Harold John Ockenga, "My Testimony and First Sermon," sermon 1, Ockenga Papers, delivered at the Austin Methodist Episcopal Church, July 23, 1923, 1–2. This "sermon" is listed as the first of the nearly three thousand manuscript sermons that make up the Harold John Ockenga sermon collection in the Ockenga Papers.

11. See Ockenga, "My Testimony." Ockenga repeats the story in a slightly expanded form in his sermon on "Samuel, or The Need of a Conversion," sermon 38, Ockenga Papers.

12. Although the preacher is not identified, the text was 1 Chronicles 11:19.

13. Ockenga, "Samuel." Ockenga first presented this sermon as a Bible study on November 30, 1925. Between December 26, 1925, and May 3, 1930, he preached the sermon a total of twenty-four times in various places. Compare Harold John Ockenga, "Life with a Vision," sermon 2205, Ockenga Papers, where he speaks of being alone in his room when he experienced the grace of God.

restless and in turmoil—uncertain about what he "was saved from" and generally ignorant of "the consequences of sin." On several occasions, after being deeply touched by a sermon, he had even raised his hand "to be remembered in prayer." Not until Galesburg, however, did he experience the assurance that he was genuinely a child of God. It was there, as he phrased it, that "Christ became a living Savior to me."[14] In later years, as his theological vocabulary expanded, he came to use the language of "predestination" and "perseverance" to describe God's sovereign work of salvation in his life. In doing so, however, he was convinced that he was in no way departing from his mother's faith. "I believe in predestination," she assured her son, "always did."[15]

A second experience, known in Wesleyan circles as the "second blessing," was also part of the Galesburg event. Having struggled with his own tendencies to "backslide" into sin and to "stray far from God," Harold John longed for a "second work of grace" in his life. Such an experience, as his mother had taught him, could help him to live in "perfect love" not only toward God but also toward other people as well. His hunger for righteousness was soon satisfied. As Harold John later testified, a "short time" after he promised God that he would enter the gospel ministry, he "experienced the second work of grace in [his] soul."[16]

This "experience of sanctification," he later wrote to a friend, is "what has meant most in my life." If his friend were to have the same experience, as "I am praying and trusting you will," it would "mean more to you than anything else in the world." For "this is the experience which made the saints of the ages and which will keep the ones today who desire to walk with God. To me the rest of these things are only a means to an end and by the grace of God I do wish to live in the holiest place he has."[17] "How beautiful the world is after the rain," he later added, "and how beautiful are our lives when He has washed them clean."[18]

Later in his ministry, in an effort to communicate to a broader evangelical audience, Ockenga abandoned some of the more distinctly Wesleyan vocabulary of these early years.[19] Never, however, does he appear to have abandoned either the importance or validity of what he had experienced at Des Plaines and Galesburg. Indeed, the famous Frank O. Salisbury portrait of John Wesley continued

14. Ockenga, "My Testimony," 2; and Harold John Ockenga, *Faith in a Troubled World* (Wenham, MA: Gordon College Press, 1972), 23–24.
15. Angie Ockenga to Harold John Ockenga, October 26, 1930, Ockenga Papers.
16. Ockenga, "My Testimony," 1.
17. Harold John Ockenga to Virginia Ray, April 26, 1927, Ockenga Papers.
18. Ockenga to Ray, May 18, 1927, Ockenga Papers.
19. A good example can be found in Harold John Ockenga, "The Second Blessing, Sanctification and Holiness," sermon 593, Ockenga Papers. On this manuscript, he crossed out the word "blessing" in the sermon title and throughout the manuscript and replaced it with the term "crisis." Rather than emphasize the language of a first and second blessing in describing justification and sanctification, by the 1930s he appears to have coalesced the various elements of redemption into the language of a single work of grace.

to hang over his desk at home throughout his ministry, and the theology of the great eighteenth-century preacher continued to inform his preaching.[20]

Call to Ministry

Harold John's third experience was closely connected to the first two. During that "final prayer meeting" in the "hotel room," he later wrote, "I covenanted with God that if he would save me I would preach the gospel."[21] The issue of God's call in his life, and the question of whether he would obey it, had been smoldering in his mind since his conversion at Des Plaines. Convinced that God was calling him into the ministry—yet drawn even more strongly toward the practice of law—he had struggled throughout his teen years with the question of what he should do with his life. Galesburg brought the matter to a head. There, as he knelt in prayer, the issue of his vocational direction was finally settled. He would become a preacher.[22]

For several weeks following his return to Chicago, Harold John told no one about his promise to enter the ministry. He thought it might be better for him to simply spend four years as a "normal young person with a normal social life in one of the big universities." Then, after graduation, he could tell his family and friends that he had decided to go to seminary rather than law school. This strategy, however, left him miserable. By February, after Alice Pfafman had taken him aside to tell him she believed God was calling him into the ministry, he knew he could no longer keep his promise to God secret from others. "It was a warm day," as he later described the scene, "and taking golf clubs to have an afternoon in the park I stopped by her house just long enough to say, 'Mrs. Pfafman—you are right. God is calling me to the ministry and I have decided to respond.' With some expression of joy which I do not recall she thanked the Lord and I left for the best game of golf I have ever played in winter or summer." Alice was so thrilled that she immediately telephoned Angie Ockenga to pass along the exciting news. "Thank God," his mother responded, "I dedicated him to the ministry before he was born."[23]

Taylor University

Knowing that Harold John Ockenga would need further education to prepare for his new calling, Alice Pfafman urged him to consider attending

---

20. The original portrait by Frank O. Salisbury, commemorating the consummation of the union of the Methodist churches on September 21, 1832, is housed in the Wesley House and Museum in London. The print, made on October 1, 1934, is now part of the Ockenga Papers.

21. Ockenga, "Samuel."

22. For a discussion of these struggles, see Lindsell, *Park Street Prophet*, 18–21.

23. Ockenga, "Samuel." See also Lindsell, *Park Street Prophet*, 21.

Taylor, a small Methodist college in Upland, Indiana.[24] Promising that she would reimburse him for all of his expenses should he find his first semester at Taylor less than satisfactory, she was able to convince him that he should abandon his plans to attend the University of Chicago and enroll instead at the much smaller holiness school. Accepting her advice, Ockenga entered Taylor in 1923. For the next four years, until his graduation with a Bachelor of Arts degree in 1927, it was his intellectual and spiritual home.[25]

Having been planted in the soil of the nineteenth-century holiness movement, Taylor had remained true to its Wesleyan heritage.[26] "Christian perfection," as John Wesley had taught in his *A Plain Account of Christian Perfection*, follows the initial experience of justification, to enable the believer to live in perfect love toward God and others. Consequently, students were continually encouraged to "hunger and thirst after righteousness" and to "go on to perfection."[27]

These themes were well known to Ockenga. Not only had he learned them at his mother's knee but he had entered college having already "experienced both of these works."[28] His years at Taylor significantly deepened his commitment to holiness. "Let me be a holy man of God through the entire 20th Century," he wrote in his journal shortly before graduation.[29] "My ambition is primarily to be a man of God," he added in writing to a close friend. "To do this I must know how to preach, pray and live. Everything else must bow to that or go."[30] By choosing to major in English and history with a minor in Biblical literature, Ockenga had been exposed to the writings and ideas of Shakespeare, Dante, Marlowe, Goethe, Hawthorne, Hugo, and others.[31] Not only did these courses help enlarge his intellectual world and broaden his perspectives

24. For the history of Taylor University, see William C. Ringenberg, *Taylor University: The First 125 Years* (Grand Rapids: Eerdmans, 1973); and Frederick Norwood and William Warren Sweet, *History of the North Indiana Conference* (Winona Lake, IN: Light and Life, 1957).

25. For a fuller discussion of the influence of Taylor upon Ockenga, see John M. Adams, "The Making of a Neo-Evangelical Statesman: The Case of Harold John Ockenga" (PhD diss., Baylor University, 1994), 97–120; and "Taylor University: Memoirs," Ockenga Papers. Ockenga, an excellent student, had attended Tilton Grammar School and Austin High School, both public institutions in the Chicago school system.

26. For an understanding of the holiness movement, see Melvin E. Dieter, *The Holiness Revival in the Nineteenth Century* (Metuchen, NJ: Scarecrow, 1980).

27. John Wesley, *A Plain Account of Christian Perfection* (Peterborough: Epworth, 1952), 112–13. See also Albert C. Outler, ed., *John Wesley* (New York: Oxford University Press, 1964), 251–305; Henry D. Rack, *Reasonable Enthusiast* (London: Epworth Press, 1989); and Kenneth J. Collins, *John Wesley* (Nashville: Abingdon, 2003).

28. Ockenga, "My Testimony," 1.

29. Harold John Ockenga, "Journal," April 10, 1927, Ockenga Papers. Ockenga's journal is a 92-page handwritten document covering the period from May 2, 1926, through September 9, 1928.

30. Harold John Ockenga to Virginia Ray, February 26, 1928, Ockenga Papers.

31. Many of Ockenga's college papers, including critical analyses of the books he was reading, can be found in the Ockenga Papers.

but they also provided an important foundation and growing vocabulary for the emerging passion of his life, the preaching of the gospel.

Ocky, as his college friends came to call him, was an outstanding student.[32] He was also a recognized campus leader.[33] Where he shone most brightly, however, was in front of an audience. Whether debating a collegiate opponent, playing a dramatic role, or delivering a prepared speech, his forensic skills impressed faculty and students alike.[34] In fact, he won a number of awards and prizes for his speaking and debating. His campus colleagues eventually dubbed him the "gifted orator from Illinois."[35]

This recognition brought him immense pleasure. Ockenga's deepest satisfactions, however, seemed to

TAYLOR UNIVERSITY
EVANGELISTIC TEAM

M. S. HAWKS, Preacher   ALVA BEERS, Preacher   H. OCKENGA, Preacher
ROY McMURRY, Cornet Soloist and Song Leader

MEETINGS
AUG. 25 TO SEPT. 6, 1925
Community Hall, Maine, N. Y.
A FULL GOSPEL FEARLESSLY DECLARED
EVERYBODY WELCOME

The Taylor Evangelistic Team (courtesy of Gordon-Conwell Libraries)

come from his preaching. While he enjoyed public speaking, drama, and debate, the proclamation of God's Word increasingly became the central focus of his life and work. God had called him to be a preacher, he was convinced, and he was determined to do everything in his power to use his college years to prepare for that important task. "I realize," he wrote in his journal, "that a man cannot excel in all things." Therefore, "he must choose his field of endeavor. I am choosing the ministry of God in preaching, praying and performing his will in social service. Though many other things may take some of my time," he concluded, "these are the ends toward which I am aiming" and these are the goals to which I shall "give my entire energy."[36]

To preach well, Ockenga was convinced, one must actually preach. Consequently, he soon joined one of Taylor's student-led gospel teams. The members

32. Ockenga graduated near the top of his class with an overall grade average of 94 on a scale of 100. The faculty recommended him for a Rhodes Scholarship at the end of his senior year. See Ockenga to Ray, May 18, 1927, Ockenga Papers.

33. Ockenga was elected class president during his freshman year and served in a variety of elected and appointed offices throughout his college career. See the *Taylor Echo*, the *Taylor Gem*, and the *Taylor University Bulletin* for accounts of his various campus activities.

34. Ockenga was a member of the Thalonian Literary Society, the Eulogonian Debating Society, and the Intercollegiate Debate Team during his Taylor years. See Lindsell, *Park Street Prophet*, 24. There appear to have been several different spellings of "Ocky."

35. See the Taylor University yearbook, the *Gem* (1925), 52, Ockenga Papers.

36. Ockenga, "Journal," May 23, 1927, Ockenga Papers.

of the Taylor Evangelistic Team, which included Alva Beers, M. S. "Billy" Hawks, Roy McMurry, and Ockenga, traveled on weekends and throughout the summers presenting the gospel in a variety of settings. By the time of his graduation, Ockenga had preached more than four hundred times in scores of churches throughout America.[37] During these years, he also kept a log of where and when he had preached a particular sermon along with a listing of the various responses that had come as a result of his preaching.[38] In addition to the activities of his own evangelistic team, Ockenga also served as treasurer (in 1925) and president (1926) of all the gospel teams. For two years, he organized their deputation work. Moreover, in addition to these outreach efforts beyond the campus, Ockenga also became an active participant in the regular evangelistic and revival services that were held each year on the campus itself.[39] In short, there were more than enough opportunities available at Taylor for a budding young preacher to practice his craft.[40]

Good preaching, Ockenga was convinced, must be undergirded by a careful study of the Bible and regular seasons of fervent prayer. Consequently, he determined that while he was a student at Taylor, he would spend an hour each morning, from 5:30 to 6:30 a.m., reading Scripture and praying. On occasions, he and the other members of the Taylor Evangelistic Team would spend an entire night in prayer.[41] In addition, Ockenga became a regular participant— and sometime leader—of the regular campus prayer meeting each Thursday evening. He was also an active member of the Holiness League, a campus organization that met each Friday evening for prayer, fellowship, and mutual edification.[42] "This morning," he wrote in his journal,

> I studied my Bible and God wonderfully opened the 6th chapter of Matthew and fed my soul. I then went to the building to prayer and Oh such a time as we had, God and I. He did a real work in my heart this morning. He melted me up and stripped me of self, and fixed my gaze upon Jesus. It was beautiful and Oh

37. For an interesting report on their meetings in Grand Ledge, Michigan, see *The Christian Witness and Advocate of Bible Holiness*, January 21, 1926, 4. "Two meetings were held every day at three and seven thirty p.m. except Monday. The afternoon services were remarkable for the spirit of prayer which was manifested. Several souls were converted and sanctified in the meetings as well as in the evening services. About ninety souls sought the Lord during the campaign, the majority seeking the blessing of sanctification" (4).

38. See, for example, Ockenga, "Samuel." The text for his sermon is 1 Sam. 3:4. His log, written in his own hand, is included with the sermon.

39. Three evangelistic campaigns were held each year on the Taylor campus. See the *Taylor Echo*, September 15, 1926, 1.

40. For some interesting reflections on preaching, see Harold John Ockenga, "How to Prepare a Sermon," *Christianity Today*, October 13, 1958, 10; and "Sermon Preparation: The Challenge of the Ministry," sermon 2709, Ockenga Papers.

41. Ockenga, "Journal," May 2, 1926, Ockenga Papers.

42. See "Holiness League" in the Taylor University yearbook, the *Gem* (1925), 56–60. Ockenga served as president of the Holiness League during the winter of 1925.

so gentle. God gave me in prayer the answer to my prayers in again tendering my heart and overflowing it. I was in a sanctified state before but was rather dry. I thank God for the refreshing and anointing.[43]

Then, as he approached his graduation in 1927, Ockenga penned the following comments: "God has been nearer to me than breathing, nearer than my very blood, and all I have to do is drop on my knees to be greatly blessed. Never was prayer so satisfying as now, or so powerful. It seems that it is my very life and I revel in it. Glory to God. I have had greater times of ecstasy but this is the best of all."[44]

Ockenga's third priority as a student, after preaching and prayer, was learning how to live out the will of God in social service. His parents had taught him the importance of sacrifice, self-reliance, and duty through their own example, and Ockenga had learned his lessons well. "We are planning our Christmas," his mother wrote one holiday season, "and our plan is not to give any gifts to the family this year." This would allow them "to give to the poor," for "our city is in terrible distress, and I should feel very guilty [if I were to] spend a lot of money on useless gifts, when so many are hungry and cold." They would have a "splendid dinner and sing [and] give thanks [that] we have plenty of comforts." "I am sure we shall not miss the gifts to each other."[45] Commending her son for his own frugality during his college years, she wrote: "I am glad you are reaping some of the good things [that] always come with sacrifice." Harold John Ockenga had "done with little, lots of times." "I cannot forget your first years at Taylor how simply you lived." Following the commendation, however, she could not resist adding a gentle reminder: "Enjoy everything you can as long as it is in a temperate way, for that is what counts."[46]

Harold Ockenga's parents also taught him to be self-reliant. By the age of nine he was earning his own spending money. By the time he entered college he had built a savings account of $800. He graduated from college debt-free, having paid the entire bill himself.[47] His mother, who spent many years of her life caring for Harold's grandmother, also taught him about duty. "I do think we should give thanks for all the blessings we have had all through the year," she wrote her son. Yet "caring for Ma has not been an easy task, for sometimes I thought I just could not stand it another minute—but God has strengthened

43. Ockenga, "Journal," May 2, 1926, Ockenga Papers.

44. Ockenga, "Journal," April 23, 1927, Ockenga Papers.

45. Angie Ockenga to Harold John Ockenga, October 26, 1930, Ockenga Papers.

46. Angie Ockenga to Harold John Ockenga, October 19, 1930, Ockenga Papers.

47. Finding employment as a dishwasher, waiter, and maintenance worker during his college years, Ockenga earned enough to cover the costs of his education. Herman Ockenga, who was opposed to his son's decision to enter the ministry, vowed that he would "not contribute a penny" to his son's education for that purpose. Following a serious heart attack (which occurred during Harold's sophomore year at Taylor University), however, Herman not only gave his life to Christ but he changed his attitude toward the vocational direction of his son. See Lindsell, *Park Street Prophet*, 21–26.

me."[48] Despite the difficulties, the descriptions of which she often included in her letters to Harold John, she never abandoned her responsibilities. It was a lesson her son remembered throughout his life.

Of even greater significance, perhaps, was the inner confidence his parents helped build into the very fabric of his character. He grew up in a world of virtually endless possibilities. Much like the huge expanse of the universe, which his mother found so endlessly fascinating, the world of Christian service seemed to stretch out before him. You are destined "for greater things," his mother often told him.[49] "I expect great things of you," she wrote, for "you were chosen to speak God's Word." Therefore, "never, never, never forget to thank him for your brilliant mind and your success" for "God has given all things to you. . . . Do his will, and do not stray away from the truth, not even in the tiniest place, in your thought."[50]

The world of sacrifice, self-reliance, and duty that his parents built for him left little space for relationships. It should come as no surprise to discover that Ockenga would later refer to himself as a lone wolf since from his earliest years his greatest struggles had come in that arena. We see this most clearly, perhaps, in his relationships with the other members of the Taylor Evangelistic Team. Often together for long periods of time while traveling during the summer and on weekends, they not only got to know each other very well but also frequently got on each other's nerves.[51] "God has used this team," Harold reflected, "to hew me close to the edges and to prune away my unnecessary and hindering attributes. I realize I have grown in grace by our fellowship and association and I can see the same changes in the others."[52]

The problem, Ockenga was convinced, emerged primarily as a result of the "sarcastic tendencies" that he often exhibited around others—a behavior pattern that he came to call his "thorn." For while his brilliant mind and quick tongue were assets in the classroom and pulpit, they quickly became destructive weapons when turned against a friend or colleague. The problem, which had damaged some of his most important friendships, was of considerable concern to the young preacher. More than once, as he readily admitted, he "broke down and cried like a baby" when called to account for his behavior.[53] The issue seemed to have erupted in particularly dramatic form on July 31,

48. Angie Ockenga to Harold John Ockenga, November 24, 1930, Ockenga Papers.

49. Angie Ockenga to Harold John Ockenga, November 9, 1930, Ockenga Papers.

50. Angie Ockenga to Harold John Ockenga, January 30, 1930, Ockenga Papers.

51. We get an interesting glimpse at the normal schedule for the evangelistic team during their summer outings from Ockenga's journal entry for July 31, 1926, Ockenga Papers: Rise at 6:30 a.m. (prayer and Bible study); 8:30–9:00 (breakfast); 9:00–9:30 a.m. (odd jobs); 9:30–2:30 p.m. (study); 2:30–3:00 p.m. (children's meeting); 3:00–4:30 p.m. (afternoon evangelistic service); 4:30–6:00 p.m. (supper and rest); 6:30–8:00 p.m. (study for service); 8:00–9:30 p.m. (service); 9:30–10:30 p.m. (relaxation); 10:30–6:30 a.m. (bed).

52. Ockenga, "Journal," May 2, 1926, Ockenga Papers.

53. Ibid.

1926. Following the evening service, a meeting at which Ockenga had preached, the other members of the evangelistic team confronted him: "They said the message was all Ockenga and not Jesus," as he later reported the event, "and that it was my old trouble showing itself. They said that I was different from everyone else and that it caused a wall to be between us." Grieved by the incident, Harold spent the following day "in meditation and prayer."

The solution to his problem, Ockenga was convinced, would once again be found in a fresh experience of God's grace. "What I need," he wrote, "is a deeper crucifixion of self. . . . [I want] the mind in me which was also in Christ Jesus. I want the fullness of Christ. There are few men who have this and yet I want it desperately. I believe I am sanctified," he concluded, but need "more."[54] Despite his heartfelt desires, there appears to be no evidence that the "thorn" was ever removed. "I confessed again," he wrote a month later, "that thing that follows me wherever I go which causes people to not like to be with me."[55] Any relief he might have experienced seemed to be only temporary.[56] Despite these struggles, he wrote, "God showed me in a new way that his grace is sufficient for me. It may be that this thorn shall never be removed and that I shall have to walk life's road alone but his grace is sufficient. I shall trust God implicitly come what may. Regardless of what God gives others I shall do the best I can and let him do the rest. May His will be done."[57]

The Search for a Lifelong Companion

Harold John Ockenga had no desire "to walk life's road alone." On the contrary, as his letters and journal regularly attest, he was deeply interested in finding the perfect companion with whom he could share his future life and ministry. He was hopeful that God would provide him with exactly the right wife. Yet he couldn't help but worry that the troubling "thorn" with which he continued to struggle might damage or delay the process. Eventually, as we shall see, God did provide not only the perfect companion but also a wonderful lifetime of marriage. Nearly a decade was to pass, however, before that August day when, in the library of the University of Pittsburgh, Harold Ockenga met Audrey Williamson, the charming coed who swept him off his feet, eventually gave him three beautiful children, and (without any question) made his life enjoyable and his ministry possible.

54. Ockenga, "Journal," June 11, 1926, Ockenga Papers.
55. Ockenga, "Journal," July 11, 1926, Ockenga Papers.
56. Nearly half a year later, for example, Ockenga wrote: "I also rather feel at this time that my work with Bill Hawks will also be over. Our personalities seem to clash considerably." See Ockenga, "Journal," December 24, 1926, Ockenga Papers.
57. Ockenga, "Journal," June 31, 1926, Ockenga Papers.

Until the day he met Audrey, Ockenga continued his troubled search for a suitable wife. Having just returned from a date with "a very charming and spiritual young lady," as he later described her in his journal, he recorded with remarkable candor that his "sarcastic tendency" had nearly wrecked the evening.[58] Although the two had been dating for nearly a year and a half while they were students at Taylor, she had made it clear that unless he found a way to deal with his problem of sarcasm, the relationship would have to end. By the end of the year, the two had finally decided to cease being "sweethearts." But they also "renewed their covenant" to keep their minds pure and their bodies chaste. It was a commitment that Harold would continue to honor throughout his lifetime. "We are both friends now," he concluded, "but lonely in the midst of many things."[59]

Another factor in their decision was Virginia Ray. While the Taylor Evangelistic Team had been ministering at the Methodist Episcopal Church in Indiana, Ockenga had spotted a young woman in the audience. On the final Sunday afternoon, they had spoken with each other and had agreed to correspond. Although Ray was still quite young, she was bright, creative, musically talented, and deeply spiritual. Most important, at least from Ockenga's perspective, was the fact that she seemed to have the potential for developing over the next five or six years into exactly the kind of person who would make an ideal pastor's wife. While their friendship eventually came to an end, their six and a half years of correspondence provide an amazing window into the life and mind of a young man during some of his most formative years. Ockenga's 115 letters, written between 1926 and 1933, serve as a kind of journal connecting his student years at Taylor, Princeton, and Westminster with his ministry at Point Breeze Presbyterian Church in Pittsburgh.[60]

As one might expect, the correspondence is filled with accounts of his daily activities and references to family and friends. "My parents mean more to me than ever before," he wrote in 1927, "and my sisters are dears. Next week mother and I shall drive down to Peoria, Illinois, and visit many of our

---

58. "All I can say is that I just lost the personal touch of God in my life. As a result it made me a little hard and gave scope for my sarcastic tendency, which is my thorn, to display itself. This showed itself to her and to others. When she told me this I broke down and cried like a baby. We talked and cried together trying to get at the root of the matter for it hurt her as much as it did me," Ockenga, "Journal," June 11, 1926, Ockenga Papers.

59. Ockenga, "Journal," January 3, 1927, Ockenga Papers.

60. The correspondence between Ockenga and Ray began on December 17, 1926, and continued until July 3, 1933. With the exception of a single poem, all 115 handwritten letters (most about four or five pages in length) were composed by Ockenga and they are rich in information about his life and work. The two correspondents had agreed that should their relationship ever end, they would return to the other all the letters they had received. Consequently, the full set of Ockenga's letters (all in their original envelopes) are now part of the Ockenga Papers. When they met Ockenga was twenty-one and Ray was fourteen. See Ockenga, "Journal," January 3, 1927.

relations. I will stay with that rich aunt about whom I told you. I believe we shall have a fine time."[61] In addition to the descriptions of daily life, the letters provide a unique view of Ockenga's inner world. The profile that emerges is of a bright, energetic, and focused young man—a passionate Christian of unquestioned integrity who is determined to serve the cause of Christ whatever the cost. It is the picture of one who loves to travel, enjoys the beauty of nature, relishes the reading of a good book, is hopelessly romantic, is fascinated by philosophical systems, finds pleasure in vigorous debate, and welcomes a difficult challenge. Ockenga reveals an unbounded zest for life, believes passionately in the importance of revival, and is willing to take risks. He reveals that he loves to walk by the ocean in the moonlight, writes poetry and enjoys art, studies the Bible and spends hours in prayer, welcomes any opportunity to hike or swim or ski or surf or play tennis, and—most of all—loves to preach.

There is no question that at the center of Ockenga's world was his love for preaching. "Thank God," he wrote in his first letter to Virginia Ray, "for the opportunity of preaching [H]is living, wonderful, thrilling gospel."[62] Ockenga lived to preach the Word—and his enthusiasm spilled over in letter after letter. "We are now through with the campaign," he wrote in the spring of 1927. "Many were either saved or sanctified, some joined the church, and tremendous crowds came. It surpassed all of our expectations."[63] "I certainly enjoy preaching," he wrote early in 1930. "These days, I feel, are a time of preparation for some large work which is ahead."[64] The correspondence also reflects Ockenga's love for the Wesleyan tradition in which he had been raised. The "experience of sanctification is what has meant most in my life," he wrote.[65] "Last week I preached in Homiletics," he wrote of his experience at Princeton, "and got things stirred up." I preached "some good old Methodist doctrine to the Presbyterians. Ha! Ha!"[66]

The central role of prayer in Ockenga's life is also expressed throughout the correspondence. "Today I have spent much time praying and meditating," he wrote. "I walked out into the country and read the Word and tonight I have a gracious feeling of peace and satisfaction in my heart, and a great anticipation of every day of the future. Praise God."[67] The letters contain some winsome evidence of Ockenga's love for the beauty of God's creation and zest for life. "I went for a long walk among the snow covered hills," he wrote of his experience on Christmas Day of 1926,

61. Ockenga to Ray, September 10, 1927, Ockenga Papers.
62. Ockenga to Ray, December 17, 1926, Ockenga Papers.
63. Ockenga to Ray, April 5, 1927, Ockenga Papers.
64. Ockenga to Ray, January 26, 1930, Ockenga Papers.
65. Ockenga to Ray, April 26 and May 18, 1926, Ockenga Papers.
66. Ockenga to Ray, November 15, 1927, Ockenga Papers.
67. Ockenga to Ray, February 26, 1927, Ockenga Papers.

and then stood watching a rapid brook as it swept down to the sea and listening to its tales of Christmas joy and sorrow. My heart was aflame with the love of Christ but mellowed with the solitude of the hour and place. But I was happy, tremendously happy! for I knew that in that place I was pleasing God, that also there were many other souls over the country whose lives were brighter and fuller because we had met, and that I was causing no one any sorrow, but some much joy. It was a great hour, I assure you.[68]

"Life is opening up before us," he wrote the following March, "with a great teeming, suffering, hungry humanity to help to God, with the great joy of doing it, and with all the beauty and satisfaction attending it. Life to me is wonderful, beautiful, and inspiring," he concluded, "and I feel more determined than ever to make the most of it."[69] "Virginia," he wrote in the fall of 1927, "my heart is just bubbling over with joy. Life is just one round of happiness which is only intermingled with the sorrow and sympathy I feel in the trouble of others whose hearts are not in tune with Jesus. My steps are ordered by the Lord and I could ask for nothing which I do not have and yet I feel the burden of humanity weighing upon me because of my love for them."[70]

Ockenga's growing fascination with missions is also reflected in the correspondence. "Lately we have had many long discussions in our room about missions," he wrote at the start of his final year of seminary. An opportunity had opened for him to go as a missionary to central China. "Won't you pray earnestly that I may know God's will in this matter?" he asked Ray. "How can I stay in towns and cities where six and seven ministers are preaching to half filled churches, when millions cry for Christ and his saving power?"[71]

A final theme at the heart of the correspondence is Ockenga's growing interest in Ray herself. On one level, his comments are those of a spiritual advisor: "It is fine that you are finding so many things to engross your time these days," he wrote late in 1927, but "I am trusting with you that they are not in any way shutting you away from close fellowship with Him because of occupying your time. I hope these days are ones of molding and shaping to you that will prepare you for the work ahead."[72] On another level, his letters seem to reflect the interests of an academic advisor or coach: "I'm so glad that you are taking up voice. It will be a great help. With that and your accomplishments on the piano you shall be some trained musician. I didn't know you were putting on drama. Let me know of your progress in this line."[73] Later he wrote, "Don't you forget to take systematic exercise every day, even at the expense of other

68. Ockenga to Ray, January 4, 1927, Ockenga Papers.
69. Ockenga to Ray, March 1, 1927, Ockenga Papers.
70. Ockenga to Ray, September 10, 1927, Ockenga Papers.
71. Ockenga to Ray, October 29, 1929, Ockenga Papers.
72. Ockenga to Ray, November 27, 1927, Ockenga Papers.
73. Ockenga to Ray, May 5, 1930, Ockenga Papers.

things. I want you to be hard and athletic. You see I spend so much time in athletics that we must be real pals in this as well as other things."[74]

The correspondence, as one might expect, also reflects Ockenga's interest in Ray as a potential wife.[75] As the years passed, however, the "ups and downs" of their friendship began to take their toll. By late 1930, Ockenga had become so concerned that he wrote to his mother to ask her advice. "Your choice is my choice," his mother responded, and "I shall love any girl you bring home to me." However, "you have been in many homes where you have seen family life, and you know our own home with its many problems" and "you know from all this that life is not a bed of roses," that "it has its ups and downs and as our Lord said we must have tribulations." No matter "how educated you are and how efficient a wife Virginia might be," only "a strong bond" will "keep that love burning." "If you are uncertain about [Virginia] before marriage, I assure you my son it will never come after marriage." Therefore, "[you should] wait until one comes to you that you know is the one and only one for you" and "I am afraid Virginia is not that one."[76]

It was not until late June of 1932 that Harold Ockenga finally took his mother's advice. "You asked me to be honest," he wrote to Ray. "There was a time when we could have made a go of things but I can't see it now. I am not in love with anyone although I go out with many girls. It seems that I have no inclination or special interest for anyone. They come and go now." So, he advised her, "you had better forget me. That oughtn't be hard since you always had so many other interests. If I don't settle down somewhere by the time you graduate I may make an effort to see you then, but I can't see any use now."[77]

Princeton Theological Seminary (1927–29)

Ockenga's graduation from Taylor University was a joyous occasion. "College is over," he wrote on June 15, 1927, and "my A.B. has been conferred."[78] By the following September, he had begun his theological studies at Princeton Theological Seminary.[79] "I had expected much," he wrote to a friend, but

74. Ockenga to Ray, August 4, 1930, Ockenga Papers.

75. By the spring of 1927, Ockenga was considering changing his name "from Harold John Ockenga to Harold John. People have too much trouble with it." "How do you like it?" he asked, "Mr. John. Mrs. John. Dr. John. Of course I'll keep my ancestral records for the family comes from the bluebloods of Holland." Ockenga to Ray, April 5, 1927, Ockenga Papers.

76. Angie Ockenga to Harold John Ockenga, December 2, 1930, Ockenga Papers.

77. Ockenga to Ray, February 26, 1928, and June 30, 1932, Ockenga Papers.

78. Ockenga graduated with a double major in history and English and with a minor in philosophy. See Ockenga, "Journal," June 15, 1927, Ockenga Papers. David Westfall preached the baccalaureate service and H. C. Morrison was the speaker at the graduation ceremony.

79. Ockenga began classes on Wednesday, September 28, 1927. For the history of Princeton Theological Seminary, see David Calhoun, *History of Princeton Seminary*, 2 vols. (Edinburgh: Banner of

Princeton "has passed all my expectations." He wrote that being there "is the greatest privilege of my life so far and I surely trust I may be worthy of it."[80] Princeton "is a most beautiful, cultured and scholastical place. I could never have obtained the privilege save in the Lord. Thus I thank Him and intend to make the most of every opportunity."[81]

By early November, Ockenga had settled into a comfortable but demanding routine. "My course has kept me busy from Monday at 6:30 a.m. till Saturday at 12:00 a.m. I have three languages, Hebrew, Greek and German, besides all the Seminary work. It is quite a load."[82] "I have noticed a great difference between the east and the west," Ockenga observed. "Here people are cold and cultured. In the west they are hospitable and friendly."[83] But he increasingly found himself falling in love with the "cold and cultured" northeast.[84] "I thank God that I was directed to this place," he wrote. "It has been a great education, a tremendous broadening, and an impetus to be true to Jesus Christ in life and teaching."[85] Nearly everything about Princeton appealed to Ockenga. He loved its gothic architecture. He was energized by its intellectual demands. He was impressed by the size and scope of its libraries. He was challenged by the brilliance of its faculty. He was dazzled by the beauty of its campus.

Some aspects of campus life, however, caused him growing concern. Princeton's "inordinate stress upon intellectual affairs," he was convinced, was undermining "individual piety." According to his own calculations, segments of the seminary community were engaged in the following practices: (1) Dancing, 10 percent; (2) Smoking, 30 percent or more; (3) Swearing, 5 percent (occasionally); (4) Theater attendance, 70 percent; (5) Card playing, 50 percent; (6) Studying on Sunday, 60 percent at least; (7) Talk of appointments to big churches with large salaries but little talk of soul salvation; (8) Virtually no evangelism; (9) No vital piety; and (10) Strife within the faculty.[86] While admitting that such an assessment presented "a rather discouraging summary,"

Truth, 1996); William K. Selden, *Princeton Theological Seminary: A Narrative History, 1812–1992* (Princeton: Theological Book Agency, 1992); Lefferts A. Loetscher, *Facing the Enlightenment and Pietism: Archibald Alexander and the Founding of Princeton Theological Seminary* (New York: Greenwood, 1983); B. B. Warfield and William Armstrong, eds., *Centennial Celebration* (Phillipsburg, NJ: P&R 2001); and David F. Wells, ed., *Reformed Theology in America: A History of Its Modern Development* (Grand Rapids: Eerdmans, 1985).

80. Ockenga to Ray, September 26, 1927, Ockenga Papers.

81. Ockenga, "Journal," October 1, 1927, Ockenga Papers.

82. Ockenga, "Journal," November 6, 1927, Ockenga Papers.

83. Ibid.

84. Ockenga's love for the East continued to deepen throughout the following years. By 1932 he would write: "The east is now home to me and it is here that I feel I belong. Strange how a few years will change one's outlook on life. The people are the same everywhere and the gospel is effective for all. But there are customs and habits here that I like." Ockenga to Ray, September 12, 1932, Ockenga Papers.

85. Ockenga, "Journal," January 18, 1928, Ockenga Papers.

86. Ibid.

Ockenga was convinced that seminary life also had its "redeeming features." The Bible was taught and honored at Princeton, although its principles were not always practiced. Much of the teaching by the seminary faculty was theologically sound. Personal devotions "kept me very near to God." And there were excellent times of prayer and fellowship with classmates such as Vic Peters and Tom Holloway. "Billy Blackstone and I are enjoying real Methodist fundamental fellowship."[87]

Taking up lodgings in room 306 in Alexander Hall, Ockenga dove into his studies with his characteristic energy and resolve.[88] "It seems that they cause one's brain to groan as they stretch it in the enlargement process," he wrote. "I never dreamed of the wealth of material there was secluded away. Never shall I run out of sermon material after seeing the sources here."[89] The Princeton faculty—including a number of internationally recognized scholars such as J. Gresham Machen, Robert Dick Wilson, Oswald Allis, Charles Erdman, Cornelius Van Til, and J. Richie Smith—encouraged their students to think deeply and prepare themselves rigorously for the various ministries to which God had called them. One professor in particular, J. Gresham Machen, became important in shaping Ockenga's thinking with his rigorous scholarship and deep commitment to Christ.[90] Through the courses he took with professor Machen—including New Testament Greek, New Testament introduction and exegesis, the life of Jesus, and Paul and his environment—and in the informal discussions and checkers matches that Machen hosted in his Alexander Hall lodgings, Ockenga's understanding of Scripture was deepened and his theological understanding was sharpened. Although Ockenga already "knew the Bible from A to Z," as his mother phrased it, he discovered in Machen a mature and gifted scholar who had much to teach the young theologian.[91]

During his two years at Princeton Theological Seminary, Ockenga distinguished himself as an outstanding student and a recognized campus leader. During his second year, he was awarded the prestigious Robert L. Maitland Prize in New Testament exegesis. Despite his academic success, he never lost his great love for preaching. He had a "fire in my bones to preach," as he phrased it, and it continued to grow "brighter and brighter and more irresistible."[92] There were plenty of opportunities to exercise his gift. For five months, during the summer between his first and second year of seminary, Ockenga trav-

87. Ibid.

88. About a dozen black loose-leaf notebooks, filled with hundreds of pages of handwritten class notes, daily Bible study notes, and sermon outlines can be found in the Ockenga Papers.

89. Ockenga to Ray, October 5, 1927, Ockenga Papers.

90. For the life of J. Gresham Machen, see Ned B. Stonehouse, *J. Gresham Machen: A Biographical Memoir* (Grand Rapids: Eerdmans, 1954) and Stephen J. Nichols, *J. Gresham Machen: A Guided Tour of His Life and Thought* (Phillipsburg, NJ: P&R, 2004).

91. For Machen's influence on Ockenga, see Adams, "The Making of a Neo-Evangelical Statesman," 134–44.

92. Ockenga to Ray, February 26, 1928, Ockenga Papers.

eled with the Princeton Evangelistic Team. Driving through dozens of states, preaching in scores of churches, and traversing thousands of miles, being on the team provided a wealth of ministry opportunities.[93]

In addition to his work on the Evangelistic Team, Ockenga was appointed by the Methodist Episcopal Conference to serve as student pastor of the First Methodist Episcopal Church of Avalon, New Jersey. Known as "The Church by the Sea," Ockenga assumed his new responsibilities on October 1, 1928.[94] Not only did the congregation thrive under his ministry but word of the remarkable young preacher also began to circulate beyond his own community. The Methodist Episcopal Church in Millville, a congregation of six hundred members, asked Ockenga when he would be finished with his seminary studies, and they invited him to preach at their church.[95] "Some summer people who are down from Philadelphia," Ockenga wrote in another letter, "told some of my people they were going to steal me for their place."[96] In addition, he began to receive invitations to preach in other churches, in the regional Rotary Club, and at a variety of conferences. When he spoke at a youth conference, two young men and two young women, all seniors in high school, "consecrated their lives to life service for Christ." Then he added, "I certainly do like the conference work."[97]

Ockenga also instituted some interesting new practices at the church. After preaching a sermon on "Robbers of God," taken from Malachi 3:8–12, he decided that the congregation should "do away with all such things as suppers, fairs, bazaars, etc., for raising money." This new "faith plan," as he called it, should even extend to the passing of the offering plate. "So now all we have is a box in the back of the church to receive whatever God sends [in]. Formerly I was to get $1100 a year and expenses here (of course it's only a student charge) but now I'll get what God sends in. If it [is] more we'll send it to missions, if less we'll abide by what the Lord sends."[98]

93. Bill Martin and Bill Blackstone were also part of the team. They drove toward the West across the Northern states and then returned Eastward across the Southern states. For descriptions of their thirteen thousand miles of travel and ministry, see Ockenga to Ray, September 12 and October 7, 1928, Ockenga Papers.

94. "I dropped you a line from Atlantic City," wrote Ockenga, "where I attended the M[ethodist] E[piscopal] Conference. They gave me a charge for next year here in New Jersey. I have someone else to fill it for the summer [while I am traveling with the Evangelistic Team] but it certainly will be nice to come back to it next year. It is small, white, and well situated. The people are of the middle class and are very spiritual. I preached there last Sunday and we had a fine time—a number were converted. [They say I can] hold it as long as I want to." Ockenga to Ray, March 17, 1928, Ockenga Papers. Ockenga served the First Methodist Episcopal Church on 34th and Dune Drive in Avalon, New Jersey, for nearly two years. On September 1, 1930, he began a one-year appointment as assistant minister of First Presbyterian Church in Pittsburgh, serving under Clarence Macartney.

95. Ockenga preached at Millville, a community of five thousand with only one church, on Sunday morning, January 12, 1929. See Ockenga to Ray, January 11, 1929, Ockenga Papers.

96. Ockenga to Ray, July 8, 1929, Ockenga Papers.

97. Ockenga to Ray, January 11, 1929, Ockenga Papers.

98. Ockenga to Ray, July 8, 1929, and January 15, 1930, Ockenga Papers.

In addition to his preaching and his work in the church, Ockenga continued to carry a full load of courses at the seminary. He had "twelve [exams] on twelve days," he wrote. "It has been a hard grind but I am happy in completing the work with good grades. Just think! I am now a senior here."[99] Rather than travel again with the Princeton Evangelistic Team during the summer, Ockenga planned to remain in Avalon to continue his ministry at the church. "In the summer," he wrote, he could "give my full time" to this ministry whereas during the winter he had only been able to serve on "week ends." Then, looking forward to the upcoming opportunity, he wrote, "large crowds" come to Avalon each summer, "as it is a high class private beach resort just 20 miles south of Atlantic City. I think it will afford a great opportunity for service among the professional class such as lawyers, doctors, professors, etc. Most of the people have fine summer houses. Then I also expect to do considerable swimming and resting."[100]

Call to the Mission Field

During the months leading up to summer, Ockenga had also decided that his future ministry would take him to the mission field. "[Let me] tell you some real news," he wrote early in May of 1929.

> I tell you in the spirit of joy and yet in the solemnity of what is deepest in my life. Jesus has definitely called me to become a foreign missionary. It has been the result of a long thought process and a season of praying it through. There is no other way for me now. When I had settled it with God and then wrote home expecting to meet opposition, as I am the only son, I found that mother had been praying for some time that I should receive the call. Isn't that wonderful?[101]

Ockenga's plan was to sail for India in four years—following the final year of seminary studies, a year of travel and study in Europe, and two years of doctoral studies at Northwestern University—to teach at the Methodist Theological College in India. The Methodist Theological College "trains college graduates

99. Ockenga to Ray, May 2, 1929, Ockenga Papers.

100. During his time at Avalon Harold led three services on Sundays, a Tuesday evening expositional Bible study, and a Thursday evening prayer meeting. In the summer, he also led morning prayers in the Avalon Hotel, where he kept a room, and offered private swimming lessons to residents of the hotel. See Ockenga to Ray, May 2 and 20, 1929, Ockenga Papers.

101. Ockenga to Ray, May 2, 1929. "I fear there is a danger" for all ministers to become "self centered," Ockenga wrote, if "we do not keep upon our faces in prayer. And when it does happen how helpless we become to help others and to do God's work. But you know people so foolishly make so much of the minister. That is one reason I am glad that I am going to the foreign field." Ockenga to Ray, July 27, 1929, Ockenga Papers. Angie Ockenga, Billy Hawks, and several members of the Taylor Evangelistic Team visited Avalon during the summer. "Mother visited my church in Avalon and I was certainly proud that she could come to the first little church I ever had." Ockenga to Ray, September 6, 1929, Ockenga Papers.

for the ministry. It will be a life of teaching, preaching, and evangelism. I am
not certain that I shall go there yet, but it looks that way."[102]

The Presbyterian Controversy

During his years at Princeton Theological Seminary, a great theological
storm was raging throughout the church.[103] "Princeton Seminary has now
split in two," Ockenga wrote on July 27, 1929,

> and most of the old faculty are organizing a new seminary. It will be called
> "Westminster." Princeton will be in the hands of the modernists. It is a sad
> story. I do not know yet where I shall go next year. I did so want to graduate
> from Princeton, but if it is modern, I'm afraid my principles will turn me else-
> where. Most of my friends are going to the new seminary. What do you think
> I should do?[104]

Not until the beginning of the fall semester was he certain what his decision
should be. "You remember I told you of the possibility of my leaving Princeton
because of the split," he wrote early in October. "Well, when I came back
[to Princeton] I found all these internationally known professors and all my
friends going to the new seminary. It was a case of taking a stand for Christ
against the modernist encroaches upon Princeton. Princeton has changed and
can never be the same, so they set forth to organize a new seminary which
would be true to God's Word."[105]

Ockenga was well aware of the enormous cost—to the faculty, his fellow
students, and his own future prospects—that such a decision represented.[106]
Nonetheless, he wrote, "I left Princeton, an assured degree, an assured Fellowship which would send me to Europe, and all the material advantages and came
here to Westminster Theological school. It was a question of taking a definite

---

102. Ockenga describes his plan in Ockenga to Ray, May 2 and October 29, 1929, Ockenga Papers.
At various times he also expressed interest in serving as a missionary in China and Africa.

103. Of the scores of studies of the fundamentalist/modernist controversy, the best source remains
George M. Marsden, *Fundamentalism and American Culture: The Shaping of Twentieth-Century
Evangelicalism, 1870–1925* (New York: Oxford University Press, 1980). On the controversy in the
Presbyterian denomination, see Bradley J. Longfield, *The Presbyterian Controversy: Fundamentalists,
Modernists, and Moderates* (New York: Oxford University Press, 1993); and Lefferts A. Loetscher, *The
Broadening Church: A Study of Theological Issues in the Presbyterian Church Since 1869* (Philadelphia:
University of Pennsylvania Press, 1954).

104. Ockenga to Ray, July 27, 1929, Ockenga Papers. The "old faculty," representing the more
conservative wing of the Princeton faculty, included J. Gresham Machen, Oswald Allis, and Robert
Wilson.

105. Ockenga to Ray, October 1, 1929, Ockenga Papers.

106. See J. Gresham Machen, "Westminster Theological Seminary: Its Purpose and Plan," *Presbyterian*, October 10, 1929, 6–10.

stand for Christ and we have done it, but at great cost."[107] "Ernest [Zentgraf], my last year's roommate and [Bill] Blackstone—that wonderful Californian— and I, are rooming together in a three room suite. It is quite lovely, a large study room, a sitting room and a sleeping room with a private bath. Billy has two large oriental rugs, and we have considerable to put in besides having it nicely furnished. So we are expecting a wonderful year together."[108] The comradery of the Westminster community, with students and faculty drawn together by clarity of purpose and the mutual sharing of some tremendous risks, created an exciting and stimulating environment in which to study and bonded the community together in a mutually satisfying fellowship.[109]

The Growing Lure of Pastoral Ministry

By the middle of his senior year in seminary, Ockenga had begun to enter- tain thoughts of a pastorate in America. While he was still open to serving as a foreign missionary, he was convinced by Frank Stevenson, president of the Westminster board, and Clarence E. Macartney, senior minister of Pitts- burgh's First Presbyterian Church, to remain in America. "If you go to the mission field," they argued, "and if other graduates here of Westminster go to the mission field, as you're planning to do, then who is going to take these churches which are the citadels of orthodoxy, and send the missionaries out? Are we going to abdicate and turn those churches over to the liberals and thus affect the mission field in an indirect way?" While their arguments eventually persuaded Ockenga to remain in the pastorate, at least "for a season," he determined to do so only on the condition that "the Lord [would make] it possible" for him "to do what both those men had said was necessary to be done, namely, to send missionaries out to the field."[110]

Moreover, a number of rather large churches were beginning to show an active interest in calling Ockenga as their pastor. The district superintendent of the Methodist Episcopal Church, however, was convinced that Ockenga was far too young to assume leadership of such substantial congregations and he was determined to block any movement in that direction. The Millville

107. Ockenga hoped to spend a term of study at the University of Berlin while he was in Europe. Ockenga to Ray, October 1, 1929, Ockenga Papers.

108. Ernest Zentgraf and Bill Blackstone both became missionaries to China under the China Inland Mission. Ockenga to Ray, October 1, 1929, and January 15, 1930, Ockenga Papers.

109. Ockenga kept a file of newspaper and magazine clippings from sources such as the *Presby- terian*, the *Christian Advocate*, and the *Methodist* reporting on the controversy and the beginnings of Westminster. He also collected pictures and institutional documents such as "The Constitution of the Alumni Association," "Our Faculty," the "Westminster Alumni Annals," R. B. Kuiper's "Practical Theology Today," and others. These can be found in the Ockenga Papers.

110. Harold J. Ockenga, *The Church God Blesses* (Pasadena and Boston: Fuller Missions Fellow- ship and Park Street Church Board of Missions, 1959), 9.

congregation of four hundred members extended to Ockenga "an official call to be their pastor" despite the fact that the district superintendent had not yet "consented." The congregation "is going to demand it," Ockenga wrote, "and I told him that if he didn't send me to [Millville] or to Allentown I would leave in the spring for Europe. Then when I come back I'll be a Presbyterian. So the fleece is out."[111]

In addition to his problems with the district superintendent, however, some influential members of the Conference of the Methodist Episcopal Church were trying to block his ordination and that of the other Westminster graduates. "We are having a wonderful time now about our ordination," Ockenga wrote with a kind of righteous relish. "The liberal members of the Conference are in charge of the educational committee and they have refused to ordain me and the others who are coming from the new Seminary. But they have no grounds for it and we are going to put up one of the biggest fights that has ever taken place in the history of the conference. We have the biggest and most influential preacher in the conference on our side and he is going to give them a time of it."[112]

The annual conference of the Methodist Episcopal Church was held in Atlantic City during the first week of March. "I think it will be a crisis time between the fundamentalists and modernists," Ockenga observed, and "most of it will rage around us who are entering from Westminster. So pray that God will give us grace, and that His will may be done in all."[113] The results of the meetings were mixed. "The Bishop," for his part, delivered "some wonderful sermons on real deep spiritual life," Ockenga wrote, and "they almost turned the Conference into a revival this morning. May God make all of our Bishops like this one is." Although a group of "liberals" tried to thwart his ordination, the conference finally voted to ordain Ockenga as a deacon. With regard to the two congregations who wanted him to come as their pastor, however, both "the District Superintendent and the Bishop have ignored the calls I have received and want me to return to Avalon. So I am taking it as Providential and am returning."[114]

Immediately following his ordination as deacon, however, two members of the conference cabinet approached Ockenga about taking on the leadership of the Chelsea-Ventnor Church in Atlantic City. While located in "the most

111. "If I am refused both of these I'm through with the Episcopacy," he wrote. It would appear that Ockenga had little quarrel with the theology of John Wesley but harbored a growing concern about the creeping modernism within the denomination and had some serious problems with its ecclesiastical polity. The Millville congregation offered him a salary of $2,000 per year and a furnished parsonage, and it was open to exactly the kind of ministry for which Stevenson and Macartney had argued. See Ockenga to Ray, January 15 and February 3, 1930, Ockenga Papers.

112. Ockenga to Ray, February 18, 1930, Ockenga Papers.

113. Ockenga to Ray, February 24, 1930, Ockenga Papers.

114. Ockenga to Ray, March 7, 1930, Ockenga Papers.

wealthy section of Atlantic City," it had long been considered "one of the hardest fields in the Conference." Three pastors had already failed to make a go of it and "there is a big chance," as Ockenga expressed it, "that I will too." The challenge was exactly what he needed, and he accepted immediately.[115] The church is just a block and a half "from the Ocean," he wrote. "Today I took two long walks on the boardwalk. The water was so blue and the sun so warm and the sand so white. They were riding horses on the beach and children were playing in the sands watched by maids. The neighborhood is wonderful." "Whether we can pull the little church out of debt," he continued, "is yet to be solved. I think it can be done."[116] "Sunday we had a fine day in the church. In the morning I preached on 'The Chambers of a Mother's Soul.' We had 65 out and in the evening there were 70 out. God is weekly increasing the congregation."[117]

Meanwhile, he had completed his final year at seminary—finishing near the top of his class, in the "first group for the year, one of four fellows in the seminary who did."[118] "It's all over now," he wrote. "I'm settled in the manse in Atlantic City and am undertaking a real program. It's hard to realize that seminary is over and that I am now facing life in earnest, but that is exactly the case."[119]

First Presbyterian Church in Pittsburgh (1930–31)

The ink had barely dried on his agreement with the Chelsea-Ventnor congregation when a letter arrived from Frank Stevenson, Westminster's Board Chairman.[120] "Dear Ockenga," he wrote,

it is important that we place one of our graduates in the First Presbyterian Church in Pittsburgh. From the letter enclosed you will see that they need an assistant minister there. Would the field and opportunities interest you? The work is hard, the rewards in the way of Sunday preaching not numerous, but the chance of learning the workings of one of the best churches in America is good. And if you would like to reach young people in a down town field, the

115. The salary was $1,500 per year with a twelve-room parsonage. Ockenga to Ray, March 11 and 25, 1930, Ockenga Papers.

116. Ockenga to Ray, March 25, 1930, Ockenga Papers.

117. Ockenga to Ray, May 14, 1930, Ockenga Papers. See also "Chambers of a Mother's Soul," sermon 72, Ockenga Papers. By the following week, the morning attendance had grown to ninety-two. See Ockenga to Ray, May 27, 1930, Ockenga Papers.

118. The Westminster Seminary graduation was held on May 6, 1930. See Ockenga to Ray, May 5, 1930, Ockenga Papers.

119. Ockenga to Ray, May 14, 1930, Ockenga Papers.

120. From reports in the *Westminster Alumni Annals* (December 1932 and December 1933) it appears that Carl McIntire assumed this charge following Ockenga's departure.

most difficult but the most satisfying type of Christian service in the world, the chance is unparalleled. You would have to become a Presbyterian.[121]

"I've been considering [a] call to Pittsburgh," Ockenga wrote after receiving a letter from Clarence Macartney outlining the details of the position.[122] "They will give me a car, $3000.00, allow me to go to the U. of Pittsburgh and will release me when I want to go. So I've been praying much about it and feel that I shall probably take it."[123] On July 19th, Ockenga was interviewed by the session of First Presbyterian Church in Pittsburgh. On July 21, the clerk of session, Robert J. Gibson, wrote to extend a formal invitation for him "to come to us as an Assistant Minister for a period of one year commencing September 1, 1930, at a salary of two hundred and fifty dollars per month."[124] By July 29, Ockenga had made arrangements for lodgings at the Young Men's Christian Association of Pittsburgh.[125] By July 30, Clarence E. Macartney had written to congratulate Ockenga on his decision to come. "I know that the decision to enter the

121. Stevenson to Ockenga, May 27, 1930, Ockenga Papers. "I thought of Blackstone for the place, but Woolley says he is going to China next year," Stevenson continued. "Some of the Princeton graduates are trying to get the position but without any luck. If you were willing to subordinate yourself to Macartney and work the job for all that is in it, I think you would find it a wise step to take. I enjoyed four years under Maitland Alexander more than any other four years of my life." Then he concluded: "You should not pull out of your present fine work until your conscience is absolutely clear. It never pays to be an opportunist and Shakespeare ought to have been hung for advising it. I am glad you see that, and I admire your attitude. On the other hand it will do no harm to talk things over with Macartney if you have the chance. I would like to see you in my old job. Do not consider it, however, unless you are sure your leaving Atlantic City will not hurt a good many souls who have confidence in you. The First Church in Pittsburgh is not the only chance you are going to have."

122. "Your work as one of the assistants here at the First Church would consist of the following: 1. Pastoral visitation; 2. Boys' Clubs and the Summer Camp in the mountains; 3. Work with the Young People's Society; 4. Work in the Sunday School. . . . The honorarium is $3000. An automobile is furnished the assistant to aid him in his calling. I have very favorable reports of your work and feel that you are the sort of man we would like to have on the Staff of the First Church." Macartney to Ockenga, June 16, 1930, Ockenga Papers. For Ockenga's reflections on the invitation, see Ockenga to Ray, June 18, 1930, Ockenga Papers.

123. By July 7 Harold would write, "Today I've got a roaming feeling about my heart that I'd like to start moving somewhere—anywhere—just to go. Yesterday was my birthday and some friends here gave me a little dinner party. It was quite nice in their lovely mansion, but somehow I wasn't there. I wasn't anywhere in particular, just roaming. . . . Another offer has come to me—to be Editor of the *Essentialist*, Associate Pastor of the First Church of Haddonfield, and Executive Secretary of the Methodist League for Faith and Life, at the same salary as the Pittsburgh offer. It is quite tempting— to begin next March. . . . Virge dear, I've had so many decisions to make this year that I sometimes feel I'd like to flee from it all. Burdened, hungry people on all sides depending on you for some help, and yet so young, so immature. God, what a position. Were it not for His strength, I would not know where to turn. No wonder there are thousands here seeking pleasure! Who can blame them? Weary, tired, hungry, heart-broken—these poor people. What a world this is." Ockenga to Ray, July 7, 1930, Ockenga Papers.

124. Gibson to Ockenga, July 21, 1930, Ockenga Papers.

125. F. C. Benner to Ockenga, July 29, 1930, Ockenga Papers.

Presbyterian ministry has meant a great deal to you," Macartney wrote, "and I pray that you may have peace and satisfaction in the course you have chosen for yourself."[126] By September 1, Ockenga had taken up his new responsibilities.[127]

"I'm quite happy," Ockenga confided to Virginia Ray, "because I feel that it is God's will and that He will bless the work. Sorry that I could not fulfill your wishes and remain a Methodist but when you call on me in Pittsburgh you'll understand why."[128] "Thanks much for the congratulations and encouragement concerning my new work," he wrote early in August. "Certainly everything in a material advantage that a young man could want shall now be mine. But I am praying that God will help me to completely forget all that and to just be a humble servant of His. I want spiritual power regardless of these other things. I would rather go hungry with Him than to have all the other advantages in the world and miss Him. Pray that God may freshly endow me with His Spirit for this new work. I realize the responsibility of it. I really feel like I were stepping into manhood now."[129]

The First Presbyterian Church was everything Ockenga had hoped it might be. "I have a private office here," he wrote, "and the church has three secretaries, with over 20 paid full time workers. Nothing could be finer. I believe it is really the beginning of my fullest opportunity. From now till I am 50 years old are the years to do creative work. I feel also that the past has accomplished much, but I expect so much more in the future. Praise the Lord for the privilege of living in this generation."[130]

In addition, Ockenga was allowed to begin his graduate studies at the University of Pittsburgh. "I will accomplish two things there in the next year," he wrote. "[I'll] get a M.A. in Arts and get my residence requirements off on a doctor's degree. Then I can take the rest of my work where I please. It seems the Lord has sent this job for a purpose. Much good can be done; my backing will be received by being in this church; great experience will be received; my education will be completed; and enough resources will be on hand to do anything I wish."[131] By 1934, Ockenga had completed the MA degree, having written his thesis on "The Role of Competition in Marx." By 1939, he had successfully completed a PhD degree at the University of Pittsburgh, having written his thesis on "Poverty as a Theoretical and Practical Problem of Government in the Writings of Jeremy Bentham and the Marxian Alternative."[132]

126. Macartney to Ockenga, July 30, 1930, Ockenga Papers.

127. On the history of the church, see Ernest E. Logan, *The Church That Was Twice Born* (Pittsburgh: Pickwick-Morcraft, 1973). For the sequence of events leading to his appointment at the church, see Ockenga to Ray, July 22, 1930, Ockenga Papers.

128. Ockenga to Ray, July 22, 1930, Ockenga Papers.

129. Ockenga to Ray, August 4, 1930, Ockenga Papers.

130. Ockenga to Ray, September 3, 1930, Ockenga Papers.

131. Ockenga to Ray, September 3, 1930, Ockenga Papers. See also Robert J. Gibson to Harold John Ockenga, July 21, 1930, Ockenga Papers.

132. Unbound copies of both of these theses can be found in the Ockenga Papers.

Furthermore, the work at the church was going well. Under Ockenga's energetic leadership, the youth ministries were thriving. "This month," he reported, "I am giving a series of five addresses in Young People's to about 125. They are to bring them face to face with Jesus Christ as their personal Saviour. I trust that the results will be accomplished. Several young men have accepted Christ this last week."[133] In addition to his work with the young people, Ockenga helped to start a men's ministry known as the Tuesday Noon Club. So successful was the venture that soon its membership exceeded two thousand and its weekly attendance was averaging about six hundred.[134]

Although Clarence Macartney rarely shared his pulpit with the staff, Ockenga had numerous opportunities to preach.[135] "I had eight speaking engagements between Saturday night and Wednesday night," he reported, "so this morning when I finished my address at the Downtown 'Y' I cancelled the remaining five preceding Easter. One can do so much, that is all. I also turned down the presidency of the Presbyterian Young People's work in Pittsburgh. It came to be too much." The key, he was learning, was to "do less and do it well."[136]

Presbyterian Ordination (January 28, 1931)

During his time in Pittsburgh, Ockenga was also ordained to the gospel ministry by the Presbytery of Pittsburgh. "My credentials and everything have gone through Presbytery and I'll be ordained Wednesday evening. Dr. Machen, the greatest fundamentalist scholar, will preach the service, and Dr. Macartney will give the charge and make the prayer. It will be an impressive and interesting service." "I will now have had the experience of ordination from a Methodist Bishop and from a Presbyterian Presbytery. And the funny thing about it is that I won't surrender my Methodist credentials until a month after I am an ordained Presbyterian clergyman."[137] The service took place at the First Presbyterian Church on January 28, 1931.[138] "The ordination service was wonderful," Ockenga later reported. "Mother came and her presence made it so much nicer. Then I had

133. Ockenga to Ray, March 2, 1931, Ockenga Papers.

134. Ernest E. Logan sent a copy of his history of the First Presbyterian Church of Pittsburgh, *The Church That Was Twice Born*, to Ockenga with the following inscription: "To Dr. Harold J. Ockenga, First Leader of the Tuesday Noon Club, which he initiated, November 4, 1930." See also Lindsell, *Park Street Prophet*, 33.

135. Ockenga often speaks in glowing terms of Macartney's preaching. Among Ockenga's papers are over fifty separately-bound sermons by Clarence Macartney on a variety of texts and topics.

136. Ockenga to Ray, March 2, 1931, Ockenga Papers.

137. Ockenga to Ray, January 22, 1931, Ockenga Papers.

138. For the arrangements and follow-up, see Harold John Ockenga to J. Gresham Machen, January 16, 1931; Machen to Ockenga, January 22, 1931 and January 28, 1931; Ockenga to Machen, January 31, 1931; and Machen to Ockenga, February 4, 1931, Ockenga Papers.

Dr. Machen, that great scholar to preach the sermon, and Dr. Macartney to give the charge. Their presentations were spiritually deep and intellectually of the best. Over 1000 people were present and it was the first Ordination service ever held in our church. God was there. People were weeping several times during the service." "All I can say in description of the whole service is that it was 'moving, challenging, inspirational, and glorious.'"[139] For his part, Machen was equally effusive about Ockenga: "Certainly your ordination was to me a very joyous occasion. I do feel profoundly thankful that the first graduating class of Westminster Seminary is represented by a man like you. I do feel great confidence that God has very rich blessings in store both for you and for those to whom you will be called to minister."[140]

Despite the enormous suc-

First
Presbyterian Church
Sixth Avenue, near Wood Street
Pittsburgh, Pa.
Clarence Edward Macartney, Minister

The Ordination of
HAROLD JOHN OCKENGA
to the Gospel Ministry by the Presbytery of Pittsburgh
Wednesday evening, January 28th, 1931

The REV. EDWARD A. CULLEY
Moderator of the Presbytery
presiding

DOXOLOGY
INVOCATION
HYMN—No. 157
THE READING OF THE SCRIPTURES—
The Rev. John K. Highberger
SOPRANO SOLO - - - - - - - Helen Bell Rush
PRAYER - - - - - - - - - - Dr. W. A. Jones
SERMON - The Rev. Prof. J. Gresham Machen, D.D.
HYMN—No. 341
THE PROPOUNDING OF THE
CONSTITUTIONAL QUESTIONS - By the Moderator
THE PRAYER OF ORDINATION - Dr. Macartney
THE LAYING ON OF HANDS BY THE PRESBYTERY
THE RIGHT HAND OF FELLOWSHIP
THE CHARGE TO THE EVANGELIST - Dr. Macartney
HYMN—No. 310
BENEDICTION

Harold John Ockenga's ordination by the Presbytery of Pittsburgh (courtesy of Gordon-Conwell Libraries)

cess he was enjoying, Ockenga continued to struggle with loneliness. Alone in his room at the end of one particularly busy Sunday, he began once again to consider "the great problems and struggles of life and existence." "What precious hours these are," he wrote, "and yet I do not like to have them come, for they make me terribly lonely."[141] At the core of his concern was his seeming inability to find a suitable wife. Although he had developed a list of twenty-five qualifications that he believed were necessary in the wife of a pastor, he seemed unable to persuade anyone who could fulfill them to join him in the venture. When Ockenga shared these concerns with his spiritual mentor, Clarence Macartney, Macartney apparently suggested

139. Ockenga to Ray, February 2, 1931, Ockenga Papers.

140. Machen to Ockenga, February 4, 1931, Machen archives, Montgomery Library, Westminster Theological Seminary. Printed in Stephen J. Nichols, ed., *J. Gresham Machen's The Gospel in the Modern World* (Phillipsburg, NJ: P&R, 2005), 29–30.

141. Ockenga to Ray, March 28, 1931, Ockenga Papers.

the name of a college student with whom he was acquainted. "So while [my sister] was still a student in college," as her missionary brother later described the sequence of events, Ockenga showed up one day at the college, presented her with a bouquet of flowers, and "asked her to be his wife, stating that Dr. Macartney had highly recommended her and that in his list of twenty-five qualifications for a wife, Bunny scored very high." For her part, as Kenneth Scott tells the story, "Bunny told him that she was highly honored by what he was asking, but replied, 'I've only met you today and don't really know you. I want to know you much better before I could give you an answer.'" Several weeks passed, her brother observed, before Ockenga "called by telephone from Toronto and again asked her if she would marry him." Evidently her answer was the same for there is no evidence that "any further communication took place."[142] Ockenga's search for a godly wife would have to continue.

Point Breeze Presbyterian Church (1931–37)

The effectiveness of Ockenga's ministry at the First Presbyterian Church soon attracted the attention of pastoral search committees in other congregations throughout the region.[143] "Soon I'll be writing to you on different stationery," he wrote early in April of 1931. "The heading will be Point Breeze Presbyterian Church. That means that I'm now pastor of another church. They called me two weeks ago and I accepted this Tuesday. The new work will begin May 1st."[144] Point Breeze "is a lovely church in the residential district of 1000 active members. It is quite a joy to me to be called to such a church, but I feel that it is in God's providence that I may begin to pour forth the Gospel that my soul contains. I'm tired of listening to others when I can be preaching. This move means a big advance in every way. It is a well known church, it has a large honorarium, a beautiful ten room brick manse, and is located in the residential district. God has been good to me." "Pray with me that God may

142. Kenneth M. Scott, *Around the World in Eighty Years* (Franklin, TN: Providence House, 1998), 94–95. I am indebted to Muriel Clement, a longtime member of Park Street Church in Boston, for drawing my attention to this delightful story.

143. For Ockenga's letter of resignation to the session of First Presbyterian Church in Pittsburgh, effective May 1, 1931, see Ockenga to the Session, April 17, 1931, Ockenga Papers. An interesting account, written twenty years later, of how the Point Breeze Presbyterian Church came to invite Ockenga to preach his first two sermons at the church can be found in Edward Sauvain to Harold John Ockenga, December 15, 1951, Ockenga Papers.

144. The Point Breeze Presbyterian Church was located on Fifth and Penn Avenues in Pittsburgh, Pennsylvania. Ockenga served as pastor of Point Breeze from May 4, 1931, until May 2, 1937. See *Congregational Register: Point Breeze Presbyterian Church* (Pittsburgh: Arthur Van Senden, 1932). A complete set of church bulletins, copies of the *Breezier*, and correspondence relating to Ockenga's call to the church are found in the Ockenga Papers. See also Ockenga to Ray, April 17, 1931, Ockenga Papers.

Order of Service

Organ Prelude—
  (a) "Toccato"
  (b) "Priere" } from "Suite Gothique" - Boellman

Doxology

Invocation and the Lord's Prayer - - Dr. James A. Kelso
  President of the Western Theological Seminary, Pittsburgh, Pa.

Hymn—157

The Reading of the Scriptures - The Rev. John K. Highberger
  Assistant Minister of First Presbyterian Church, Pittsburgh, Pa.

Anthem—"Festival Tedeum" - - - - Buck

Prayer - - - - - - Dr. W. A. Jones
  Associate Minister of First Presbyterian Church, Pittsburgh, Pa.

Sermon - - - - Dr. Clarence E. MacCartney
  Pastor of First Presbyterian Church, Pittsburgh, Pa.

Solo—"The Earth is the Lord's" - - - Lynnen
  Mr. Clyde Miller, Baritone

The Propounding of the Constitutional Questions - Dr. Kelso

The Prayer of Installation - - - Dr. Thomas Watters

The Charge to the Pastor - - Dr. J. Gresham Machen
  Professor, Westminster Theological Seminary, Philadelphia, Pa.

The Charge to the People - - Dr. Donald MacKenzie
  Professor, Western Theological Seminary, Pittsburgh, Pa.

Hymn—388

Benediction (People Seated) - Rev. Harold John Ockenga

Organ Postlude—"Grand Choeur" - - - Guilmant

Installation of Harold John Ockenga as pastor of Point Breeze Presbyterian Church in Pittsburgh (courtesy of Gordon-Conwell Libraries)

bless in this new undertaking. Dr. Macartney is back of me in my decision," Ockenga continued. "The die is now cast and plenty of work is here—but I thrive on work."[145]

Harold's installation as pastor of the Point Breeze Presbyterian Church on May 8, 1931, was a memorable event. Clarence Macartney gave the sermon and J. Gresham Machen offered the pastoral charge.[146] Using 2 Kings 19 as his text and focusing on the "threatening letter" that had come to Hezekiah, the King of Judah, Machen warned the young pastor of a "threatening letter" that he, as the newly installed pastor of the Point Breeze congregation, now held in his own hand—a letter signed "by men who are dominating the political and social life of the world" and who are determined to destroy all "who hold to the Gospel of Christ."[147] "To-day, all over the world,"

145. Ockenga to Ray, April 17, 1931, Ockenga Papers.

146. Ockenga to Machen, April 16, 1931; Machen to Ockenga, April 20, 1931; Ockenga to Machen, May 9, 1931; and Machen to Ockenga, May 13, 1931, Ockenga Papers. For an account of the installation in his parent's local periodical, see "Called to a Large Church," *Austinite*, May 15, 1931, 14. See also Harold John Ockenga, "Point Breeze Church," *Presbyterian Banner*, May 14, 1931, 28.

147. A stenographic transcript was prepared by someone at the Point Breeze Presbyterian Church and a copy of it sent to Machen. He telegraphed Ockenga with the message: "Greatly appreciate transcript of address just received but please note that I do not want to have the address printed." Four days later he followed the telegram with a letter of explanation, noting his concerns that "the

he argued, "public opinion is overwhelmingly against the gospel of Jesus Christ"—among literary and intellectual leaders, on the faculties of universities, and even among those who dominate "the life and machinery of the churches."[148]

"Now, my brother, when you receive their threatening letter," he continued, "there are three things that you can do with that letter." You can "obey" it and "surrender your faith." You can "refuse to read it" and "dig your head like an ostrich in the sand." Or "you can take that letter and read it from beginning to end" and then "spread it open in the presence of Almighty God." It is the third option, Machen was convinced, to which God has called the shepherds of the flock. "If we are not standing in opposition in the presence of a hostile world, we are no true disciples of Jesus Christ." Do not be afraid of controversy, he advised. "The teaching of our Lord is full of controversy—because he set his righteousness sharply in opposition to the false righteousness of the Scribes and Pharisees. Now when the great revival comes upon the church, for which we long, things may happen that we do not know.[149] The Spirit moves when He will and how He will, and we cannot command His coming, but about one thing that will happen when the Spirit moves in power in the Church of Jesus Christ, I think we can be perfectly sure. When that happens, the miserable, feeble talk about the avoidance of controversy on the part of Christian men and preachers of Jesus Christ, will all be swept away as with a mighty flood. A man on fire with a message never speaks in a way like that; never speaks with the indifferent manner of the world, but proclaims his gospel in the presence of the world of enemies, briefly and nobly in the presence of everything that is lifted up against the Gospel of Jesus Christ." "When Hezekiah laid that letter in the presence of God, God sent an answer to Hezekiah through the greatest of the prophets, Isaiah the son of Amoz. Now He will send an answer to you if you lay the threatening letter of a hostile world before Him in your ministry to-day."[150]

---

stenographic report" of his charge had been sent "entirely without explanation as to the person by whom the report had been made or the purpose for which it was intended. So I became a little alarmed lest it should be used for printing. The report is quite extraordinarily good, but of course, like even the best of stenographic reports, it would have to be revised before it could be sent to a printer. In the second place, there are reasons why I should be very loathe to publish this address. I do not know that any such thing was in view. But if it is desired, will you please communicate with me before anything is done." See Machen to Ockenga, telegram, May 19, 1931; Machen to Ockenga, May 23, 1931; and the stenographic copy of Machen's "Charge to the Pastor" in the Ockenga Papers. What is likely the copy Ockenga sent to Machen can be found in the Machen Archives, Montgomery Library, Westminster Theological Seminary. For a printed version of the text, see Nichols, *J. Gresham Machen's The Gospel in the Modern World*, 34–42.

148. J. Gresham Machen, "The Charge to the Pastor," delivered at Point Breeze Presbyterian Church, May 8, 1931, typed manuscript, Ockenga Papers.

149. See Ockenga's later address on "The Great Revival," *Bibliotheca Sacra*, April–June 1947, 223–35.

150. Machen, "Charge to the Pastor."

"The whole world is your province as a preacher of the Gospel of Christ," Machen continued. "Be interested in the teachings of science, in literature, in philosophy and art." "Do not be content with a superficial study of this Holy Book, but be a scribe who has become a disciple of the Kingdom of God. Do not be content merely with a chance acquaintance with the Book, but seek to study it in the light of the grand, exegetical tradition of the Christian Church." If these instructions were followed, Machen concluded, "you will know that nothing, no hostility of the world, no adverse decisions of souls and bodies of the visible church, no defections, no hostility can ever separate you from the great heritage that God has given you and these people in this Book."[151]

Machen's words made a profound impression on the young preacher. Machen's charge became in a way a kind of manifesto for Ockenga's future ministry: Preach fearlessly. Don't be afraid of controversy. Center your ministry on Christ. Know your Bible thoroughly. Open yourself to science, literature, philosophy, and art. Be confident that you are secure in the hands of the sovereign God.[152] With these convictions in mind, Ockenga threw himself into the ministry at Point Breeze with enormous enthusiasm. "I've been working so hard," he wrote after the first month of ministry, "that my head is in a whirl. This week I have two more theses to get in, have sermons to get out, have the general assembly in Pittsburgh, and next week we're putting on a general calling campaign. Meetings every night. Many friends came to town for the assembly and I had to entertain them, which was a joy."[153] After completing a year and a half of ministry, he wrote: "Last Sunday we received 15 adults into membership. That makes 150 in 1 1/2 years. And our emphasis is laid upon real conversion and church attendance. Everything is progressing splendidly in the church work and we have much to be thankful for."[154]

Ockenga's nearly six years at Point Breeze were foundational for his future ministry. Under his energetic leadership the congregation prospered. Church membership, after the rolls were substantially trimmed of "dead wood," grew once again to nearly a thousand. Attendance on Sundays grew to about three hundred and fifty in the mornings and about two hundred and fifty in the evenings. A regular prayer meeting was established, drawing an average of seventy participants. The Sunday school increased to nearly four hundred. The youth programs burgeoned. A sixty-voice choir and a paid quartet were added. And in the midst of an economic depression, the mortgage was retired and the church

151. Ibid.

152. For the influential role that Machen played as one of Ockenga's primary mentors, see their exchange of some thirty letters and telegrams between January 16, 1931, and January 21, 1935, Ockenga Papers.

153. Ockenga to Ray, June 2, 1931, Ockenga Papers. Ockenga's sister Myrtle also lived at the manse, helping to care for the house and providing entertainment for many events at the church.

154. Ockenga to Ray, October 11, 1932, Ockenga Papers.

buildings were renovated.[155] This was quite an achievement for a young man who for most of his ministry at Point Breeze was still in his twenties.[156]

The Perfect Companion

"I've only had two Pittsburgh dates," Ockenga wrote early in 1930, "and both were flops. I may get up nerve to try it again. Guess I'm destined to be a batch."[157] His mother, while ready to embrace anyone her son decided to marry, had also made it clear that he should be exceedingly careful in his selection. Make sure, she had advised, that you are certain she is the "one and only one" God has intended for you. Marriage is difficult enough under the best of circumstances, but it is impossible when the match is not in accordance with God's sovereign purposes.[158] Not until August of 1934 did the "one and only one" enter Ockenga's life. While eating at the restaurant in the Hotel Webster in downtown Pittsburgh, he spotted a beautiful young woman. Tanned by the summer sun and dressed in sparkling white, she not only caught his eye but also stole his heart. Two days later, while reading a German treatise by Karl Marx as he prepared for his comprehensive exams in the library at the University of Pittsburgh, Ockenga saw her again. This time he seized the opportunity, introduced himself, and eventually drove the young lady home in his wire-wheeled Dodge coupe.[159]

The young woman was Audrey Williamson. A native of Lee, Massachusetts, she was also a student at the University of Pittsburgh, completing a bachelor of science degree and preparing herself for a teaching career.[160] Over the next ten days the two spent many hours together in Pittsburgh. When Williamson left for her vacation in Canada, Ockenga followed her to the summer resort in Limberlost where she was staying. There, while hiking, swimming, dining, and enjoying each other's company, they both fell deeply in love. By the time they left Limberlost, they were officially engaged.

On August 6, 1935, almost exactly a year after their meeting in the university library, Harold Ockenga and Audrey Williamson were married. The wedding,

155. Lindsell, *Park Street Prophet*, 34–37. See also Ockenga to Ray, May 4, 1931, Ockenga Papers.

156. A chronological summary of "Events of Significance in the Last Five Years," handwritten by Harold John Ockenga (1931 to 1936), is in the Ockenga Papers. Ockenga was succeeded at the Point Breeze church by Donald A. Spencer, who assumed his responsibilities on Sunday, May 2, 1937. The church bulletin for that date can be found in the Ockenga Papers.

157. Ockenga to Ray, January 15, 1930, Ockenga Papers.

158. Angie Ockenga to Harold John Ockenga, December 2, 1930, Ockenga Papers.

159. Although the writer is not identified, a brief description of these events, titled "The Way Dr. Ockenga Met Mrs. Ockenga," is included in the Ockenga Papers. See also Lindsell, *Park Street Prophet*, 39.

160. Williamson's mother came from Virginia (of English and German ancestry). Her father came from West Virginia and was of Scottish descent. Both parents had grown up as Methodists, which influenced Ockenga's later openness to Pentecostalism.

held at the Point Breeze Church, was the social event of the year. "Rev. Harold John Ockenga, former assistant pastor of the First Presbyterian Church and pastor of the Point Breeze Presbyterian Church for five years, will wed a pretty teacher of the Wightman school at an August wedding ceremony," the papers announced.[161] The church was packed and the wedding service, led by Williamson's pastor, went off without a hitch.

Following the ceremony, to the delight of everyone present, the young couple left for a few days in Eaglesmere before boarding the *Bremen* for

Audrey Williamson and Harold John Ockenga (courtesy of Park Street Church, Boston)

a six week honeymoon tour of the British Isles, Holland, Germany, Switzerland, and France. Over the subsequent years, God brought three beautiful children into their home.[162] Audrey proved to be an ideal wife—the "one and only one" for whom Harold's mother had prayed so many years. "I finally took the leap," Harold wrote for the class news section of the *Westminster Alumni Annals*, "and am delighted. Life is very different. The Lord gave me a very wonderful wife."[163]

There is a delightful irony, of course, at the heart of their happy relationship. In the early 1950s, as Ockenga was preaching at the Army Chapel Center in Tokyo, he took up the theme of "falling in love with Jesus Christ." To illustrate the point he was making, as one of his listeners later described the sermon, Ockenga asked the question: "How do you know you have found the woman you are looking for to be your wife? Do you sit down and make a list of twenty-five characteristics you want in your wife and then score each potential spouse against that list? Is that how you know?" Then answering his own question, Ockenga answered, "Of course not! Why, when I first saw my wife—it was in a library—my heart flipped and I fell in love with her and I said to myself, 'That's the person I'm going to marry.' And we have been in love ever since. When you're in love, you know it!"[164]

161. Unidentified newspaper clippings of the wedding can be found in the Ockenga Papers.

162. The couple's children were named Audrey Starr, Aldryth Sabra, and Harold John Ockenga Jr. For a fuller description of these events, see Lindsell's description in the *Park Street Prophet*, 39–44.

163. The *Westminster Alumni Annals* 6, no. 1 (January 1936): 8. The annals also reported that several of Ockenga's Westminster classmates, including Robert S. Marsden, Billy Blackstone, and Carl McIntire, had also participated in the wedding.

164. Scott, *Around the World in Eighty Years*, 95.

Poised for National Leadership

With a new wife, a thriving church, the support of some powerful friends, a growing list of academic degrees, and a string of ministerial successes behind him, Harold John Ockenga seemed ready for the "greater things" his mother had predicted for him. He would not need to wait long. Within a year he would assume his new responsibilities as pastor of the historic Park Street Church in Boston—a pulpit that would catapult him into national prominence and earn him the nickname "Mr. Evangelical."

3

THE GRAND VISION

Park Street Church, in the heart of Boston, seemed to be exactly the right place for Harold John Ockenga to exercise his considerable gifts.[1] Surrounded by educational, historical, and cultural institutions, John Winthrop's "city on a hill" and the magnificent Park Street spire that pierced the sky at Boston's very center appeared to be a perfect match for the brilliant thirty-one-year-old preacher. "I don't know a more fortunate young man in America than yourself in receiving a call to a church like Park Street," wrote Arcturus Zodiac Conrad, known by most of his parishioners as A. Z. Conrad, the man who had served as pastor of the church since 1905. "It is an ideal place to take up the ministry with the expectation of a full development."[2]

While Conrad was beloved by the congregation, his advancing age and deteriorating health had made the search for his successor a matter of some urgency.[3] "I began three years ago," Conrad wrote in the summer of 1936,

> to seriously and prayerfully determine in my own mind the best man to carry on at Park Street Church. With a very wide acquaintance among ministers and

1. For the history of Park Street Church, see H. Crosby Englizian, *Brimstone Corner* (Chicago: Moody, 1968); Harold John Ockenga, "The Unique and Unparalleled Position of Park Street Church in Boston's Religious History," sermon 663; and Harold John Ockenga, "The Foundations of Park Street Church," sermon 2085, preached on February 22, 1969, at Park Street Church, Ockenga Papers.

2. Conrad to Ockenga, September 11, 1936, Ockenga Papers. Born November 26, 1855, Conrad served as pastor of Park Street Church from 1905 until his death on January 22, 1937. Under his ministry, several religious revivals occurred: in 1906, 1909, 1920, and 1928. Ockenga was being called to serve as copastor with Conrad.

3. See, for example, Conrad to Emery, February 2, 1934, Ockenga Papers.

laymen, I was able to get abundant information regarding many men.[4] You have heard of many of them. I am perfectly clear that the Reverend Harold Ockenga is the man whom I would like to see called as Co-Pastor. He is a fine scholar with a genial personality and more nearly fills every requisite for the Pastor of our church than any man I know.[5]

An unofficial meeting of the church board was called for Thursday evening, August 13, to "informally discuss the future in regard to the pastorate and the financing of any proposed changes."[6]

The Call to Park Street Church

At the conclusion of morning worship on August 16, 1936, the church board met to establish a general committee[7] for the purpose of recommending a copastor.[8] On August 21, the congregation voted to officially authorize the committee's activities and membership.[9] On August 27, the committee met and "unanimously voted to extend a call to Dr. Harold John Ockenga to come to Park Street Church and act as Co-Pastor with Dr. Conrad," to appoint a "committee of three" (consisting of George M. Watson, Cramer Hudson, and Morton Campbell[10]) to meet with the candidate to "go over everything

4. Among those in whom the congregation had expressed an interest were Aquilla Webb, Harry Rimmer, Donald G. Barnhouse, Stewart Robinson, Burleigh Cruikshank, F. P. McConkey, Roy Vail, Martin Anderson, Andrew Richards, John McComb, David McClennan, and Harold Laird. See "Report of the General Committee to the Special Meeting of Park Street Church Held Tuesday, September 15, 1936," 3–4; and brown packet of letters and other materials marked "Park Street Church, M. C. Campbell, Harvard Law School," Ockenga Papers.

5. Conrad to the official members of the Park Street Boards, undated copy, Ockenga Papers. Conrad had been hand-picked by his predecessor, John Lindsay Withrow, and had served as copastor with him until Withrow's death. Conrad was proposing that the boards adopt the same procedure for his successor and he offered to relinquish $4,000 of his annual salary to make it possible.

6. Letter to members of the board of deacons, the board of trustees, and the prudential committee, August 6, 1936, Ockenga Papers.

7. Also known as the "committee of discovery and recommendation."

8. The search committee consisted of George M. Watson (chair of the board of trustees), Charles W. Barker (chair of the prudential committee), Grace Walizer (president of the Women's Benevolent Society), Alvin J. Shartle, Charles H. Chenoweth, and Christina Grant in addition to the entire board of deacons (Nathan Dennett, Morton Campbell, Stiles Kedy, J. Cramer Hudson, George Morland, Harry Finley, John Lincoln, Peter MacPhee, Angus MacEachern, Willard Armes, Martin Shamlian, Bror Grondal, Robert Carson, George Tupper, and Paul Bowler).

9. Search Committee to members of Park Street Church, September 5, 1936, Ockenga Papers. The congregation voted on August 21 to approve the committee with the addition of three members nominated from the floor: Mrs. Anna Nicholson, Mrs. Harriet Hemenway, and Mrs. Archibald Mackay.

10. Campbell, a professor at Harvard Law School, outlined "several indispensable qualifications for our minister: (1) He must really have the Christian virtues, including the willingness to efface self in achieving the good of the church and Christ's Kingdom; (2) He must be Trinitarian in doctrine and evangelical in attitude and practice, and must accept the authority of the Bible; (3) He must have power in the pulpit;

with him regarding salary and everything important," and to "present him with a call to the Park Street Church pulpit as Co-pastor with Dr. Conrad, subject to the vote of the church."[11] On September 2, the committee of three met with the candidate. On September 4, the committee of three presented its written report to the general committee.[12] On September 15, the congregation gathered to hear the "Report of the General Committee" and to vote on its recommendations.[13]

Harold John Ockenga was no stranger to Park Street. Between 1934 and 1936 the congregation had heard him preach seven times.[14] Nonetheless, the "committee of three" and the general committee undertook their responsibilities with great care and much prayer. In talking with people in Pittsburgh, they had discovered that their

Park Street Church, Boston (courtesy of Garth M. Rosell)

candidate "was beloved by everyone" in the Point Breeze Church, that "he had worn well in his pastorate of five years," that "he had a fine influence with the young people," that he always gave preeminence to "the Kingdom of Heaven rather than personal interest," and that his wife, Audrey, was "a fit helpmate"

---

(4) He must have unusual pastoral qualities; (5) He should be between thirty-five and fifty years of age; (6) And it is highly desirable that he have a vision of the universality of the Kingdom, and hence a zeal for missions, home and foreign." Campbell to Clarence Macartney, February 13, 1934, Ockenga Papers.

11. See "Minutes of the August 21, 1936, Congregational Meeting," Ockenga Papers.

12. See "Report of Sub-Committee of Three" (September 4, 1936), Ockenga Papers. The report was signed by its chairman, Morton Campbell, and its secretary, J. Cramer Hudson. Copies were also given to Conrad and Ockenga.

13. A fourteen-page "Stenographic Report of the Meeting" was taken by Marion Clark. For the announcement of the special meeting see Newton and Tupper to members of Park Street Church, September 5, 1936. For the committee's five-page report to the congregation see "Report of the General Committee." All of these documents are in the Ockenga Papers.

14. Ockenga had preached two sermons during the summer of 1934, one in the spring of 1936, and four in the summer of 1936. As early as February 1934, Clarence Macartney had written to Morton Campbell to commend Ockenga: "He is about thirty years of age, of strong personality, and a remarkably able speaker for so young a man. He is, of course, thoroughly loyal and zealous as to the faith once delivered to the saints. He has done a great deal of travelling, and is thoroughly informed as to the great movements in the Church and in the world. I feel he is worthy of your consideration, although he comes under the limit you set, thirty-five years of age." J. Gresham Machen gave a similarly strong endorsement: "I understand that Mr. Ockenga has splendid congregations and that he is known to be a really outstanding preacher." See Macartney to Campbell, February 24, 1934; and Machen to Campbell, February 21, 1934, Ockenga Papers.

in his work.[15] They had examined his theology and found him to be thoroughly orthodox.[16] "Your committee believes that Mr. Ockenga is a man of deep spiritual and intellectual power, and that he has the will and capacity of growth both in mind and spirit." Consequently, "after due deliberation the General Committee unanimously recommends to the Church that it call the Rev. Harold J. Ockenga, of Pittsburgh, Pennsylvania, as co-pastor."[17] By the close of the meeting, the congregation had voted officially to extend a call and had established a four person committee to work out the details.[18]

"Beloved Brother in Christ," the committee's letter to Ockenga began, "on the evening of September 15, 1936, Park Street Church voted unanimously to ask you to become Co-Pastor with Rev. Dr. A. Z. Conrad." "Of the history of Park Street Church you are more or less familiar," they continued. "For more than a century and a quarter it has borne a consistent testimony to the truth of the Gospel of our Lord Jesus Christ and we are sure you will faithfully maintain that testimony. We have prayed earnestly that God's Will might be done and we feel confident that we are in harmony with His Will in thus calling you."[19] "Brethren," Ockenga responded in a telegram, "Divine urgency to accept call. Appreciate unanimity. Await contract."[20]

While arrangements for such matters as office location and secretarial support were worked out rather quickly,[21] the issue of Park Street's radio ministry

15. Of Audrey Ockenga the session of Point Breeze Presbyterian wrote: "We do not forget the place that is left vacant in our church life and in our affections by the one whom our pastor so recently selected as his helpmeet. In that short period Mrs. Ockenga has endeared herself to all of us. Quietly, modestly, she has won us all, and it is with poignant feeling that we lose her from our midst." See session of Point Breeze Presbyterian Church, "An Appreciation," published in the Sunday Bulletin, October 18, 1936, Ockenga Papers.

16. During the interviews, Ockenga affirmed both the "Confession of Faith and By-Laws of Park Street Church" and "The Westminster Confession of Faith."

17. "Report of the General Committee," Ockenga Papers.

18. Of 240 votes cast, Ockenga had received 228 (with votes of two or three assigned to Laird, Barnhouse, Rimmer, Johnson, and McComb). Forming the committee were George Tupper (chair), J. Cramer Hudson, George M. Watson Jr., and Morton C. Campbell. Ockenga's annual salary was to be $6,000, he was to receive a two-month vacation each summer, and have a personal secretary. See "Stenographic Report," 7 and 10.

19. Committee to Ockenga, September 18, 1936, Ockenga Papers. The letter is signed by all four members of the committee.

20. Ockenga wrote this response, which was sent subsequently by telegram, on the back of the Special Delivery envelope in which the letter of call had been sent. George Tupper, in his response on September 21, thanked Ockenga for his telegram "which we interpret as an acceptance of your call to Park Street Church." With the letter, Tupper enclosed two copies of the contract. Although it is clear that Ockenga was not fully satisfied with the terms of the contract, the records are not sufficiently complete to reconstruct the reasons why. In any case, Ockenga signed the contract and by September 25 he had written George Watson indicating that he had "accepted the call." All of these documents can be found in the Ockenga Papers.

21. Ockenga was given Conrad's upstairs office, including the Globe-Wernicke bookcases, and Marion R. Clark, who had been Conrad's secretary for sixteen years, was to continue to assist Ockenga. See Conrad to Ockenga, September 11, 1936, Ockenga Papers.

remained very much in question. "You have certainly been keeping me posted on what is happening in Boston," Ockenga wrote Conrad early in November. "This must be a considerable effort on your part and I greatly appreciate it. Your last letter touched me deeply. I am so sorry that you continue in such pain."[22] Although he disliked bothering Conrad further, there was a problem he felt he had to address before coming to Boston, the matter "of the radio."

"Everything seems to point to my coming," he continued, "as I could interpret the events which took place." But "a number of events" have since thrown "a cloud over that clearness so that I definitely wavered and thought of withdrawing my acceptance. When the news got out that I had decided to go," in fact, "there was a tremendous protest on every hand—from church members, outside friends, board of education, ministers, etc. They all felt that my ministry was here. Then the church had a protest meeting and pled with me to stay. You see," he continued, "I took this church at a low point and with a large debt and at the bottom point in the depression. Now we have no debt, and are able to do things. Yesterday, we had 350 in Sunday School, five hundred in morning church, fifty in young peoples and 300 in evening attendance. One man offered to pay the full expense of broadcasting every Sunday evening and two Sunday mornings a month permanently. This was 1800.00 a year. He laid down his first check on condition that I stay. Ten others guaranteed 5,000.00 for an increase in our budget. They offered me personally another thousand a year, two months vacation, any further secretarial aid I might need, another assistant . . . and any other reasonable thing I might suggest. Letters poured in, tears were shed, etc."[23]

"Now I withstood all that and carried the dissolution through Presbytery, because I believed God wanted me to go to Boston. You can readily see that this was on a spiritual basis for materially every advantage is to stay here. Since investigating the Boston field I find that the salary offered me is not even equivalent to the salary here which I have been receiving ever since I was 25 years old and all through the depression."[24] "Still I felt that I should come. And to make things clear let me say that I will not accept any increase from the Boston church now, if offered. Material considerations have not influenced my decision to come."[25]

"But this is what disturbs me!" he continued. "I am deeply concerned about the lack of faith and vision on the part of those back of this movement." If the church "hasn't faith enough" to continue the radio ministry it has had for many years, such a decision "is not much of a recommendation for a new

22. Ockenga to Conrad, November 2, 1936, Ockenga Papers.
23. Ibid.
24. Ockenga's reference here relates to Boston's high cost of living: including telephone, automobile, housing, etc. In addition, he estimated that his salary would be reduced by nearly $500 (without computing the additional $1,000 each year he had just been offered at the Point Breeze Church).
25. Ockenga to Conrad, November 2, 1936, Ockenga Papers.

man. Now I am quite willing to stop the radio if it is not self-supporting after the first year. After all the radio is not the church, and a great work can go on without it. But I insist that the church should not take a backward step just as a new pastor comes in." Therefore, unless "you and the committee give me assurance that the church will keep [its radio ministry] another year, which symbolizes an attitude to me, I shall seriously consider a re-call [to Point Breeze] and will send my resignation to Park Street Church if I decide in its favor." "I have surrendered every point to your committee which concerned any material consideration," he concluded. This, however, is "a matter of principle." "My action will depend on your reply."[26] Needless to say, the radio ministry was continued and has continued to this day.

Harold John Ockenga's ministry at Park Street began officially on November 15, 1936. "Your sermon this morning was a masterpiece," Conrad wrote in a letter to his new colleague. "It was magnificently delivered. How I thank God that he directed me to you. We will have a very sweet fellowship together, after which, I trust for many many years, our loving Lord will give to you two the complete charge and leadership in that dear church, whose worth and beauty and influence will grow on you as the years pass."[27]

Installation of the New Minister (November 18, 1936)

On Wednesday evening, November 18, 1936, Harold John Ockenga was formally installed as copastor of Park Street Church.[28] Conducted under the authority of the Suffolk West Association of Congregational Churches and moderated by the Rev. Dr. Ralph Rogers of Auburndale, it was an impressive event.[29] Clarence E. Macartney, Ockenga's old friend and mentor from Pittsburgh, delivered the sermon, titled "God in History." "What we need today," Macartney proclaimed, "is a living faith in God," not a God who is removed from his people but one "who is in the midst of them." "With some people," he said, "God is like one who sits hidden in a watch tower on the battlefield of time, waiting anxiously to see if what men and nations do shall fit in with

26. Ibid.

27. Conrad to Ockenga, November 15, 1936, Ockenga Papers. The Presbytery of Pittsburgh, of which Ockenga was a member, granted him permission to "labor outside the bounds" in accepting the Park Street pastorate. Thereafter, he continued to submit annual reports of his ministry at Park Street and to request annual renewal of this permission. See, for example, Ockenga to the Presbytery of Pittsburgh, January 29, 1946, Ockenga Papers.

28. A report of the proceedings can be found in "Dr. Ockenga is Formally Inducted as Co-Pastor of Park Street Church," *Boston Herald*, November 19, 1936.

29. Participants in the installation service included Andrew Richards, Clarence Macartney, Nathan Wood, Clarence Dunham, Edward Byington, Edward Camp, Ralph Rodgers, J. Lee Mitchell, William MacDuffie, and Harold John Ockenga. A. Z. Conrad, who was seriously ill at the time, was unable to attend.

His plan and purpose. But, according to the Scriptures, God acts before men act and before nations act."[30]

"There has been a tendency in some quarters in the church," he continued, "to display a feeling of consternation, almost panic, at the hostile and anti-Christian forces that are working in the world today. Men are saying: 'Lo, here!' 'Lo, there!' and every unfavorable condition in colleges, in labor, in youth, in the home, in politics, in international relationship, is at once declared to be a challenge to the church. How would it do," Macartney asked in conclusion, "to change our tone and proclaim the church of the living God as a challenge to the evil and the unbelief and the godlessness of this present generation?"[31]

Having observed his life and ministry for the past five years, both Clarence Macartney and Ockenga's former parishioners at the Point Breeze Presbyterian Church were convinced that he would continue to set exactly that "tone" for the Park Street congregation. "Mr. Ockenga has succeeded in welding together a congregation with the one aim, namely to make Point Breeze Church a power for Christian good in this community. He has preached the Word that is able to make us wise unto salvation" and "he has endeared himself to church officers and members alike by his understanding sympathy and helpful counsel." "Men who are capable of filling the large places in the scheme of things are not numerous," the Session of Point Breeze continued, "and we believe Mr. Ockenga to be one of these." "Life is progress, and progress must be upward. The larger the field the greater the opportunities to do good and serve the Master."[32]

Although Ockenga could never have known it at the time of his installation, his ministry at Park Street Church in Boston was to continue for the next thirty-two years.[33] During those three decades, his name and that of Park Street Church became virtually synonymous. Moreover, Park Street Church itself came to be recognized around the world as one of evangelicalism's most prominent pulpits.[34]

"The larger the field," his friends at Point Breeze had predicted, "the greater the

30. Quotations are taken from a newspaper report of the event, "Dr. Ockenga is Formally Inducted."

31. Ibid.

32. See session of Point Breeze Presbyterian Church, "An Appreciation." "I send you and Mrs. Ockenga my hearty and affectionate GOD BLESS YOU," wrote A. Z. Conrad some six weeks after the installation. I pray that the coming year will "bring you unprecedented joy and success. I do congratulate you on the wonderfully fine start you have made in your Pastorate. It makes me very very happy." Conrad to Ockenga, January 1, 1937, Ockenga Papers. A few weeks later, on January 22, 1937, the faithful old pastor died.

33. For a delightful summary of his ministry at Park Street, including a number of historic pictures, see "Reviewing 32 Years of Ministry," *Park Street Spire*, special issue, June 1969, Ockenga Papers.

34. During his time at Park Street, Ockenga was regularly invited to assume the leadership of other churches and educational institutions. While Harold and Audrey struggled over several of these calls, they could never bring themselves to leave New England. See the correspondence from places such as the First Presbyterian Church in Seattle, Lake Avenue Congregational Church in Pasadena, the First Presbyterian Church in Pittsburgh, Fuller Theological Seminary in Pasadena, the Moody

opportunities to do good and to serve the Master." In seizing that opportunity, Ockenga helped Park Street to see its ministry as "not just congregation-wide, or city-wide, or even area-wide," but increasingly "world-wide."[35]

Park Street Church became a kind of microcosm or visible embodiment of a major segment of the larger evangelical movement itself. Under Ockenga's energetic leadership, the congregation embraced and sought to live out in its daily activities the core values that had given shape and direction to the American evangelical movement since its beginnings in the Great Awakening: the centrality of the cross, the church, the authority of the Bible, the necessity of conversion, the importance of spiritual renewal, and the task of worldwide evangelization.

These were the themes to which Ockenga returned again and again during his ministry at Park Street Church, as the nearly three thousand manuscript sermons in the Ockenga Papers make absolutely clear.[36] J. Gresham Machen, his friend and theological mentor, had charged him to be "a preacher of the Gospel of Christ." "Do not be content," he had warned, "with a superficial study of this Holy Book." But always "keep your contact with the grand central tradition of the church of Jesus Christ."[37]

The Centrality of the Cross

The Bible specifically declares, Ockenga often reminded his congregation, that Jesus Christ is the foundation of the church.[38] Yet, as his mentor had suggested, our "affirmation concerning Christ" can only be "made within the Biblical witness and the confession of the Apostles' Creed."[39] Consequently,

Memorial Church in Chicago, Westmont College in Santa Barbara, and many others—all seeking to lure Ockenga into pastorates or presidencies. Materials can be found in the Ockenga Papers.

35. Quotations are taken from one of the many tributes recorded at the end of Ockenga's thirty-two-year ministry. See "Every Once In Awhile," *Park Street Spire*, special issue, June 1969, Ockenga Papers.

36. Manuscripts of these sermons, numbered consecutively, can be found in the Ockenga Papers. In addition to this core collection, there are numerous miscellaneous sermons, outlines of sermons in notebooks, printed sermons, handwritten sermons, and recorded sermons available in the collection. Hundreds of these recorded sermons, originally recorded on magnetic tape, are now available in CD format.

37. J. Gresham Machen, "The Charge to the Pastor," delivered at the installation of Harold John Ockenga at Point Breeze Presbyterian Church, May 8, 1931, Ockenga Papers.

38. Ockenga preached scores of sermons and sermon series that were centered on Jesus Christ and his atoning work on the cross. For example, see Harold John Ockenga, "The Glory of the Cross," unnumbered sermon; "Established in Christ," sermon preached December 8, 1940; "Our Exalted Lord and the Fullness of Life," sermon preached February 7, 1943; and "The Atonement," sermon preached January 7, 1945, Ockenga Papers.

39. Harold John Ockenga, "The Nature of God," *United Evangelical Action*, November 1, 1945, 7–8. Since the time of the ancient councils of the Christian church, from Nicaea (AD 325) to Chalcedon (AD 451), the discussion of Christology and the Trinity have been closely related as the Nicene Creed and the Formula of Chalcedon clearly indicate. For a discussion of the first four councils of the

Ockenga believed, as followers of Christ, the members of Park Street Church were declaring publicly and unequivocally that their allegiance was to the triune God. "Boston has always been as conscious of Park Street Church's Trinitarian testimony," he concluded, "as a pedestrian on the common is conscious of the magnificent spire ever pointing toward heaven."[40]

Park Street Church had been founded in 1809, after all, precisely because so many of Boston's congregational churches had decided to abandon their allegiance to historic trinitarianism in favor of the increasingly attractive Unitarian alternative.[41] Even its location on the Boston Common and the architecture of its building, called by Henry James "the most interesting mass of brick and mortar in America," was designed to symbolize the beauty and permanence of its historic faith.

The Church

Of greater importance than the physical building, Ockenga was convinced, is the presence of the living God within the true church, the body of Christ. "If the Church is compared to a building which is being fitly framed together," he argued, "there are materials necessary for such purposes." These "living stones," those who have "been born of the Spirit," become "part of a corporate group, of a congregation, of a body. Together the believing individuals are constituted a Church of God."[42]

Understood in this manner, the church should be viewed not as an organization but as an "organism formed of spiritually quickened individuals united to Jesus Christ, fulfilling His purpose of redemption in the world." The church's "purity must be derived from its faithfulness to the Word and its practice of the Sacraments. Its universality must include all believers. Its apostolicity must be derived from direct connection with the Holy Spirit who called and anointed the apostles. Its unity must be by relation to and submission to the Lord Jesus Christ."[43]

---

church, see Philip Schaff and Henry Wace, eds., *The Seven Ecumenical Councils*, in *A Select Library of Nicene and Post-Nicene Fathers of the Christian Church* (Grand Rapids: Eerdmans, 1971); J. N. D. Kelly, *Early Christian Creeds* (New York: Longman, 1972); and Jaroslav Pelikan, *Credo: Historical and Theological Guide to Creeds and Confessions of Faith in the Christian Tradition* (New Haven: Yale University Press, 2003).

40. Harold John Ockenga, "The Foundations of Park Street Church," sermon 2085, preached on February 22, 1959, Ockenga Papers.

41. See Harold John Ockenga, "The Unique and Unparalleled Position of Park Street Church in Boston's Religious History," published by Park Street Church, Ockenga Papers. For the growth of Unitarianism, see Conrad E. Wright, *The Beginnings of Unitarianism* (North Haven, CT: Archon Books, 1976); and Sydney E. Ahlstrom, *An American Reformation: A Documentary History of Unitarian Christianity* (Middletown, CT: Wesleyan University Press, 1985).

42. Ockenga, "The Foundations of Park Street Church."

43. Ibid.

At the center of everything, of course, is Christ. "God has given a means for the believer to take each hurdle in this course of the Christian life. That instrument is the person of the Lord Jesus Christ. For sins we have the propitiation of the Cross of Christ, for sin we have the burial and resurrection of Christ, for suffering we have identification with Christ, and for Satan's system, worldliness, we have the transforming of our minds into the image of Christ. God establishes believers," Ockenga was convinced, "by the preaching of Jesus Christ."[44]

The Authority of the Bible

The unique authority of the Bible was another theme to which Ockenga returned again and again throughout his ministry.[45] "The Bible is the Word of God," he declared. "It is the watershed of modern theological controversy. On the right of this mountain peak are all those who believe that the Bible is the revelation of God and is infallibly inspired. They may differ on many details of interpretation of that revelation, but they agree as to its authority. On the left," he continued, "are all those who reject the Bible as the primary authority in faith and life, substituting for it any one of several forms of authority ranging from the human mind to the common experience and agreement of the church." Yet it is "only on the basis of the Bible as the Word of the Lord" that believers can ever hope to have "agreement on Christ, on the way of salvation, and on ecclesiastical matters."[46]

"Therefore," he declared to his Park Street parishioners, "the Bible is the Christian's one and only standard." By it we can "test all doctrines" and believe "only that which is in accord with God's revealed Word." The Bible, moreover, "judges" our lives, so that we can obey "its precepts and principles," and conform our lives to its godly teachings. "Bible Christians take the Word of God seriously" and they seek to apply it in every arena of life. "'Thy Word have I hid in my heart,'" he concluded, "'that I might not sin against Thee.'"[47]

44. Harold John Ockenga, "Established in Christ," sermon preached at Park Street Church, December 8, 1940, and published by the church, Ockenga Papers.

45. See, for example, Harold John Ockenga, "The Inspiration of the Bible," sermon preached February 7, 1932; "Bible Christians," sermon preached December 13, 1936; "What is the Christian's Authority? The Church or the Bible?" sermon preached on March 23, 1945; "Who Gave us our Bible?" sermon preached on October 2, 1949; "Learning the Holy Scriptures," sermon preached October 16, 1966, Ockenga Papers.

46. For the address and quotations, see Harold John Ockenga, The Word of the Lord, The Campbell Morgan Bible Lectureship: Third Lecture, July, 1951 (Glasgow: Pickering and Inglis), 3. Another address, of the same name but slightly different content, was delivered the previous month at Calvin College and Seminary's Calvinistic Conference, held from June 3–5, 1951, in Grand Rapids. Originally published in the Presbyterian, it was reprinted in a twenty-four-page pamphlet, a copy of which can be found in the Ockenga Papers.

47. Harold John Ockenga, "Bible Christians," preached at Park Street Church, December 13, 1936, Ockenga Papers.

The Necessity of Conversion

A fourth theme to which Ockenga returned repeatedly throughout his Park Street ministry was the necessity of spiritual conversion or new birth.[48] "It is very gratifying to me," he told a Sunday evening audience at Park Street, "to notice the powerful way in which the Spirit of God is awakening the consciences of men to their lost condition and to the need of their being saved." Consequently, his intention in preaching that evening was simply "to remove all ground from under you and leave you with no other hope but Jesus Christ." Many of you "have resisted long enough. You have said 'No' to God sufficiently. It is now time for you to examine your heart, remembering that the eternal choice of life and death rests upon you now. For this purpose," he concluded his opening remarks, "I am turning my attention to this matter of conversion and for every inquirer who is honest before God I intend to make it plain enough for you that you may be saved."[49]

Following his intriguing introduction, Ockenga proceeded to spell out in detail the "meaning of conversion," the "hindrances to true conversion," and the "way of conversion." Those who are truly converted, he argued from the writings of the apostle Paul, will "be justified" before God, will experience "peace with God," will have "access to this grace," and will "have the Holy Spirit shed abroad" in their hearts. Moreover,

> such a saved one will immediately become useful in the matters of the kingdom. He will seek first the kingdom of God and His righteousness. Such a saved one will then become the instrument in the salvation of others. He will know that he that converteth a sinner from the error of his ways shall save a soul from death and shall cover a multitude of sins. The movements of God's blessing upon communities are carried by one person. A visitor will come to a community touched by God and will carry the blessing back to another community. Thus it will spread from place to place like fire spreads when sparks are carried by the wind and dropped first in one field or forest and then another.

Therefore, he asked his listeners, "Can you say before God and this company I believe I am converted? If you cannot now is the time to settle that matter."[50]

48. See, for example, Harold John Ockenga, "The Contrite Heart," sermon 530; "Repentance Toward God and Faith Toward the Lord Jesus Christ," sermon 638; "Forgiveness of Sins as Taught in the Bible," sermon 772; "Repentance Unto Life," sermon 1561; "The Conversion of a Sinner," sermon 1723; "The Renaissance of the Soul," a sermon pamphlet published by Park Street Church; and "The Doctrine of the Great Awakening and of the New Awakening—Regeneration," in Harold John Ockenga, *The Great Awakening* (Boston: Fellowship, 1940), Ockenga Papers.

49. Harold John Ockenga, "I Believe I Am Converted," sermon 780, Ockenga Papers.

50. Ibid.

The Importance of Spiritual Renewal

A fifth major theme of Harold John Ockenga's preaching was the need for revival.[51] "We are experiencing the mercy drops of God's blessing," he declared in 1947, "but we await the great revival."[52] And "what is the great revival?" he asked.

> It is the time when God's work is unusually prospered, quickened, enlarged, and vitalized. The normal, usual, expected progress of Christian work may be witnessed in many places. The great revival is only witnessed periodically in Christian history. The great revival marks a condition when men give primary interest and attention to the things of God above their livelihood, above their intellectual pursuits, and above their social interests. A terror of wrongdoing descends upon them. A passion for repentance seizes them. A desire for salvation characterizes them.[53]

Genuine revival, Ockenga was convinced, is always the work of the sovereign God: for it is "God's work to forgive sin, with the concomitant blessing of deliverance from evil habits, assurance of salvation, and enjoyment of spiritual blessings"; it is "God's work to rebuild and strengthen the church as His witness in the world"; and it is "God's work to bring in everlasting righteousness."[54] People can prepare themselves for the blessings of revival by genuine repentance, united believing prayer, and the faithful preaching of God's Word—but no one other than God can create genuine spiritual awakening. Such blessings come only when and where the sovereign Lord of the universe chooses to send them.[55]

Harold John Ockenga was fascinated by revival history. His library was filled with books about the great revivals and their leaders. His sermons were loaded with the stories of revivals and those who were touched by them. Furthermore, he prayed daily that God would once again touch New England with the fresh winds of his Spirit. "All progress in Christian things," he believed, "is made by revivals."[56] As a student of revival history, Ockenga knew of the many "seasons of refreshing" that had marked New England's past.[57] While

51. See, for example, Harold John Ockenga, "When A Revival Prevails," sermon 637; "Reformation and Revival," sermon 1157; and *The Great Awakening*, Ockenga Papers.

52. Harold John Ockenga, "The Great Revival," presented at the W. H. Griffith Thomas Memorial Lectures at Dallas Theological Seminary and published in *Bibliotheca Sacra*, April–June 1947, 223–35.

53. Ibid., 223. For a helpful listing of resources for the study of revival, see Richard Owen Roberts, *Revival Literature: An Annotated Bibliography with Biographical and Historical Notices* (Wheaton: Richard Owen Roberts, 1987).

54. Ockenga, "The Great Revival," 224.

55. For a study of the biblical foundations for revival, see Walter C. Kaiser Jr., *Revive Us Again: Biblical Insights for Encouraging Spiritual Renewal* (Nashville: Broadman & Holman, 1999).

56. Ockenga, "The Great Revival," 225.

57. See Ockenga, *The Great Awakening*; Martin Moore, *Boston Revival, 1842* (Boston: John Putnam, 1842); Garth M. Rosell and Richard A. G. Dupuis, eds., *The Memoirs of Charles G. Finney: The*

only God can produce such times of blessing, Ockenga was well aware of the impact they could have on both the church and society. "The result of a revival is always a higher ethical standard through the changed lives of the people. Those who have been adulterous, profane, wicked men become righteous, sanctified men." Furthermore, he was convinced, a genuine revival also "affects the church, calling it back to the centrality of the Cross and redemption in its message and worship, rather than to the practice of formalism. Withal, there comes a new awakening to the heart of the church and a new conviction of Christian truth and life to the masses with the first breath of revival."[58]

The analogy may be drawn between revivals and waves of the sea, he suggested.

> The individual waves gather momentum, swell to fullness, and then break upon the sands only to have the water retard and be gathered into another wave. Underneath the waves is the constant, actual progress of the incoming tide. Thus the divine progress likewise is made through successive waves of revival back of which is the rising tide of divine work. Similarly all human progress in national, intellectual, economic, or political movements is made in waves which rise, spend their force, fall back, and have their place taken by another. This periodic ebb and flow may be traced in all the realms of life, but underneath them there is the tide of progress.[59]

"The conditions of our day constitute an alarming demand for such a revival," Ockenga was quite certain. There are those who "say we have plenty of time." There are those who claim that revival "will not happen in our day. But I say the time is shorter than you think. We stand in need of the great revival."[60]

The Task of Worldwide Evangelization

A final theme to which Ockenga returned with regularity was the task of worldwide evangelization.[61] In 1935, when he took up his new responsibili-

Complete Restored Text (Grand Rapids: Zondervan, 1989); H. M. Grout, ed., *The Gospel Invitation: Sermons Related to the Boston Revival of 1877* (Boston: Lockwood, Brooks and Co., 1877); Arcturus Z. Conrad, ed., *Boston's Awakening* (Boston: The King's Business, 1909); Keith J. Hardman, *Seasons of Refreshing* (Grand Rapids: Baker Books, 1994); and many others.

58. Ockenga, "The Great Revival," 228. See J. Edwin Orr, "Revival and Social Change," *Fides et Historia* Spring 1974, 1–12.

59. Ockenga, "The Great Revival," 225. Contrast Timothy L. Smith, "My Rejection of a Cyclical View of 'Great Awakenings,'" *Sociological Analysis* 44 (Summer 1983): 97–102.

60. Ockenga, "The Great Revival," 234–35.

61. See, for example, Harold John Ockenga, "The Christian Apologetic for Missions," sermon 1096; "Life with a Vision," sermon 2205; and "What Twenty-Five Years of Missionary Conferences Have Taught Me," preached on the occasion of the 25th Annual Missionary Conference at Park Street in 1964, sermon 2540, Ockenga Papers. See also Harold John Ockenga, *The Church God Blesses*, a

ties at Park Street, the congregational budget for missions was $2,235 and the budget for general church expenses stood at $18,885. By 1969, the year of his retirement, the missions budget had climbed to $366,549 and the general church budget to $153,550. Over the thirty-two years of his ministry a total of $5,759,900 was given to support hundreds of missionaries and mission projects around the world.[62]

"This single congregation of 2200," Ockenga wrote in 1959,

> is building a greater church, one composed of people who are black and yellow and brown and white in skin and drawn from fifty nations on five continents and the islands of the sea through the preaching of its 120 missionaries on whose labors the sun never sets. Today these countless multitudes join with us and the assembly in heaven in thanking God for the vision, faith, courage and consecration of those 26 persons who originally formed this congregation and erected this building and commenced this testimony on "Jesus Christ, the one foundation, other than which no man can lay."[63]

Much of this growth, of course, came as a result of the faith pledges that became the hallmark of the annual missionary conferences that were launched in 1940 and that over the years became one of the most prominent features of congregational life at Park Street.[64] Undergirding these important events was Ockenga's regular preaching on the sacred obligation of Christians to be involved in the spreading of the gospel throughout the world. "Park Street Church is orthodox," he said, "but its orthodoxy did not make the church."[65] "Park Street Church has a famous building," he continued, "but this is not the source of its fame." "Park Street Church is an historical church"—where "William Lloyd Garrison gave his orations against slavery," and where "Charles Sumner gave his great oration on the war system of the

---

series of four messages on missions delivered at Fuller Theological Seminary, September 30 to October 3, 1958, and published jointly by Fuller Missions Fellowship and Park Street Church Board of Missions (Pasadena and Boston: Fuller Missions Fellowship and Park Street Church, 1959). For several years, during the early 1940s, Park Street Church also published the *Missionary Quarterly of Park Street Church*. Issues for April 1941 and February 1943 are available in the Ockenga Papers.

62. Statistics are taken from June A. Jenkins, ed., "Reviewing 32 Years of Ministry," *Park Street Spire*, June 1969, 10. Programs for many of the annual conferences can be found in the Ockenga Papers.

63. Ockenga, "The Foundations of Park Street Church."

64. Oswald J. Smith, pastor of the Peoples Church in Toronto, helped introduce the concept of the faith pledge to Park Street: those who attended the missionary conferences were encouraged to "step out on faith" and make a pledge for the support of the Park Street's missionaries and missionary program, trusting God that he would enable them to meet their obligation during the subsequent year. Smith was one of the guest speakers at the first conference in 1940 and also at subsequent gatherings.

65. Park Street's "original creed," Ockenga continued, "was the Westminster Confession of Faith and the Apostles' Creed. It has not veered from its orthodoxy in the many years of its existence. Out of this orthodox movement came scores of other Congregational Churches which are Trinitarian but Park Street Church is not known primarily for its orthodoxy."

nations," and where the hymn "America was first sung," and where "many national organizations" such as "the American Education Society, the Prison Reform Society, the Handel and Haydn Society," and "the Animal Rescue League" were constituted—"but it is not famous for these events." Rather, "Park Street Church is known for its missionary activity." "Go to Egypt, to Ethiopia, to Kenya, to Tanganyika, to South Africa, to the Congo, to Nigeria, to Liberia, to Ecuador, to Brazil, to Bolivia, to Mexico and to thirty or more other nations and you will find the work of the missionaries of Park Street Church."[66]

Ockenga's preaching was not confined to a discussion of evangelicalism's six core values. Indeed, his sermons included systematic expositions of biblical books; biographical studies of biblical and historical characters; doctrinal sermons on major theological themes; topical series on prayer, the person and work of the Holy Spirit, and the cost of discipleship; historical sermons on such topics as Park Street's heritage or the rich legacy of Protestantism; and a wide range of interpretive sermons on contemporary political, social, and ecclesiastical issues. Many years he preached a special sermon on the political, social, religious, and economic events of that particular year in light of Scripture.[67]

Yet there can be little question that the themes that most deeply fired Ockenga's imagination, engaged his energies, and dominated his preaching were precisely the same passions as those that had energized modern evangelicalism since its beginnings in the revivals of America's Great Awakening. What Jonathan Edwards and the New Lights of the eighteenth century had so vigorously defended against Charles Chauncy and the Old Light detractors, Harold John Ockenga was prepared to defend and promote in mid-twentieth century America and throughout the world.[68]

The bitter battles between fundamentalism and modernism that had dominated much of American religious life during the early decades of the twentieth century had separated much of the evangelical community from its rich heritage.[69] While many of Ockenga's contemporaries were ready to join hands with likeminded believers, fragmentation and distrust seemed ready to thwart any attempt at united evangelical action. "I keenly feel this position of a lone

66. Ockenga, "What Twenty-Five Years of Missionary Conferences Have Taught Me."
67. See, for example, Harold John Ockenga, "The Events of 1936 in the Light of the Scripture," sermon 503, Ockenga Papers.
68. In "A New England Harvest," sermon 1120, for example, Ockenga comments that they "are committed to the same gospel that the Puritans preached." Throughout its history, Park Street Church has "stood like a rock on orthodox, Biblical, evangelical Christianity."
69. For an understanding of these events and their aftermath, see George M. Marsden, *Fundamentalism and American Culture: The Shaping of Twentieth-Century Evangelicalism, 1870–1925* (New York: Oxford University Press, 1980); Joel A. Carpenter, *Revive Us Again: The Reawakening of American Fundamentalism* (New York: Oxford University Press, 1997); and George M. Marsden, *Reforming Fundamentalism: Fuller Seminary and the New Evangelicalism* (Grand Rapids: Eerdmans, 1987).

wolf, as I have sometimes been called," Ockenga asserted, "but I recognize that there are many lone wolves in the ministry today who in a measure have been greatly blessed by God in their own particular fields of endeavor. Yet I see on the horizon ominous clouds of battle which spell annihilation unless we are willing to run in a pack."[70]

The Corrosive Influence of Modernism

Only a united effort, Ockenga was convinced, would be able to counter the corrosive influences of modernism. "Tragic as it is," he wrote, "the controversy between Christianity and Modernism is necessary." Indeed, if "the present, powerless, depleted, diminished Church is again to enjoy God's blessing and receive times of refreshing from on high," words reminiscent of his theological mentor J. Gresham Machen,

> that church must purify itself from the hoary heresies of antiquity and from the questionable ethics of many of its leaders. In order to do this we must acquaint ourselves not only with the teachings of the Bible but with the movements that are supporting the Bible. Then it falls to us to withdraw all membership, influence and financial support from Modernistic organizations and throw it one hundred percent toward Bible Christianity.[71]

Consequently, the question should not be "Are we seeking unity?" but "What is the nature of the unity we seek?" Genuine unity "can only exist when compatible things are joined together." The cross that "unites Christians," Ockenga continued, "separates them" from all others. "Christ has no concord with the devil" nor does the true believer have anything to do "with an infidel." Yet true believers "recognize each other across denominational and sectarian lines," they "speak the same Biblical language," and they "enjoy fellowship with one another." Their unity is "organic and spiritual" rather than "organizational" or "hierarchical." A "cathedral," to use Ockenga's image, "is a unity but it is not constructed by identical blocks of stone, nor is the temple of God constructed of uniform specimens of humanity." Fundamentalists call for "interdenominationalism." Modernists call for "ecumenicity." Yet "we must not seek uniformity but the unity of spiritual communion of the saints. The nature of the unity Christ seeks is a vital mystical union of believers in the life of Christ and with one another."[72]

70. Harold John Ockenga, "The Unvoiced Multitudes," in *Evangelical Action! A Report of the Organization of the National Association of Evangelicals for United Action, Compiled and Edited by the Executive Committee* (Boston: United Action Press, 1942).

71. See Harold John Ockenga, "Our Most Subtle Enemy, or Modernism," printed sermon, Ockenga Papers.

72. Harold John Ockenga, "The Nature of the Unity We Seek," sermon 1673, Ockenga Papers.

The New England Evangelistic Association and the New England Fellowship

By the time Harold John Ockenga arrived in Boston, the kind of biblical unity for which he yearned was already in full operation. Since its founding in 1889, the Evangelistic Association of New England had been sponsoring cooperative efforts in evangelism throughout the region.[73] In 1929, the efforts of the New England Evangelistic Association were augmented by the establishment of the New England Fellowship. Quietly and largely unheralded, J. Elwin Wright and his parents had been building a network of evangelical Christians throughout the region since the early decades of the twentieth century.[74] The purpose of the New England Fellowship, as that network came to be called, was to assist evangelical Christians "to publish, broadcast, preach and teach the fundamentals of the Christian faith."[75] By 1936, the year Ockenga was installed as pastor of Park Street Church, the New England Fellowship was already facilitating scores of joint ventures in conferences, camps, evangelistic services, youth gatherings, radio outreach, publications, and vacation Bible schools.[76]

Headquartered at his Rumney, New Hampshire, conference center, New England Fellowship's founder and president J. Elwin Wright became "a tireless advocate for evangelical cooperation."[77] A graduate of the New York Missionary Training College for Home and Foreign Missions, an institution founded by A. B. Simpson and later renamed Nyack College, the unassuming and indefatigable Wright was a perfect complement to Park Street's dashing young pastor. Although they could not have known it at the time, their friendship and the close working relationship they forged during the late 1930s was to take on special importance during the 1940s and 1950s in the establishment of some of evangelicalism's most prominent organizations.[78]

---

73. Known in more recent years as Vision New England, the Evangelistic Association of New England had since its founding in 1889 sought to join Christians throughout New England in the task of rural and city evangelism, hospital visitation, and lumber camp work. The organization was headquartered at Tremont Temple in Boston.

74. The story of the New England Fellowship (NEF) is told by J. Elwin Wright's gifted assistant, Elizabeth Evans, in *The Wright Vision: The Story of the New England Fellowship* (New York: University Press of America, 1991).

75. *The Constitution and By-Laws of the New England Fellowship* (1937), typed four-page document, Ockenga Papers.

76. The New England Fellowship had offices at Park Street Church and at its main conference center in Rumney, New Hampshire. For a listing of NEF activities, see John Bolton to Harold John Ockenga, February 5, 1937; J. Elwin Wright to Ockenga, February 8, 1937; and the foldout map of New England, listing the scores of sites in which the NEF was engaged in a variety of ministries, Ockenga Papers.

77. The description of Wright is taken from Randall Balmer, "James Elwin Wright (1890–1973)," in *Encyclopedia of Evangelicalism*, rev. and exp. ed. (Waco: Baylor University Press, 2004), 769.

78. The NAE was the most important of these new organizations. For the role of Wright and Ockenga in its formation, see Arthur H. Matthews, *Standing Up, Standing Together: The Emergence*

In August of 1929, when the first conference for pastors and Christian workers was held at Rumney, such possibilities were little more than distant dreams.[79] But those who gathered that summer represented several of New England's denominations and seemed able to "submerge their unessential differences and unite in perfect fellowship in a period of worship, spiritual inspiration, and prayer."[80] Subsequent Rumney conferences only served to reinforce Wright's growing passion for evangelical cooperation and fellowship.

Over the next decade attendance at the Rumney conferences grew rapidly and the list of speakers began to look like a "Who's Who" of evangelical Christianity: William Bell Riley, pastor of the First Baptist Church in Minneapolis; A. Z. Conrad, pastor of Park Street Church in Boston; Merrill C. Tenney, professor at Gordon College and later dean of the Graduate School at Wheaton College; R. G. Lee, pastor of the Belleview Baptist Church in Memphis, Tennessee; Harold Paul Sloan, pastor of the Methodist Episcopal Church in Haddonfield, New Jersey; Jack Wyrtzen, founder of Word of Life; H. H. Savage, founder of the Maranatha Bible Conference in Michigan; Mrs. Charles Cowman, author of the devotional classic *Streams in the Desert*; Curtis Lee Laws, editor of the influential *Watchman-Examiner*; Gleason Archer, Clarence Roddy, and George Ladd, all of whom would later teach at Fuller Theological Seminary; Will Houghton, pastor of Calvary Baptist Church in New York City; Walter Maier, radio preacher for the Lutheran Layman's League; Walter Kallenbach, the blind evangelist; and Harry Ironside, pastor of Moody Church in Chicago were but a few of the many who made their way to Rumney.[81]

Also numbered among the speakers was Harold John Ockenga. At the first Rumney Youth Conference in the summer of 1936, while still pastor of the Point Breeze Presbyterian Church in Pittsburgh, Ockenga and his new bride spent a week together at Rumney while he preached to the 120 young people who had gathered for the conference that summer. It was on this occasion that the Ockengas and Wrights first met.[82] Later that year, their friendship was renewed as Ockenga took up his new responsibilities at Park Street Church.

---

of the National Association of Evangelicals (Carol Stream, IL: National Association of Evangelicals, 1992).

79. The first conference was held from August 15–25, 1929. For a description, see Evans, *The Wright Vision*, 19–31.

80. Matthews, *Standing Up, Standing Together*, 6. In 1929, as a result of this conference, the older First Fruit Harvester Association that had been founded by J. Elwin Wright's Pentecostal father was transformed into the New England Fellowship. For the story, see Evans, *The Wright Vision*, 1–18.

81. For information on the Rumney Conference Grounds (including programs, facilities, and speakers), see Evans, *The Wright Vision*, 19–31.

82. Ibid., 56.

The National Association of Evangelicals

Since the time of the Puritans, New England had provided leadership for the evangelical movement. By 1940, due in large measure to the successful ministries of the New England Fellowship, it appeared poised to do so again. Indeed, at the Rumney Pastors Conference in 1939, the participants requested the NEF leadership to explore whether or not there was interest across the country in establishing "a national association based on the principles of the Fellowship."[83] At the 1941 conference, Wright reported that such an interest was not only apparent but that it also seemed to be growing. As a result, the 1941 conference adopted the following resolution: That as delegates to the New England Fellowship Pastors Conference, "[we] feel a deep concern that the evangelical and evangelistic denominations, missions, associations, churches, and other religious organizations of America find some workable basis of co-operation and co-ordination which will enable them to present a united front against the inroads of modernism, infidelity, and atheism." Consequently, "[we] resolve that it is the unanimous conviction of this Conference that immediate steps be taken by responsible leaders of these evangelical groups to bring into existence a central and representative organization operating under an appropriate name designating its purpose, through which evangelical Christians may become vocal."[84] By the following October, Wright had persuaded Will Houghton, president of Moody Bible Institute in Chicago, to call and host a gathering of evangelical leaders to discuss the possibility of establishing a national organization on essentially the same principles as those that undergirded the New England Fellowship.[85]

Carl McIntire, Harold John Ockenga's friend and former classmate at Westminster Theological Seminary, was among the sixteen leaders who attended that meeting.[86] Just a few weeks earlier, on September 17, 1941, McIntire and his colleagues, McAllister Griffiths and Harold S. Laird,

83. Ibid., 115. For minutes, publications, programs, pictures, and Ockenga's extensive correspondence relating to the establishment of the NAE, see the Ockenga Papers. Additional resolutions and mandates by the conference and the New England Fellowship Board followed the 1939 action.

84. Evans, *The Wright Vision*, 115–16.

85. Those who gathered at Moody Bible Institute on October 27–28, 1941, included V. Raymond Edman, president of Wheaton College; Harry Ironside, pastor of Moody Church; Charles E. Fuller, radio pastor; Horace F. Dean, vice-president of the Philadelphia College of the Bible; Ralph T. Davis, head of the Africa Inland Mission; William Ward Ayer, radio preacher; Stephen Paine, president of Houghton College; T. J. Bach, secretary of the Scandinavian Alliance; H.C. Crowell, member of the MBI staff; Charles A. Porter, associate pastor of Moody Church; Ernest M. Wadsworth, secretary of the Great Commission Prayer League; Carl McIntire, McAllister Griffiths, and Harold S. Laird, all representing the newly established American Council of Christian Churches (ACCC); Will Houghton, president of Moody Bible Institute; and J. Elwin Wright, who was elected to chair the meeting.

86. McIntire had been part of Ockenga's wedding party.

had helped establish a similar organization in New York City, named the American Council of Christian Churches (ACCC).[87] Founded for the purpose of defending and promoting biblical orthodoxy, the new ACCC was especially concerned about what many in the organization believed to be the growing influence of the Federal Council of Churches.[88] "The Federal Council," McIntire argued in a *Christian Beacon* editorial, controls both "the appointment of Protestant chaplains" and the use of the "free time" that is donated by radio stations for use by Protestant churches. But, he argued, "the Federal Council does not represent all the Protestant churches in America, although it claims that prerogative and is recognized as such by many organizations and institutions."[89] Consequently, there was an immediate need for a national organization to give voice to evangelical concerns and to check the growing power of organizations like the Federal Council that they feared were increasingly being dominated by the forces of modernism.[90] In fact, the reason McIntire and his colleagues had come to Chicago was to persuade those who had gathered at the Moody Bible Institute to join their new venture.[91]

Everyone at the meeting was convinced that such an organization was urgently needed. "The Federal Council of Churches very well represents liberal Protestantism," argued William Ward Ayer, one of the participants and a radio preacher himself, but it does not represent "evangelical Protestantism."[92] Of special concern was the matter of access to the radio airwaves. At that time, the Federal Communications Commission allocated free radio time to Roman Catholics, Jews, and Protestants. Since the Federal Council became the de facto arbiter of who received the Protestant assignments, one can understand why William Ward Ayer, Charles E. Fuller, and even Harold John Ockenga might become concerned that they were, in effect, being systematically shut out of

87. The ACCC initially included the Bible Presbyterian Church and the Bible Protestant Church. Several additional denominations joined later. See Louis Gasper, *The Fundamentalist Movement, 1930–1956* (Grand Rapids: Baker Academic, 1981), 21–39.

88. The Federal Council of Churches, later to be known as the National Council of Churches, was established in December of 1908 in Philadelphia. Making up its initial membership were thirty-three denominations representing about eighteen million American Protestants. See Charles S. MacFarland, *Christian Unity in the Making: The First Twenty-Five Years of the Federal Council of the Churches of Christ in America, 1905–1930* (New York: Federal Council of Churches, 1948); J. Elwin Wright, *How Modern is the Federal Council?* (New York: Fellowship, 1947); and Carl McIntire, *Twentieth-Century Reformation* (Collingswood, NJ: Christian Beacon Press, 1944).

89. Carl McIntire, "Federal Council," *Christian Beacon*, August 15, 1940, 2. The ACCC was eventually able to secure concessions on both the awarding of free radio time and the appointment of military chaplains.

90. For an example of the growing concern over the Federal Council of Churches, see W. Lee Rector, "The Federal Council of Churches: An Infidelistic, Modernistic, and Unpatriotic Organization Now Operates to Destroy 'The Faith,'" (Ardmore, OK: First Orthodox Baptist Church, n.d.).

91. See Matthews, *Standing Up, Standing Together*, 14.

92. Quotation from the *New York Times*, March 22, 1937.

the process.[93] In addition to their concerns about the growing power of the Federal Council of Churches, the ACCC and New England Fellowship also shared a common commitment to historic orthodoxy.[94] Indeed, the doctrinal positions of the ACCC and the New England Fellowship were remarkably similar.[95]

The two groups divided, however, on three issues of enormous importance. The first issue related to membership. McIntire had limited membership in the ACCC to denominational entities. Wright, on the other hand, was convinced that membership should be open to all denominations, missionary organizations, associations, congregations, and individuals who shared a common mission and who were able to sign a common statement of faith. A second issue, closely related to the first, was the question of whether or not the organizations should welcome the burgeoning Pentecostal movement.[96] McIntire and his colleagues were wary of Pentecostalism, the movement that had emerged with such power during the Azusa Street revival of 1906,[97] considering it "obnoxious, perhaps subversive, and likely to result in a hybrid fundamentalist movement."[98] They were not alone, of course. As recently as 1928, the World's Christian Fundamentals Association had gone on record "as unreservedly opposed to Modern Pentecostalism, including the speaking in unknown tongues, and the fanatical healing known as general healing in the atonement, and the perpetuation of the miraculous sign-healing of Jesus and

---

93. See Tona J. Hangen, *Redeeming the Dial: Radio, Religion, and Popular Culture in America* (Chapel Hill: University of North Carolina Press, 2002).

94. The preamble of the ACCC constitution calls its member denominations to give "witness to the glory of God and the historic faith of the church universal, including adherence to these truths among others, equally precious: the full truthfulness, inerrancy, and authority of the Bible, which is the Word of God; the holiness and love of the one sovereign God, Father, Son, and Holy Spirit; the true deity and sinless humanity of our Lord Jesus Christ, His virgin birth, His atoning death, 'The just for the unjust,' His bodily resurrection, His glorious coming again; salvation by grace through faith alone; the oneness in Christ of those He has redeemed with His own precious blood; and the maintenance in the visible church of purity of life and doctrine." Reprinted in Gasper, *The Fundamentalist Movement*, 23.

95. J. Elwin Wright, when asked about his theological position, liked to say simply that it was the same as the Apostles' Creed. The theological affirmations of the New England Fellowship can be found in Evans, *The Wright Vision*, 14.

96. For excellent introductions to the movement, see Vinson Synan, *The Holiness-Pentecostal Tradition: Charismatic Movements in the 20th Century* (Grand Rapids: Eerdmans, 1997); Grant Wacker, *Heaven Below: Early Pentecostals and American Culture* (Cambridge, MA: Harvard University Press, 2001); Larry Martin, *The Life and Ministry of William J. Seymour* (Joplin, MO: Christian Life Books, 1999); Cecil M. Robeck Jr., ed., *Charismatic Experiences in History* (Peabody, MA: Hendrickson, 1985); and Cecil M. Robeck Jr., *The Azusa Street Mission and Revival* (Nashville: Nelson, 2006).

97. For an eyewitness account of the revival, see Frank Bartleman, *Azusa Street: The Roots of Modern-day Pentecost* (South Plainfield, NJ: Bridge, 1980).

98. Carl McIntire, *The Testimony of Separation* (Collingswood, NJ: Christian Beacon Press, 1946), 61. I discovered this quotation in Gasper, *The Fundamentalist Movement*, 30.

His apostles, wherein they claim the only reason the church cannot perform these miracles is because of unbelief."[99]

J. Elwin Wright, on the other hand, was inclined to welcome Pentecostals with genuine warmth and enthusiasm. His parents, Joel and Mary Wright, had "studied the writings of John Wesley," the movement's spiritual father,[100] and by 1892 had left the Free Will Baptists, "joined the Free Methodist Conference," and taken "his first pastorate as a Free Methodist" pastor in Barre, Vermont. During these years in Vermont, the family had come in contact with a number of Pentecostal believers and had been profoundly influenced by them.[101] Largely due to his parents' influence, J. Elwin Wright had grown up with an appreciation for the Pentecostal movement. His commitment to the task of uniting New England's evangelicals, as Elizabeth Evans has suggested, may have inclined him toward a more "moderating position on the nature of tongues,"[102] as reflected in the little article on the subject he published in 1922,[103] but it certainly did not seem to dampen his enthusiasm for welcoming his Pentecostal brothers and sisters into the fold.

Like Wright, Ockenga was also inclined to include holiness and Pentecostal groups in the new organization. His own roots in Wesleyan holiness provided an important bridge across which Pentecostal and holiness denominations could cross from "isolation to cooperation," as historian Edith L. Blumhofer has argued.[104] Such openness would come at a cost. "I thought it would be well to drop you a few lines," wrote J. Roswell Flower, general secretary of the Assemblies of God, to Ockenga in 1943, "since I have seen the reports of the recent convention" disparaging the NAE "because of its inclusion of such church groups as the Free Methodists, the Sixth Principle Baptists, the Assemblies of God, and the 'Pentecostal or 'Tongue' Holiness Groups.'" "We

99. Edith L. Blumhofer, *The Assemblies of God: A Chapter in the Story of American Pentecostalism*, vol. 2 (Springfield, MO: Gospel Publishing House, 1989), 17. For a helpful discussion of the relation between the Assemblies of God and the NAE, see pp. 13–52.

100. For a discussion of the Wesleyan roots of modern Pentecostalism, see Donald Dayton, *Theological Roots of Pentecostalism* (Peabody, MA: Hendrickson, 1991). Compare Howard A. Snyder, *The Divided Flame: Wesleyans and the Charismatic Renewal* (Grand Rapids: Francis Asbury, 1986).

101. Evans, *The Wright Vision*, 2.

102. This was the assessment of Wright's longtime colleague, Elizabeth Evans, in *The Wright Vision*, 7.

103. "Speaking in tongues is a sign and not the evidence of the baptism of the Holy Ghost," Wright wrote in 1922. "I am only stating what has always been my position from the early days of the Pentecostal movement. The recent articles in various Pentecostal magazines advocating the 'tongues as the evidence' theory have led me to believe that the time has come when I must take a more definite and public stand in regard to the matter," J. Elwin Wright, *The Baptism of the Holy Ghost and Its Relation to Speaking in Tongues* (Rumney, NH: First Fruit Harvesters Association, 1922), 1. For a discussion of "initial evidence" see Gary B. McGee, ed., *Initial Evidence* (Peabody, MA: Hendrickson, 1991).

104. Edith L. Blumhofer, "From Isolation to Cooperation: The Assemblies of God and the New Evangelicals," in *The Assemblies of God*, 13–32. Blumhofer argues that the Assemblies of God were largely isolated from other evangelical groups prior to 1940.

wish to assure you," he continued, "that the Assemblies of God desire no great prominence in this movement, although we are interested in its success, and we do purpose to promote the cause with all resources available to us. We recognize that this association has done a new thing in the earth by the recognition of groups formerly excluded from 'Fundamentalist' associations. Whether this course has been wise or not remains for the future to tell us."[105]

Looking back across the decades, the answer to Flower's intriguing question seems obvious. Given the fact that modern Pentecostalism—and its charismatic offspring—represents the largest and fastest-growing movement in the history of the Christian church, with a worldwide membership of nearly six hundred million after only a century of existence, makes one wonder where evangelicalism would be today without it.[106] Less than fifty years after the founding of the National Association of Evangelicals for United Action (NAE), in fact, over seventy-six percent of its total membership by "denominational families" was made up of churches representing either the Pentecostal or the Holiness Traditions.[107]

A third issue dividing the leaders in Chicago was McIntire's insistence on the principle of separation.[108] Only those denominations that were willing to renounce modernism and separate themselves from the Federal Council of Churches, he declared, were welcome to join the American Council.[109] J. Elwin Wright, on the other hand, envisioned an organization like his own New England Fellowship that would be substantially more flexible.[110] The "movement toward unity," he wrote,

> is proceeding all over the world in spite of denominational bigotry, prejudice and incompetency. Its force was demonstrated well in the recent pastors' conference at Rumney, where sixteen denominations were represented but where the delegates came not as official representatives of their various communions but of the body of Jesus Christ. There was a delightful and spontaneous unity which was effortless. Diversity was notable in the leadership. The chairman

---

105. Flower to Ockenga, May 26, 1943, Ockenga Papers. For a continuing discussion see Flower to Ockenga, June 1 and 10 and October 8, 1943, Ockenga Papers.

106. See David B. Barrett, Todd M. Johnson, and Peter Crossing, eds., "Missiometrics 2005: A Global Survey of World Mission," *International Bulletin of Missions Research* 29, no. 1 (January 2005): 27–30.

107. Matthews, *Standing Up, Standing Together,* app. E, 175.

108. For an excellent discussion of the separatist impulse, see Carpenter, *Revive Us Again,* 33–88.

109. See McIntire, *The Testimony of Separation.* A lively discussion of this issue was to continue within the NAE itself. See, for example, James E. Bennet to Harold John Ockenga, October 15, 1943, Ockenga Papers.

110. The New England Fellowship tended to adopt the famous epigram, "In necessariis unitas, in dubiis libertas, in omnibus caritas" (In essentials, unity; in non-essentials, liberty; and in all things, charity). The saying is usually attributed to St. Augustine. Its origin has also been attributed to Martin Luther, Richard Baxter, and many others. Some scholars believe it originated with Repertus Meldenius in a 1627 tract published in Germany.

was a Presbyterian. The opening address was given by a Methodist. The other principal speakers were Episcopalian, Lutheran, Baptist and Congregational. The final speech was given by the pastor of a church undenominationally related. [111]

"The victory," Wright was convinced, "was in the fact that no one was asked to surrender his convictions." Indeed, he concluded, "it is on a platform of this breadth that unity must come. We never have believed alike on all points and we never will until Christ removes the veil from our eyes. I regard it as absolutely certain that those who accept His Word and rely on His atoning blood for salvation will inevitably be driven together by the pressure of the apostasy of this age."[112]

While a substantial portion of the meeting was given to a discussion of McIntire's proposal, it became increasingly apparent that thirteen of the sixteen participants wanted to move in Wright's more inclusive direction. McIntire, Griffiths, and Laird, sensing that "there was nothing to be gained by their further presence," withdrew from the discussions. Before they left, however, the group had extended to McIntire and his colleagues an invitation to attend the organizational meeting that they were planning to hold in St. Louis the following April.[113]

A National Conference for United Action Among Evangelicals was convened on April 7, 1942, at the Hotel Coronado in St. Louis, Missouri.[114] The conference was opened, on the morning of April 7, with an address to about one hundred and fifty delegates by J. Elwin Wright. "For a number of years," Wright remarked, "many of us have been asking, 'Why does not someone start a movement to create some sort of central committee or office which will provide a clearing house for evangelicals in relation to matters of common concern?'" Then briefly reviewing the events that had led to the St. Louis gathering, he called on the delegates to answer that question by declaring their "essential solidarity as evangelicals," resolving "to go forward together unitedly for the truth," cultivating "a spirit of love and consideration toward those with whom we differ on less essential matters," and pledging "to God and each other" to henceforth "avoid carping and unkind criticism of our brethren of like precious faith." If they did so, he concluded, the prayer of Jesus may "yet be fulfilled."[115]

---

111. J. Elwin Wright, *The New England Fellowship Monthly*, July–August 1940, 8–9.
112. Ibid.
113. Matthews, *Standing Up, Standing Together*, 15.
114. A collection of documents from the early history of the NAE can be found in *Evangelical Action! A Report of the Organization of the National Association of Evangelicals for United Action*, compiled and edited by the Executive Committee (Boston: United Action Press, 1942).
115. J. Elwin Wright, "An Historical Statement of Events Leading Up To The National Conference at St. Louis," in *Evangelical Action!* 3–16.

Delegates at the National Conference for United Action Among Evangelicals held at the Hotel Coronado in St. Louis in April, 1942 (courtesy of Wheaton College Archives and Special Collections)

While Wright's comments were received with appreciation, Ockenga's keynote address, "The Unvoiced Multitudes," absolutely electrified the delegates. "Gentlemen," the Park Street prophet began, "we are gathered here today to consider momentous questions" and perhaps to even "arrive at decisions [that] will affect the whole future course of evangelical Christianity in America."[116] "Evangelical Christianity has suffered nothing but a series of defeats for decades," Ockenga lamented. In virtually every arena of culture, evangelical Christianity has been placed on the defensive. The "terrible octopus of liberalism, which spreads itself throughout our Protestant Church, . . . [has dominated] innumerable organizations, pulpits, and publications, as well as seminaries and other schools." The "poison" of materialism in educational institutions has spoiled "the testimony and message of the majority of our young preachers today." The "floods of iniquity" have poured over America "in a tidal wave of drunkenness, immorality, corruption, dishonesty, and utter atheism." Look around you, he suggested to the delegates. What you will see are Christians who are "defeated, reticent, retiring and seemingly in despair." If ever was needed "some organ to speak for the evangelical interests, to represent men who, like myself, are 'lone wolves' in the church" it was certainly today. Such defeat and despair, however, are no longer necessary. Like the dawning of a glorious new morning, dispelling the darkness and despair of a long and painful night, Ockenga threw open the windows of hope. Is it possible, he asked, that a new day is dawning? "Can such an organization" as we have been discussing "be launched here which will be the vanguard of the movement? I answer unqualifiedly, it can." "Are we in earnest?" he asked. "Are

116. Harold John Ockenga, "The Unvoiced Multitudes," in *Evangelical Action!* 19–39.

we teachable?" "Are we clean?" "Are we willing to dissolve any organizational connection which we may have in order that we, as a group, may adequately represent evangelical Christianity to this nation? If we are," he concluded, then "the day has dawned and the hour has struck inaugurating a new era in evangelical Christianity."[117]

Something remarkable happened that April morning. Harold John Ockenga began his address as the bright young pastor of Park Street Church. By the time his address ended, it was apparent to nearly everyone in the room that the resurgent evangelical movement had found its new leader. It was as if his years of study, long vigils of prayer, experience of God's forgiveness and grace, deep love for preaching, fascination with travel, dark nights of the soul, yearnings for holiness, love for the gospel, and commitment to truth all came together in a single moment. By the close of the St. Louis Convention, the delegates had chosen Ockenga to serve as the first president of its new organization, the National Association of Evangelicals for United Action.[118]

Assisted by J. Elwin Wright, the organization's new promotional secretary, Ockenga took up the new responsibilities with his characteristic zest. The task of building a functioning national organization where nothing had existed before seemed to energize both Ockenga and Wright. Indeed, by September 9, 1942, they had gathered the executive committee together in New York City's Pennsylvania Hotel to begin wrestling with a flood of issues about which decisions needed to be made. It was only the first of a string of meetings that were held that winter and spring.[119]

Among the tasks facing the leadership of the new organization were the establishment of committees,[120] the setting up of regional and national offices,[121] the raising of a budget,[122] the adoption of a statement of faith,[123]

---

117. Ibid.

118. The NAE was not officially established until the meeting of the International Constitutional Convention for United Evangelical Action at the LaSalle Hotel in Chicago on May 3–7, 1943.

119. See executive committee meeting minutes, National Association of Evangelicals for United Action, September 9, 1942; January 6 and May 20, 1943, Ockenga Papers.

120. Fourteen committees were established: constitution, missions, radio, evangelism, war service, education, moral reform and social service, separation of church and state, publications, problems of evangelical literature, resolutions, finance, fields of endeavor and policy, and fraternal relations. The 108 individuals who were appointed to serve on these committees include many key names from early-1940s evangelicalism, including Torrey Johnson, Stacey Woods, Bryant Kirkland, Paul Rees, Harry Rimmer, Lewis Sperry Chafer, Robert B. Munger, and Thomas Zimmerman. Typed listing in Ockenga Papers.

121. See typed listing of "District," "Superintendent," and "Secretary" in Ockenga Papers.

122. For budget reports see Ockenga Papers.

123. The committee adopted a seven point statement: (1) We believe the Bible to be the inspired, the only infallible, authoritative word of God; (2) We believe that there is one God, eternally existent in three persons: Father, Son, and Holy Ghost; (3) We believe in the deity of Christ, in His virgin birth, in His sinless life, in His miracles, in His vicarious and atoning death through His shed blood, in His bodily resurrection, in His ascension to the right hand of the Father, and in His personal return

National Association of Evangelicals Executive Committee. Clockwise from head of table: Harold J. Ockenga, J. Elwin Wright, R. J. Bateman, John W. Bradbury, J. Alvin Orr, Leslie R. Marston, James T. Rider, William W. Ayer, Alex H. Sauerwein, Ralph T. Davis, H. M. Shuman, J. J. Taylor, J. Williston Smith, and Gertrude D. Clark (courtesy of Gordon-Conwell Libraries)

the development of membership policies and procedures, the planning of national and regional conferences, the necessary preparations for a constitutional convention, matters of incorporation, and issues relating to publicity and publications.[124]

The executive committee also set out a detailed rationale to explain why they had felt compelled to establish the NAE. "In April 1942," the rationale began, "more than one hundred and fifty ministers and laymen, meeting at St. Louis, Mo., coming from all sections of the United States, were led to form

in power and glory; (4) We believe that for the salvation of lost and sinful man regeneration by the Holy Spirit is absolutely essential; (5) We believe in the present ministry of the Holy Spirit by whose indwelling the Christian is enabled to live a godly life; (6) We believe in the resurrection of both the saved and the lost; they that are saved unto the resurrection of life and they that are lost unto the resurrection of damnation; (7) We believe in the spiritual unity of believers in Christ. This version appeared on the back of the membership application cards for the new organization. A slightly shorter version can be found in the executive committee meeting minutes, September 9, 1942, 5; copies of both in the Ockenga Papers.

124. For discussion of these various concerns and the decisions that were made, see executive committee meeting minutes for September 9, 1942, and January 6 and May 20, 1943, Ockenga Papers.

this organization for the following reasons, which we believe properly and imperatively called it into existence." Among the reasons that followed were three central concerns: that there are "millions of earnest Christians in America who are not represented by any other organization or inter-church group"; that some of the "interdenominational Protestant church organizations" that do exist "have so far departed from 'the faith once for all delivered to the saints' that many millions of us cannot give to them our allegiance"; and that many earnest Christians "feel deeply the propriety and necessity that the unvoiced millions who hold the evangelical doctrines of the Holy Scriptures should be articulate and vocal." "We therefore," they concluded, "most earnestly invite all Christians who share these positions, to unite with us." Such a show of evangelical solidarity, they were convinced, would advance their "ideals and teachings," bring glory to God, and "greatly hasten the evangelization of the masses."[125]

Ockenga's Burgeoning Network

Harold John Ockenga's election as the first president of the NAE thrust him almost immediately into national prominence. During the thirteen months between the St. Louis Convention in April of 1942 and the Chicago Constitutional Convention in May of 1943, Ockenga not only crisscrossed the country on behalf of the fledgling organization but he also carried on a rapidly expanding correspondence with many of evangelicalism's most important leaders.[126]

Ockenga had met a few of these individuals before. Now, however, he found himself in regular contact with leaders like C. Stacey Woods, general secretary of Inter-Varsity Christian Fellowship;[127] John Bradbury, editor of the *Watchman-Examiner*;[128] J. Roswell Flower, general secretary of the General Council of the Assemblies of God;[129] Clarence Bouma, professor of ethics and apologetics at Calvin Seminary;[130] J. E. Jaderquist, executive secretary of the Bible House of Los Angeles;[131] Percy B. Crawford, pastor and director of the Young People's Church of the Air;[132] Charles E. Fuller, director of the Old Fashioned Revival Hour;[133] Frederick T. Ellis, national secretary for England's Faith for the Times

125. The full text can be found in the executive committee meeting minutes, September 9, 1942, 4–5, Ockenga Papers.

126. Correspondence files in the Ockenga Papers.

127. Woods to Ockenga, May 5, 1943, Ockenga Papers. See also A. Donald MacLeod, *C. Stacey Woods and the Evangelical Rediscovery of the University* (Downers Grove, IL: InterVarsity, 2007).

128. Bradbury to Ockenga, May 11, 1943, Ockenga Papers.

129. Flower to Ockenga, May 25, 1943, Ockenga Papers.

130. Bouma to Ockenga, May 27, 1943, Ockenga Papers.

131. Jaderquist to Ockenga, May 10, 1943, Ockenga Papers.

132. Crawford to Ockenga, June 3, 1943, Ockenga Papers.

133. Fuller to Ockenga, June 7, 1943, Ockenga Papers.

Campaign;[134] Paul W. Rood, president of the World's Christian Fundamentals Association;[135] Donald Grey Barnhouse, pastor of Tenth Presbyterian Church in Philadelphia;[136] Bob Jones, founder of Bob Jones College;[137] and a host of others. "This has been a herculean undertaking," Ockenga later reflected, "in writing, speaking, travel, answering questions, organizing and meeting innumerable people. Personally, I have traveled through thirty-four states and have been absent from my local work for ten weeks." Yet these travels had opened his eyes to the needs and opportunities confronting the American church and they had convinced him that great numbers of believers were "waiting for the clear cut, definite, sane and progressive leadership" that could "inaugurate a new era for Christian influence and effectiveness" throughout the world.[138]

International Constitutional Convention for United Evangelical Action, LaSalle Hotel in Chicago, Illinois (May 3–7, 1943)

By the time Harold John Ockenga rose to give the presidential address on May 4, he was well known to most of the nearly one thousand delegates who had gathered that morning at Chicago's LaSalle Hotel.[139] *United Evangelical Action*, the official publication of the NAE, carried the full text of Ockenga's address to the assembled delegates.[140] Like his St. Louis speech the year before, his "Christ for America" address in Chicago not only galvanized and energized those who had gathered that morning but it came to serve, as his "Unvoiced Multitudes" had done in 1942, as a kind of manifesto for the movement.[141]

Ockenga clearly referenced the events of World War II in his address. "This nation is passing through a crisis which is enmeshing western civilization. Confusion exists on every hand. We are living in a very difficult and bewildering time." Yet he was convinced, "America not only will survive this war, but will emerge chastened, serious as to government, religion and morals and ready for an advance under the proper type of leadership." Ockenga argued that an

---

134. Ellis to Ockenga, June 19, 1943, Ockenga Papers.

135. Rood to Ockenga, July 8, 1943, Ockenga Papers.

136. Barnhouse to Ockenga, July 13, 1943, Ockenga Papers.

137. Jones to Ockenga, July 10, 1943, Ockenga Papers.

138. Harold John Ockenga, "Christ for America," *United Evangelical Action*, May 4, 1943, 3–4, 6. The convention program is also included in this issue on p. 7.

139. For an account of the proceedings, see Matthews, *Standing Up, Standing Together*, 49–58; and Evans, *The Wright Vision*, 115–19.

140. Ockenga, "Christ for America."

141. Horace F. Dean, national chairman of Christ for America, wrote both J. Elwin Wright and Harold John Ockenga following the Constitutional Convention to express his concern about the confusion that might arise in Ockenga's choice of title for his presidential address. The problem seems to have been resolved with a good spirit of cooperation. See Dean to Wright, May 6, 1943, and Dean to Ockenga, May 13, 1943, Ockenga Papers.

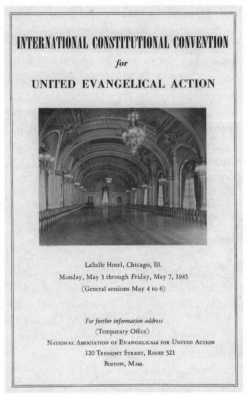

LaSalle Hotel, Chicago, Ill.
Monday, May 3 through Friday, May 7, 1943
(General sessions May 4 to 6)

For further information address
(Temporary Office)
NATIONAL ASSOCIATION OF EVANGELICALS FOR UNITED ACTION
120 TREMONT STREET, ROOM 521
BOSTON, MASS.

Program for the International Constitutional Convention for United Evangelical Action, LaSalle Hotel, Chicago, May 3–7, 1943 (courtesy of Gordon-Conwell Libraries)

instrument capable of meeting "the need of this crisis hour in our nation and the world" was in hand. The NAE "is the only hopeful sign on the horizon of Christian history today. If we who are gathered here meet our responsibility this week it may well be that the oblique rays of the sun are not the rusty red of its setting but are the golden rays of its rising for a new era."[142]

Not only did Ockenga's presidency of the NAE make him the movement's most important young leader but the eloquence of the speeches he delivered at its early conventions also established him as evangelicalism's most trusted voice. During the 1940s and 1950s, in fact, it was rare that a new initiative was taken or a new organization established without an opening address by Ockenga.[143]

When one reads through his addresses one after the other, it is difficult to miss the distinctive pattern of their design. Ockenga's speeches characteristically began with the crisis of civilization punctuated by quotations from intellectuals such as Pitirim Sorokin or Karl Marx and ended with the hope of God's kingdom. They started with exegesis and finished with application. They painted a dark backdrop of moral and cultural decay and then splashed on the bright colors of God's sovereign grace. They opened with impending disaster and closed with the dawning of a glorious new era. Taken by themselves, these structural patterns cannot fully explain the enormous emotional impact Ockenga's

142. Ockenga, "Christ for America," 3–4, 6.

143. These included the NAE, Fuller Theological Seminary, and Gordon-Conwell Theological Seminary to name but a few. For the astounding range of new organizations and initiatives, see Wesley K. Willmer, J. David Schmidt, and Martyn Smith, *The Prospering Parachurch: Enlarging the Boundaries of God's Kingdom* (San Francisco: Jossey-Bass, 1998).

addresses tended to have on those
who heard them. Even the brilliance of his mind, the breadth of
his knowledge, and the sharpness of
his rhetoric cannot fully account for
their influence. Rather, what seemed
to make his addresses so unusually
powerful was his ability to articulate clearly and persuasively what so
many of his listeners were already
thinking and feeling. In essence, his
voice was their voice—more refined
and polished to be sure, but no less
familiar.[144]

The Grand Vision

All great moral leaders embody
in some sense the deepest hopes and
aspirations of those who choose to
follow them. For those who felt
marginalized, Ockenga was a self-
described lone wolf who sought to
gather them together in a pack. For

Oil painting of Harold John Ockenga in academic regalia (courtesy of Gordon-Conwell
Libraries)

those who had grown weary of old battles and ineffective strategies, he offered a fresh new beginning. For those who felt powerless against the rising
tide of evil, he called for united evangelical action. For those who wanted to
spread the gospel around the globe, he shared their passion for worldwide
evangelization. For those who yearned for revival, he was a leader whose
deepest desire was the arrival of genuine spiritual awakening.

"What the Communist party is in the vanguard of the world revolution,"
Ockenga argued in his stunning but now largely forgotten address "Resurgent
Evangelical Leadership," "the evangelical movement must be in the world
revival."[145] And what is an evangelical? he asks. "An evangelical is a Christian" who affirms unreservedly the historic doctrines of the faith, as reflected
in the Apostles' and Nicene Creeds, who is "zealous for practical Christian
living," and who seeks "the conversion of sinners" through evangelistic and
missionary outreach. Furthermore, he argued, evangelicalism "should be

144. For an example, see G. H. Montgomery, "Observation of Convention of Evangelicals," a
twenty-three-page report on the NAE's Constitutional Convention, Ockenga Papers.
145. Harold John Ockenga, "Resurgent Evangelical Leadership," undated manuscript, Ockenga
Papers. The address was published in *Christianity Today*, October 10, 1960, 11–15.

differentiated from other movements," most notably, from Roman Catholicism, modernism, and fundamentalism. "The history of the last five decades has been largely under the aegis of a triumphant modernism," a movement that "developed a new theology concerning Christ, man, sin, salvation, the Church and the Church's mission." Against the advance of modernism, Ockenga continued, came a "fundamentalist reaction" and the start of the "modernist-fundamentalist controversy." Unfortunately, "time revealed certain weaknesses in the fundamentalist cause"—namely, energies on behalf of "the great offensive work of missions, evangelism and Christian education" were diverted in an effort to defend the faith "against the constant and unremitting attacks of the modernists and liberals." Eventually, "the liberals took over the control of the denominations and began a series of acts of discrimination, ostracism and persecution of the evangelical." As a result, fundamentalism sadly became little more than "a holding tactic, impotent in denominational machinery and indifferent to the societal problems which were rising in the secular world."[146]

Theologically, of course, "there is a solidarity of doctrine between fundamentalism and evangelicalism." Indeed, "the evangelical defense of the faith theologically is identical with that of the older fundamentalists." Furthermore, Ockenga continued, fundamentalism and evangelicalism share "a common source of life for they belong to one family." Evangelicals owe a great debt to fundamentalism, and it

> is a mistake for an evangelical to divorce himself from historic fundamentalism as some have sought to do. These older leaders of the orthodox cause paid a great price in persecution, discrimination, obloquy and scorn which they suffered at the hands of those who under the name of modernism repudiated biblical Christianity. For decades these fundamentalists were steadfast to Christ and to biblical truth regardless of the cost. They maintained the knowledge of orthodox Christianity through Bible schools, radio programs, Christian conferences and Bible conferences. In the true New Testament sense, they were witnesses, or martyrs. Most of these leaders were well known to me personally. I speak of men such as James M. Gray, Lewis Sperry Chafer, Arnold C. Gaebelein, R. C. Haldeman, Harry Ironside, J. Gresham Machen, J. Alvin Orr, Clarence Edward Macartney, Walter Meier, Robert Dick Wilson, W. B. Riley, Charles E. Fuller, Robert Shuler, Oswald T. Allis, Harry Rimmer, only to mention a few. These were great defenders of the faith.[147]

Despite his appreciation for the efforts of the old fundamentalist stalwarts of the early twentieth century, it seems clear that Ockenga's inspiration came primarily from even older sources—namely, from the great stream of historic

---

146. Ibid.

147. Ibid. For a similar argument, see Richard J. Mouw, *The Smell of Sawdust: What Evangelicals Can Learn From Their Fundamentalist Heritage* (Grand Rapids: Zondervan, 2000).

Christianity that mentors like J. Gresham Machen had taught him to love and from the rich heritage of evangelicalism that had emerged in the revivals of America's Great Awakening. "The evangelical has general objectives he wishes to see achieved," Ockenga argued. Included among these are a winning of "new respectability for orthodoxy in academic circles by producing scholars who can defend the faith on intellectual grounds," the recapturing of "denominational leadership from within the denominations rather than abandoning those denominations to modernism," reform of the social order, and "a revival of Christianity in the midst of a secular world which faces desperate problems."[148]

For these to be accomplished, he was convinced, there had to be "evangelical cooperation," the publication of "a new literature expressing the orthodox position," and the "training and feeding of evangelical ministers into the churches." Furthermore, evangelicals could not rely on "piecemeal action by fragmented groups." Rather, they needed a united and "up-to-date strategy for the evangelical cause." Such a strategy must be "based upon the principle of infiltration." Modernists "have been using this strategy for years. They have infiltrated our evangelical denominations, institutions and movements and then have taken over the control of them. It is time for firm evangelicals to seize their opportunity to minister in and influence modernist groups."[149]

Despite fundamentalism's important contributions, Ockenga was convinced that the movement had made one enormous strategic mistake. In the heat of battle, especially following the Scopes Trial in 1925, fundamentalism had tended to turn inward, to "circle the wagons," so to speak, and to adopt a strategy of withdrawal. Fearing that their sons and daughters would "lose their faith," for example, many parents had pulled their children out of the increasingly liberal universities, enrolling them instead in Christian liberal arts colleges or Bible schools.[150] Many others, discouraged by what they believed to be the growing strength of modernism in the mainline denominations, chose to sever their ties with those bodies and to seek more likeminded fellowship in evangelically oriented congregations.[151] Those who had once been participants in the ecumenical revolution now found themselves increasingly estranged from its structures and programs.[152] Still others, sensing what they believed to be the moral and cultural decay within America's institutions, withdrew from the

148. Ibid.

149. Ibid.

150. See Virginia L. Brereton, *Training God's Army: The American Bible School, 1880–1940* (Bloomington: Indiana University Press, 1990); William Ringenberg, *The Christian College*, 2nd ed. (Grand Rapids: Baker Academic, 2006); Conrad Cherry, *Hurrying Toward Zion: Universities, Divinity Schools and American Protestantism* (Bloomington: Indiana University Press, 1995); and George M. Marsden, *The Soul of the American University* (New York: Oxford University Press, 1994).

151. See Bradley J. Longfield, *The Presbyterian Controversy* (New York: Oxford University Press, 1993).

152. See J. I. Packer, "Why I Left," *Christianity Today*, April 5, 1993, 33–36.

public square. In contrast to this strategy of withdrawal, Ockenga called on a new generation of evangelical Christians to infiltrate the very institutions that so many of the old stalwarts had felt compelled to abandon. Ockenga pled with his followers to penetrate every institution with the transformative power of God's wonderful truth, to apply in every arena of human existence the life-giving power of biblical Christianity, and to spread the gospel to every corner of the globe.

Before such a grand vision could become a reality, Ockenga was convinced there had to be a great revival. "We realize," he observed, "that we are at the ebb-tide of revival waves. Darkness has engulfed our age. Sin, fear, hate, doubt, distrust, and despair characterize the dominant mood of this day." Yet we need not despair for there is also in our day "a regrouping of forces for a new advance. In the ebb there is always the gathering of the swell before moving forward, and that swell is gathering now."[153] Within three years the great revival for which he yearned would sweep like a mighty river through Boston, across America, and around the world.

While the NAE would provide the cultural vision and much of the organizational savvy for the great mid-twentieth-century evangelical renaissance, it would not be the primary source of its explosive growth. Rather, to the surprise of nearly everyone, the tens of thousands of new converts that eventually populated the burgeoning evangelical movement would come primarily from the massive youth revivals of the 1940s. Led by a gifted, fun-loving, and somewhat unlikely "band of brothers" and centered in the work of an increasingly global organization known as Youth for Christ International, the movement not only breathed new life into dry bones but it also helped to change the religious landscape of America.

153. Ockenga, "The Great Revival," 223–35.

4

✳✳✳✳✳✳✳✳✳✳✳✳✳✳✳✳✳✳✳✳✳✳✳✳✳✳✳✳✳✳✳✳✳✳✳✳✳

A BAND OF BROTHERS

Throughout most of its history, both colonial and national, the United States has been a land of farmers, merchants, and small shopkeepers.[1] By the end of the nineteenth century, however, America's largely rural and agrarian economy had begun giving way to the urbanized and industrialized patterns characteristic of the twentieth century.[2] As thousands of immigrants poured into America's cities, seeking jobs in factories and a new life in what they believed to be a land of promise, America's cultural patterns also began to change.[3]

New heroes, often symbols of America's growing wealth, power, and influence, began to replace revered icons of a bygone age. A new awareness of the larger world, especially for the thousands of young soldiers who had served in World War I, began to replace the relative isolation of earlier years. And a new restlessness, especially among America's young people, opened the door for what Frederick Lewis Allen has called America's "revolution in manners and morals."[4]

1. See Samuel Eliot Morison, *The Oxford History of the American People* (New York: Oxford University Press, 1972); Sydney E. Ahlstrom, *A Religious History of the American People* (New Haven: Yale University Press, 1972); Bernard Bailyn, *The New England Merchants in the Seventeenth Century* (New York: Harper Torchbooks, 1955); John Rupnow, *The Growing of America: 200 Years of U. S. Agriculture* (Atkinson, WI: Johnson Hill, 1975); and Carl Bridenbaugh, *The Colonial Craftsman* (Chicago: University of Chicago Press, 1964).

2. These transitions, of course, created enormous controversy. See Samuel P. Hays, *The Response to Industrialism, 1885–1914* (Chicago: University of Chicago Press, 1968); Norman Pollack, *The Populist Response to Industrial America* (New York: Norton, 1966); Norman J. Ware, *The Labor Movement in the United States, 1860–1890* (New York: Vintage, 1964); and Robert H. Wiebe, *The Search for Order, 1877–1920* (New York: Hill and Wang, 1967).

3. For a classic study of American immigration, see Oscar Handlin, *The Uprooted: The Epic Story of the Great Migration That Made the American People* (Toronto: Little, Brown, 1990).

4. Frederick Lewis Allen, "The Revolution in Manners and Morals," in *Only Yesterday: An Informal History of the 1920's* (New York: Harper & Row, 1964), 73–101.

"What most distinguishes the generation who have approached maturity since the debacle of idealism at the end of the War," observed the noted journalist Walter Lippmann, "is not their rebellion against the religion and the moral code of their parents, but their disillusionment with their own rebellion. It is common for young men and women to rebel," he reflected, "but that they should rebel sadly and without faith in their own rebellion, that they should distrust the new freedom no less than the old certainties—that is something of a novelty."[5]

The Rise of Evangelical Youth Movements

Whatever helped to produce America's moral revolution, there can be little doubt that the eroding morality of the roaring 20s and the growing restlessness among the youth of the land were producing a deepening concern within the Christian community.[6] Unwilling to leave the future of their young people to chance, a growing number of Christian leaders began to develop strategies for reaching them more effectively. Among the earliest of the leaders were Lloyd Bryant, Percy Crawford, Paul Guiness, Walter Smyth, Oscar Gillian, Jim Rayburn, Stacey Woods, and Jack Wyrtzen.[7]

Christian ministry to young people was, of course, nothing new. Throughout the eighteenth, nineteenth, and early twentieth centuries, a variety of organizations had been established to evangelize, disciple, and prepare young men and women for Christian service. Among the better known of these were the Sunday School Movement (1781),[8] the Young Men's Christian Association (1844),[9] the Young Women's Christian Association (1858),[10] the Christian Endeavor Society (1881),[11] the Student Volunteer Movement (1886),[12] the World Wide Baraca Philathea Union (1892/1893),[13] and the World's Student Christian Federation

5. Walter Lippmann, *A Preface to Morals* (1929; repr., New York: Time-Life Books, 1964), 16.

6. Among the possible causes of what Frederick Lewis Allen liked to call the "revolution in manners and morals," perhaps the most frequently noted are the new freedoms made possible by the automobile, the advent of movies, the availability of magazines, the "eat, drink and be merry" atmosphere following the end of World War I, and the growing disillusionment over "the war to end all wars" itself.

7. For a helpful introduction to the youth movements of the 1930s and 1940s, see Bruce Shelley, "The Rise of Evangelical Youth Movements," *Fides et Historia*, January 1986, 47–63.

8. See Robert W. Lynn, *Big Little School: Two Hundred Years of the Sunday School* (Birmingham, AL: Religious Education Press, 1980).

9. See L. L. Doggett, *History of the Young Men's Christian Association* (London: International Committee of the Young Men's Christian Associations, 1909).

10. See Mary W. Sims, *The First Twenty-Five Years* (New York: Woman's Press, 1932).

11. See Francis E. Clark, *World Wide Endeavor: The Story of the Young People's Society of Christian Endeavor* (Philadelphia: Gillespie, Metzgar and Kelley, 1896).

12. See Nathan D. Showalter, *The End of a Crusade* (Metuchen, NJ: Scarecrow Press for the ATLA Monograph Series, 1997).

13. See Ann Elizabeth Olson, *A Million for Christ: The Story of Baraca Philathea* (South Hamilton, MA: The Ockenga Institute, 2004).

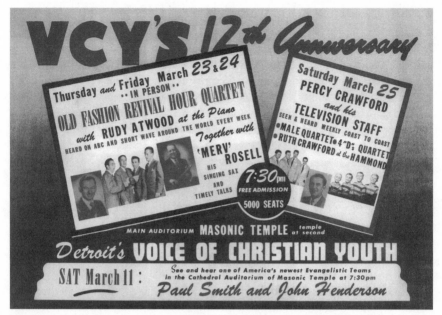

Advertising flyer for the Voice of Christian Youth (courtesy of Gordon-Conwell Libraries)

(1895).[14] Augmenting the work of these organizations, while not always specifically aimed at ministry to young people, were scores of summer Bible conferences, Christian camping programs, denominational youth programs, religious periodicals, radio broadcasts, denominational and ecumenical campus ministries, local church youth groups, Bible colleges, Christian liberal arts colleges, theological seminaries, and a wide array of missionary organizations.

With the arrival of the 1920s and 30s, however, Christian ministries to young people seemed to take on a renewed sense of urgency. Scores of new organizations, geared primarily to evangelize and disciple young men and women, were established throughout North America during the decades between World War I (1914–18) and World War II (1939–45): including the Inter-Varsity Christian Fellowship of Canada (1928),[15] the Christian Youth Campaigns for America (1929),[16] the Young People's Church of the Air (1930), the Navigators (1933), the Christian Service Brigade (1937), the Voice of Christian Youth (1937), Young Life Campaign (1937), Pioneer Girls (1939),

14. See John R. Mott, *The World's Student Christian Federation* (New York: Association Press, 1947).

15. For a fuller story of Inter-Varsity Christian Fellowship, see C. Stacey Woods, *The Growth of a Work of God* (Downers Grove, IL: InterVarsity, 1978); Jim Howard, *Student Power in World Evangelism* (Downers Grove, IL: InterVarsity, 1970); and Paul A. Bramadat, *The Church on the World's Turf* (New York: Oxford University Press, 2000).

16. See James C. Hefley, *God Goes to High School* (Waco: Word, 1970), 13–27.

the Inter-Varsity Christian Fellowship of the United States (1941),[17] and Word of Life (1941).

There were significant differences between the organizations, often reflecting the personalities and interests of their founders. Some ministries, like Dawson Trotman's Navigators, worked primarily with military personnel.[18] Others, like Betty Whitaker's Pioneer Girls, were more gender specific.[19] Jim Rayburn's Young Life Campaign sought to reach kids through relationships and friendship evangelism[20] while Percy Crawford focused more attention on radio and television.[21] Jack Wyrtzen's Word of Life sponsored enormous rallies, such as those that packed New York City's Madison Square Garden with twenty thousand kids, while the Christian Service Brigade tended to emphasize weekly Bible studies and community service projects.[22] Henrietta Mears, director of Christian Education at the Hollywood Presbyterian Church, centered much of her work on developing Christian leaders within the local church or at the Forest Home Conference Center she helped establish, while Oscar Gillian concentrated the ministry of the Voice of Christian Youth on sponsoring large interdenominational youth rallies.[23]

Despite the differences in emphasis, most of the ministries shared two primary goals: evangelism and discipleship. From Lloyd Bryant's New York City ministry in 1929, considered by some to have been the first youth rally outreach in America,[24] to Jack Wyrtzen's amazingly successful efforts, which began in the same Christian and Missionary Alliance Gospel Tabernacle in

17. See Keith and Gladys Hunt, *For Christ and the University: Story of Inter-Varsity Christian Fellowship in the United States of America, 1940–1990* (Downers Grove, IL: InterVarsity, 1991).

18. See Betty Lee Skinner, *Daws: A Man Who Trusted God* (Colorado Springs: NavPress, 1993).

19. See S. A. Robertson, "A Description of Pioneer Girls: An International Religious Club Program" (PhD diss., Northern Illinois University, 1977).

20. See Shelley, "The Rise of Evangelical Youth Movements," 52–55.

21. In January of 1921, Pittsburgh's Calvary Episcopal Church broadcast its Sunday service over KDKA, the first known broadcast of a church service over America's first radio station. By 1925, seventy-one of six hundred radio stations were being operated by churches or religious organizations. The first radio network, NBC, was launched in 1926. The following year Congress passed the Radio Act of 1927, allocating free time to three faith groups: Catholic, Protestant, and Jewish. Since the Protestant allocation was controlled by the Federal Council of Churches, the action eventually helped to encourage the establishment of the NAE. For a fascinating discussion of these developments, see Tona J. Hangen, *Redeeming the Dial* (Chapel Hill: University of North Carolina Press, 2002), esp. 21–36. For Percy Crawford's work, see Crawford to Ockenga, June 3, 1943, Ockenga Papers. In 1950, Crawford began broadcasting the first coast-to-coast television program. He also helped establish the Atlantic City Victory Center (an outreach ministry to military personnel); the Pinebrook Bible Conference in Stroudsburg, Pennsylvania; and Kings College in Briarcliff Manor, New York.

22. See George Sweeting, *The Jack Wyrtzen Story* (Grand Rapids: Zondervan, 1960); Paul Heidebrecht, *The Brigade Trail* (Wheaton: Christian Service Brigade, 1987).

23. See Earl O. Roe, ed., *Dream Big: The Henrietta Mears Story* (Wheaton: Regal, 1991); Hefley, *God Goes to High School*, 20.

24. Hefley, *God Goes to High School*, 19.

1941, the central focus remained essentially the same. Moreover, many of these ministries were connected through the generous support of benefactor Herbert J. Taylor. While president of an aluminum company in Chicago, Taylor's vision and generosity provided a substantial portion of the financial support for many of the new organizations. Without his assistance, youth ministry in America might have developed quite differently.

The Emergence of Youth for Christ

The collective impact of these ministries has been enormous. And some of them—along with newer organizations such as World Vision (1950), Campus Crusade for Christ (1951), the Fellowship of Christian Athletes (1954), Youth with a Mission (1960), Focus on the Family (1977), and Promise Keepers (1990)—are still active today. But during the 1940s, no ministry was more successful in reaching young people than Youth for Christ. Its explosive growth was breathtaking, its global vision was ahead of its time, and its influence surprised even its most ardent supporters.[25] The ministry of Youth for Christ helped prepare the way for the religious revivals that swept across America and around the world during the early 1950s. Not only did it provide the "Mid-Twentieth Century Awakening," as historian J. Edwin Orr described the revivals of the 1950s, with much of its leadership and nearly all of its most prominent evangelists but it also provided the infrastructure for the most successful urban crusades.[26] With rare exception, the cities with the strongest Youth for Christ presence in the 1940s became the cities most deeply touched by the revivals of the 1950s. "The origins of Youth for Christ," historian Bruce Shelley observed, "are almost impossible to trace."[27] The first president of Youth for Christ, Torrey Johnson, thought the movement might be rooted in Jack Wyrtzen's ministry in New York City, Oscar Gillian's ministry in Detroit, Walter Smyth's ministry in Philadelphia, Dick Harvey's ministry in St. Louis, or Roger Malsbary's ministry in Indianapolis—but did not know for sure. What was known, Johnson was convinced, was that "Youth for Christ is a miracle of God in its origin, in its development, and in its results." The

25. For the story of Youth for Christ, see Mel Larson, *Young Man On Fire: The Story of Torrey Johnson and Youth for Christ* (Chicago: Youth Publications, 1945); Torrey Johnson and Robert Cook, *Reaching Youth for Christ* (Chicago: Moody, 1944); Joel A. Carpenter, *Revive Us Again: The Reawakening of American Fundamentalism* (New York: Oxford University Press, 1997), 161–76; Hefley, *God Goes To High School*; and Mervin Rosell, "Remembering Youth for Christ," *Northwestern Pilot*, November 1949, 42–43, 58.

26. J. Edwin Orr, *The Second Evangelical Awakening in America* (London: Marshall, Morgan & Scott, 1952), 160.

27. Shelley, "The Rise of Evangelical Youth Movements," 48.

Spirit of God seemed to be moving in such a way that "here and there they began to start."[28]

On May 29, 1943, in Indianapolis, for example, a Christian and Missionary Alliance evangelist named Roger Malsbary launched "a combination broadcast-rally in the old English Theater," the very first "to bear the name Youth for Christ in the United States."[29] Over the next two years, similar rallies were established in St. Louis, Kansas City, Minneapolis, Chicago, Toronto, Winnipeg, Los Angeles, Denver, Seattle, Miami, Detroit, Boston, Philadelphia, Washington, D.C., and a number of additional locations. Perhaps the most important of these, given its central role in the future of the movement, was the launching in 1944 of what came to be known as "Chicagoland Youth for Christ." George Beverly Shea, who had worked with Jack Wyrtzen in New York City before moving to Chicago to become part of Moody Bible Institute, had repeatedly urged Torrey Johnson to launch a similar work in Chicago. "Torrey," he said, "there should be a 'Youth for Christ' meeting in Chicago every Saturday night. You're the man to get it started."[30] Although Johnson worried about whether he should add another task to his already busy pastoral schedule, he worried even more about what would happen if he failed to do so. On April 13, 1944, while attending the NAE annual meeting in Columbus, Ohio, he made his decision to move forward with the launching of Chicagoland Youth for Christ.[31]

To everyone's surprise, on Saturday evening, May 27, 1944, Chicago's Orchestra Hall was filled to the rafters for the first of what would be twenty-one successive rallies held in that building. Bob Cook led the singing, Doug Fisher played the organ, Rose Arzoomanian was the soloist, and a gifted young evangelist named Billy Graham was the speaker. The success of that first rally, to everyone's delight, was repeated again and again throughout the following months.

Youth for Christ Victory Rally (October 21, 1944)

What brought Chicagoland Youth for Christ to national prominence, however, was not so much the successful Orchestra Hall gatherings as it was the massive "Victory Rally" that was held on October 21, 1944, at the Chicago Stadium. "Torrey emceed, world champion indoor miler Gil Dodds testified, Bev Shea and Rose Arzoomanian sang, and Merv Rosell preached."[32] Following the service, Torrey Johnson scribbled a quick note on the inside cover of

28. Torrey Johnson, "God Is In It!" presidential address, July 29, 1945, in the Billy Sunday Auditorium, Winona Lake, Indiana. Copy of sermon from the Archives of the Billy Graham Center, Wheaton College, Wheaton, Illinois.

29. Hefley, God Goes to High School, 21.

30. Johnson and Cook, Reaching Youth for Christ, 10.

31. For an introduction to the life and ministry of Torrey Johnson, see Larson, Young Man on Fire. For Johnson's decision to launch the Chicagoland Youth for Christ, see esp. p. 79.

32. Hefley, God Goes to High School, 23.

Youth for Christ Victory Rally at Chicago Stadium (courtesy of Gordon-Conwell Libraries)

his new book, *Reaching Youth for Christ*, and handed it to the speaker: "My Dear Brother in Christ, Merv Rosell, 'You did a bang-up job on our Victory Rally tonight before 28,000.' Torrey Johnson—Rom. 1:16."[33]

With the growing success and prominence of Youth for Christ, rallies began to spread to many additional cities. The most popular preachers—including youth evangelists such as Billy Graham, Merv Rosell, Chuck Templeton, Hyman Appelman, Jack Shuler, Jimmie Johnson, Bob Cook, Torrey Johnson, T. W. Wilson, Percy Crawford, and Jack Wyrtzen—were in constant demand. With the explosive growth of the movement, it became increasingly apparent that some sort of national organization was needed to coordinate its activities and to respond to the growing number of requests for information and help.

Roger Malsbary, director of Youth for Christ in Indianapolis, was the first to suggest the idea of holding an organizing convention. After several preliminary meetings, a "Temporary Youth for Christ International Committee" was established (with Torrey Johnson serving as its chairman), a temporary office was set up in Chicago, two staff members were hired (Billy Graham as Youth for Christ's first full-time evangelist and organizer and Clyde Dennis as the first editor of the *Youth for Christ* magazine), and plans were laid for the "First Annual Convention of Youth for Christ International."[34]

First Annual Convention of Youth for Christ (July 22–29, 1945)

The meetings were held from July 22 to 29, 1945, on the Winona Lake Conference Grounds. "Being convinced that we are witnessing a visitation

33. The note was written on the inside cover of Johnson and Cook, *Reaching Youth for Christ*, Mervin E. Rosell Papers.

34. "Minutes of the First Annual Convention," Youth for Christ International, July 22–29, 1945, Winona Lake Conference Grounds, Winona Lake, Indiana. These have been deposited at the Archives of the Billy Graham Center. Just two months before these meetings, on Memorial Day, Chicagoland Youth for Christ's largest rally was held at Soldier Field. Percy Crawford was the preacher and Merv Rosell gave the invitation.

First Annual Convention
of Youth for Christ on the
Winona Lake Conference
Grounds, July 22–29, 1945
(courtesy of Gordon-
Conwell Libraries)

of the Spirit of God in convicting and regenerating power among the youth, such as has not been seen in recent times," the founding constitution began, "we propose to group ourselves in an association to be known as Youth for Christ International." The document outlined four major objectives: "(1) To promote and to help Youth for Christ everywhere; (2) To encourage evangelism among youth; (3) To emphasize radiant, victorious Christian living; and (4) To foster international service through existing agencies."[35]

Torrey Johnson was elected president; Dick Harvey, vice-president; George Wilson, secretary; and Walter Block, treasurer. North America was divided into ten regions to be directed by ten regional vice presidents: Bob Pierce, Pacific Northwest; Hubert Mitchell, Pacific Southwest; Rex Lindquist, Rocky Mountain; Richard Harvey, Central; Dan Iverson, South; John Huffman, New England; Ed Darling, Great Lakes; Walter Smyth, Eastern; Charles Templeton, Eastern Canada; and Watson Argue, Western Canada.[36]

After his election as president, Torrey Johnson addressed the large crowd assembled in the Billy Sunday Tabernacle. The "pessimists" tell us "that the days of revival are past," declared Johnson, but "the rising tide" of revival "is everywhere round about us. Our brother Hyman Appelman has experienced it. John R. Rice, Merv Rosell, Jack Shuler, some older and some younger, are experiencing this thing in the rising tide of evangelism and revival that is coming back."[37]

35. "Constitution of Youth for Christ International," Articles I and II, in the "Minutes of the First Annual Convention."

36. Listing of officers is taken from "Minutes of the First Annual Convention."

37. Torrey Johnson, "God Is In It!" sermon delivered at the Billy Sunday Tabernacle in Winona Lake, Indiana, on Sunday morning, July 29, 1945. A copy of the sermon, along with "Minutes of the First Annual Convention," Youth for Christ International, July 22–29, 1945, Winona Lake Conference Grounds, Winona Lake, IN, can be found in the Archives of the Billy Graham Center.

"We propose to join hands with these evangelists" and "we're going to work together" in "city-wide revivals," Johnson promised. The evangelists "won't [even] have to call an organizational meeting. We will already have a city-wide representation of businessmen, youth leaders and pastors to iron out all the details and difficulties. These fellows are on their toes and know what the score is!" What they were praying for were "great old-fashioned city-wide revivals—not just one or two here and there—but we want to reach all the large cities and rural areas." "America cannot survive another twenty-five years like the last twenty-five," Johnson declared. "If we have another lost generation after this war like at the close of the last war, America is sunk. At the close of the last war we did not reach our servicemen. They came home and they were disillusioned and unhappy. They fell into sin, and now we have a generation of young people who do not know where they stand." Soon "our soldiers, sailors, marines, and airmen" will be coming home, Johnson observed. "Do you know who is going to run the world after the war? Don't think for a minute that we're going to do it—that's nonsense." Rather, Johnson proclaimed, we "are going to sit on the side-lines" while "the 14,000,000 service men and women" who lived through "the hell of Guadalcanal" or survived "the invasion of Normandy" or made it beyond "the Anzio beachhead"—they are the ones "who will rule this country. We have to reach them for Christ, or God help us."[38]

While Youth for Christ's regular use of military language ("crusade," "campaign," and "victory") and wartime imagery ("foxholes," "stars," and "stripes") might seem a bit foreign to some who are living today, it flowed quite naturally from a generation that remembered World War I, experienced World War II, and would soon live through the war in Korea. Almost everyone at every Youth for Christ rally had a friend or family member in the military or had experienced the loss of a loved one. Consequently, it was a rare American Youth for Christ rally that did not display the American flag and regularly link matters of faith and patriotism in its sermons and music. Not until the 1960s were such close connections seriously questioned.[39] Whatever the effects of war, the depression, and social change on the national consciousness, many evangelical leaders were convinced that God had called them to reach as many people with the gospel of Christ as their energies, resources, and

38. Johnson, "God Is In It!" James L. Stokesbury estimates that a total of sixteen million Americans served in World War II including four hundred thousand who were killed and five hundred thousand who were injured. He estimates that a total of seventy million had, at one point or another throughout the war, borne arms. See Stokesbury, A Short History of World War II (San Francisco: HarperCollins, 2001), 377–89.

39. Virtually all of America's patriotic songs, from "America" (first sung at Park Street Church in Boston) to Irving Berlin's "God Bless America," also make the link between faith and patriotism. It is interesting to note that the words, "under God," were added to our national pledge of allegiance to the flag and that the nation's motto, "In God We Trust," were both officially established by Congress during the 1950s.

opportunities would allow. No one would prove to be more effective in doing so than Billy Graham.

Billy Graham

In his autobiography, *Just As I Am*, Billy Graham wrote about the years he spent growing up in Charlotte, North Carolina. With disarming candor and winsomeness he described his family, his boyhood dreams, his conversion, the beginnings of his lifelong friendship with the Wilson brothers, the Tuesday evening Bible studies he attended at the home of "Mommy" Jones, his decision to enroll at Bob Jones University, and a host of other interesting events of his early life.[40] Spilling from each page is an unmistakable zest for life. "I get a kick out of just being alive," he later declared. "Life to me is a glorious, exciting adventure!"[41] Following his conversion in 1934, Graham recalled, "other revivalists and evangelists came through Charlotte" and "I went to hear most of them."[42] Among those who preached in Charlotte during those years were two young evangelists, Jimmie Johnson and Merv Rosell. "Just out of college," Graham wrote of Johnson, "he was young and handsome, and his devotion to Christ flashed in his dark eyes as he preached the gospel in all of its power to the crowds that came to hear him." Not only did Johnson stay at the Graham home while he was in Charlotte but he was also responsible for Graham's first public testimony of his Christian faith. It occurred at the Monroe, North Carolina, jail when Johnson, whom Graham had driven from Charlotte to Monroe, called upon him for a word of testimony. With his "knees knocking," as Graham later described the event, he got up and spoke to "the ten or so prisoners" who were at the service.[43]

Merv Rosell also preached in Charlotte during those years, having first been introduced to the South in the summer of 1936 by William Bell Riley, pastor of the First Baptist Church and president of the Northwestern Schools in Minneapolis, Minnesota.[44] In the spring of 1936, during his senior year at Northwestern Theological Seminary, one of the three institutions of the Northwestern Schools that Billy Graham would later serve as president, Merv Rosell was enrolled in Riley's homiletics class. When Rosell's turn came to preach, he did so with great "energy and feeling." Following the sermon,

40. *Just As I Am: The Autobiography of Billy Graham* (San Francisco: HarperSanFrancisco, 1997), esp. 3–111. See also Grady Wilson, *Billy Graham as a Teen-Ager* (Wheaton: Miracle Books, 1957).

41. Quotations are from the *Boston Daily Globe*, January 1, 1950, 9.

42. Graham, *Just As I Am*, 32.

43. Ibid.

44. See William Vance Trollinger Jr., *God's Empire: William Bell Riley and Midwestern Fundamentalism* (Madison: University of Wisconsin Press, 1990); and the *Northwestern Pilot,* memorial issue, January 1948. Ten reels of William Bell Riley microfilm are part of "Collection 95, Supplement 1" in the Archives of the Billy Graham Center.

before dismissing the class, Riley said: "Rosell, I'll see you in my office." Fearful that he was being "called on the carpet," the twenty-four-year-old student was shaking by the time he arrived at his instructor's office. "Professor Riley," he asked, "did I preach too fervently or loudly?" "Oh, that sermon," Riley replied, "it touched my heart and it touched my life. What are you doing this summer? I'd like to have you travel with me in the South. Could you take the summer and spend it with me down in Memphis and Dothan and other places in the South?" "I would be honored," Rosell replied.[45]

Riley and Rosell's first stop on their southern tour was the famous Belleview Baptist Church in Memphis, Tennessee, pastored by Robert G. Lee.[46] When Riley was losing his voice and felt he would not be able to preach, he announced to a packed sanctuary that he had brought along "a young lad from my homiletics class who will preach in my place." Although he had already been preaching for five years in the Midwest, Rosell's very first sermon in the South was from one of the region's most famous pulpits.[47] "The South just seemed to adopt me," Rosell later commented. "Merv Rosell," as Jimmie Johnson phrased it, "is the most Southern Northern boy we know." For nearly a decade, Rosell focused most of his ministry in the South.[48] He and Johnson—like scores of other young evangelists during the late 1930s and early 1940s—traveled from town to town preaching in churches tiny and large, in open fields, in tabernacles, and in tents of all sizes.

Not only did the Riley/Rosell trip cement a lifelong friendship but Riley also took special care to introduce Rosell to his wide circle of southern friends: Bob Jones Sr., Robert G. Lee, John C. Cowell, John R. Rice, Robert C. McQuilkin, and evangelists Jimmie Johnson, Fred Brown, Joe Bamberg, and John Gamble, among others. Rosell and Johnson, in particular, hit it off immediately, developing a friendship that would continue throughout their lifetimes. Not only did they work together in revival meetings throughout the South during the 1930s but they also collaborated in helping start a daily radio program in 1938, *Your Daily Devotional Program*, that aired at 7:15 each morning from WPTF, Raleigh, North Carolina's fifty-thousand-watt radio station, and they jointly compiled and edited an early book of fourteen Bible studies, titled *Voices of Victory*, that had been used on the broadcast.[49] It was also through

45. Oral history interview with Mervin E. Rosell, "Memories of Dr. William Bell Riley," conducted August 15, 1992, Rosell Papers.

46. See John E. Huss, *Robert G. Lee: The Authorized Biography* (Grand Rapids: Zondervan, 1967).

47. Merv Rosell's first revival campaigns, at the age of nineteen, were all held in Minnesota: Rochester, Spring Valley, Brownsdale, and Austin. Curtis Akenson, a classmate at Northwestern and later pastor of the First Baptist Church in Minneapolis, often joined him for these early meetings.

48. Accounts are taken from an oral history interview with Mervin E. Rosell, August 15, 1992, Rosell Papers.

49. Jimmie Johnson and Merv Rosell, *Voices of Victory Via Air: Radio Studies* (St. Paul, MN: Northland, 1942).

Advertisement for the World Vision Conference (courtesy of Gordon-Conwell Libraries)

Johnson that Rosell came to know the Pattersons, the Grahams, the Wilsons, and others in the Charlotte community. "We thank God for the day that Jimmie Johnson brought you and Vi and the baby into our home," Vernon Patterson later reminisced. "Our home was your headquarters, I believe, for about two years."[50]

A Band of Brothers

The growing friendship and evangelistic collaboration between Jimmie Johnson and Merv Rosell, while incidental by itself, is significant in that it is illustrative of a process that was taking place not only throughout the South but also across America during the late 1930s and early 1940s. Scores of young evangelists including Johnson, Rosell, Jack Shuler, Fred Brown, Jack Wyrtzen, Percy Crawford, Torrey Johnson, Bob Cook, Cliff Barrows, Billy Graham, Grady Wilson, T. W. Wilson, Bob Pierce, Bob Evans, and Chuck Templeton—all of whom had been born after the turn of the century—began to join hands in the task of worldwide evangelization.

Often thrown together at youth rallies, revival meetings, or summer conferences, they came to know and trust each other. Sometimes ridiculed or dismissed by the "cultured despisers" of their day, they found encouragement in the company of like-minded colleagues. Increasingly caught up in the revivals that began breaking out during the 1940s, especially in connection with the growing success of Youth for Christ, they shared sermons and ideas,

50. Patterson to Rosell, July 1, 1982, on the occasion of Rosell's seventieth birthday, Rosell Papers. For Vernon William Patterson (1892–1991), a North Carolina businessman, see the Papers of Vernon William Patterson (Collection S) in the Archives of the Billy Graham Center. For the Wilson brothers, Grady and T. W., see Graham, *Just as I Am*, 663–64, 667–78.

song leaders and musicians, laughter and prayer, defeats and victories. In short, by the mid-1940s a recognizable "band of brothers" was beginning to emerge within the evangelical movement. While they all had their own personalities and styles, to be sure, they were drawn together by intense loyalties, deep friendships, and a shared mission. Meanwhile, the grand old leaders of evangelism—preachers such as William Bell Riley (1861–1947), Billy Sunday (1862–1935), Harry Ironside (1876–1951), Charles E. Fuller (1887–1969), Bob Jones Sr. (1883–1968), John R. Rice (1895–1980), Harry Rimmer (1890–1952), Robert "Fighting Bob" Shuler (1880–1965), Oswald Smith (1889–1986), and others born before the turn of the century—were anxious both to encourage their younger colleagues in the work of evangelism and to pass on to them some of the hard-earned insights they had gained during their own ministries.

Books like William Bell Riley's *The Perennial Revival* were published and conferences like the "How to Have a Revival" week on the Winona Lake Conference Grounds during the summer of 1945 were held.[51] Realizing that their own ministries would soon be drawing to a close, many of these older leaders increasingly engaged in preparing the next generation for the important task to which they had given their own lives. Riley, for example, in his book *The Perennial Revival*, borrowed the apostle Paul's admonition to Timothy to use as his own dedication at the front of the new volume: encouraging those whom he was mentoring to "Preach the word; be instant in season, out of season; do the work of an evangelist, fulfill thy ministry." Older evangelists including Charles E. Fuller, Bob Jones Sr., and Oswald Smith encouraged the younger evangelists by showing up as special guests at their meetings. "Ma" (Mrs. Billy) Sunday and Homer Rodeheaver, both of whom had been part of Billy Sunday's ministry earlier in the century, also wrote to the young evangelists and visited their crusades as special guests.[52] "I will never forget," Ma Sunday wrote to Merv Rosell, "dear old Philadelphia and elsewhere I've visited you." She would often "pray for you and your party."[53]

With the rise of Youth for Christ came a growing need for preachers who could connect with the thousands of young people who crowded into the rallies, were able to hold youths' attention throughout the often lengthy sermons, and could persuade their listeners of the need to come in repentance

51. See William B. Riley, *The Perennial Revival* (Philadelphia: Judson, 1933); and Robert J. Wells and John R. Rice, eds., *How to Have a Revival* (Wheaton: Sword of the Lord, 1946). The Winona Lake conference was sponsored by Sword of the Lord and featured twenty-five lectures by Hyman Appelman, Joe Henry Hankins, Jesse Hendley, Bob Jones Sr., John R. Rice, and Robert J. Wells.

52. See Homer Rodeheaver, *Twenty Years With Billy Sunday* (Winona Lake, IN: Rodeheaver Hall-Mack, 1936). "Your address Sunday afternoon . . . was one of the very finest and most practical and most needed messages of the entire conference," wrote Rodeheaver. "While you were preaching, I caught little glimpses of Billy Sunday and if Jack Shuler does not prove to be the one, in case a Billy Sunday picture is made, I feel you could do it." Rodeheaver to Rosell, July 21, 1953, Rosell Papers.

53. W. A. Sunday to Rosell, June 26, 1952, Rosell Papers.

Newspaper advertisement for the Chicagoland Youth for Christ (courtesy of Gordon-Conwell Libraries)

to Jesus Christ. Although scores of gifted young evangelists—the emerging "band of brothers"—were engaged in successful ministries by the mid-1940s, only a handful rose to special prominence in the mid-twentieth-century spiritual awakening. Those who did often admitted they were not necessarily the most gifted preachers, the most brilliant thinkers, or even the most winsome personalities. While any fair-minded observer would judge people like Billy Graham, Percy Crawford, Merv Rosell, Hyman Appelman, and Jack Wyrtzen to be genuinely remarkable individuals, the evangelists themselves were without exception convinced that anything of value they accomplished was because of God's power rather than any human abilities they might possess. Indeed, they believed that it was downright dangerous to claim even the smallest credit for what was happening, since to do so was to risk the immediate loss of God's hand of blessing on their ministry.

One of the characteristics shared by most of the 1940s evangelists was their sense of wonder at what God was doing around them. They knew that they could not have produced it by themselves. Indeed, there is a winsome sense of humility that pervaded their personal conversations and correspondence. "God is tremendously blessing here in Britain," Billy Graham wrote in a letter to Merv Rosell in November of 1946. "In six weeks God has given us nearly two thousand souls. However, we have had some sad flops too."[54] Billy Graham had first visited Europe, during March and April of 1946, to help launch the ministry of Youth for Christ in England, Ireland, Scotland, Sweden, and Norway.[55] During a second trip, from October of 1946 through March of 1947, he and his team conducted scores of campaigns and rallies throughout England and Wales and helped prepare for the First British Youth

---

54. Graham to Rosell, November 27, 1946, Rosell Papers.

55. The team, led by Torrey Johnson, consisted of Chuck Templeton, Stratt Shufelt, Wesley Hartzell, and Billy Graham. For a description, see Graham, *Just As I Am*, 98–101.

Violette Rosell, Chuck Templeton, Connie Templeton, Bob Evans, Billy Graham, Ruth Graham, and Merv Rosell (courtesy of the Billy Graham Center Archives at Wheaton College)

for Christ Conference that was scheduled to be held in Birmingham from March 26 to 28, 1947.[56]

The correspondence during those months is filled with humor and gentle ribbing. "You're about the swellest guy I have ever known—you're tops with me, I'm not kidding! If I could get a great big smile and wear a pair of glasses and learn to toot a horn and could write a book for young people with my picture on the front," Graham wrote, poking a bit of fun at his old friend Rosell, "then I'd be like you. Boy! I guess I am doomed just to an ordinary existence however."[57]

Graham's reference was to the cover of Rosell's new book, *Challenging Youth for Christ*.[58] The Zondervan Publishing House had sent Billy Graham several hundred copies of the book for distribution in England. "They were snapped up while I was taking them to the book table," Graham reported in a letter to Rosell. "You have no idea how tremendously your books would go in Britain. I strongly suggest that you get Zondervan to release all rights except in America and let me give it to my good friends Marshall, Morgan & Scott. They could sell literally thousands throughout the empire."[59]

In addition to their friendly ribbing, the letters reflect how serious these young evangelists were when it came to the ministry they were convinced God had entrusted to them. "I wish we had time to have a long talk," Graham wrote with

56. Graham, *Just As I Am*, 101–11.

57. Graham to Rosell, November 27, 1946, Rosell Papers.

58. Mervin Rosell, *Challenging Youth for Christ* (Grand Rapids: Zondervan, 1945).

59. Graham to Rosell, February 21, 1947. See also Pat Zondervan to Rosell, February 18, 1947; Zondervan to Rosell, March 5, 1947; Zondervan Publishing House to Marshall, Morgan & Scott, March 5, 1947; and Ted W. Engstrom to Rosell, January 9, 1946, Rosell Papers.

reference to Rosell's upcoming meetings in Winston-Salem, North Carolina. "As you know, the South is much on my heart. Somehow I have never had a very good reception in the South. I am praying that that might change because it is one of the great burdens of my soul."[60] "I tell you the truth," Graham observed, "when I say that I have been spending more time in study, preparation and prayer than ever before in my life. We have had all types of problems, obstacles and barriers to overcome," he continued, "but God is seeing us through. You and I are pals and I am counting on you tremendously to call upon people everywhere to pray. We are here at a most crucial time—much is at stake."[61]

"I feel that during these days of study, preparation and experience, I have learned many profitable spiritual lessons," Graham continued. Then, shifting back into a more lighthearted mood, he reflected: "By the way, I have numerous invitations to various parts of the Empire and am thinking seriously of a tour of South Africa next winter. What do you think? I wish we could go together on a tour! You could preach, lead the singing, play and sing, and I could take the collection!! Looking forward to hearing from you straight away and as the British would say 'Cheerio.' Your Pal."[62]

Billy Graham's ministry in Europe is reflective of the growing priority evangelicals were giving to the task of worldwide evangelization. While evangelicalism had always stressed global missionary outreach, the two world wars had combined to invest the task with a renewed sense of urgency. "At the beginning of the 1940s," wrote Mel Wyma, "World War II shook that generation to their roots. Sides were taken and hordes of our sterling young men were sent to fight a battle from which they would never return. It was considered the patriot's duty to offer his life to fight for the cause. No one considered him a fanatic. During this time, God brought about events that also united men and women in a battle—for the souls of men."[63]

Convinced that "something must be done to reach the unreached," a team of seven young men, all but one of whom were from Saginaw, Michigan, went as missionaries to Bolivia early in 1943 to work with the Ayore Tribe.[64] "The men had entered the Bolivian wilderness," the *Chicago Daily Tribune*

60. Graham to Rosell, February 21, 1947, Rosell Papers.

61. Graham to Rosell, November 27, 1946, Rosell Papers. The "band of brothers" often spoke of each other as "Pals." See the inscriptions in Billy Graham, *Calling Youth to Christ* (Grand Rapids: Zondervan, 1947) where he wrote "To My Pal 'Merv,' With thanksgiving for your comradeship in presenting the claims of Christ—Billy Graham, Aug 27, '47"; and *Revival in Our Time: The Story of the Billy Graham Evangelistic Campaigns* (Wheaton: Van Kampen, 1950) where he wrote "To My Dear Pal and Friend Merv Rosell, With Love, Appreciation, and Affection—Billy Graham, Psa 16:11."

62. Graham to Rosell, February 21, 1947, Rosell Papers.

63. Mel Wyma, "A World To Reach," *Brown Gold* 49, no. 9 (January–February 1992): 3–5. This anniversary edition of *Brown Gold*, the official magazine of New Tribes Mission, marked the 50th year of New Tribes Mission, founded in 1942 in Chicago, Illinois, by Paul Fleming, Cecil Dye, Robert Williams, and Lance Latham. Mel Wyma was New Tribes Mission's foreign secretary.

64. Ibid., 3.

reported, "to teach the old fashioned gospel based on the biblical command of St. Matthew 28:19—'Go ye therefore and teach all nations.'" "Two months ago," the article continued, five of the seven missionaries "plunged into the green jungle after leaving the last outpost at Robere, 300 miles east of Santa Cruz, Bolivia. The region is inhabited by one of the last savage Indian tribes" who "shoot poisoned arrows from their primitive bows and blow pipes and wield tomahawks of aboriginal type. No word or trace of the five men has been received since then."[65] "Heartache, disappointments, and discouragements marked the beginning of the New Tribes Mission," reflected its founder Paul Fleming, but God's "presence overshadowed each trial, and by His strength we kept looking ahead. We were a group of young men with nothing but faith in God. We had built all our hopes on one fact: God wanted to reach a world, and He was looking for men through whom He could accomplish that task. We determined to be such men, limited only to the miraculous working power of the Holy Spirit."[66]

Although the missionaries were never found, Jean Dye, a linguist and the wife of one of the five who had gone missing, went to live in Bolivia, learned the language of those who many believed had killed her husband, and sought to reach them with the gospel. In May of 1947, nearly three and a half years after her husband and his companions had last been seen, Jean made her first contact with the Ayores. Building on the work of two Bolivian Christians and a Mexican missionary named Joe Morina, who had for many months been leaving small gifts along the paths for the Ayore people, Jean Dye and her companions caught their first glimpse of several tribal warriors. "They always come over the hill," Joe Morina had assured her, and "here they come now." The scene could hardly have been more dramatic. "If I die," Jean remarked, "I die." "Where are your women?" Jean asked the warriors in their own language when they reached the place they were standing. "Back in the bush," they replied. "Call them," she requested, for "they have nothing to fear." Face to face with "one of the fiercest tribes of South America," according to one account, Jean told them "she loved them" and opened the door "to the winning of these people to Christ." "We thank you Lord for bringing 'Whana' back," one member of the tribe later prayed, "to prove that she is not angry with us for killing her husband."[67]

65. "American Missionaries Lost," *Chicago Daily Tribune*, Wednesday, January 12, 1944. The missionaries were carrying no "weapons of any sort" despite their knowledge that members of this tribe "have beheaded other white men" and "have severed explorers' arms." Merv Rosell, a close friend of Paul Fleming and a member of the New Tribes Mission board, volunteered to serve on a "search party" to look for the missing missionaries.

66. Wyma, "A World to Reach," 4.

67. The account is taken from a letter written by Guy W. Playfair (Jean Dye's father) to Sylvia Nethercott (his sister-in-law), on December 22, 1955, following a visit with Jean in South America. A copy can be found in the Rosell Papers.

Like the story of the five missionaries who were murdered in 1956 by the Auca Indians in Ecuador, told so vividly by Elisabeth Elliot in her book *Through Gates of Splendor*, the loss of the five missionaries in Bolivia a decade earlier inspired a whole generation of missionary recruits and helped foster a global vision for evangelical Christians.[68]

Youth for Christ Congress on World Evangelization

Few organizations were more deeply committed to worldwide evangelization than Youth for Christ International. From its earliest years, as its name makes clear, its vision had been global in scope. Even before the organization had been officially established, youth rallies had been springing up in cities around the world. Consequently, it seemed appropriate to Torrey Johnson and his colleagues that the very first International Youth for Christ Congress on World Evangelization should meet outside of North America. The gathering, held in Beatenberg, Switzerland, from August 10 through 22 of 1948, was certainly one of the most important youth gatherings of its kind ever to have been held. The list of delegates, representing forty-six nations, includes many key leaders of twentieth-century evangelicalism.[69] "The burden of this conference is the final and complete evangelization of the entire world in our generation." We "are not here for a vacation," the participants were reminded, and "we are not here to trifle with time and opportunity." Rather, "the Holy Spirit has brought us together for Prayer, for Bible Study, for heart-searching, and for waiting upon God. May it please HIM to give us a new and greater insight into the task of world evangelization and the means by which it can be accomplished NOW!"[70]

"May we go from the Alpine heights of Beatenberg down to the world of men, conquering and to conquer. May it please GOD through this conference to do a 'new thing' in our day—the effects of which shall never die until we see HIM face to face!" From 6:30 in the morning, with the "rising bell," to 9:30 or 10:00 in the evening, following a season for "repentance," "confession of sin," "fullness of the Holy Spirit," and personal "consecration," the delegates, who spoke at least eighteen different languages, remained focused on the task at hand. Following the conference, some of the delegates stayed in

---

68. Elisabeth Elliot, *Through Gates of Splendor* (Carol Stream, IL: Tyndale, 1986).

69. For an account of the conference, see Hefley, *God Goes to High School*, 42–57. "The registration list read like a who's who in evangelical circles," as Hefley described Beatenberg, including "Bob Jones, Jr., Stephen W. Payne, Harold Ockenga, Paul Freed, Bob Pierce, Merv Rosell." See esp. p. 42. For Ockenga's report to his Park Street Church congregation on the conference, see his sermon "Beatenberg," sermon 1442, Ockenga Papers.

70. "World Conference on World Evangelization," August 10–22, 1948, Beatenberg Bible School, Beatenberg, Switzerland, sponsored by Youth for Christ International, seven pages of program materials; copy in Rosell Papers.

Europe for a time to speak at Youth for Christ rallies or to preach in churches throughout the region.[71] Upon returning home, many of the American delegates were involved in follow-up meetings, youth rallies, and special conferences. Among the delegates who reported on the International Youth for Christ Congress on World Evangelization to their home congregations was Harold John Ockenga.[72]

The explosive growth of Youth for Christ, whose ministry was touching the lives of tens of thousands of young people by the late 1940s, helped prepare the way for the massive citywide crusades of the early 1950s. In his presidential address in 1945, Torrey Johnson had promised that Youth for Christ would "join hands" with the evangelists in the promotion of "city-wide revivals." The band of brothers "won't [even] have to call an organizational meeting," he predicted, since Youth for Christ will already have in place—in virtually every city around the globe—the leadership and infrastructure to make all the necessary contacts and arrangements.[73] By the late 1940s, it was clear that Torrey Johnson's promise was being fulfilled. Furthermore, the friendships between a growing band of brothers that had been forged on the Youth for Christ circuit were providing tested leadership for America's emerging spiritual awakening.

71. Oswald Smith, for example, preached forty-two times during the six weeks following the conference in Switzerland, Holland, Belgium, France, Germany, and Italy. See Oswald Smith, "The Miracle of Youth for Christ in Europe," *Peoples Magazine*, First Quarter, 1949, 10–21.

72. Harold John Ockenga, "Beatenberg." Ockenga also continued a lively correspondence with Youth for Christ leaders such as Torrey Johnson, Bob Cook, and Robert Evans. Their letters can be found in the "Youth for Christ" folder, Ockenga Papers.

73. Torrey Johnson, "God Is In It!"

5

※※※※※※※※※※※※※※※※※※※※※※※※※※※※※※※※

A MID-TWENTIETH-CENTURY
AWAKENING

From the earliest years of the NAE, its leaders had been praying for revival.[1] "The one thing which impressed me," wrote Harold John Ockenga following his presidential travels in 1942 on behalf of the new organization, "[is] the hunger and longing for revival" among the "ministers and leaders" with whom he met. These yearnings were further confirmed the following spring as those who had gathered in Chicago for the Constitutional Convention concluded their meetings "with all the delegates on their knees praying for revival."[2] Yet the "Great Revival" for which Ockenga and his colleagues were praying was not to come for another seven years.[3] When it finally did arrive at the end of 1949, it seemed to burst on the scene as a surprise to everyone.[4]

1. See, for example, "Association Plans Nation-Wide Revival," *United Evangelical Action*, May 4, 1943, 1.

2. Harold John Ockenga, "America's Revival is Breaking," sermon 1577, Ockenga Papers. Ockenga first preached this sermon to the Park Street congregation on November 28, 1949, just a month before the start of the great Boston Revival. In slightly revised form, he preached it again on eleven occasions and in eleven locations during the subsequent months of 1950.

3. Harold John Ockenga, "The Great Revival," *Bibliotheca Sacra*, April–June 1947, 223–35. Compare Harold John Ockenga, "America's Revival is Breaking."

4. For Ockenga's account of the revival, see Harold John Ockenga, "The Mid-Century Church," sermon 1576, Ockenga Papers.

"The last world-wide awakening," observed historian J. Edwin Orr, "began in the middle of the nineteenth century."[5] Lasting for more than fifty years, from 1857 until the beginning of World War I, revival fires continued to spread, touching Scandinavia, England, Scotland, Wales, Korea, Canada, and the United States through the ministry of faithful lay Christians and preachers such as Charles G. Finney, Dwight L. Moody, Hudson Taylor, Evan Roberts, W. J. Seymour, J. Wilbur Chapman, "Gipsy" Smith, and Billy Sunday.[6]

Since the end of those revivals, the church had experienced nearly four decades of "spiritual famine." The "rise of totalitarian dictatorships," the "dominance of theological compromise," and the "outbreak of the World Wars," during an era that Orr liked to call "the forty years of dearth," continued to undermine the efforts of Christians around the world to provide a "spiritual witness" within their communities. Yet "when the enemy comes in like a flood, the Spirit of the Lord raises up a standard against him." Indeed, J. Edwin Orr was convinced, the beginnings of a "Mid-Twentieth Century Awakening" were increasingly apparent "all over the world."[7] It is difficult to argue with Orr's conclusion. Between 1940 and 1960 for example, church affiliation in America increased by an incredible twenty percentage points, from forty-nine percent to an unprecedented sixty-nine percent of the total population. Moreover, during roughly the same period the amount of money spent by churches and synagogues on construction of buildings skyrocketed from twenty-six million dollars annually in 1945 to well over a billion dollars annually by 1960.[8] Furthermore, as even a cursory review of evangelical publications will reveal, reports of religious revivals throughout America and around the world can be found in abundance.[9]

5. J. Edwin Orr, *The Second Evangelical Awakening in America* (London: Marshall, Morgan & Scott, 1952), 202. Orr dated its beginnings during the "Prayer Revivals" of 1857–58.

6. For a discussion of these revivals, see Keith J. Hardman, *Seasons of Refreshing: Evangelism and Revivals in America* (Grand Rapids: Baker Books, 1994); Earle E. Cairns, *An Endless Line of Splendor: Revivals and Their Leaders from the Great Awakening to the Present* (Wheaton: Tyndale, 1986); Kevin Adams and Emyr Jones, *A Diary of Revival* (Nashville: Broadman & Holman, 2004); Kathryn T. Long, *The Revival of 1857–58: Interpreting an American Religious Awakening* (New York: Oxford University Press, 1998); and J. Edwin Orr, *The Light of the Nations: Evangelical Renewal and Advance in the Nineteenth Century* (Grand Rapids: Eerdmans, 1965).

7. Orr, *The Second Evangelical Awakening in America*, 202.

8. Statistics are taken from Sydney E. Ahlstrom, *A Religious History of the American People* (New Haven: Yale University Press, 1972), 952–53. For a more detailed breakdown of statistical trends, see George Gallup Jr. and D. Michael Lindsay, *Surveying the Religious Landscape: Trends in U.S. Beliefs* (Harrisburg, PA: Morehouse, 1999), esp. 1–20.

9. See L. Nelson Bell, "1951, Year of Decision," *Northwestern Pilot*, January 1951, 113; "The Pilot News Section," *Northwestern Pilot*, January 1951, 125–27; *Moody Monthly*, October 1954; "Revival Reports," *Youth for Christ* magazine, special revival issue, October 1950, 34–79. See also Joel A. Carpenter, *Revive Us Again: The Reawakening of American Fundamentalism* (New York: Oxford University Press, 1997), 211–32.

Billy Graham became the best known of the revival leaders during the 1950s, to be sure, but he was by no means alone. A "multitude of God-blessed ambassadors of the cross such as Merv Rosell, Jack Shuler, John R. Rice, Bob Jones, [and] Hyman Appelman," declared the editor of *United Evangelical Action*, were being used by God to proclaim the glorious gospel of Jesus Christ around the globe.[10] One might add the names of Percy Crawford, T. W. Wilson, Jack MacArthur, Guy Libbey, Gregorio Tingson, Floyd Ankerberg, Jack Wyrtzen, Borris Bessmertney, Bob Cook, Torrey Johnson, Charles E. Fuller, Grady Wilson, Robert Evans, Cliff Barrows, Jimmie Johnson, Oswald Smith, Pete Riggs, and others.

The "mercy-drops" of revival had been falling throughout the 1940s, largely as a result of the ministry of organizations such as Youth for Christ, but 1949 and 1950 brought a veritable downpour of spiritual awakening.[11] Reports of revival came from Africa, India, Indonesia, the Philippines, Korea, Japan, China, the Soviet Union, Europe, and Latin America.[12] Similar reports of enormous crowds and thousands of conversions came from the provinces of Canada and from almost every state across America.[13] "It seems apparent," wrote Bill Bright, "that the Lord is preparing His ministers in every denomination for the times of refreshing that lie ahead. Especially in the Pacific Coast States there are ever-increasing groups of ministers meeting quietly but faithfully for the simple purpose of intercession, interceding with God for a revival of religion."[14] Led by Armin Gesswein, a Lutheran pastor in the Los Angeles area, weekly prayer meetings for this purpose were launched in 1941. By 1945, nearly fifty pastors had joined the meetings.

As a result of these prayer gatherings, about 120 Presbyterian, Baptist, Methodist, Holiness, Pentecostal, United Brethren, Lutheran, and independent ministers gathered at the Pacific Palisades Conference Grounds in September of 1948 for a two-and-a-half-day Revival Conference. "It was a time in the heavenlies," wrote Norman Grubb, with "not a breath of controversy or theological argument."[15] A second Pacific Palisades Conference was held the following year. This time over four hundred pastors and many of their spouses gathered to hear the preaching of Harold John Ockenga and the revival teaching of J. Edwin

10. James DeForest Murch, "1951–The Evangelical Year–1951," *United Evangelical Action,* January 1, 1952, 10–11.

11. The reference, of course, is to the well-known hymn based on Ezekiel 34:26, "There Shall Be Showers of Blessing," by Daniel W. Whittle (1840–1901).

12. See Orr, "World Survey of Spiritual Awakening," in *The Second Evangelical Awakening in America,* 202–9.

13. See Carpenter, *Revive Us Again,* 315–16nn69–70; app. D, "The Movement in Evangelism," in Orr, *The Second Evangelical Awakening in America,* 188–201; and "Revival Reports," 34–79.

14. Bill Bright, "The Movement Among Ministers," reprinted from the *Awakening* bulletin in app. A in Orr, *The Second Evangelical Awakening in America,* 160–65.

15. For a fuller discussion of these prayer initiatives, see Norman Grubb's report in *Life of Faith,* February 16, 1949, and reprinted in app. A in Orr, *The Second Evangelical Awakening in America,* 161–63.

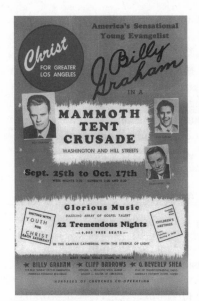

Poster for the Billy Graham Los Angeles Crusade in 1949 (courtesy of Gordon-Conwell Libraries)

Orr and to pray together for a fresh touch of spiritual awakening. "There was a great moving of the Spirit," reported Claude Jenkins, the executive secretary of Christ for Greater Los Angeles, "with the spirit of Revival being carried out from the conference to many areas."[16]

The prayers of those who had gathered at the Pacific Palisades Conference Grounds seemed to have been answered with the arrival of Billy Graham in September of 1949.[17] Having just come from the College Briefing Conference in the nearby San Bernardino Mountains—a gathering of "some 500 students from colleges and universities all over the West" that Billy Graham would later describe as "one of the richest spiritual experiences of my life" and "the turning point of my ministry"—he began his Los Angeles Crusade on September 25, 1949.[18]

Only thirty years old when the meetings began, Graham was already a well-known speaker on the Youth for Christ circuit.[19] But the six-thousand-seat "canvas cathedral with the steeple of light," erected at the corner of Washington and Hill Streets in Los Angeles broadened his ministry to many new segments of the community.[20] Christ for Greater

16. Claude C. Jenkins, "First Signs of Revival: Unusual Stirrings in California," first published in *Life of Faith*, May 25, 1949, and reprinted in Orr, *The Second Evangelical Awakening in America*, 162–63. Additional prayer conferences for revival were held on the Pacific Palisades Conference grounds, and in Seattle, Tacoma, San Francisco, Minneapolis, Philadelphia, Chicago, and many other locations; see 163–65.

17. For an account of the meetings, see William Martin, *A Prophet with Honor: The Billy Graham Story* (New York: William Morrow, 1991), 106–20.

18. For a fuller description of the College Briefing Conference, held during September of 1949 at Forest Home, see Orr, *The Second Evangelical Awakening in America*, 188. In addition to Graham, the speakers at that conference included Henrietta Mears, Dave Cowie, Bob Munger, Dick Halverson, Louis Evans, J. Edwin Orr, and Dad Elliott.

19. As president of Northwestern Schools in Minneapolis and vice-president of Youth for Christ International, Billy Graham had preached at scores of YFC rallies in America and Europe and had (with his team of Cliff and Billie Barrows and George Beverly Shea) led citywide campaigns in Grand Rapids, Michigan; Des Moines, Iowa; Charlotte, North Carolina; Augusta, Georgia; Altoona, Pennsylvania; and other locations prior to the Los Angeles meetings. In Los Angeles, as Mel Larson described it, "things 'just bubbled over.'" See Mel Larson, "Tasting Revival in Los Angeles," in *Revival in Our Time* (Wheaton: Van Kampen, 1950), 11.

20. A number of well-known Hollywood stars, for example, came to Christ as a result of his preaching and personal witness. See Orr, *The Second Evangelical Awakening in America*, 187.

Los Angeles, under the leadership of Claude Jenkins and Clifford Smith, provided the primary impetus for the crusade, and hundreds of churches throughout Southern California were official sponsors of the meetings.

Billy Graham's Los Angeles Crusade tent (taken from *Revival in Our Time: The Story of the Billy Graham Evangelistic Campaigns* [Wheaton: Van Kampen, 1950])

Originally scheduled for twenty-two nights, from September 25 through October 17, the extended meetings continued for eight weeks, with services each evening at 7:30 and each Sunday at 3:00 and 8:30 p.m. By the close of the crusade, over three hundred and fifty thousand people had attended the seventy-two meetings and three thousand individuals had professed Christ as personal savior.[21] "Many of us have prayed and worked for years toward a real heaven-sent revival," observed Charles E. Fuller at the close of the meetings, and they were now "permitted to see that revival in our midst. Reports are coming to us from other parts of the world of a similar working of the Holy Spirit in convicting and converting power. Let us praise God and pray on for revival to spread throughout the length and breadth of our land, for surely His coming draweth nigh."[22]

The Boston Revival

Encouraged by friends like Charles Fuller, who spoke of Billy Graham as "a godly, humble young man,"[23] Harold John Ockenga invited Graham to Boston for a New Year's Eve youth rally at the six-thousand-seat Mechanics Hall in Boston and a eight-day evangelistic series to be held at Park Street Church. Allan Emery, whose own father had been instrumental in bringing Billy Sunday to Boston a generation earlier, agreed to serve as general chairman for the meetings. While Graham's meetings were officially sponsored by more than one hundred local Protestant churches, the primary support for the meetings came from Emery, Harold John Ockenga, the New England Fellowship, the Evangelistic Association of New England (now Vision New England), Youth

21. Figures are taken from Larson, "Tasting Revival at Los Angeles," in *Revival in Our Time*, 11. See also Martin, *A Prophet with Honor*, 106–20.

22. Dorothy C. Haskin, "Spiritual Awakening in California," *Moody Monthly*, January 1950, 328–29.

23. Fuller to Ockenga, December 29, 1949, Ockenga Papers.

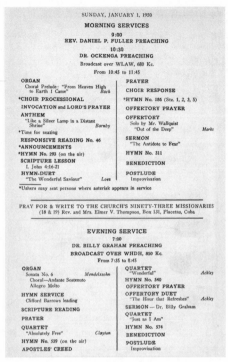

SUNDAY, JANUARY 1, 1950

MORNING SERVICES

9:00

REV. DANIEL P. FULLER PREACHING

10:30

DR. OCKENGA PREACHING

Broadcast over WLAW, 680 Kc.

From 10:45 to 11:45

ORGAN Choral Prelude: "From Heaven High to Earth I Came" *Bach*	PRAYER
	CHOIR RESPONSE
*CHOIR PROCESSIONAL	*HYMN No. 186 (Stz. 1, 2, 3, 5)
INVOCATION and LORD'S PRAYER	OFFERTORY PRAYER
ANTHEM "Like a Silver Lamp in a Distant Shrine" *Barnby*	OFFERTORY Solo by Mr. Wallquist "Out of the Deep" *Marks*
*Time for seating	
RESPONSIVE READING No. 46	SERMON "The Antidote to Fear"
*ANNOUNCEMENTS	
*HYMN No. 293 (on the air)	HYMN No. 311
SCRIPTURE LESSON I. John 4:16-21	BENEDICTION
HYMN-DUET "The Wonderful Saviour" *Loes*	POSTLUDE Improvisation

*Ushers may seat persons where asterisk appears in service

PRAY FOR & WRITE TO THE CHURCH'S NINETY-THREE MISSIONARIES
(18 & 19) Rev. and Mrs. Elmer V. Thompson, Box 131, Placetas, Cuba

EVENING SERVICE

7:00

DR. BILLY GRAHAM PREACHING

BROADCAST OVER WHDH, 850 Kc.

From 7:35 to 8:45

ORGAN Sonata No. 6 *Mendelssohn* Choral—Andante Sostenuto Allegro Molto	QUARTET "Wonderful" *Ackley*
	HYMN No. 540
	OFFERTORY PRAYER
HYMN SERVICE Clifford Barrows leading	OFFERTORY DUET "The Hour that Refreshes" *Ackley*
SCRIPTURE READING	SERMON — Dr. Billy Graham
PRAYER	QUARTET "Just as I Am"
QUARTET "Absolutely Free" *Clayton*	HYMN No. 574
HYMN No. 539 (on the air)	BENEDICTION
APOSTLES' CREED	POSTLUDE Improvisation

Sunday, January 1, 1950, worship bulletin for Park Street Church, Boston (courtesy of Park Street Church)

for Christ, Tremont Temple, and Park Street Church.[24]

As the meeting approached, even the most optimistic could not have imagined the remarkable events that were about to take place. The young preacher who had been scheduled to lead the crusade, the thirty-one-year-old Billy Graham, was then relatively untested and largely unknown in the churches of New England.[25] Despite the fact that Graham's enormously successful eight-week crusade in Los Angeles had just ended, expectations in Boston remained surprisingly modest, and publicity was sparse. Paid advertisements for the New Year's Eve service—such as one that appeared in the *Boston Herald* on Saturday morning announcing that the "dynamic, enthusiastic" young evangelist had "thrilled thousands in Los Angeles"—were even more difficult to locate.[26]

The New Year's Eve service at Mechanics Hall, however, changed everything. The six thousand who jammed the hall, along with the hundreds of people

24. The first meeting was scheduled for Mechanics Hall, a six-thousand-seat facility, to be held on New Year's Eve, December 31, 1949. See Lawrence Dame, "Evangelist Here to Vie with New Year's Fun," *Boston Herald*, December 31, 1949, 14; "We May Spend Selves into Depression, Graham Says," *Boston Daily Globe*, January 10, 1950, 1, 14; and Martin, *A Prophet with Honor*, 123–41. By April of 1950, the publishers of Van Kampen Press had produced a fascinating little book, *Revival in Our Time: The Story of the Billy Graham Evangelistic Campaigns*, with help from Charles E. Fuller, Harold John Ockenga, C. Wade Freeman, J. Edwin Orr, Mel Larson, Don Hoke, Jerry Bevan, and Cliff Barrows. For the Boston revival, see esp. 28–33.

25. The *Boston Daily Globe*, in its issues from March 26 to April 4, 1950, published a ten-part series on "The Life Story of Billy Graham" written by Joseph F. Dinneen. The *Boston Post*, on January 13, 14, and 15, 1950, published a three-part series on Dr. Graham's life written by Allen Thomason and later produced an eight-page *Boston Post Souvenir Edition* on the "Life Story of Rev. Billy Graham," one hundred sixty five thousand copies of which it distributed free of charge.

26. See the *Boston Herald*, December 31, 1949, 7. Billy Graham, Cliff Barrows, George Beverly Shea, and Grady Wilson arrived in Boston on December 30 and held a service at Park Street Church that evening. For a description of these events, see "Evangelist Warns Boston to Repent or Be Destroyed," *Boston Daily Globe*, December 31, 1949, 9; and *Revival in Our Time*, 26–31.

who were turned away, suddenly made the event front page news. "Evangelist Graham Draws 6000," proclaimed the *Boston Herald*, and "more than could be counted hit the sawdust trail," reported the *Boston Daily Globe*.[27] The *Boston Post*, in its Sunday edition, carried a full report of the four-hour meeting along with a detailed description of the service, a listing of its major participants, and a dramatic picture of the crowd that had filled Mechanics Hall to overflowing.[28]

One of the speakers that evening was Harold John Ockenga. In his address, "The Mid-Century Turning Point," he told his listeners that they were standing "at the division of the century." Looking back, he reminded his listeners of the "stupendous changes" of the past fifty years. Then, looking ahead, he pointed to "overwhelming evidence" that "God is visiting America." In Los Angeles, he continued, "the young evangelist speaking in this hall tonight, Billy Graham, began what was announced and planned to be a three-week campaign in a tent holding 5,000 people. From the beginning the tent was packed. Later 1,500 more chairs were added and night after night for eight weeks the tent was filled and people stood by the thousands."[29] Turning his attention back to Boston, Ockenga then laid before the assembled crowd the possibilities that stretched out before them. "The hour for revival has struck. New England is ripe for evangelism. The same yearning which is seen over the land is experienced here," Ockenga declared. "Yesterday has gone. Tomorrow is uncertain. We have only today. Now is the time. Let us redeem it. Let us use it. Let us make it the vehicle of a glorious future in which Christian truth and experience will be spread abroad to become incorporated in the lives of us all."[30]

Billy Graham's sermon toward the close of the evening touched the crowd of young people deeply. "The young evangelist," reported the *Boston Herald*, "chose as his text the warning of the prophet Amos: 'Prepare to meet thy God, O Israel, or perish.'" At the end of his sermon he called on his listeners to make a new start and invited those who wished to respond to his invitation to come forward. "More than 500 in the audience raised their hands to indicate their desire to be saved, and 400 came forward to pray with Dr. Billy."[31]

At the end of the evening, Ockenga rose to announce to the crowd the arrival of the new year. Having witnessed the remarkable events of the evening, however, he also told the audience that they were part of something much

27. W. E. Playfair, "Evangelist Graham Draws 6000 from 'Eve' Celebration," *Boston Herald*, January 1, 1950, 1, 5; and "Graham Scores Typical Revelry of New Year's Eve," *Boston Daily Globe*, January 1, 1950, 1, 9.

28. *Boston Post*, January 1, 1950, 15.

29. Harold John Ockenga, "The Mid-Century Turning Point," sermon 1448, preached at Mechanics Hall, December 31, 1949, Ockenga Papers.

30. Ibid.

31. Playfair, "Graham Draws 6000," 1, 4. A photograph of the Mechanics Hall crowd can be found on p. 4.

larger than a single service. In the face of enormous national and international problems, "millions of Americans believe an old-fashioned spiritual revival could preserve our God-given freedoms and way of life." There were indications "from coast to coast that America is on the verge of such an awakening." America must therefore fall upon its knees in repentance and prayer.[32] New England, Ockenga believed, would lead the nation once again as it had so many times in the past. "God has come to town," Ockenga was convinced. "The revival has broken in Boston" and if "New England can receive such a shaking of God under this stripling who like David of old went forth to meet the giant of the enemy, then we believe that God is ready to shake America to its foundations in revival."[33] Graham later added that "if staid, conservative New England" could have a revival, it "would sweep west until it takes the whole country by storm."[34]

The Surprising Work of God

What Boston was experiencing, Ockenga was convinced, was nothing short of the kind of "surprising work of God" that had come to New England two centuries earlier under the ministry of George Whitefield and Jonathan Edwards. The linkage with Edwards and Whitefield is significant. By "revival," Ockenga argued, "I do not mean what we have often called revivals in the churches, where we set up a meeting and bring in a preacher and call it a 'revival.' I am talking now about a heaven-sent, Holy Ghost revival given in the sovereignty of God with no human explanation for it whatsoever."[35] Since his arrival in Boston in 1936, Ockenga had been praying for such a revival. He had brought well-known evangelists to preach at Park Street Church each year. He had himself preached revival services on a regular basis. He had even helped to plan an anniversary celebration of George Whitefield's ministry in New England in the mid-eighteenth century.[36] Yet none of these efforts had produced the kind of genuine revival that he believed was absolutely essential if the grand vision was to become a reality. Indeed, New England had not seen such a revival, he was convinced, since the Great Awakening two centuries earlier.

At Mechanics Hall, however, Ockenga sensed that his longstanding prayers and the prayers of many others were finally being answered. "New England," Graham was persuaded, was "on the verge of a great sweeping revival such as

32. *Boston Post*, January 1, 1950, 15.

33. Harold John Ockenga, "Boston Stirred by Revival," *United Evangelical Action*, January 15, 1950, 4.

34. "Graham Urges N.E. Revival to Sweep U.S.," *Boston Herald*, January 8, 1950, 1.

35. Harold John Ockenga, "Is America's Revival Breaking?" *United Evangelical Action*, July 1, 1950, 3–4, 8, 13–15. Transcribed address delivered at the 8th Annual Convention of the National Association of Evangelicals in Indianapolis, April 18, 1950, Ockenga Papers.

36. See Harold John Ockenga, *The Great Awakening* (Boston: Fellowship, 1940).

it has not seen since the days of Jonathan Edwards."[37] Before the New Year's Eve Service had ended, in fact, Mechanics Hall had already been secured for a service the following day, and plans were underway to find larger facilities throughout the city for the eight days of meetings that had originally been scheduled for Park Street Church. "Because hundreds of persons were turned away from the jam-packed Mechanics Building," reported the *Boston Post* in its Sunday edition, "it was announced last night that Rev. Billy Graham will speak again in the same hall at 3:00 p.m. today."[38] Well before the appointed hour arrived, Mechanics Hall was once again full, and later that same evening more than two thousand were turned away from Park Street Church.[39] Like Jonathan Edwards before him, Graham was both surprised and a little terrified by what God seemed to be doing in Boston. Although "he believed God had been at work in Los Angeles," William Martin reports, "he also knew that months of preparation, thousands of dollars spent on promotion, and a windfall of publicity had contributed to that campaign's success. But in Boston, with little preparation or publicity, the response was similar."[40]

Following the Mechanics Hall service, in fact, Graham met with Ockenga and Emery and asked them to pray that God would keep him from taking even "the smallest credit" for what was happening in Boston since he knew that if he did, his "lips would turn to clay." "Emery was astonished," as Martin tells the story. "Instead of praying for the various problems we might foresee, such as finances, follow-up, converts, or anything else, here, after this unexpected triumph, Billy's concern was that the Lord keep his hand on him" so that he might "continue moment to moment to give God the glory."[41] "No person or organization," Graham later told a gathering of pastors at Park Street Church as the Boston revival neared its conclusion, "is needed to bring about a true and great revival." Genuine spiritual awakening, Graham concluded, comes only from "God Himself."[42] Authentic revival, Ockenga would have added, occurs "with no human explanation for it whatsoever."[43]

Such an affirmation, however, was not intended to release the Christian community from any responsibility. While true revival comes only from above, there is plenty for the church to be doing here on earth. Indeed, as Graham affirmed repeatedly throughout the meetings, God has established the necessary "conditions for revival" and Christians are responsible to do all they can to fulfill them. Four conditions, he was convinced, were of special importance: repentance, prayer, the unity of God's people, and obedience to God's Word.

37. Playfair, "Graham Draws 6000," 1.
38. *Boston Post*, January 1, 1950, 9.
39. "Graham Scores Typical Revelry," 1, 9; and Ockenga, "Is America's Revival Breaking?" 4.
40. See Martin, *A Prophet with Honor*, 123–41.
41. Ibid., 124.
42. "Billy Graham Meetings May Continue Here," *Boston Daily Globe*, January 14, 1950, 1, 3.
43. Ockenga, "Is America's Revival Breaking?" 3.

The first task, Graham told a capacity crowd in Boston's Opera House, is repentance. "Repent, repent, repent, repent your sins," he warned the audience, "or you're going to die." God's judgment is coming, "and every man, woman and child is going to stand before the Great White Throne of God, and you won't get to heaven unless you repent of your sins." Such repentance, he continued, requires "a profound sorrow" for your sins, a willingness to renounce your sins, a "confession" of those sins, and a genuine faith in Christ. "You can't go on living the same old way" as you did before and still consider yourself a Christian, he concluded, "it just can't be done."[44]

The second condition for revival is prayer. "If we have a prayer meeting all over the city," Graham told the Wednesday night audience at Mechanics Hall, "in homes, in offices, in churches and in clubs, we are going to have an old Holy Ghost revival that will shake New England." If Christians would "put everything secondary to prayer," he continued, "we will see a revival" in Boston greater than anything the city has known since the days of Billy Sunday.[45] Calling on the Christian community to create a "wall of prayer"[46] or "a chain of prayers,"[47] he asked Christians to give "a half hour day and night" to prayer for revival.[48] In his own schedule, which was filled from early morning to late at night, he practiced what he preached, giving at least an hour each day to pray for God's Spirit to be poured out upon Boston.[49]

The third condition for revival is the unity of the Christian community. People from "many churches will join you in the revival meetings," he told an audience at Park Street Church, "and many will find their way to Christ in this city because some ministers and leaders of various churches forget their differences of creed and join hands for the great purpose of bringing souls to God."[50] A "great wave of spiritual awakening is in progress across the nation," he was convinced, but it could not succeed unless God's people were willing to join hands in prayer and common purpose.[51] Graham was delighted to report at the close of the Boston meetings that they had been "a triumph in interdenominational co-operation."[52]

44. "Graham Tells Flock to 'Repent or Perish,'" *Boston Herald*, January 10, 1950, 1, 3; and *Boston Post*, January 13, 1950, 15.

45. "Week of Prayer in Boston asked by Evangelist Graham," *Boston Daily Globe*, January 5, 1950, 1, 17, 31. Billy Sunday preached in Boston in 1917. See the *Boston Herald*, January 15, 1950, 1, 5B.

46. "Graham Jams Opera House," *Boston Herald*, January 13, 1950, 20.

47. "Denounces 'Jelly Fish' Christians," *Boston Post*, January 3, 1950, 1.

48. *Boston Daily Globe*, December 31, 1949, 9.

49. "Billy Graham Urges Pastors to Appeal to the Common Man," *Boston Sunday Globe*, January 1, 1950, 1, 54; and Ian Menzies, "Billy Graham Feels Like Wet Dishrag After Sermon," *Boston Sunday Globe*, January 8, 1950, 1.

50. *Boston Daily Globe*, December 31, 1949, 9.

51. Lawrence Dame, "Billy Graham Rally Tomorrow," *Boston Herald*, December 30, 1949, 1, 9.

52. *Boston Post*, January 18, 1950, 2.

The fourth condition for revival is the study of and obedience to the Bible. "I don't believe you can go year in and year out being a Christian without reading the word of God." Centering his own preaching on Scripture, he not only filled his sermons with the phrase "the Bible says," but he also commended his listeners for their diligent reading and study of Scripture. "I am glad to see so many people with Bibles here tonight."[53]

The next twelve months, Graham told his listeners, "will determine the destiny of America." They would experience either "revival or the judgment of God." Revival is the "only force that can save us from destruction." For revival to come, however, Christians throughout New England would need to fulfill the conditions God had established for spiritual awakening: repentance, prayer, unity, and obedience to Scripture. If they determine to do so, a great revival could sweep across Boston and New England and spread from there to touch the entire world.[54]

What came to be called the New England Mid-Century Revival took place in two distinct phases: from December 31 to January 16 and from March 17 to April 23. The first phase was held exclusively in Boston. When Graham returned in March and April, however, the work fanned out to touch the major cities of all six New England states. By the time both phases of the crusade had ended late in April, tens of thousands had attended the meetings and over nine thousand had made public professions of faith in Christ.[55]

During the first two weeks of the crusade, Billy Graham and his team, which then included Cliff Barrows and Grady Wilson, focused their attention on Boston. Living in the Hotel Bellevue, they maintained a demanding daily schedule.[56] On a typical morning, as reported by the *Boston Daily Globe*, Graham read the newspapers, responded to the "flood of correspondence" that had accumulated, answered "more than 30 phone calls" and made "at least the same number," "lunched with local churchmen," prepared his evening sermon, and "devoted more than an hour to prayer." This "ceaseless merry-go-round" of activity, as the reporter called it, was tackled with "speed, with patience and with an individual pleasantness" that left all who came in contact with him "invigorated." To keep in shape, the reporter continued, the "tall, athletic evangelist, who weighs in at a healthy 170 pounds," did daily calisthenics, took frequent walks through the Boston Common, played golf and tennis, drank plenty of orange juice, and took vitamin pills.

53. *Boston Daily Globe*, January 5, 1950, 1, 21.

54. *Boston Daily Globe*, December 31, 1949, 5.

55. Harold Lindsell, *Park Street Prophet: A Life of Harold John Ockenga* (Wheaton: Van Kampen, 1951), 155–56.

56. "Thousands of Corrupt Want Revival to End, Billy Graham Asserts," *Boston Daily Globe*, January 15, 1950, 1, 55. In addition to his regular team, several local artists were added to help with the music. Franklin MacKerron coordinated the choirs and his wife Eleanor played the piano for the meetings. Paul Pretiz played the organ.

Such a grueling schedule could not help but take its toll. "His spell-bound audiences see him pacing, gesticulating, pouring out energy like an unleashed spring," as the reporter phrased it, but what most do not see is the "physical and mental strain" that accompanied such activities. Graham admitted he often felt "like a wet dishrag" at the close of a meeting and would sometimes lie awake for three or four hours in the night, unable to sleep. "I would give anything to be able to sleep." "If I continue this pace and God does not give me a longer span of years than most," he said, "my life will be short."[57]

Most of the leaders of the crusade were relatively young. The "greybeards" of the revival, as one reporter labeled them, were nearly all in their twenties and early thirties. Harold John Ockenga, the elder statesman, was in his mid-forties, but Billy Graham, George Wilson, and Allan Emery were all thirty-one; Cliff Barrows was twenty-six; Eleanor MacKerron, the pianist, was twenty-nine; Paul Pretiz, the organist, was twenty-three; and Tal McNutt, the director of Youth for Christ in Boston, was twenty-four. "The present Boston campaign," reported the *Boston Daily Globe*, "has doubtless captured much of its zeal and impetus from the young men and women who have been at work both on and off stage here since the movement's beginning on New Year's eve." In at least this sense, the Boston meetings were an extension of the youth movements that had been sweeping America throughout the previous decade. "Salesmanship requires youth," as one observer phrased it, and when the "enthusiasm, energy and fervor" of young people is properly harnessed, it can work "wonders."[58]

In addition to youthfulness, the Boston meetings were also marked by joyous enthusiasm. Graham preaches, wrote one reporter, "as if he had found the glorious secret of eternal life and felt that it was too precious to be kept from others—that he must share it with the world." "I get a kick out of just being alive," Graham often remarked. "Life to me is a glorious, exciting adventure!" "This is the greatest business in the world," added Allan Emery, the general chairman for the crusade, "the business of bringing souls to Jesus Christ."[59] Graham admitted that he did "grieve" that so many are kept from this joy by the deceptions of "the Devil," and it is true that America's "wild, sinful way of living must be a stench in the holy nostrils of God." Yet God offers each sinner a "great new start." "Jesus Christ can solve all your problems," he often told his listeners. "He can lift your burdens and bring peace to your heart. Christ can transform your life so that you can begin . . . as a new person."[60]

Whatever the reasons for their interest, thousands of people from across New England made their way to the meetings in Boston. Over the first two

57. Menzies, "Graham Feels Like Wet Dishrag," 54; and "Graham Urges Pastors to Appeal to the Common Man," 1, 54.
58. "We May Spend Selves into Depression," 1, 14.
59. "Fill Opera House for Revival," *Boston Post*, January 13, 1950, 15.
60. "Graham Scores Typical Revelry," 1, 9.

weeks (including the twenty services held at Mechanics Hall, the Opera House, and the Boston Garden) more than one hundred fifteen thousand had attended the meetings and some three thousand "decision cards" had been signed, according to an estimate by Allan Emery.[61]

The final service was held on January 16 at the Boston Garden. "In the greatest revival meeting New England has seen in the present generation," reported the *Boston Daily Globe*, "a capacity crowd of 16,000 filled every seat in Boston Garden last night, and more than 5,000 were turned away." At the close of the service, "from every corner and from the highest galleries in the great sports auditorium, 3,000 converts streamed down to the platform in response to the dynamic young preacher's plea to accept Christ."[62] "No great sporting event, no appearance of any champion team," not even the presence of "Winston Churchill or any other great national or international figure," added a report in the *Boston Post*, had been able to attract "bigger or more enthusiastic throngs inside and outside the huge structure" than had Billy Graham.[63]

"Not in my generation," Graham told the audience, "has there been such a moving of God's Spirit." This "is not the doing of any preacher," he continued, and it is certainly "not the doing of Billy Graham." Rather, it is "the miracle that God Himself has done to bring to New England the chance for full salvation."[64]

Using the Old Testament story of Noah as his major focus, Graham drew a parallel between Noah's time and his own. The "philosophers, scientists and modernists" then, much like today, "refused to believe that disaster could sweep the world." But "when the cloud came and the rain started and the water rose," he continued, then "thousands came, pounding at the door of the Ark, begging Noah to let them come in and be saved." They had lost their chance, but God has mercifully "left the door open for you tonight," and you can be saved if you would but "come into the Ark now." Upon hearing the invitation, as a *Boston Post* reporter described the event, individuals "of all races, creed[s], color[s] and economic strata moved steadily to the front of the hall." A "man in tattered clothing, the knees of his trousers worn through, walked behind a woman wearing an expensive fur coat."[65]

"Down from every balcony and corner in the vast building came white-haired men, girls of high school age, mature women from whose eyes tears

61. See the *Quincy Patriot Ledger*, January 17, 1950. Extensive coverage of the Boston meetings was provided by the city's three major newspapers. Between December 30, 1949, and January 17, 1950, the *Boston Daily Globe* carried twenty-seven articles, the *Boston Post* included twenty-four articles, and the *Boston Herald* published twenty articles.

62. "16,000 Jam Graham's Closing Revival," *Boston Daily Globe*, January 17, 1950, 1. Front page reports were also carried in Boston's other major newspapers.

63. Allen Thomason, "Garden Packed for Big Revival Rally," *Boston Post*, January 17, 1950, 1, 8.

64. "16,000 Jam Graham's Closing Revival," 1.

65. Thomason, "Garden Packed," 1, 8.

were falling," wrote a *Globe* reporter, "yet there was, among those many hundreds, no seeming hysteria. Those who cried looked as if they shed tears of relief or happiness." Others "walked forward quietly, serenely, as if they knew a long time ahead that they were ready to look for the better life that Graham told them Christ offered."[66] The three thousand who came forward, in repentance for their sins, each received a small paperback copy of the Gospel of John. Graham then prayed with them and encouraged them to read their Bibles daily (starting with five readings of the Gospel of John), pray regularly, tell someone else about Christ, and, if they were not already a member, join a local church.[67]

At the close of the service, the audience stood to sing once again the chorus that had become a kind of theme song for the meetings: "Send a great revival to my soul; Send a great revival to my soul; Let the Holy Spirit come and take control; Yes, send a great revival to my soul." Many were convinced that revival was exactly what God had sent to Boston. The following morning, while reflecting on the gathering at the Boston Garden, Graham commented: "The huge rally on Monday night at the Garden was the greatest revival meeting I have ever witnessed or participated in. More converts came forward to receive Jesus Christ than at any other evangelistic meeting I ever held." Indeed, what happened in Boston over those two weeks "has greatly inspired me to continue in the great work of Jesus."[68]

Graham Returns

When Harold John Ockenga announced to the Boston Garden crowd on Monday evening that Billy Graham had agreed to return to New England in March and April, they burst into applause.[69] Even before the service was over, plans were already underway for phase two of the New England Mid-Century Crusade. Unlike the first visit, these meetings would be held throughout the region and would involve "extensive preparations" by "hundreds of people." Traveling to all six of the New England states, Graham preached in over twenty cities during the five-week crusade. By the great closing rally on the Boston Common, an additional six thousand individuals had signed the cards indicating their "acceptance of Jesus Christ as their personal Savior."[70]

While there was some opposition to the meetings, it was remarkably subdued. A Unitarian pastor in Manchester, New Hampshire commented that he

66. "16,000 Jam Graham's Closing Revival," 1, 4.
67. Thomason, "Garden Packed," 1, 8.
68. "Dr. Graham and Wife to Visit Niagara Falls," *Boston Post*, January 18, 1950, 2.
69. Thomason, "Garden Packed," 8.
70. See Lindsell, *Park Street Prophet*, 156–57.

did not approve of "such an emotional orgy" as a revival.[71] Yet his concerns and those of others are almost impossible to find in the nearly five hundred reports of the meetings that were published in New England's newspapers. While other preachers, from Jonathan Edwards and George Whitefield to Billy Sunday, had run into a storm of controversy, Graham's welcome throughout New England seemed to be extended with relatively little dissent.[72] This is not to suggest that opposition to the meetings was entirely absent. "There are thousands in Boston who wish this revival would hurry and get over," Graham told one of his audiences. "Moral pollution and political corruption would like to drive us from Boston. They don't want a revival. They don't want people to be saved. They hate the Gospel." Indeed, "there are thousands of young people in Boston tonight who are living on the husks of the swine. You'll find them in the night clubs, saloons, cocktail lounges, parked in automobiles and houses of ill fame."[73]

The spiritual warfare to which Graham referred, while certainly formidable, is not reflected in the published reports of the meetings.[74] Coverage of Graham's meetings was overwhelmingly positive. Indeed, as Harold Lindsell has suggested, the publicity accorded Graham's New England Crusade was "without precedent." The "Boston papers ran front page headlines almost daily" and "local papers went all out to give journalistic coverage to the greatest series of meetings that had hit New England since the days of George Whitefield."[75]

Everyone seemed to be fascinated by Billy Graham. Newspapers scrambled to provide their hungry readers with background stories about the exciting young evangelist.[76] These reports seem to point to five central reasons for Graham's appeal to the people of New England: his winsome personality, his personal integrity, his commitment to moral purity, his biblical preaching, and his "unction" from God. "Dashing and good-looking," as Grace Davidson from the *Boston Post* described him, "this swashbuckling Southerner in his chic gray suit with draped lapels and bright blue and orange tie" looked as if he "belonged in the star's dressing room of a musical comedy rather than in a pulpit." Boston "has seen many evangelists through the decades, from the aged to children, all nationalities and types, from Billy Sunday to Aimee Semple McPherson," she continued, but "never before" has it seen someone

71. Earl Banner, "Graham Calls Manchester 'Difficult Town Spiritually,'" *Boston Daily Globe*, evening edition, April 3, 1950.

72. For the criticisms of George Whitefield by some of Harvard's academics, see Alan Heimert and Perry Miller, eds., *The Great Awakening: Documents Illustrating the Crisis and Its Consequences* (Indianapolis: Bobbs-Merrill, 1967), 183–364.

73. "Thousands of Corrupt Want Revival to End," 1, 55.

74. For a discussion of Billy Graham's approach to criticism, see Garth M. Rosell, "Grace Under Fire," *Christianity Today*, November 13, 1995, 30–34.

75. Lindsell, *Park Street Prophet*, 157.

76. See, for example, Dinneen, "The Life Story of Billy Graham," and Thomason "Life Story of Rev. Billy Graham."

like Billy Graham.[77] His Southern charm and engaging personality, as reporters were quick to note, won him hundreds of new friends throughout New England.

Even more impressive to the somewhat cynical reporters, however, was Graham's personal integrity. During his first press conference in Boston, a sparsely attended event, one of the reporters asked Billy Graham "how much money he expected to garner" from his meetings in Boston.[78] Graham responded that since the Northwestern Schools, where he served as president, paid him $8,500 a year, he would take no income at all from the crusade. In fact, he told the reporters, a committee from the Park Street Church planned to "release a full, audited financial statement" as soon as the meetings had ended.[79] Unwilling to let the matter rest, the reporter continued to press Graham "to admit he expected to get rich from his campaigns." Pulling a crumpled telegram from his pocket, one that the hotel bellman had delivered to him a few moments earlier, he handed it to the reporter and commented: "Sir, if I were interested in making money, I would take advantage of something like this." The telegram, according to Allan Emery, "offered Graham a substantial sum—'something like $250,000 to star in two Hollywood films.' As the reporters passed it around, judging both it and Billy Graham to be authentic, their attitude visibly changed."[80]

Early in his ministry, during the 1948 evangelistic meetings in Modesto, California, Graham had called the members of his team together to discuss ways in which they could fortify themselves more fully against the "lust of the flesh, and the lust of the eyes, and the pride of life" (1 John 2:16 KJV). As described by Graham's biographer, William Martin, the Elmer Gantry image attached to American evangelism, which Sinclair Lewis had "assembled from skeletons and scraps found in the closets of real-life evangelists," was well known by Graham. So he asked his colleagues to identify "all the things that have been a stumbling block and a hindrance to evangelists in years past" so that together they might establish effective means of avoiding them. Out of that discussion emerged the "Modesto Manifesto," as it came to be known, a set of practical guidelines for maintaining moral purity and avoiding even "the appearance of evil" amid the lures of money, sex, and power. Realizing that such rigorous standards would be impossible to keep without God's help, they joined together in fervent prayer asking the Holy Spirit to guard them from those dangers. The fact that Graham's ministry has been preserved from

77. *Boston Post*, December 30, 1949, 3.

78. I am indebted to Allan Emery Jr. for his eyewitness account of this event as reported in Martin, *A Prophet with Honor*, 124–25.

79. For a report on this audit, see the *Boston Daily Globe*, March 26, 1950, 1, 44.

80. In addition to Allan Emery's account, as recorded by Martin, information on the finances of the New England Crusade can be found in "Graham Hits 'Profit' Critics," *Boston Herald*, January 11, 1950.

even the whisper of immorality is evidence that these precautions have been honored and their prayers have been answered.[81]

In addition to his charming personality, personal integrity, and commitment to moral purity, New Englanders were also attracted to the fact that Graham preached with a special sense of authority. Early in his ministry, among the pines of the Forest Home conference grounds in California, Graham had come to the conviction that the Bible is the very Word of God. Questions as to its authority had been troubling the young preacher for weeks. Knowing that the matter must be settled in his mind if he ever hoped to preach with authority and power, he wrestled with his doubts until he was able to pray: "Father, I am going to accept this as Thy Word—by *faith*! I'm going to allow faith to go beyond my intellectual questions and doubts, and I will believe this to be Your inspired Word."[82] That simple prayer transformed Graham's ministry—convincing him, once and for all, of the Bible's absolute authority. That conviction also transformed Graham's preaching, enabling him to proclaim the gospel to his New England audiences with power and authority.

More important than any of these other traits, Graham was convinced, was the touch of God upon his life. Without this divine "unction," this anointing from above, he believed that "his lips would turn to clay." Graham was well aware that there were already in New England many who could out-preach, out-think, and out-organize him. Such comparisons, however, were beside the point. Whatever abilities he might possess, he was absolutely certain that without God's hand upon him, his ministry would immediately collapse. Indeed the greatest fear of true servants of God is that God's hand of blessing will be taken from them—that God's power will no longer be present in their lives and ministries. This is the reason that Graham has been so fearful of ever claiming even the slightest credit for the work he is doing. Far from reflecting a false modesty, it is the stark and frightening realization that all genuine spiritual awakening is the work of God alone. Those who steal God's glory from him will soon find themselves stripped of authority and power.

The Mid-Century Campaign

Whatever the reasons for his popularity, people from across New England flocked to the meetings. The team of Graham, Grady Wilson, Cliff Barrows, George Beverly Shea, Jerry Bevan, Carlton Booth, Ted Smith, and Harold John Ockenga visited many towns and villages throughout the six New England

81. I have developed these themes more fully in Rosell, "Grace Under Fire," 30–31.
82. *Just As I Am: The Autobiography of Billy Graham* (San Francisco: HarperSanFrancisco, 1997), 139.

states. The grueling schedule allowed thousands of people throughout the region to hear the message.

The climax of Graham's New England Crusade came in a series of Boston-area services that were held between April 19 and 23, 1950. From Wednesday through Saturday at 7:30 p.m., services were held at the Boston Garden.[83] At 5:00 p.m. on Friday, a special service was held in the Rockwell Athletic Cage at the Massachusetts Institute of Technology.[84] The final service was held on the Boston Common on Sunday afternoon at 3:30.[85] "Entering the lion's den of science," as a *Boston Herald* reporter phrased it, Billy Graham "electrified" the MIT faculty, students, and guests who had gathered in the school's Rockwell Athletic Cage. "We have humanized God and deified man," Graham told "the friendly audience," and we "have worshipped at the throne of science." Deep down in our souls, however, "we must admit that we have no answer to the dilemma facing our civilization." "We find ourselves with bombs that can destroy vast sections of the human race," he continued, "and the other power has them too." But "we do not have the moral guts to control scientific discovery." "I believe there is a way out," he concluded. "I believe that God can intervene" if we are "willing to let Him." We must "have a spiritual awakening. If students here became as fanatical about God and Christianity as students in Europe are about Communism, we could turn the world upside down." But first "you must give your heart and soul to Christ."[86]

The final service of Graham's New England Crusade was held on Sunday afternoon at the Boston Common. "Fifty thousand persons ignored wet, 46-degree weather yesterday afternoon" to attend the closing service, the *Boston Daily Globe* reported.[87]

83. Transcripts of the sermons were made and duplicated by James O. A. Luckman from Park Street Church. Copies of the sermon for April 19 (Text: Nahum 1:3; Title: "God's Great Hurricane") and April 20 (Text: Daniel 6; Title: "Daniel in the Lion's Den") are from the Rosell Papers.

84. For coverage of the MIT service see Lawrence Dame, "1500 Brave Students Receive Billy Graham MIT Message," *Boston Herald*, April 22, 1950; and "3000 Tech Men Cheer Dr. Graham," *Boston Post*, April 22, 1950.

85. Newspapers estimated that between forty thousand and fifty thousand were in attendance. See the front page reports in the *Boston Daily Globe*, *Boston Herald*, and *Boston Post*, April 24, 1950.

86. Quotations are taken from the *Boston Herald*, April 22, 1950. Graham also spoke at Brown University during his meetings in Rhode Island. See Paul Stevens, "6000 Crowd Halls For Revival in R.I.," *Boston Herald*, April 14, 1950.

87. Ian Menzies, "14,000 at Garden, MIT Hear Graham Glorify Home Life," *Boston Daily Globe*, April 22, 1950, 1, 3; Robert P. Allen, "Billy Warns U.S. of 'Strike-Outs,'" *Boston Sunday Globe*, April 23, 1950, 1, 48; and *Boston Post*, April 24, 1950, 1. While hundreds of photos were taken of this event, to my knowledge only one set of moving pictures was taken of the Boston Common gathering. Merv Rosell, described by his good friend Billy Graham in a *Boston Daily Globe* interview as "one of the greatest evangelists preaching today," had come to Boston to attend the final week of the crusade. Seeing the enormous crowd that had gathered, Cliff Barrows handed Rosell his Bell and Howell camera and asked him to get some pictures of the service. This historic film is now housed with the Rosell Papers.

Billy Graham at the Boston Garden in 1950

Speaking from a lectern near the Soldiers and Sailors Monument, the location from which George Whitefield had spoken to a crowd of twenty-three thousand in 1740, Graham began by presenting a five-point peace plan. America, he declared, "must maintain strong military power for defense"; "must strengthen organizations like the F.B.I. for internal protection"; must maintain "economic stability for security"; must maintain "confidence in each other, race with race, creed with creed, color with color, remembering that we are all Americans and that America is the nation that has made every man a king"; and must meet God's demands for "repentance of sins, individual faith in Jesus Christ, national humility and a united prayer for peace."[88] He then called on the crowd to wave white handkerchiefs as a demonstration to President Truman and the world that the Christians in America want peace not war. Harold John Ockenga then led the huge crowd in a prayer for peace.[89] Unlike Whitefield, who had no microphone,

88. Wording is taken from Harold John Ockenga, "The Mid-Century Campaign," a report on Billy Graham's ministry in New England, Ockenga Papers. For an analysis of Graham's political involvements see Eric J. Paddon, "Modern Mordecai: Billy Graham in the Political Arena, 1948–1980" (PhD diss., Ohio University, 1999).

89. The prayer, specially written for the occasion, was led by Ockenga and voiced by everyone present: "O God our Father, in whose hands is our destiny, have mercy upon Thy people. We acknowledge that we deserve Thy wrath and that we are in danger of judgment. In the Bible, Thou hast promised to hear our prayer, to forgive our sin, and to heal our land, if we humble ourselves, if we pray to Thee, and if we turn from our wicked ways. We wish to meet these conditions and

Billy Graham rally on the Boston Common, 1950 from the Harold
John Ockenga Papers

"powerful amplifiers carried [Graham's] message to hundreds parked in cars along Charles and Beacon streets and to a scattering of people leaning out of hotel windows along the skyline across the Public Garden."[90]

Following the singing of "America," led by Cliff Barrows, Billy Graham rose to speak a second time. Taking "his text from Amos: 'Prepare to meet thy God,'" as Ockenga later described the event, he "began to preach on 'Shall God Reign in New England?' It was a great sermon and, at the conclusion of it, hundreds and hundreds of hands were raised signifying the desire on the part of people to accept Christ as Savior."[91]

"I'm praying for a righteous peace," Graham told his listeners, "but I see little hope for it unless we have an old-fashioned, heaven-sent, Holy Ghost revival." Characterizing America as "the most sinful nation in all history," he called upon his listeners to repent and "turn to Christ while there is still time." At the end of the sermon, Graham asked all those who wanted "to accept Christ as personal Savior" to wave once again their white handkerchiefs. In response, as reported by the *Boston Daily Globe*, "white cloths fluttered up" throughout "the great outdoor congregation."[92]

Following the meeting on the Boston Common, Harold John Ockenga commented on the events he had been witnessing over the first four months of 1950. "All of New England has been ringing with revival," he declared. Thousands of prayer meetings had been held, scores of services had been conducted, and over nine thousand conversions had been recorded. As a result of the meetings, "churches have been quickened, the ministers have been encouraged, the

---

to claim this promise. Our corruptions have brought violence upon us. O Righteous One, let our repentance and sorrow for sin, and our faith in Christ, bring peace to us, and to our nation. Let Christ reign over us, over New England, over America, and finally over the world, for Jesus' sake. Amen." George McKinnon, "40,000 Respond to Graham in Peace Rally on Common," *Boston Daily Globe*, April 24, 1950, 1–2; and "Dr. Ockenga Leads Crowd at Revival in Prayer for Peace," *Boston Daily Globe*, April 24, 1950, 1.

90. McKinnon, "40,000 Respond to Graham," 1–2.

91. Ockenga, "The Mid-Century Campaign," Ockenga Papers.

92. McKinnon, "40,000 Respond to Graham," 1–2.

people have been revived and hundreds of members have joined the churches. It has initiated a new era of evangelical co-operation and of power—spiritual power—in New England."[93]

The original intentions, Ockenga admitted, were "to start in one church and to continue there for eight days, but God broke through and the greatest halls were necessary throughout the whole of New England. We can say that for two hundred years there has been no such movement in New England. George Whitefield was the last man who stirred New England in such a way." Then, expanding the vision beyond the region, Ockenga drew his conclusions:

> Now we envisage that what has occurred in Boston, especially the great concluding rallies and the peace rally on the Boston Common, will launch a pattern for all America so that a peace offensive may be launched on the basis of righteousness, revival and prayer which will roll back the tides of sin and will obtain Divine mercy for our country in the hour of its crisis. Let millions of people pray for peace, but let them seek peace through righteousness and revival of Christian faith.[94]

Beyond the immediate results, the Boston revival had enormous importance for the future of the evangelical movement itself. For it was the Boston revival perhaps more than any other that established Billy Graham's reputation as the outstanding evangelist of his time. It was the Boston revival, conducted in the shadow of some of America's leading academic institutions, that established Graham's credibility as one who could hold his own in any context. It was the Boston revival, uniting the exuberance of Youth for Christ with the sophistication of the NAE, that helped join the Christian community in a powerful new coalition. And it was the Boston revival, as new friends came to know and trust each other, that produced a cadre of leaders that would guide evangelicalism for the next fifty years.

Of perhaps greatest importance in that regard was the lifelong friendship that the Boston revival helped establish between Billy Graham and Harold John Ockenga. This new coalition, forged in the revival fires of New England, was to provide essential leadership for the burgeoning evangelical movement for more than a generation.

93. Ockenga, "The Mid-Century Campaign." For a shorter version of his reflections, see Harold John Ockenga, "Afterthoughts on Boston," in Orr, *The Second Evangelical Awakening in America*, 191–93.

94. Ibid.

6

★

THE FLOODTIDE OF REVIVAL

Billy Graham's meetings in Los Angeles and Boston seemed to portend the beginning of a new era in evangelism. By the close of the Los Angeles Crusade, for example, the Christ for Greater Los Angeles Committee was already making plans for eight follow-up campaigns throughout Southern California. The largest of these, conducted by Merv Rosell from June 4 through 25 of 1950, drew a total attendance of one hundred and fifty thousand and recorded thousands of conversions.[1]

The same "canvas cathedral" that Graham had used for the Los Angeles meetings was once again "filled to capacity night after night," with "9000 on hand the opening Sunday afternoon." Claude Jenkins, who had directed Graham's earlier crusade, "declared [Rosell's] Greater Long Beach campaign to be the most successful 1950 revival effort."[2]

Scores of additional revivals began to break out in nearly every region of America. For example, Torrey Johnson, the first president of Youth for Christ, led meetings in Oakland, California, attended by over one hundred thousand people with nearly one thousand conversions.[3] Jack Shuler's six-week campaign

1. Figures taken from J. Edwin Orr, *The Second Evangelical Awakening in America* (London: Marshall, Morgan & Scott, 1952), 196–97.

2. "Thousands Accept Christ as More Than 100,000 Attend Long Beach Crusade," *Youth for Christ* magazine, special revival issue, October 1950, 56–57, 73.

3. Orr, *The Second Evangelical Awakening in America*, 195.

in Ft. Wayne, Indiana, drew seventeen thousand people to the closing rally and nearly one thousand "came forward for salvation and reclamation."[4] Jimmie Johnson's twenty-three day crusade in Memphis, Tennessee, drew a total of seventy thousand people and 726 "decisions for Christ" were recorded.[5] Religious revivals, encouraged by groups such as InterVarsity, Campus Crusade, Youth for Christ, and the Navigators, also began to break out at a number of colleges and seminaries including Bethel College in St. Paul, Minnesota; Northern Baptist Theological Seminary; Wheaton College in Wheaton, Illinois; North Park College; Asbury College; Seattle Pacific College; Simpson Bible College; Baylor University; and Houghton College.[6]

Furthermore, reports of revivals began to pour into America from around the world as the awakening began to touch places like Belgium, Japan, Ireland, New Zealand, Spain, India, Czechoslovakia, Italy, Guatemala, Finland, Holland, Germany, Sweden, Wales, Switzerland, and Austria.[7] While scores of evangelists were involved in "America's Mid-Century Awakening," as J. Edwin Orr labeled it, among the most prominent were two old friends, Merv Rosell and Billy Graham. Merv Rosell, for example, led major campaigns during 1950 in Long Beach, Kansas City, Des Moines, Chicago, and Phoenix, in addition to shorter meetings in other locations. Hundreds of thousands packed the cities' largest arenas, concert halls, and "canvas cathedrals" to attend the services and many thousands of those who came made decisions for Christ.[8]

In Kansas City, for example, over two hundred thousand people crowded the twelve-thousand-seat Municipal Auditorium during the twenty-two days of Rosell's campaign. On the opening Sunday, nearly twenty-five thousand people arrived for the service. Many of those who could not get in for the first service waited outside and then filled the auditorium for a hastily-called second service. By the end of the campaign, 5,300 decisions for Christ had been recorded.[9]

4. "Shuler at Zollner Stadium," in *Youth for Christ* magazine, October 1950, 59.

5. "Revival Reports," *Youth for Christ* magazine, October 1950, 36–37.

6. J. Edwin Orr, *Campus Aflame: A History of Evangelical Awakenings in Collegiate Communities* (Wheaton: International Awakening Press, 1994), 169–84.

7. Reports from all of these locations can be found in "YFC Around the World," *Youth for Christ* magazine, October 1950, 8–71.

8. For accounts of these revivals, see Orr, "The Emergence of Mervin Rosell," in *The Second Evangelical Awakening in America,* 198–201; J. Edwin Orr, *Good News in Bad Times: Signs of Revival* (Grand Rapids: Zondervan, 1953), 183–85; *Northwestern Pilot,* January 1951, 125–26; and *Youth for Christ* magazine, special revival edition, October 1950, 44–79.

9. The Kansas City for Christ Crusade held from July 22 to August 13, 1950, attracted "more than 200,000 persons [who] have prayed, sobbed, listened and witnessed before the Lord in the project sponsored by churches throughout Greater Kansas City." See "Faith as the Key," *Kansas City Star,* August 13, 1950. A report of the opening services, including a picture of the overflow crowd, was carried on the front page of the *Kansas City Times;* see "Throng to Pray: 25,000 in Three Crowds," *Kansas City Times,* July 24, 1953, 1. The Crusade received substantial coverage in the *Kansas City Star* and the *Kansas City Times.* See also Orr, *The Second Evangelical Awakening in America,* 198–99.

Meeting in what Charles E. Fuller described as "the largest tent ever erected anywhere,"[10] the Iowa for Christ Crusade drew an estimated attendance of one hundred and fifty thousand. Rosell's three-hour service on September 4, 1950, held in the tent and concluded with prayer on the Iowa state house steps, was attended by over thirty thousand. "This is a momentous occasion in the history of Iowa," declared Governor William S. Beardsley at the final gathering. "We urge the people of this State to seek God in this crisis time."[11]

"More than 400 churches in the Chicago area are supporting the first citywide revival campaign here in several years," wrote a reporter for the *Chicago Herald-American*. Rosell, "who is compared to Billy Sunday or Billy Graham," the reporter continued, "has stirred men, women and children in Portland, Los Angeles, Kansas City and Des Moines." Meetings were held at 7:30 each evening and at 3:00 p.m. each Sunday in Orchestra Hall on Michigan Boulevard. Sunday evening services were also held at Moody Memorial Church.[12]

During the month of November, 1950, the Arizona for Christ Crusade was held in a "canvas cathedral" at Seventh and Oak Streets in Phoenix. Sponsored by over eighty churches in the Phoenix area, the meetings drew a total attendance of more than ninety thousand. "Every night for almost three weeks," reported the *Arizona Republic*, "the big tent . . . has been filled with some 3,000 people trying to get closer to God. . . . Inside the canvas cathedral, Merv Rosell captures the people with the practiced genius of a symphony conductor."[13]

A Decade of Evangelism

Scores of additional citywide meetings were held throughout the following years in cities including Philadelphia, Oakland, Tacoma, Denver, Dallas, Boston, Topeka, and many others both in America and throughout the world. In Philadelphia, for example, 886 churches united to sponsor a two-week "Mervin Rosell Area-Wide Evangelistic Campaign." Walter H. Smyth, the chairman for the crusade, observed that it had been a long time since he had witnessed such "a spirit of unity" among the pastors as was reflected in their unanimous and

10. This was actually three large tents combined, allowing ten thousand to be seated inside and another ten thousand to be seated outside. The "canvas cathedral" used both by Graham and Rosell in Los Angeles and Long Beach was actually a combination of two large tents erected side-by-side. Charles E. Fuller and "Ma" Sunday, wife of the famous evangelist Billy Sunday, were among the guests attending the meetings.

11. Governor Beardsley's comments and a picture of the event were carried on the front page of the *Des Moines Register*. See "30,00 Stand on Statehouse Steps in Prayer for Troops in Korea," *Des Moines Register*, September 4, 1950. See also "Revival News," *Youth for Christ* magazine, October 1950, 35.

12. Stanley Pieza, "Youth-for-Christ Crusade Opens Here Saturday," *Chicago Herald-American*, September 14, 1950, 6.

13. "Rosell Captures Crowd's Attention Like Musician; Speaks to 90,000," *Arizona Republic*, November 24, 1950, 27.

Merv Rosell Crusade in Philadelphia (courtesy of Gordon-Conwell Libraries)

enthusiastic vote in favor of holding the campaign. Methodists, Presbyterians, Baptists, Pentecostals, Mennonites, Christian and Missionary Alliance, Church of the Brethren, and others were solidly behind the effort.[14]

In addition to the regular team of Howard and Ada Skinner, Hilding Halvorsen, Karl Steele, and Cy Jackson, other friends including Charles E. Fuller, Stuart Hamblen, and Oswald Smith came to help out in the process.

"A year ago," wrote Merv Rosell late in 1950, "I was able to write with conviction and assurance" that I was "expecting revival." But now we can actually see with our own eyes that an "avalanche of blessing is gathering force to thunder into every valley of our nation." We dare not "touch its shining glory." Rather, "we kneel in awe and worship the God of this heavenly hurricane. . . . Don't be discouraged because your city is small and 'out-of-the-way,'" he cautioned his readers. God often "puts His finger on the insignificant and makes it magnificent. Remember Wesley's Aldersgate; Finney's Adams; Livingstone's Kirk of Shotts; Evan Robert's wee land of Wales." They were "little places" with "ordinary men," but they were touched

14. Walter H. Smyth to Mervin E. Rosell, March 14, 1951, and telegram from Smyth to Rosell, March 14, 1951, Rosell Papers.

by a great God. "Revival can come to your town," Rosell was convinced, if faithful Christians would follow the three instructions outlined by evangelist Reuben Archer Torrey: "(1) Let a few Christians get thoroughly right with God (This is prime essential); (2) Let them bind themselves in prayer for revival until God opens the heavens and comes down; and (3) Let them put themselves at God's disposal to use as He sees fit in winning others to Christ. That is all." In "real revival," Rosell concluded, "nothing is impossible; no one is untouchable! Its molten flow fuses folk anywhere and forges unbreakable links in a chain of soul-winning, home-healing and nation-mending. Revival is God-unlimited!"[15]

Billy Graham

While many other evangelists played significant roles in the Mid-Twentieth Century Awakening, none spoke to more people, witnessed more conversions to Christ, or exerted a greater influence than Billy Graham. With rare natural abilities, winsomeness, dedication to the task of worldwide evangelization, and good old-fashioned hard work, Graham emerged from the meetings in Los Angeles and Boston as the most prominent and influential evangelist of the twentieth century.[16] "Almost a half century later," Billy Graham reflected in his autobiography, "it is impossible to re-create the nonstop activity and excitement that engulfed us during those months following our meetings in Los Angeles and Boston. At times I felt almost as if we were standing in the path of a roaring avalanche or a strong riptide, and all we could do was hold on and trust God to help us."[17] Throughout the whirlwind months of 1950, Graham had conducted successful crusades in Columbia, Portland, and Atlanta and had preached in a variety of additional venues throughout New England, the Midwest, the West, and the South. Over one and a half million people had heard Billy Graham in person, and nearly fifty thousand had committed their lives to Christ.[18]

15. Merv Rosell, "Revival Can Come to Your Town," *Youth for Christ* magazine, October 1950, 51, 76–79.

16. Graham's rapid rise to international prominence as America's best-known and most-loved evangelist caused some jealousy and resentment among a few of the other evangelists. My own father, however, remained passionately loyal to his old friend and he would not allow so much as a day to pass without fervently praying for God's continued blessing upon Billy Graham and his team. A signed picture of Graham hung prominently in his office for as long as I can remember.

17. *Just As I Am: The Autobiography of Billy Graham* (San Francisco: HarperSanFrancisco, 1997), 172.

18. See Donald E. Hoke, "Harvesting at the Revival in Columbia," in *Revival in Our Time: The Story of the Billy Graham Evangelistic Campaign* (Wheaton: Van Kampen, 1950), 41–49; Graham, *Just As I Am*, 172–87; Curtis Mitchell, *Those Who Came Forward: Men and Women Who Responded to the Ministry of Billy Graham* (Philadelphia and New York: Chilton Books, 1966); and John Pollock, *Crusades: 20 Years with Billy Graham* (Minneapolis: World Wide Publications, 1969).

Furthermore, by the end of 1950, with another New Year's Eve rally at Mechanics Hall in Boston,[19] the "Hour of Decision" radio broadcasts had been launched, a new film ministry had been started, the evangelistic team had been enlarged, and the Billy Graham Evangelistic Association had been established.[20] It was during the Portland Crusade, held from July 23 through September 4 in a specially-constructed "wooden cathedral" seating twelve thousand, that the Billy Graham Evangelistic Association was formed.[21] Having begun to collect money for their new radio ministry, the "Hour of Decision," the Graham team realized they would need to establish a nonprofit organization to oversee and distribute the funds. With the help of his old friend George Wilson, articles of incorporation for the Billy Graham Evangelistic Association were drawn up and processed. Billy and Ruth Graham, Cliff Barrows, Grady Wilson, and George Wilson became the charter members. They later expanded the board to include new friends such as Allan Emery and Harold John Ockenga.[22]

A modest one-room office was secured in Minneapolis, a secretary was hired, and George Wilson was appointed to oversee the operation. For nearly four decades, Wilson oversaw the expansion of Billy Graham's ministries.[23] Billy Graham's public ministry has been well documented and needs little comment here.[24] Suffice it to say that between the Los Angeles campaign in 1949 and the New York City Crusade in 1957, including major preaching missions to Asia,[25] the British Isles,[26] and Europe,[27] Billy Graham became a household name around the world. With far more to do than he could possibly do by himself, Graham increasingly turned to trusted friends to carry forward

19. Continuing the tradition, two hundred Boston churches united to invite Merv Rosell to conduct an evangelistic crusade at Mechanics Hall from New Year's Eve of 1952 through January 11, 1953. See Harold John Ockenga to Merv Rosell, March 22, 1952; and Allan C. Emery to Merv Rosell, September 26, 1952; Rosell Papers.

20. For Graham's interesting descriptions of the origins of these various initiatives, see Graham, *Just As I Am*, 172–87.

21. For a description of these meetings and pictures of the construction of the tabernacle, see "Graham Portland Crusade Second Largest in American History as 632,000 attend; 9,000 Converts," *Youth for Christ* magazine, October 1950, 34–39.

22. See the files relating to the Billy Graham Evangelistic Association in the Ockenga Papers.

23. For a more detailed description of the beginnings of the Billy Graham Evangelistic Association, see Graham, *Just As I Am*, 181–87; William Martin, *A Prophet with Honor: The Billy Graham Story* (New York: William Morrow, 1991), 123–41; and Stanley High, *Billy Graham* (New York: McGraw-Hill, 1956), 151–68.

24. See esp. Graham, *Just As I Am*; and Martin, *A Prophet with Honor*.

25. See Graham, *Just As I Am*, 263–81.

26. See George Burnham, *Billy Graham: A Mission Accomplished* (New York: Revell, 1955); Tom Allan, ed., *Crusade in Scotland* (London: Pickering & Inglis, 1955); Edward O. England, *Hallowed Harringay* (London: Victory, 1955); *Moody Monthly*, October 1954; and John R. Rice, "God's Power in Scotland," *Sword of the Lord*, May 20, 1955, 1–2.

27. See Graham, *Just As I Am*, 239–59.

his expanding evangelistic vision. "During the past few months we have been re-evaluating our entire ministry," he wrote in a letter to Merv Rosell, and "we believe that the time has come for a group of us evangelists to work more closely together." Since "you and I have discussed on several occasions the possibility of working more closely together," he continued, "I would like to propose the possibility of your coming with us on a full-time basis." Primarily "you would carry on in your great God-given evangelistic efforts throughout the world," but "from time to time perhaps we could work together in a crusade so that our hearts might stay close together."[28] Although Rosell declined the

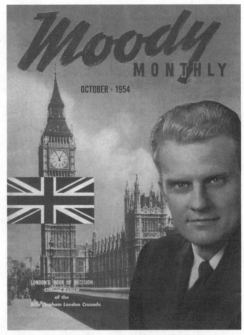

Billy Graham on the cover of *Moody Monthly*

invitation, it served to further strengthen an important relationship in the old band of brothers.

The New York Crusade (1957)

Billy Graham's New York City Crusade, which continued for sixteen weeks from May 15 through August 10, was a turning point in American evangelism.[29] Over two million people attended the meetings, more than sixty-one thousand came forward at the invitations, and about thirty-five thousand wrote to indicate that they had made a decision as a result of the telecasts.[30] Despite the tens of thousands who found peace with God during the summer of 1957, however, the New York Crusade tended to deepen the divisions within the evangelical community itself. At issue was Billy

28. Graham to Rosell, July 1, 1958, Rosell Papers.

29. For accounts of the sixteen-week crusade, see George Burnham and Lee Fisher, *Billy Graham and the New York Crusade* (Grand Rapids: Zondervan, 1957); Martin, *A Prophet with Honor*, 225–51; and Graham, *Just As I Am*, 297–324. For a sampler of Graham's sermons, see Billy Graham, *The Challenge: Sermons From the Historic New York Crusade* (New York: Pocket, 1972).

30. Figures are taken from Graham, *Just As I Am*, 321.

Billy Graham New York City Crusade at Yankee Stadium, May 15 to August 10, 1957 (courtesy of Gordon-Conwell Libraries)

Graham's apparent willingness to cooperate in his New York Crusade with individuals, churches, and ecclesiastical organizations whose orthodoxy was considered "suspect."[31]

Concerns about separation from apostasy and worldliness were nothing new. They had frequently surfaced in the earlier debates over "come-outism" and ecumenical cooperation. By and large, however, the great Mid-Twentieth-Century Awakening between 1949 and 1955 had remained relatively free of controversy.

"My heart was greatly refreshed," wrote John R. Rice in 1955, after spending a week with Billy Graham and his evangelistic team.

> I had seven wonderful days with them in the great All-Scotland Crusade. I saw thousands of people claim Christ as Saviour with an average of 400 people coming forward each night in Kelvin Hall, with approximately 900 claiming Christ publicly in Edinburgh in one afternoon meeting in Tyne Castle Stadium, and with telegraphed reports coming in of thousands of people claiming Christ in the relay services in some 2,000 auditoriums over the British Isles where people

31. Robert O. Ferm, *Cooperative Evangelism: Is Billy Graham Right or Wrong?* (Grand Rapids: Zondervan, 1958), 18–19.

listened to the Kelvin Hall services transmitted by telephone lines and broadcast by loud speakers.

"Thank God," wrote Rice, "for the wonderful results of the Scotland Campaign."[32] Despite Rice's glowing report, questions were beginning to circulate about Billy Graham's evangelistic strategy. "Did Billy Graham really take Dr. Bonnell, a liberal Presbyterian pastor of New York City, to Scotland as his guest? Does Billy use the Revised Standard Version of the Bible or the King James Version? What is Billy's attitude toward modernism and modernists? What is Billy Graham's doctrinal position concerning the verbal inspiration of the Bible and other great fundamentals?"[33]

Concerns over these and other questions continued to escalate during the months following the Scotland Crusade. Convinced that God was leading him "to help put evangelism back into the hands of good, old-time, orthodox preachers," the founder and chairman of the board of trustees of Bob Jones University began to develop "a list of evangelists who will not knowingly accept an invitation under any modernistic sponsorship." Writing to a number of evangelists, including graduates of Bob Jones University, he invited them to sign and return an enclosed form if they wished to be included on the list.[34]

His plan was to write to "approximately forty thousand pastors in the United States and Canada" to let them know that such a list was available at their request should they wish help in identifying an "uncompromising evangelist" to lead "an evangelistic campaign" in their own congregation or "a united campaign with other evangelical groups." "I am not trying to run your business or the business of any other pastor," Jones assured the pastors. "I have no axe to grind. I do not want anything except to make whatever contribution I can to the cause for which you stand and for which I stand."

Deepening Divisions

During the New York Crusade in 1957, the early fissures had broadened into a deep ravine. "Although Billy Graham began weakening his position prior

32. Rice, "God's Power in Scotland," 1–2, 6–7. Billy Graham, M. R. Dehaan, V. Raymond Edman, Louis Talbot, Pat Zondervan, Merv Rosell, and a number of others were listed as members of the "Co-operating Board" of the *Sword of the Lord*.

33. Rice, "God's Power in Scotland," 7. Rice raised these questions at the end of his article and responded to them in the following issue, continuing to defend Billy Graham as "God's anointed man" who is "being used tremendously" in the great revivals of the day.

34. Jones to Merv Rosell, January 19, 1956; Jones to "Dear Friend," undated mimeographed letter "to our own Bob Jones University graduates who are in evangelistic work" and "later we may send a letter to some good evangelists who are not graduates of Bob Jones University"; and Jones to "My Dear Brethren," undated mimeographed letter "to approximately forty thousand pastors in the United States and Canada"; copies of the letters and the return form for evangelists can be found in the Rosell Papers. See also Martin, *A Prophet with Honor*, 239–51.

to 1957," argued Ernest Pickering, "it was in that year that the major turning point in his career was reached." "The participation of outright liberals in a great campaign such as this was a first in American evangelism."[35] Perhaps even more damaging was the fact that Graham's New York Crusade was officially sponsored by the Protestant Council of the City of New York, an affiliate of the National Council of Churches that represented all but a few of the Protestant churches within the greater New York metropolitan area.[36]

By the close of the New York Crusade, it was clear that a line had been drawn in the sand. Fundamentalists like Bob Jones, Carl McIntire, and John R. Rice, eager to guard the purity of the church, planted their flag on the separatist side. Evangelicals like Billy Graham, Carl F. H. Henry, and Harold John Ockenga, eager to see the gospel proclaimed to as many people as possible, remained open to cooperation whenever it could be done without theological compromise. "The New York crusade did not cause the division between the old Fundamentalists and the New Evangelicals," argued William Martin, but "it did provide an event around which the two groups were forced to define themselves."[37]

Throughout 1957, increasing space in the *Sword of the Lord*, the independent Christian weekly founded by Rice in 1934, was given to articles critical of Billy Graham's ministry. "For more than a year," Merv Rosell wrote in a letter to John R. Rice during the summer of 1958, many of us have been "deeply concerned about the growing clouds of incompatibility among the family of believers."[38] Those of us who are "generally classed as the 'generation of younger evangelists' have watched and listened with sincere admiration to the 'senior evangelists' who led the way in crusading for Christ. They urged us to pray that some day our generation might see 'some young man chosen of God to lead thousands to Christ in another great sweep of evangelism.'" God answered that prayer, he continued, and laid "his hand on such a man whom I have known since his boyhood days in Charlotte. Almost every other evangelist, old and young, has sat with tears in his eyes to thank God for the amazing Crusades in London, Glasgow, or some American city." Indeed, "those years, in the early fifties, seemed like a 'golden age.' Deep and true friendships bound us all together. Crowds beyond our greatest faith were attending all of our Crusades and the harvest was bountiful. Editors, like yourself, were extending our ministries to tens of thousands. It seemed every man of God was honestly praying for every other servant of Christ. Good memories!"[39]

35. Ernest D. Pickering, *The Tragedy of Compromise: The Origin and Impact of the New Evangelicalism* (Greenville, SC: Bob Jones University Press, 1994), 49–76, quotation from p. 55. For a contrasting perspective, see Ferm, *Cooperative Evangelism*, esp. 48–94.
36. For a discussion of these developments, see Martin, *A Prophet with Honor*, 220–24.
37. Ibid., 224.
38. Rosell to Rice, August 22, 1958; for Rice's response, see Rice to Rosell, September 3, 1958, Rosell Papers. Rosell had been a member of the honorary board since July 30, 1952.
39. Rosell to Rice, August 22, 1958.

"Then came the gradual, insidious division (for one cause or another)," Rosell lamented, "which set 'brother against brother' until I found in each city two opposing camps of my own friends. No longer did I see the shining eyes of God's men who talked only of Christ. Now, they whispered to me, 'Are you against that young evangelist or against those critical writers?'" The letter continued: "Beloved Dr. W. B. Riley chose me to travel with him in my youth and carefully taught me, in those tender years, that every man—even the great ones of his day—had a weakness or failure. He urged me to keep my eyes on Christ, not on the failures of men. Consequently, I have persistently refused to become a party to criticism. When God vindicates, we need not be vindictive. Often I read this to myself: 'Therefore, thou art inexcusable, O man, whosoever thou art that judgest: for wherein thou judgest another, thou condemnest thyself; for thou that judgest doest the same things . . . and thinkest thou this, O man . . . that thou shalt escape the judgment of God?' (Romans 2)."[40]

Then, after requesting with deep regret that his name be removed from the *Sword of the Lord* cooperating board, Rosell concluded: "I have not changed my theology, my calling or my purpose in life. There is no compromise, if I know my heart, just equal loyalty to all my friends. Because I have a deep conviction that I can serve Christ best by prayer and intercession, I prefer not to 'sign' even the unkind criticism of one friend against another."[41]

While not true of all the participants in the debates, there is a profound sadness that runs through the evangelical literature of the late 1950s. Having begun the decade with such optimism and hope, many evangelicals found themselves increasingly discouraged by the deepening rifts within the family. While Billy Graham's great crusades were to continue with enormous success for many more decades—and the ministry of other gifted evangelists would continue to flourish—America's era of united citywide crusades seemed largely to have passed by the end of the 1950s. Increasingly, evangelism's center of gravity seemed to be shifting from North America to other parts of the world. The changes, as we will see, were to have a profound impact on the future direction of the evangelical movement. What did not change was the continuing priority given to evangelism within the movement itself. For evangelicals like Harold John Ockenga and Billy Graham, the spread of the gospel around the globe remained the primary driving passion and central concern. The purpose of unity was mission. The goal of cooperation was the spread of the gospel to as many men, women, boys, and girls as could possibly be reached before the return of Christ.

40. Ibid.
41. Ibid.

7

✳✳✳

RECLAIMING THE CULTURE

W hile deepening divisions would become painfully apparent by the close
of the 1950s, setting brother against brother, a spirit of buoyant optimism seemed to pervade the first half of the decade. Encouraged by America's
emerging spiritual awakening, its ranks swelled by tens of thousands of new
converts, the American evangelical movement seemed unstoppable.

Harold John Ockenga, for his part, was quite sure that 1950 would go down
in history "as the year of heaven-sent revival." It is true, Ockenga conceded, that
the "Philistines" have invaded America, infecting its universities with relativism,
its churches with worldliness, and its society with crime, rape, and violence.
But Scripture assures us that "times of refreshing" will come and now, at long
last, "America's hour has struck." We don't "have to wait" until "next year." We
"don't have to wait ten years." We "don't have to pray anymore, 'Lord, send a
revival.' The revival is here!"—"Revival is the solution to all our problems."[1]

Ockenga's comments reflected the conviction, shared by many of his evangelical colleagues, that the grand vision of reclaiming the culture for Christ
could not be achieved without the arrival of an "old-fashioned, heaven-sent
revival." After all, the movement itself had begun in the midst of the Great
Awakening of the eighteenth century. Now, two centuries later, it appeared to
Ockenga that the surprising work of God was once again opening the way for

1. Harold John Ockenga, "Is America's Revival Breaking?" *United Evangelical Action*, July 1, 1950,
3–4, 8, 13–15. For examples of the scope of these revivals, see J. Edwin Orr, *The Second Evangelical
Awakening in America* (London: Marshall, Morgan & Scott, 1952); and *Youth for Christ* magazine,
special revival issue, October 1950.

a whole new era in the spread and effectiveness of biblical Christianity. "The evangelical defense of the faith theologically," Ockenga insisted, "is identical with that of the older fundamentalists." Evangelicals and fundamentalists differed, however, on matters of strategy and goals. With regard to strategy, Ockenga and many of his colleagues believed that they must abandon their propensity to withdraw from the culture and its institutions and commit themselves rather to the "principle of infiltration." From modern military campaigns we have learned "that the frontal attack," as Ockenga liked to phrase it, "is not very effective. The French Maginot line was circumvented," referring to the invasion of France by the Germans during World War II, and was thereby rendered obsolete.[2]

"The Communists," though, "used the principle of infiltration" when fighting in Korea, Indo-China, and Tibet, and as a result were far more successful. "We evangelicals need to realize that the liberals, or modernists, have been using this strategy for years. They have infiltrated our evangelical denominations, institutions and movements, and they have taken over control of them." The time has come, Ockenga concluded, for evangelicals to reverse the process by joining "hands with evangelicals everywhere" and seizing the "opportunity" to "infiltrate" those same denominations, institutions, and movements with the salt and light of biblical Christianity.[3] The reason for adopting such a strategy, Ockenga was convinced, was the importance of achieving four essential goals: the reform of society, the renewal of the church, a return to intellectual respectability, and the spread of the gospel around the globe.[4] It is to these important tasks, as the following chapters will suggest, that the evangelical movement turned its attention with both energy and courage.

The Reform of Society

During the summer of 1946, Carl F. H. Henry began preparing a series of lectures designed to "'perform surgery' on Fundamentalism." Following

2. Harold John Ockenga, "Resurgent Evangelical Leadership," *Christianity Today*, October 10, 1960, 11–15.

3. Ibid. In his influential book *Christ and Culture* (Expanded 50th anniversary issue; San Francisco: HarperSanFrancisco, 2001), H. Richard Niebuhr suggested that at least five different "types"—or "zones" as historian Martin Marty prefers to call them—have characterized Christianity's understanding of the relationship between the church and culture throughout its history. While all five of these can be found, often in overlapping configurations, within evangelicalism, Ockenga's "principle of infiltration" seems at first glance to fit most easily into the fifth: "Christ the Transformer of Culture." Like the Puritans before him, Ockenga and many of his evangelical colleagues saw their task as nothing less than the reclaiming for Christ's kingdom the whole of God's creation. The purpose of infiltration, therefore, was to prepare the way so that individual lives and cultural institutions might ultimately be transformed by the power of the gospel.

4. Ockenga, "Resurgent Evangelical Leadership," 11–15.

a "trial run at Gordon College of Theology and Missions," the eight essays were published as *The Uneasy Conscience of Modern Fundamentalism.*[5] "A tract for the times," as Henry called it, the little eighty-nine-page book "made quite a stir."[6]

When Henry wrote *The Uneasy Conscience* at the age of thirty-four, "evangelicals were still a beleaguered minority," he later reflected, "straining to break out of their cultural ghetto, firming their identity against both modernism and neo-orthodoxy, and struggling for academic acceptance and literary achievement." During the 1920s, 1930s, and 1940s, Henry argued, the "fundamentalists were devoting their best energies to unmasking the theological defects of Protestant liberalism," namely "its empirical disavowal of miracles" and its "notions of inevitable progress and of humanity's intrinsic goodness. Their usual approach was to scorn modernist efforts for a new social order." Meanwhile, for their own part, the fundamentalists "sponsored no program of attack on acknowledged societal evils and ignored serious reflection on how an evangelical ecumenism might impinge on the culture crisis." Rather, they concentrated almost exclusively on "evangelism" as "the solution to every problem."[7]

The great eighteenth- and nineteenth-century heritage of American evangelicalism, however, was deeply rooted in social reform, as historian Timothy L. Smith so clearly demonstrated in his pioneering book, *Revivalism and Social Reform.*[8] Smith's basic argument is deceptively simple: America's mid-nineteenth-century religious revivals, reinforced by a passionate quest for personal and corporate holiness, unleashed a flood of evangelical social activity, mobilizing tens of thousands of new recruits for the battles against slavery, poverty, and greed. Far from abandoning their longstanding commitment to sound theology, biblical authority, personal holiness, and the missionary mandate, these nineteenth-century evangelicals believed that it was precisely because of those commitments that they were obligated, to borrow the words of the prophet Micah, to "act justly and to love mercy and to walk humbly" with their God.

Indeed, it was their love of the Bible—with its repeated instructions to care for the poor and needy, to be honest in business dealings, to look after

---

5. Carl F. H. Henry, *The Uneasy Conscience of Modern Fundamentalism,* with a foreword by Richard J. Mouw (Grand Rapids: Eerdmans, 2003). The book, first published by Eerdmans in 1947, was dedicated to T. Leonard Lewis, president of the college, with an introduction written by Harold John Ockenga.

6. Description and quotations are from Carl F. H. Henry, *Confessions of a Theologian: An Autobiography* (Waco: Word, 1986), 112–13.

7. Carl F. H. Henry, "The Uneasy Conscience Revisited: Current Theological, Ethical and Social Concerns," *Theology, News and Notes,* December 1987, 3.

8. See esp. Timothy L. Smith, *Revivalism and Social Reform* (Baltimore: Johns Hopkins University Press, 1980; Eugene, OR: Wipf & Stock, 2005); Norris Magnuson, *Salvation in the Slums,* with a new introduction by Garth M. Rosell (Eugene, OR: Wipf & Stock, 2005); and Donald W. Dayton, *Discovering an Evangelical Heritage* (New York: Harper & Row, 1976).

widows and orphans, and to treat the neighbor as one might wish to be treated—that made so many evangelical Christians willing to risk their lives and fortunes in their quest to fight injustice, care for the needy, reform prisons, and rid the nation of the scourge of slavery. Christians have suffered mightily over the centuries in their efforts to preserve "the faith once delivered to the saints." But their deep desire to obey Scripture, as the work of Timothy Smith and others has so clearly demonstrated, has also been for many believers a powerful engine for change and an enormous motivation for social reform.[9]

Given evangelicalism's historical commitment to social justice, in both America and Britain, how are we to make sense of fundamentalism's seeming disinterest in such matters?[10] The answer, according to sociologist David O. Moberg, can be found in what he called the "Great Reversal."[11] As modernists became increasingly identified with the Social Gospel movement, many fundamentalists abandoned the language of social reform.[12] When modernists talked about building the kingdom of God on earth, many fundamentalists focused increased attention on the rapture of the church and the prospect of a better life in heaven.[13] The modernist pastors preached about social injustice, the fundamentalist preachers tended to concentrate their message on the important work of evangelism.[14]

It is possible, of course, that the "Great Reversal" was more a matter of rhetoric than of reality. As historian Norris Magnuson demonstrated in his superb study, *Salvation in the Slums*, substantial numbers of evangelical Christians remained vigorously active in social ministries—especially among the burgeoning immigrant populations in America's expanding cities—at the very time that social gospel language was falling out of favor within fundamentalist communities.[15] While modernists may have talked more about social action, evangelical Christians in the Salvation Army, in scores of city missions, and on the mission fields of the world continued

9. The preceding two paragraphs are taken from my introduction to the 2005 edition of Smith, *Revivalism and Social Reform*.

10. For example, see the Clapham group and its most famous member, William Wilberforce. See William Wilberforce, *A Practical View of Christianity*, edited by Kevin C. Belmonte with a foreword by Garth M. Rosell and an introduction by Charles Colson (Peabody, MA: Hendrickson, 1996); and Kevin Belmonte, *Hero for Humanity: A Biography of William Wilberforce* (Colorado Springs: NavPress, 2002).

11. The term "Great Reversal," as Moberg acknowledges in the preface, was actually borrowed from Timothy L. Smith. For his helpful argument, see David O. Moberg, *The Great Reversal: Evangelism and Social Concern*, rev. ed. (Philadelphia and New York: Lippincott, 1977), 11, 30.

12. See Ronald C. White and C. Howard Hopkins, *Social Gospel: Religion and Reform in a Changing America* (Philadelphia: Temple University Press, 1975).

13. See Timothy P. Weber, *Living in the Shadow of the Second Coming: American Premillennialism, 1875–1925* (Chicago: University of Chicago Press, 1987).

14. See Henry, "The Uneasy Conscience Revisited," 3–9.

15. See Magnuson, *Salvation in the Slums*.

to feed the hungry, find shelter for the homeless, and provide concrete help for those in need.

Many of these, like the members of Boston's Clarendon Street Church, clearly remembered the passionate calls to social engagement by evangelical pastors such as their own Adoniram Judson Gordon.[16] "Into our doors," he had reminded his listeners as early as 1887, the "populations of the Old World are pouring by the hundreds of thousands every year." The church, moreover, "is the one institution in which every man's wealth is under mortgage to every man's want." Consequently, he warned, "as surely as darkness follows sunset, will the alienation of the masses follow sanctimonious selfishness in the church. If a Christian's motto is, 'Look out for number one,' then let him look out for estrangement and coldness on the part of number two." It is not "an orthodox creed that repels the masses, but an orthodox greed."[17] Whatever the reasons for fundamentalism's seeming indifference to social issues, by the 1930s it was increasingly apparent that modernism had become identified with the social gospel whereas fundamentalism had become more exclusively identified with evangelism.[18]

"The first prominent spokesman calling for a revival of interest in social issues," argued David Moberg, "was Carl F. H. Henry." Calling for a "new reformation," Henry's *Uneasy Conscience of Modern Fundamentalism* spelled out "the implications of personal regeneration for social as well as individual problems."[19] Henry minced no words in his indictment of fundamentalism for its lack of an adequate social agenda. "The great majority of Fundamentalist clergymen, during the past generation of world disintegration," he wrote, "became increasingly less vocal about social evils." How many of you, he asked a group of evangelical pastors, over the course of the past six months "have preached a sermon devoted in large part to a condemnation of such social evils as aggressive warfare, racial hatred and intolerance, the liquor traffic, exploitation of labor or management, or the like?" "Not a single hand," he reported, "was raised in response." "For the first protracted period in its history," Henry lamented, "evangelical Christianity stands divorced from the great social reform movements."

16. For an excellent study of Gordon, see Scott M. Gibson, *A. J. Gordon: American Premillennialist* (Lanham, MD: University Press of America, 2001).

17. A. J. Gordon, "Individual Responsibility Growing Out of Our Perils and Opportunities," in *National Perils and Opportunities: The Discussions of the General Christian Conference of the Evangelical Alliance* (New York: Baker & Taylor, 1887), 379–90. I am indebted to Grant Wacker for bringing this fascinating article to my attention. For an expanded version of this discussion, see my introduction to Magnuson, *Salvation in the Slums*.

18. See Moberg, *The Great Reversal*, 204–5. For a helpful analysis of the continuing patterns, see Robert Wuthnow, *The Struggle for America's Soul: Evangelicals, Liberals, and Secularism* (Grand Rapids: Eerdmans, 1989), esp. 19–38.

19. Moberg, *The Great Reversal*, 160.

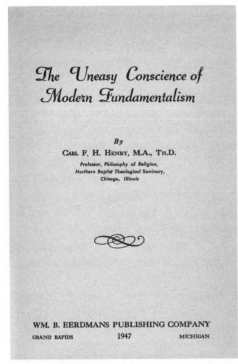

The Uneasy Conscience of Modern Fundamentalism

By
CARL F. H. HENRY, M.A., TH.D.
Professor, Philosophy of Religion,
Northern Baptist Theological Seminary,
Chicago, Illinois

WM. B. EERDMANS PUBLISHING COMPANY
GRAND RAPIDS   1947   MICHIGAN

Title page from Carl F. H. Henry's *The Uneasy Conscience of Modern Fundamentalism*

While affirming fundamentalism's theological orthodoxy, realistic assessment of a fallen human nature, and commitment to the supernatural work of God, Henry criticized the movement for "its spirit of independent isolationism," "overly-emotional type of revivalism," "tendency to replace great church music by a barn-dance variety of semi-religious choruses," and, most especially, "ethical irresponsibility." "It is not fair to say that the ethical platform of all conservative churches has clustered about such platitudes as 'abstain from intoxicating beverages, movies, dancing, card-playing and smoking,'" Henry remarked, "but there are multitudes of Fundamentalist congregations in which these are the main points of reference for ethical speculation."[20]

"If evangelicals believe that the enduring corrective of modernity's badly-skewed ethical and epistemic compass is the self-disclosed God and his moral agenda," Henry reflected forty years after *Uneasy Conscience* was published,

> they had better say so in this crucial turning-time in America. Otherwise they may soon find themselves aliens in a once promised land. We may even now live in the half-generation before hell breaks loose and, if its fury is contained, we will be remembered if we are remembered at all, as those who used their hands and hearts and minds and very bodies to plug the dikes against impending doom.[21]

Had Harold John Ockenga been present when Henry questioned the evangelical pastors, at least one hand would have been raised. Indeed, long before the 1947 publication of *The Uneasy Conscience*, Ockenga had preached numerous times on every one of the issues on Henry's list—racial hatred and

20. Henry, *The Uneasy Conscience*, 1–11.
21. Henry, "The Uneasy Conscience Revisited," 9.

intolerance, exploitation of labor, the liquor traffic, aggressive warfare—and many more besides.

Racial Prejudice

While he was still in his twenties and pastor of the Point Breeze Presbyterian Church in Pittsburgh, for example, Ockenga had already addressed the issue of racial prejudice.[22] Throughout history, Ockenga admitted, "the race problem has been the source of hatred, murder, and innumerable cruel wars," yet the "rise and expansion of the white race is one of the most sordid chapters" in that history. "Brutality, frauds, pillage, plunder, cruelty, knavery, and human horror, have followed in its trail. The white man appropriated whatsoever he desired," Ockenga continued. "One need not be a student to recognize how the brown, yellow, and black peoples have been browbeaten and robbed of life and liberty by white exploitation."[23]

"In America we have the peculiar condition of the presence of many racial groups, intermingling in economic and social life. Into our country have been poured the accumulated hatreds of the ages," Ockenga lamented, "until racial prejudice is one of the greatest problems and sins of our country." There is "no excuse for the treatment which the predominant Nordics in America have accorded to other racial groups. No stain is darker upon our shield of justice than the treatment of the negro."[24]

Yet "all of mankind," Ockenga continued, "are members of the same human family." We are united in our sinfulness, we are all of one blood, we all bear the image of God, and we all stand in need of salvation. Through his work on the cross, Christ "has broken down the middle wall of partition" so that there is no longer "Jew or Gentile, black or white, bond or free, but all men are one in Christ." "Herein, rests the great truth of the Christian family. Whereas, humanly speaking, we are all members of the human family through birth; we through the new birth become members of the Christian family." Christ's redemption "is the secret of the regeneration of the world, and it is the solution for race prejudice."[25]

Ockenga's convictions about racial injustice, while perhaps unusual for his historical era, would hardly have sounded strange to his evangelical heroes, John Wesley and Charles G. Finney.[26] Wesley for example, whose

22. Harold John Ockenga, "Race Prejudice," sermon preached at Point Breeze Presbyterian Church, October 14, 1934, Ockenga Papers. See also Harold John Ockenga, "God's Answer to the Question, 'Am I My Brother's Keeper?'" sermon 854, preached at Park Street Church, October 4, 1942; and "The Christian Faces Segregation and Other Social Problems," undated sermon 2050, Ockenga Papers.

23. Ockenga, "Race Prejudice."

24. Ibid.

25. Ibid.

26. See Harold John Ockenga, "The Warmed Heart of John Wesley and Methodism," undated sermon preached at Park Street Church; and Ockenga, "The Secret of America's Greatest Revivalist," sermon on Charles G. Finney preached at Park Street Church in 1937, Ockenga Papers.

life and thought had profoundly shaped Ockenga's mother's faith and his own, had "attacked slavery as a contradiction of humanity, reason, and natural law."[27] Do not "be weary of well doing," Wesley had written in a letter to William Wilberforce supporting his efforts to bring an end to the slave trade throughout the British Empire. "Go on, in the name of God and in the power of his might, till even American slavery (the vilest that ever saw the sun) shall vanish away before it." Then referring to a tract he had just read that morning by "a poor African," Wesley continued, "I was particularly struck by that circumstance that a man who has a black skin, being wronged or outraged by a white man, can have no redress; it being a 'law' in all our colonies that the *oath* of a black against a white goes for nothing. What villainy is this?"[28]

Ockenga, of course, was well aware of Wesley's writings on the subject of slavery. His 1934 sermon "Race Prejudice," in fact, seems to draw some of its inspiration from Wesley's 1774 tract, *Thoughts upon Slavery*. It is God's intention, Wesley had argued, that "every child of man," indeed "every partaker of human nature," should enjoy the benefits of liberty. "Let none serve you," he wrote, "but by his own act and deed, by his own voluntary choice." So "away with all whips, all chains, all compulsion! Be gentle toward all men. And see that you invariably do unto every one, as you would he should do unto you." Since it is God, Wesley was convinced, "who hast mingled of one blood, all the nations upon earth," it is the church's obligation to place itself clearly on the side of mercy, justice, and truth.[29]

In addition to the influence of Wesley, Ockenga also drew inspiration from the man whom he considered "America's greatest revivalist." God's work is hindered, Charles Finney had argued a century earlier, "when ministers and *churches take wrong ground in regard to any question involving human rights.*" "The time has come," Finney continued, when we must hear the "cries of lamentation, mourning and woe. Two millions of degraded heathen in our own land stretch their hands, all shackled and bleeding, and send forth to the church of God the agonizing cry for help." For far too long, the church has "taken the wrong side on the subject of slavery," allowing "prejudice to prevail over principle." Indeed, it is time we called this "abomination by its true name"—and recognized that slavery is a great "sin."[30] Ockenga would certainly have agreed.[31]

27. Leon O. Hynson, *To Reform the Nation: Theological Foundations of Wesley's Ethics* (Grand Rapids: Francis Asbury, 1984), 49.

28. Wesley to Wilberforce, February 24, 1791, in *John Wesley*, ed. Albert C. Outler (New York: Oxford University Press, 1980), 85–86.

29. John Wesley, *Thoughts Upon Slavery* (London: R. Hawes, 1774), 29–53.

30. Charles G. Finney, *Lectures on Revivals of Religion*, ed. William G. McLoughlin (Cambridge, MA: Harvard University Press, 1960), 287–89. See also Garth M. Rosell and Richard A. G. Dupuis, eds., *The Memoirs of Charles G. Finney* (Grand Rapids: Zondervan, 1989), 411–31.

31. While it is beyond the scope of this study, a systematic analysis of Ockenga's early writing and preaching on social issues could provide some useful perspectives on the development of evangelical

Poverty

While Ockenga was concerned about racial relations, he was even more troubled by the problem of poverty.[32] Having grown up in Chicago under the shadow of a world at war, he had observed firsthand both the excesses of the "Roaring 20s" and the grinding poverty and winding breadlines that followed the 1929 crash of the stock market. While his own family had not suffered the kinds of dislocations that had touched many homes during that period, Ockenga was aware of its impact on many within the congregations he served throughout the early years of his own pastoral ministry.[33]

During his years in Pittsburgh, for example, he began a serious study of the causes of poverty and its possible cure. Having enrolled as a master of arts student at the University of Pittsburgh, he selected as his thesis topic a study of the role of competition in Karl Marx. "The 1929–34 economic crisis has stimulated a revival of Marxism," he observed in the introduction to his thesis. Marx had "prophesied that periodic crises were inevitable under the capitalist system" and he was convinced that "capitalism contains the inherent forces which will destroy it as a system." Since "competition" is the most important of these "inherent forces," Ockenga chose to make that the focus of his thesis. "The work of this thesis," he wrote at the conclusion of his study, "is merely an analysis of the two kinds of competition—in capitalism and in communism. It is not an evaluation of either."[34]

Building on these theoretical foundations, Ockenga used his doctoral studies at the University of Pittsburgh to focus more particularly on poverty. "Why become so agitated over poverty, as if you could banish it from the world?" he asked in the foreword to his doctoral thesis, titled "Poverty as a Theoretical and Practical Problem of Government in the Writings of Jeremy Bentham and the Marxian Alternative." While "poverty is an abiding fact," he wrote in response to his own question, it is incumbent upon all of us to seek "the most fruitful means of mitigating its evils." Although "we are not to give a panacea to end poverty," he argued, "we are to examine ways and means of meeting the perennial problem."[35]

---

attitudes and practices with respect to personal and social ethics, and be a helpful addition to the important work that has already been done on Carl F. H. Henry's *Uneasy Conscience*.

32. See, for example, Ockenga, "The Man Hit By A Depression," sermon preached at Point Breeze Presbyterian Church, June 21, 1931; and "God and the Depression," sermon preached at Point Breeze Presbyterian Church, April 17, 1932, Ockenga Papers.

33. See Robert S. McElvaine, *The Great Depression: America 1929–1941* (New York: Three Rivers, 1993); and Studs Terkel, *Hard Times: An Oral History of the Great Depression* (New York: Norton, 2000).

34. Harold John Ockenga, "The Role of Competition in Marx," MA thesis, University of Pittsburgh, 1934, 1, 135; typed manuscript copy in the Ockenga Papers.

35. Harold John Ockenga, "Poverty as a Theoretical and Practical Problem of Government in the Writings of Jeremy Bentham and the Marxian Alternative" (PhD diss., University of Pitts-

The two most influential approaches to poverty, Ockenga was convinced, were those represented by Jeremy Bentham on the one side and Karl Marx on the other. The first alternative, which he called "the classical doctrine," rejected "minimum wage laws, doles and relief by government" and called for a "system of poorhouses, non-governmental interference and self-dependence." It was, he observed, "the prevailing method of treating poverty in America till recent years." The second alternative, which Ockenga labeled "radicalism," "demands that the government shall take over the regulation of individual and business life by means of housing, public works, social security, wage legislation, agricultural planning and industrial regulation in price fixing and production processes."[36]

Although Ockenga did not state his own preference in the thesis, he seems to have rejected both the utilitarian philosophy of Bentham and the radical philosophy of Marx. Rather than adopting either alternative, Ockenga was quite sure that the solution to the "social question," as he liked to call it, could be found in Scripture. "God has not left us without guidance," he declared, but has "given us principles" by which to solve our problems. Using as his outline the familiar slogan of the French revolution, "Liberty, Equality, and Fraternity," Ockenga spelled out for his Park Street parishioners in 1943 the competing nature of "liberty and equality," the mediating capacity of "fraternity," and the absolute necessity of God's transforming work on the cross.[37]

In all human relationships, be they parent and child, husband and wife, or employer and employee, God regards each party—"the great or the small," the "servant or master," the "black or white," the "male or female"—with exactly the same care and concern. "There is no respect of persons with God," Ockenga declared. "There is no difference out of Christ," for all are "sinners" in need of salvation. "There is no difference in Christ," for all are "Christians and children of God." Consequently, from the divine perspective, all individuals are both free and equal. "Christianity unqualifiedly teaches equalitarianism as well as liberty, but it teaches a third principle which brings these together," namely, "fraternity."[38]

"Liberty must be modified if it is to be harmonized with equality," Ockenga continued, "and equality must be adjusted and give way before liberty, but these conceptions must do their compromising within the range of the family." The "rights, liberties and positions" that are often demanded "outside the family" simply "have no meaning inside the family." Indeed, the "French had it right. The motto must include the three, liberty, equality, and fraternity." The problem, of course, is that individuals often "do not think as Christians, and

burgh, 1939), 7; typed manuscript copy in the Ockenga Papers. See also "Abstract of a Doctor's Dissertation," *University of Pittsburgh Bulletin* 36, no. 4 (January 15, 1940): 1–9.

36. Ockenga, "Poverty as a Theoretical and Practical Problem," 7, 17–18.

37. Harold John Ockenga, "The Solution to the Social Problem," sermon preached at Park Street Church, October 10, 1943, Ockenga Papers.

38. Ibid.

they do not believe in human brotherhood." The only adequate solution is the cross of Christ. When a person "has an experience of Christ at the cross, accepting Him as his Savior, and through Him returning unto the father's house, he becomes a member of the household of Faith. From him are removed his hates, his antipathies, his pride, and his rebellion."[39]

"What would happen" to "employer-employee" relations, "race consciousness," "social inequality and injustices," and "class conflicts," Ockenga asked, if people were to gather at the foot of the cross? The result, Ockenga was convinced, would be the overthrow of "exploitation, injustice, and oppression." True Christianity begins "with our vertical relationship to God" but it must always include our "horizontal relationship with men." Since "what we do to men, we do to God," God will hold us "responsible for our deeds." "Christianity is the most practical element in life," Ockenga concluded. "Embrace Christ and the crux of the social question is removed."[40]

The Problem of War

"Because we do not have peace between individuals, between classes, or between nations," Ockenga told his Point Breeze Presbyterian congregation in 1935, "[I will] defend my sister against assault, my city against criminals, and my nation against revolution or enemies. We must have an army as surely as police and if we enjoy the safety and protection we should also bear the responsibility."

"Although the mass slaughter of modern war is repulsive," he continued, I can "have no sympathy with these ultra pacifists." While we must do everything in our power to avert war, Ockenga concluded, there are "conditions," drawn from classic "just war theory," under which wars can appropriately be fought. Indeed, "some things are worse than war."[41]

The Abuse of Alcohol

Throughout his early ministry, Ockenga also addressed issues relating to the manufacture, distribution, and abuse of hard liquor. Drawing once again on his Wesleyan roots, Ockenga warned his Park Street congregation of the "awful menace, that soul-destroying menace, that life-killing menace, alcohol," a substance that "has taken more lives than all our wars" and "more money than all of our worship of God, our education of our children, and the entertainment that we enjoy."

39. Ibid.
40. Ibid.
41. Quotations are taken from Harold John Ockenga, "The Bible and War," sermon preached at Point Breeze Presbyterian Church, November 10, 1935. See also Ockenga, "War—Are We Dupes of the Munition Makers?" sermon preached at Point Breeze Presbyterian Church, November 11, 1934, Ockenga Papers. Ockenga was for a time a reserve chaplain in the Navy.

After developing a biblical and historical argument for total abstinence, Ockenga challenged his hearers to commit themselves to a five point program to end the production, distribution, and use of alcohol. "First," he said, "accept Christ in your life and make him Lord of your life. Christ and liquor will have no part one with another." Second, allow your life "to be filled with the Spirit." Third, "talk with the children in the church and the home and warn them of the evils of drink." Fourth, commit to "abstinence" and "write in your Bible, 'I will abstain from all alcoholic beverages.'" Fifth, call upon government to "step in" to regulate and control "the liquor traffic." Although, he added, "I am a Libertarian and believe that government control should be reduced to the least common denominator," this is a case where "evil" practices are "violating" human "rights and privileges." So, he concluded, "I challenge you as Christians tonight to fight this thing in the church, to fight it in your home, fight it in society, fight it by the ballot, fight it with local option, fight it with your influence, fight it with your testimony all down the line, and God knows how many souls by that you may save from hell and turn to him."[42]

Additional Issues

In addition to such issues as racial prejudice, poverty, war, and the liquor traffic, Harold John Ockenga regularly addressed a wide variety of other social and political concerns—from capital punishment, crime, and international aid to mental health, divorce, and communism—throughout his ministry in the 1930s and 1940s.[43] "Recently, while preaching a sermon on 'The Influence of the Church in the Labor Crisis,'" he wrote in his introduction to Henry's *The Uneasy Conscience of Modern Fundamentalism*, "I evoked a comment from a Christian soldier. Said he, 'I became a political liberal on my knees, though I am a Fundamentalist in faith. Why must the church be on the wrong side of every major social issue?'" Well, Ockenga responded, "if the Bible-believing Christian is on the wrong side of social problems

42. Quotations are taken from Harold John Ockenga, "America's Great Menace," undated sermon 1861. See also Ockenga, "Liquor: What is Following Prohibition?" sermon preached at Point Breeze Presbyterian Church, October 21, 1934, Ockenga Papers.

43. See, for example, Harold John Ockenga, "Crime," sermon preached at Point Breeze Presbyterian Church, October 28, 1935; "The Evaluation of Capital Punishment," sermon preached at Park Street Church, January 3, 1965; "The Christian View of Marriage, Separation and Divorce," sermon preached at Point Breeze Presbyterian Church, October 7, 1934, and at Park Street Church, November 17, 1940; "Mental Health," sermon preached at Point Breeze Presbyterian Church, May 20, 1934; "God and the Struggle for Bread," sermon preached at Point Breeze Presbyterian Church, June 28, 1936; "The Movies," sermon preached at Point Breeze Presbyterian Church, September 30, 1934; "Communism and the Christian Faith," undated sermon; "The Dual Allegiance of Christians," sermon preached at Park Street Church, November 22, 1964; and "The European Crisis," sermon preached at Point Breeze Presbyterian Church, October 8, 1933, Ockenga Papers.

such as war, race, class, labor, liquor, imperialism, etc. it is time to get over the fence to the right side. The church needs a progressive Fundamentalism with a social message."[44]

The Root Problem

Since both Ockenga and Henry believed that social problems are rooted in human rebellion against God, beginning with Adam and Eve's disobedience in the garden, they were convinced that only the atoning work of Christ on the cross was sufficient to forgive sins, tame the rebellious heart, and bring genuine peace with God. Consequently, the fundamental solution to human sinfulness and the starting point for all genuine social reform is the transforming power of the gospel. "The evangelical task," as Henry phrased it, "primarily is the preaching of the Gospel, in the interest of individual regeneration by the supernatural grace of God, in such a way that divine redemption can be recognized as the best solution of our problems, individual and social."[45] Unlike many of their contemporaries, Ockenga and Henry seemed to understand the nature of evil in corporate as well as individual terms. Indeed, Henry concluded his *Uneasy Conscience of Modern Fundamentalism* with a plea for the understanding of Christianity as both "a life view" and "a world view." While individual Christians are responsible to apply biblical principles in every aspect of their daily lives, the Christian community must also join hands in collective efforts to address difficult structural evils such as racism, crime, and injustice. The principal reason for the establishment of the NAE, after all, was to encourage and facilitate united evangelical action.

To neglect the great social issues of the day, therefore, was simply not an option. Those who had abandoned the public square needed to be reminded of Christ's command to be "salt and light" in an increasingly corrupt world. Those who had given up on the political process needed to be reminded that genuine change is possible through wise and wholesome laws. Those who expected immediate results needed to be reminded of the need for hard work over many years. Those who thought they could achieve great goals by themselves needed to be reminded of the importance of Christian community. Those who had grown cynical and pessimistic needed to be reminded that the gospel is still able to transform individual lives, to renew decaying institutions, to motivate individuals for a lifetime of benevolence, and to provide hope in a world of despair. "Christianity," Ockenga argued, must be the "mainspring" in the reform

44. Ockenga, "Introduction," in Henry, *The Uneasy Conscience*, xx. See also Harold John Ockenga, "Labor, or What Ails the Workingman?" sermon preached at Point Breeze Presbyterian Church, September 16, 1934, Ockenga Papers. I was unable to locate a sermon that might fit the "recently preached" description to which Ockenga referred in the introduction.

45. Henry, *The Uneasy Conscience*, 88–89.

"of the social order. It is wrong to abdicate responsibility for society under the impetus of a theology which over-emphasizes the eschatological."[46]

The Renewal of the Church

Evangelicalism's second major goal, as Harold John Ockenga described the agenda in his article on *Resurgent Evangelical Leadership*, was the renewal of the church. Under the "unremitting attacks of the modernists," fundamentalists were maneuvered into a defensive position, Ockenga argued. "Gradually," as they withdrew from their churches and began to circle the wagons, "the liberals took over control of the denominations." As the ecclesiastical power of the modernists increased, so too did their programs of "discrimination, ostracism and persecution" against the fundamentalists. Finding themselves increasingly "impotent in denominational machinery" and seemingly determined to remain largely "indifferent to the societal problems," Ockenga concluded, fundamentalism was "defeated in the ecclesiastical scene."[47]

The main problem as Ockenga saw it was fundamentalism's "erroneous doctrine of the Church." He argued that "2 Corinthians 6:14–17 was used to justify the continuous process of fragmentation." While their doctrinal orthodoxy was certainly commendable, fundamentalism's separatist mentality was wrongheaded and dangerous. Indeed, by placing almost all of their energy on the tasks of contending for the faith and avoiding any appearance of being "yoked together with unbelievers," fundamentalism had in Ockenga's opinion neglected the church's God-given responsibilities for "missions, evangelism, education and worship." Small wonder, he concluded, that "fewer and fewer great scholars were found in the evangelical ranks as the decades passed."[48]

While Harold John Ockenga remained committed to theological purity, he was equally passionate about the need for evangelical unity. "Cooperation without compromise," had become a byword for the NAE. Difficult as it might be to achieve, Ockenga and his colleagues remained unwilling to yield either purity or unity. There were many, of course, who remained equally convinced that Ockenga and his colleagues were abandoning purity in their quest for unity. "One of the chief differences between New Evangelicals and Fundamentalists," argued Ernest Pickering in his book, *The Tragedy of Compromise*, "concerns the views of each regarding what we call 'ecclesiastical separation.' Fundamentalist separatists believe that there should be complete separation from all churches and fellowships of churches that tolerate unbelief or compromise with error." The NAE, on the other hand, advocated "cooperation without compromise." "Although few would dispute the accuracy of the first word in

46. Ockenga, "Resurgent Evangelical Leadership," 6.
47. Ibid., 11–15.
48. Ibid.

describing the NAE," Pickering suggested, "many would raise serious questions about the last two."[49]

Although the issue of ecclesiastical separation had been simmering for years, it came to a full boil following Ockenga's convocation address "The Challenge to the Christian Culture of the West" at the inauguration of Fuller Theological Seminary in 1947.[50] After describing the enormous challenges facing the church in the wake of the tragic decline of Christian influence in western culture, Ockenga sketched a rationale for establishing the new seminary. Fuller

"United Action" in a Nut-Shell (courtesy of Wheaton College Archives and Special Collections)

Theological Seminary, he declared, was being established to capture the burgeoning west "for evangelical Christianity"; "restate the principles of western culture"; "specialize in apologetic literature"; "rebuild the foundations of society"; "lay hold upon and grapple" with the great issues of the day; reclaim "our Christian heritage"; produce scholarly books; promote and maintain the highest possible "spiritual and intellectual standards"; provide "lectureships" by "visiting professors from abroad"; help meet the "shortage of preachers in every major denomination"; train "preachers, . . . missionaries, evangelists, educators," and "leaders in every phase of Christian endeavor"; and provide "leadership in social, educational and civic responsibility."[51]

Then, shifting his attention from the larger goals to the more particular policies that would guide the new institution, Ockenga declared:

49. Ernest D. Pickering, *The Tragedy of Compromise: The Origin and Impact of the New Evangelicalism* (Greenville, SC: Bob Jones University Press, 1994), vii, 21.

50. Harold John Ockenga, "The Challenge to the Christian Culture of the West," convocation address at the inauguration of Fuller Theological Seminary, Pasadena, California, October 1, 1947, Ockenga Papers.

51. Ibid.

We intend to be ecclesiastically free. To cooperate with all evangelical denominations. It is our intention and desire that our students may come from the
Denominations and may go back to the Denominations to cooperate, to take a
place of leadership, to infuse evangelical conviction and life and to strengthen
the church that is. *We repudiate the "Come-outist" movement which brands all
Denominations as apostate.* We expect to be positive in our emphasis, except
where error so exists that it is necessary for us to point it out in order to declare
the truth. This positive emphasis will be on the broad doctrinal basis of a low
Calvinism. We expect to develop a social theory which will express our Christian conviction on the burning issues of the hour.[52]

While most of Ockenga's address was quickly forgotten, this single paragraph—and most especially the single sentence which has been identified
by italics—seemed to take on a life of its own. "We cannot but be deeply
disturbed," wrote the editor of the *Presbyterian Guardian*, "by some of this
language." While granting that Ockenga may have been speaking "unguard-
edly," he "gives the impression that he and the new seminary are irrevocably
opposed to ecclesiastical separation under any circumstances. He seems to say
that it is immaterial in which denomination men preach so long as they preach
the Gospel." "The seminaries which are established upon the Scriptures," he
continued, "face a solemn challenge today, not only to furnish ministers who
can effectively proclaim the Gospel, but who also will labor for the purity of
the church, regardless of the opposition that may emerge on that account."
It is our hope, he concluded, that Fuller Seminary will "stand unflinchingly"
for "the supremacy of Christ's Word; and that it will resist, rather than drift
along with, the current of ecclesiastical indifferentism which is sapping the
vitals of organized Christianity."[53]

The editor of the *Presbyterian Guardian* was not alone in expressing
his concerns. Scores of letters, editorials, phone calls, and faculty discussions followed Ockenga's address—each with its own agenda and point of
view. Even Billy Hawks, Ockenga's old friend and colleague on the Taylor
Evangelistic Team, wrote of his concerns. "I wish you would come and see
me," he wrote in December of 1947. "I feel like weeping and lamenting

---

52. Italics have been added. See Ockenga, "The Challenge to the Christian Culture of the West,"
10–11, Ockenga Papers. A slightly different wording of this paragraph appeared in the Fuller Theological Seminary's *Bulletin* following the address: "May I say just a word about our policy? We do not
intend to be ecclesiastically bound. We will be free. But we are ecclesiastically positive. In our church
relationships though we are inter-denominational, we do not believe and we repudiate the 'come-outism' movement. We want our men to be so trained that when they come from a denomination, whatever
that denomination is, they will go back into their denomination adequately prepared to preach the
Gospel and to defend the faith and to positively go forward in the world of God."

53. Ned B. Stonehouse, "Fuller Seminary and Separatism," *Presbyterian Guardian*, February 10,
1948, 35. For another interesting example, see James E. Bennet to Carl F. H. Henry, a letter from a
New York attorney, published under the title, "Bennet Defends Come-Outers to Seminary Professor,"
Christian Beacon, November 1, 1947, Ockenga Papers.

and mourning over you. Everything that I read spoken against you touches me to the quick, yet some of the things you are doing only cause me grief and heaviness of heart." It "grieves me Harold to see you giving way here a little and there a little to policies that will be the ruination of our country." You "ought to be a trumpet of God in America," yet you "are fast succumbing" to the "inclusivistic trends that will sink us into the sea of oblivion spiritually as surely as it has the countries across the sea." "Christ will spew lukewarm men out of his mouth." Therefore, he concluded, I must "plead with you to stand out against the policy mongers of our day. Combination is weakness! Separatism is Power! in the sight of God."[54]

"Concerning one brief statement of my address given at the 1947 Convocation of Fuller Seminary," Ockenga wrote in response to his critics, "some misunderstanding, misinterpretation, and misquotation have occurred. Wide circulation," he continued, "has been given to a partial statement—'We repudiate the come-outism movement'—without considering the context of the statement."[55] Some had interpreted his comments, Ockenga reflected, "as a repudiation of fundamentalism or as a criticism of the independent church movement," or as a ruling-out of every kind of "separation movement" or as an attack on "the independence and sovereignty of the local church." None of these meanings was intended. Rather, Ockenga argued, his comments were aimed at those

ORGAN PRELUDE   *Great Hymns of the Faith*
        GEORGE BROADBENT *at the Manual*

All Hail the Power of Jesus Name   ELLOR
        REVIVAL HOUR CHORUS
        H. LELAND GREEN, M.S.E., *Directing*

Invocation   CARL F. H. HENRY, M.A., TH.D.

How Firm a Foundation   KEITH
        Congregational Hymn
WELCOME   ⎫
THE BIRTH OF THE SEMINARY   ⎬ CHARLES E. FULLER, D.D.
PRESENTATION OF THE FACULTY   ⎭

There Is a Fountain   COWPER
        REVIVAL HOUR QUARTET
        Congregation uniting for last stanza

SCRIPTURE   EVERETT F. HARRISON, A.M., TH.D.

PRAYER   WILBUR M. SMITH, D.D.

My Heavenly Father Watches Over Me   GABRIEL
        REVIVAL HOUR QUARTET
        WILLIAM MacDOUGALL, *Soloist*
ANNOUNCEMENTS, REGISTRATION, OFFERING

Sanctus   GOUNOD
        REVIVAL HOUR CHORUS
        JOSEPH BARCLAY, *Soloist*

ADDRESS: "The Challenge to the Christian Culture of the West"
        PRESIDENT HAROLD JOHN OCKENGA
        PH.D., D.D., L.L.D., LITT.D., HUM.D.

CLOSING REMARKS

BENEDICTION   HAROLD LINDSELL, A.M., PH.D.

Fuller Theological Seminary's opening convocation, October 1, 1947 (courtesy of Fuller Theological Seminary Library Archives)

---

54. William S. Hawks to Harold John Ockenga, December 11, 1947, Ockenga Papers. Hawks was then pastor of the Bible Presbyterian Church in East Orange, New Jersey. For Ockenga's response see Ockenga to Hawks, December 12, 1947, Ockenga Papers.

55. Harold John Ockenga, "Come-Outism," manuscript article in the Ockenga Papers. This and subsequent quotations are taken from this article.

who first "set themselves up in judgment upon churches and denominations," proclaiming one or another of them "apostate" and then demanding "that other evangelicals" leave those denominations or face the charge that they are disloyal to God's Word. When evangelicals within those denominations "do not respond by 'coming out,' because they do not believe that their denominations are apostate," they are labeled "compromisers," "pussyfooters," and "disloyal" by the "come-outers." Rather than respecting the prayerful decisions of fellow believers, Ockenga lamented, the come-outers "criticize, attack, and discomfit" those "who are doing God's work and will."[56]

What seemed to concern Ockenga most deeply was the "assumed right" of the come-outers "to sit in judgment upon their brethren who have continued to labor in the denominations which have been labeled apostate." Not only did "such divisive 'come-outism'" bring "reproach upon the entire evangelical cause," it was also in clear violation of scriptural teaching. Although the church in Corinth was "guilty of division, carnality, drunkenness, and spiritual insubordination," Ockenga argued, the apostle Paul "called the members 'saints,' and he did not advocate that believers come out of the church." Ockenga was convinced that each Christian had an obligation not only to follow his or her own conscience in such difficult decisions but also to honor the decisions of others even though he or she might strongly disagree with the choices that were being made.[57]

In making his case against come-outism, Ockenga was once again working from what he believed to be biblical principle rather than personal experience. However, as historian George Marsden posed the question in his superb study of Fuller Seminary, if evangelicals like Harold John Ockenga were really convinced "that the mainstream denominations were not apostate," why did they not choose to "work through the denominational agencies" rather than investing such enormous energy in creating a whole set of new "transdenominational evangelical agencies" such as Fuller Seminary, the NAE, and *Christianity Today*?[58] When asked why he and his colleagues had decided to start new ventures such as Fuller Theological Seminary, Ockenga tended to offer his standard reply. "We needed new wineskins," he would answer. When great movements of God's Spirit take place within human history, such as the Protestant Reformation of the sixteenth century, the Wesleyan revival of the eighteenth century, or the evangelical resurgence in the twentieth century, the old forms are sometimes unable to contain them. While we should avoid abandoning existing structures too quickly, Ockenga cautioned, there are unique moments in human history when new theological movements require new academic expressions to undergird and support them. The 1940s was precisely such a

56. Ibid.
57. Ibid.
58. George M. Marsden, *Reforming Fundamentalism: Fuller Seminary and the New Evangelicalism* (Grand Rapids: Eerdmans, 1987), 95.

time, and organizations such as the NAE and Fuller Theological Seminary were precisely such wineskins.[59]

The World Council of Churches

This pattern can perhaps be most clearly illustrated by Ockenga's uneasy relationship with the World Council of Churches. The first assembly of the World Council of Churches, scheduled from August 22 through September 5 of 1948, was held in Amsterdam, Holland.[60] "I received your very gracious invitation to become an official and accredited visitor at the First Assembly of the World Council of Churches," Ockenga wrote to the World Council Headquarters in April of 1948, and "I accept this with pleasure and plan to be present."[61] Inspired by the success of the International Missionary Conference held in Edinburgh in 1910, considered by most to be the starting point of the modern ecumenical movement, John R. Mott, William Temple, Willem Adolf Visser't Hooft, and others envisioned "a world Christian body that would link the churches together in unity, mission and service."[62] While a variety of gatherings had been held during the 1930s and 1940s, focusing largely on mission, doctrine, and action, it was not until 1948 that the World Council of Churches was officially established. Taking as its theme, "Man's Disorder and God's Design," the gathering in Amsterdam stirred enormous interest around the world.[63]

Having had their quarrels with the Federal Council of Churches, established in 1908 for the purpose of expressing more fully "the unity of the Christian church" and of increasing its influence in "matters affecting the moral and social condition of American society," leaders in both the NAE and the ACCC had reason to view the upcoming meetings in Amsterdam either with guarded optimism, extreme caution, or outright hostility.[64] "In a recent study of the World Council," wrote the editor of *United Evangelical Action*, "we reached the conclusion that evangelicals must view its rise with alarm." Of primary concern, wrote editor James Murch, was the fear that the council

59. See, for example, Ockenga, "The Distinctives of Seminary Education," a lecture delivered on October 5, 1971, at Gordon-Conwell Theological Seminary, Ockenga Papers.

60. See "First Assembly of the World Council of Churches," *Bulletin* no. 4 (June 1948); and Eleanor K. Browne to Delegates, Alternates, Accredited Visitors, Fraternal Delegates, and Observers, instructional letter with an enclosure, "Towards Amsterdam, August 1948," March 1948, Ockenga Papers.

61. Harold John Ockenga to Willem Adolf Visser't Hooft, April 20, 1948; see also Henry Smith Leiper to Ockenga, April 7 and May 16, 1948, Ockenga Papers.

62. P. A. Crow, "World Council of Churches," in *Dictionary of Christianity in America*, ed. Daniel G. Reid, Robert D. Linder, Bruce L. Shelley, and Harry S. Stout (Downers Grove, IL: InterVarsity, 1990), 1273–75.

63. A classic study of the movement is H. E. Fey, ed., *A History of the Ecumenical Movement*, 2 vols., 4th ed. (1967, 1970; repr., Geneva: Consul Oecumenique, 1993).

64. In 1950, the Federal Council of Churches merged with about a dozen other organizations to form the National Council of Churches.

was "theologically weak," power hungry, and inadequately committed to the authority of "the infallible Word of God and the Christ who is Lord and King of His Church." If the World Council turned out to be "Babylon instead of Jerusalem," he concluded, it is hoped that evangelicals will have "the courage to withdraw."[65]

"I have just read with sorrow and amazement your editorial" wrote Henry Smith Leiper, the associate general secretary of the American Committee for the World Council of Churches, after reading the February 15 issue of *United Evangelical Action*. "Is not an 'evangelical' a 'bearer of good news?'" he asked at the close of his lengthy defense of the WCC. "It would be a pleasure to read good news from your pen about your brethren in a world where one would suppose that the words of the Master are more than ever applicable: 'Those who are not against us are for us.'"[66]

Given the grand vision of reclaiming the culture for Christ, to which Ockenga and his evangelical colleagues seemed so clearly committed, one might have expected that they would have enthusiastically welcomed the challenge of infiltrating and helping to shape a new organization such as the World Council of Churches.[67] In reality, however, few if any of the evangelicals who attended seemed ready to "roll up their sleeves" and do the hard work that would be necessary to achieve such a goal. Rather, what they seemed prepared to do, as many had done in their relationship with the mainline denominations, was to find their fellowship and expend their energy in organizations old and new over which they could exercise more immediate control. While it is true that limitations of space made it impossible for more than a handful of American evangelicals to secure invitations to attend the World Council meetings as official delegates or visitors, there was certainly no shortage of conference opportunities for the hundreds of evangelicals who traveled to Europe that summer. Ockenga, for example, not only attended the World Council of Churches meetings in Amsterdam but also participated in International Youth for Christ Congress on World Evangelization in Beatenberg, Switzerland (August 10–22, 1948), the European Conference of the International Fellowship of Evangelical Students in Lausanne, Switzerland (August 7–16, 1948), the National Association of Evangelicals Conference of Evangelical Leaders in Clarens, Switzerland

65. James DeForest Murch, "As Amsterdam Nears," *United Evangelical Action*, February 15, 1948, 12–13. Murch provided six primary reasons for his position: (1) the WCC will not be purely evangelical; (2) it will not be strictly Protestant; (3) it will inevitably become a super-church; (4) it will be a political pressure group; (5) it will ostracize dissident churches; and (6) it will be the means of dividing churches in which there is disagreement concerning it.

66. Henry Smith Leiper to James DeForest Murch, March 22, 1948, Ockenga Papers.

67. For a detailed description of the proceedings of the World Council meetings in Amsterdam, see David D. Baker's account, "The World Council Constituted," *Advance*, October 1948, 22–23. The WCC was officially formed on August 23, 1948, by vote of the 400 delegates from 135 churches in 40 countries.

(August 7–11, 1948), and the Remonstrant Brotherhood consultation at Hilversum, Holland (August 20–21, 1948). In addition, he preached at a number of locations throughout Europe as his schedule allowed, and he preached every Sunday in August at D. Martin Lloyd-Jones's Westminster Chapel in London.[68] While it is clear that Ockenga and his colleagues were genuinely interested in the World Council meetings, their most satisfying fellowship and most enthusiastic participation was reserved for the other conferences and meetings that tended to cluster around it.

The Roman Catholic Church

In addition to the growing divisions between the evangelical movement and the World Council of Churches, Ockenga and his colleagues were casting a wary eye in the direction of the Roman Catholic Church. During the summer of 1947, a year before the World Council of Churches meeting in Amsterdam, the United States secretary of war invited fourteen prominent church leaders from America on a tour of Europe. Three Roman Catholic priests, one Jewish rabbi, and ten Protestant ministers—including representatives from both the NAE and the ACCC—were part of the official mission. The itinerary, overseen by the chief of chaplains, included visits to the World Council in Geneva and to the pope at the Vatican.

Harold John Ockenga, who represented the NAE on the tour, reported on the experience in a sermon he delivered at Park Street Church following his return.[69] "Modern air transport made possible an unusual achievement," Ockenga marveled, "interviewing Pope Pius XII, titular head of the Roman Catholic Church, and Dr. Visser't Hooft of the World Council of Churches at its headquarters at Geneva on the same day."[70] Then describing their visit with the pope, Ockenga told his congregation that following brief comments from Pope Pius XII and a response by Methodist Bishop Corson, he had shaken the pope's hand and asked him a question: Is the Roman Catholic Church still opposed to communism as affirmed by his predecessor, Pope Pius XI? "The Pope then launched on an extemporaneous speech," Ockenga continued, "in which he declared" that since "the church was supernaturalistic and communism was naturalistic and materialistic," the two remained "irrevocably irreconcilable." "Is that absolute," Ockenga asked? "Yes, absolute," the pope responded.[71]

68. Lloyd-Jones to Ockenga, October 18 and December 8, 1947, Ockenga Papers. The organizational meeting of the International Council of Christian Churches also met in Amsterdam during August, but Ockenga did not attend. Program materials and correspondence regarding the various conferences and meetings can be found in the "World Council" folder in the Ockenga Papers.

69. Harold John Ockenga, "My Visit With the Pope: Relief and Religious Freedom in Italy," sermon preached on October 5, 1947, Ockenga Papers.

70. The meetings were at 9:00 a.m. in the Vatican and 4:30 p.m. in Geneva.

71. Quotations taken from Ockenga, "My Visit With the Pope," 14–15.

Although the three Roman Catholic priests had declined the invitation to meet with Visser't Hooft in Geneva, only the representative of the ACCC, had refused to see the pope. His concern grew out of a request by the Protestant pastors of Rome that their fellow Protestants on the team refuse to meet with the pope. Fearing that such a meeting would only serve to reinforce an erroneous image of rapprochement between Protestants and Roman Catholics, Rome's Protestant pastors were convinced that the Vatican's persecution of Protestants throughout Italy would remain as strong as ever. "How different it would have been," commented the editor of the *Christian Beacon*, "had the American Protestants stood with these Italian men, and encouraged them in their stand, rather than being a party to helping break their spirit and their resistance."[72]

For those who live in the aftermath of the enormous changes within the Roman Catholic Church as a result of the reformist Second Vatican Council, called by Pope John XXIII during the early 1960s, it is often difficult to understand the deep suspicion and antagonism that existed between Roman Catholics and Protestants throughout the 1940s and 1950s.[73] Ockenga himself, called to minister in America's most dominantly Roman Catholic geographical region,[74] had more than a few run-ins with Boston's Catholic leadership during the course of his Park Street ministry: from the famous "Boston incident" in 1951[75] when Ockenga officially protested a Roman Catholic Mass that was planned for the Boston Common to the intense debates in 1960 over a Roman Catholic candidate's bid for the White House.[76]

The Second Vatican Council had a profound impact on relations between Roman Catholics and Protestants in general and on Harold John Ockenga in particular.[77] "I think there is a tremendous wind of change . . . blowing

72. "One Protestant," editorial in the *Christian Beacon*, reprinted in the *Gospel Witness and Protestant Advocate*, September 11, 1947, Ockenga Papers.

73. For an understanding of Vatican II, see Austin Flannery, ed., *The Basic Sixteen Documents of Vatican Council II: Constitutions, Decrees, Declarations* (Northport, NY: Costello, 1995); David F. Wells, *Revolution in Rome* (Downers Grove, IL: InterVarsity, 1972); G. C. Berkouwer, *The Second Vatican Council and the New Catholicism* (Grand Rapids: Eerdmans, 1965); Norman Geisler and Ralph E. MacKenzie, *Roman Catholics and Evangelicals: Agreements and Differences* (Grand Rapids: Baker Academic, 1995); and Charles Colson and Richard John Neuhaus, eds., *Evangelicals and Catholics Together* (Dallas: Word, 1995).

74. Ockenga estimated that Boston, during his ministry there, was seventy-eight percent Roman Catholic. See Harold John Ockenga, "The Charge to the Church," sermon preached at Park Street Church, October 2, 1966, 3, Ockenga Papers.

75. See "State Official Answers Park Street Minister," *Pilot*, July 14, 1951; Harold John Ockenga to Francis E. Kelly (Massachusetts Attorney General), July 10, 1951; and Kelly to Ockenga, July 5, 1951, Ockenga Papers.

76. Harold John Ockenga, "Religion, Politics and the Presidency," sermon preached at Park Street Church, June 5, 1960, Ockenga Papers.

77. For reflections on Vatican II, see Harold John Ockenga, "The Second Vatican Council," sermon preached at Park Street Church, September 23, 1962, Ockenga Papers.

in the Roman Catholic Church," Ockenga told his Park Street congregation in 1966, and "the Vatican Council probably has been the instigating force of this." However we might view these changes, he continued, "something is happening and it is certainly much different than it was twenty years ago." The changes are evident in an abundance of "little things," he continued. Not only has Billy Graham been warmly welcomed at Catholic institutions such as Boston College, Ockenga observed, but Boston's Cardinal Cushing has also spoken positively of his ministry. Near the front door of Park Street Church, Ockenga recounted with some amazement, a Roman Catholic priest recently "took my hand in both of his and said, 'I hear good things about your preaching.'"[78]

While Ockenga welcomed the friendlier atmosphere, he also warned his listeners against the erosion of doctrine. "Though new breezes are blowing through the ancient halls of the Roman Church, we do know that the basic claims and teachings are unchanged. Reform is touching Rome," he was sure, "but not on the final and ultimate questions." Evangelicals should welcome the "spiritual renewal," "new emphasis upon Bible scholarship, Bible translation and Bible reading," and "inclusion of the laity" that were occurring within Roman Catholicism. "Yet," he concluded, "we have no expectation of Rome changing its dogmatic teaching, its absolute claims, and its intolerant ways."[79]

The Attack Becomes Personal

Given Ockenga's deep roots in the Wesleyan holiness movement, it must have been jolting when he returned from the 1947 tour of Europe to learn that his personal behavior had come under attack. While he had often been criticized for the strong positions he had taken on matters of biblical principle and theological orthodoxy, his personal ethics had remained essentially beyond question.

Throughout the months of autumn, as New England's leaves turned from green to a glorious array of yellows, reds, and oranges, a flurry of letters arrived in Ockenga's Park Street Church postbox asking if the rumors swirling about him were really true. "You are probably aware of the rumors relative to your personal actions while on the European trip this summer," wrote one concerned friend. Other letters added the specifics: that Ockenga had insisted on visiting the pope despite the objections of the Protestant clergy in Rome, that he had made "obeisance" to the Pope when the delegation had visited him in the Vatican, that he was seen drinking "intoxicating liquor" at meals and receptions, that he had attended the opera and theatre in Paris,

78. Ockenga, "The Charge to the Church."
79. Ockenga, "The Second Vatican Council."

and that he had purchased "cigarettes in the P.X. and then sold them on the black market."[80]

Although Ockenga remained publicly silent on the matter, he confided to friends how deeply grieved he was over the behavior of those who claimed to be part of the family of faith. "If it is necessary for me to co-operate with evangelicals who lie, misrepresent and do such harm to their brethren," he lamented, "then I personally will kiss goodbye to the evangelical movement. I am sick and tired of it all." With regard to the specific allegations, Ockenga wrote: "I shook the Pope's hand and made no other form of obeisance whatsoever"; "I did not smoke"; "I have never drunk any liquor except once when my father gave me some whiskey to show me what it was, as a boy, and on two occasions when I tasted champagne, once with my wife on our wedding tour and once this summer in the company of our whole group when several of us had a discussion concerning the taste of champagne"; "I believe in total abstinence, preach it and practice it"; "I did not trade cigarettes on the black market," although he admitted he did give away the free cigarettes that were distributed to the delegation; he went to the theatre with "members of the commission" to "ascertain what our men were imbibing in Class A and B clubs under the Army [and] the Red Cross"; "I went to the opera in Europe at the invitation of the generals"; and finally, he added, when I am at home, my wife and I attend the opera and we have occasionally gone "to the movies, probably once in a year or once in eighteen months. I haven't been more than nine times in ten years."[81]

Ockenga's behavior, in short, was always carefully circumscribed. While he embraced life with zest, joy, curiosity, and delight; relished a beautiful sunset; loved to swim, hike, and ski; enjoyed music and the arts; adored his wife's paintings; loved literature and read broadly, regularly, and deeply; loved to think and analyze and probe interesting ideas; was fascinated by travel, architecture, and history; and loved to meet interesting people and debate ideas with them—nonetheless, he remained even more passionate about the need for personal holiness and purity of life. Consequently, it was not the specific content of the rumors that most deeply troubled Ockenga. As one who was unusually straightforward about his beliefs and practices, he had always welcomed genuine questions and honest correction. Rather, what disturbed him was the attitude toward culture that the charges seemed to betray. "I think that these fundamentalists are doing irreparable harm to our movement," he confided to a friend, "by identifying Christianity with 'Thou shall not.' They have lost all the joy out of Christianity and Christian living. They have made it negative. They are dividing to absurdity and I assure you that I myself will have nothing to do with that kind of movement."[82]

---

80. Quotations from letters in a file titled "European Tour Correspondence," Ockenga Papers.
81. Ibid.
82. Ibid.

Christ and Culture

By adopting what Ockenga believed was a Christ against culture position, to borrow H. Richard Niebuhr's helpful categories, separatists like those in the ACCC had gained a substantial strategic advantage over Ockenga and his evangelical colleagues.[83] Like many in the early church, they came to see themselves as a persecuted minority in a largely pagan society. Since the culture was beyond hope of repair—indeed it stood under the certain judgment of a righteous God—their task was primarily to evangelize, gather a faithful remnant, and keep themselves "unspotted from the world" until the glorious return of Christ and the rapture of the church. While Ockenga and his colleagues were certainly aware of the dangers of a fallen creation, they refused to withdraw from culture or to abandon creation to the Evil One. Rather, they were convinced that Christ could transform culture. Since the whole of creation belongs to God, their task was to help reclaim the culture for Christ by serving as "light and salt" in a dark and decaying world.[84] They were, as they liked to phrase it, to be "in the world but not of it."

Such a position, however, left them vulnerable to the charge that they had compromised the "faith once delivered to the saints." In their efforts to reclaim the culture for Christ, they increasingly heard the complaint—often by old friends and former colleagues—that they had sacrificed the purity of the church in their misguided quest to restore its unity. Rather than attempting to infiltrate the mainline denominations and the ecumenical organizations, their critics repeatedly told them, they should withdraw from those apostate structures and throw in their lot with the faithful remnant. Any "compromise with apostasy or on doctrine," wrote the president of the ACCC, "invariably leads downward to compromise on worldliness and finally with sin."[85] It is a slippery slope, the separatists were convinced, that can only lead to a tragic and painful fall.

Even more serious than the charges of their critics were the almost invisible dangers lurking within the evangelical movement itself. While there can be little doubt that Ockenga, Henry, and other evangelical leaders were genuinely committed to the task of reclaiming the culture for Christ, their tendency to build a wide range of parachurch organizations that they could immediately control rather than infiltrating and seeking to transform the older and sometimes moribund institutions that were outside of their control seemed to lead future generations of evangelicals in quite a different direction from that which the first generation of leaders intended to travel. Rather than pouring their considerable energies and resources into reentering and reenergizing the mainline denominations, the ecumenical organizations, the universities, the halls

83. Niebuhr, *Christ and Culture*, 45–82.
84. Ibid., 190–229.
85. W. O. H. Garman to Harold John Ockenga, June 10, 1948, Ockenga Papers.

of government, the criminal justice system, the social service agencies, and the professions, for example, many evangelicals seemed content to operate mainly and sometimes exclusively within their own subculture. Complicating matters was the fact that many of these new organizations seemed to be remarkably successful.[86] Indeed, the more prominent those organizations became, the more comfortable many of them seemed to be with the surrounding culture. While there were exceptions, to be sure, the camel of cultural captivity was able to get its nose under evangelicalism's burgeoning tent so subtly that few seemed to notice the stakes of identity begin to loosen.[87]

"During the 1960s I somewhat romanced the possibility," Carl F. H. Henry later reflected, "that a vast evangelical alliance might arise in the United States to coordinate effectively a national impact in evangelism, education, publication and sociopolitical action," but "by the early 1970s the prospect of a massive evangelical alliance seemed annually more remote, and by mid-decade it was gone."[88]

---

86. On the growth and influence of the parachurch, see Wesley K. Willmer, J. David Schmidt, and Martyn Smith, *The Prospering Parachurch: Enlarging the Boundaries of God's Kingdom* (San Francisco: Jossey-Bass, 1998).

87. I borrowed the image of the camel and tent from C. C. Goen's superb introduction to *The Great Awakening*, vol 4. of *The Works of Jonathan Edwards* (New Haven: Yale University Press, 1972), 11. The original passage reads: "It contained a built-in equivocacy whereby the Arminian camel could get its nose under the Puritan tent so unobtrusively that few of the insiders noticed when the stakes of orthodoxy began to loosen."

88. Carl F. H. Henry, "American Evangelicals in a Turning Time," *Christian Century*, November 5, 1980, 1058–62.

8

✳✳✳✳✳✳✳✳✳✳✳✳✳✳✳✳✳✳✳✳✳✳✳✳✳✳✳✳✳✳✳✳✳✳✳✳✳✳

RENEWING THE MIND

From his earliest years, Harold John Ockenga had been fascinated by the life of the mind. With the encouragement of his parents, he became a voracious reader, a first-rate scholar, a recognized author, and an avid collector of books. By the time he assumed his responsibilities as pastor of Park Street Church in Boston, he had accumulated four earned degrees, including master of arts and doctor of philosophy degrees from the University of Pittsburgh, and an enormous personal library. After more than three decades of ministry at Park Street, he had published fifteen books and hundreds of sermons and articles, and was widely recognized as one of Boston's most respected intellectual leaders.[1]

"He intimidated me," observed Billy Graham, reflecting on the early years of their friendship. "I worried that with my simple preaching I might be an

---

1. Harold John Ockenga's published volumes, in chronological order, are *These Religious Affections* (1937), *Our Protestant Heritage* (1938), *Have You Met These Women?* (1940), *Everyone That Believeth* (1942), *The Comfort of God* (1944), *Our Evangelical Faith* (1946), *The Spirit of the Living God* (1947), *Faithful in Christ Jesus* (1948), *The Word of our Lord* (1951), *The Church in God* (1956), *Protestant Preaching in Lent* (1957), *Power Through Pentecost* (1959), *Women Who Made Bible History* (1962), *No Other Lord* (1969), and *Faith in a Troubled World* (1972). The title of Ockenga's MA thesis is "The Role of Competition in Marx" (1934) and his PhD dissertation is "Poverty as a Theoretical and Practical Problem of Government in the Writings of Jeremy Bentham and the Marxian Alternative" (1939). For a listing of articles, sermons, and chapters written for books, see John M. Adams, "The Making of a Neo-Evangelical Statesman: The Case of Harold John Ockenga" (PhD diss., Baylor University, 1994), 205–18.

embarrassment to his sophistication and scholarship." However, "as we got to know each other," Graham continued, "I came to realize that Harold was a rare blend of intellectual ability and deep personal piety. Harold was looked on as *the* evangelical intellectual leader, not only in New England but also in the United States."[2]

The academic achievements and intellectual aspirations of Ockenga and many of his closest friends, including colleagues such as Edward John Carnell and Carl F. H. Henry, raise a number of important questions for those who have tended to see evangelicalism as one of the major wellsprings of America's anti-intellectual tradition.[3] This focus on the intellect was the third of evangelicalism's four goals.

In his Pulitzer Prize–winning volume *Anti-Intellectualism in American Life*, Richard Hofstadter observed that since "religion was the first arena of American intellectual life," it also became "the first arena for an anti-intellectual impulse." Tensions between "the mind and the heart"—or, to put it another way, between the "intellect" and the "emotions"—Hofstadter argued, have existed throughout human history. What is unique about the American experience, however, is that in the New World—with its lack of traditional establishments—the creative balance between "mind and heart" quickly gave way to the dominance of "emotions" over "intellect." Indeed, it was in America, Hofstadter was convinced, that "enthusiasm and revivalism won their most impressive victories."[4] There is sufficient truth in Hofstadter's assertions to make any evangelical uncomfortable. While most would reject Gerrard Winstanley's characterization of universities as "standing ponds of stinking waters,"[5] there are plenty of contemporary evangelicals who remain deeply suspicious of higher education.[6] The "Great Reversal," as sociologist David Moberg described fundamentalism's rapid withdrawal from culture,

2. *Just As I Am: The Autobiography of Billy Graham* (San Francisco: HarperSanFrancisco, 1997), 167.

3. See, for example, R. A. Knox, *Enthusiasm* (Oxford: Oxford University Press, 1958). Edward John Carnell had earned doctorates from both Harvard University and Boston University. Carl F. H. Henry had earned doctorates from both Northern Baptist Theological Seminary and Boston University.

4. Richard Hofstadter, *Anti-Intellectualism in American Life* (New York: Vintage, 1962), 55–56. For a critique of the popular notion that American revivalism is characterized by a "triumph of heart over head," see Garth M. Rosell, "Charles G. Finney: His Place in the Stream of American Evangelicalism," in *The Evangelical Tradition in America*, ed. Leonard I. Sweet (Macon, GA: Mercer University Press, 1997), 131–47.

5. Winstanley was a seventeenth-century English dissenter. His colorful comment is quoted in Hofstadter, *Anti-Intellectualism in American Life*, 58. See also H. Richard Niebuhr, *The Social Sources of Denominationalism* (Cleveland and New York: Meridian, 1965), chaps. 2 and 3.

6. For an understanding of why many evangelicals are wary of university education, see George M. Marsden, *The Soul of the American University: From Protestant Establishment to Established Non-belief* (New York: Oxford University Press, 1994); and George M. Marsden and Bradley J. Longfield, eds., *The Secularization of the Academy* (New York: Oxford University Press, 1992).

helped shape evangelical perceptions of American education at least as profoundly as they influenced attitudes toward mainline denominations, ecumenical organizations, and issues of social justice.[7]

Edwards and Chauncy Revisited

The beginnings of the modern evangelical movement, as we have already seen, can be traced at least as far back as the Great Awakening of the eighteenth century. While the division between New Lights and Old Lights focused primarily on whether one tended to favor the revivals or to oppose them, as illustrated in the lively debates between Jonathan Edwards and Charles Chauncy, a growing tension had also begun to appear between those who relied on the Bible as their ultimate authority and those who had come to view reason as a sufficient standard. Such a conclusion does not imply either that the eighteenth century rationalists had forsaken the Bible or that the evangelicals had abandoned reason. Like others in his day, for example, Jonathan Edwards made full use of all four components in what has come to be known as the Wesleyan Quadrilateral—scripture, tradition, reason, and experience.[8] While Edwards considered all four resources to be of value, however, the Bible remained for him and his evangelical colleagues the final court of appeals on all matters great and small.

There can be little question that Harold John Ockenga believed that he stood firmly in the tradition of Jonathan Edwards.[9] Both men loved the Bible and joyfully placed themselves under its authority. Both relished the life of the mind and spent many hours in reading, study, and reflection. Both enjoyed the beauties of God's creation and loved to walk and pray among the hills and trees. Both welcomed religious revivals and defended them as gracious gifts from a sovereign God. Both were committed to the spread of the gospel around the world and prayed regularly for its achievement. Both married godly women with greater social graces than their own. Both served as college presidents and were well educated themselves. Both strongly affirmed the importance, as Billy Graham phrased it, of combining intellectual ability and deep personal piety.

Such commitments, while helping give shape and direction to the evangelical movement as a whole, have also produced continuing divisions within the evangelical ranks over issues of pedagogy. While Richard Hofstadter was undoubtedly

7. David O. Moberg, *The Great Reversal: Evangelism and Social Concern*, rev. ed. (Philadelphia: Lippincott, 1977).

8. Donald A. D. Thorsen, *The Wesleyan Quadrilateral: Scripture, Tradition, Reason and Experience as a Model of Evangelical Theology* (Grand Rapids: Zondervan, 1990); and W. Stephen Gunter, Scott J. Jones, Ted A. Campbell, Rebekah L. Miles, and Randy L. Maddox, *Wesley and the Quadrilateral: Renewing the Conversation* (Nashville: Abingdon, 1997).

9. See Harold John Ockenga, "Jonathan Edwards and New England, or The Apologetic of Protestantism," sermon 589, preached at Park Street Church in 1938, Ockenga Papers.

correct in identifying anti-intellectualism as a problem for evangelical Christians, to say nothing of the American culture as a whole, a far more important debate within evangelicalism centers on the question of *what kind of education* evangelical Christians believe they should be providing for their children. While pockets of anti-intellectual sentiment can be identified in every era of evangelical history, the vast majority of evangelicals seem again and again to have embraced both formal and informal education as an important part of the evangelical project. Had this not been the case, many of our nation's colleges and universities would never have been founded. Indeed, often as a result of America's evangelical revivals, throughout the eighteenth and nineteenth centuries in particular, scores of institutions of higher education were established.[10]

Charles G. Finney, the towering figure in the early history of Oberlin College and one of Harold John Ockenga's spiritual heroes, came to symbolize evangelicalism's profound commitment to the life of the mind.[11] While primarily known as a revivalist and social reformer, Finney spent much of his time in the classroom and some fifteen years serving as president of one of America's most important educational institutions.[12] An outspoken advocate of higher education, Finney often counseled his students to "Read, study, think, and read again. You were made to think. It will do you good to think; to develop your powers by study. God designed that religion should require thought, intense thought, and should thoroughly develop our powers of thought."[13] "Do not understand me to disparage learning," Finney remarked. "The more learning the better," if it is the "right kind" of learning. "God forbid that I should say a word against an educated ministry," he continued, but "let education be of the right kind," educating a person *"for the work."* "Do not let education be such" that when students graduate "after spending six, eight, or ten years in study, they are not worth half as much as they were before they

10. William Ringenberg, *The Christian College*, 2nd ed. (Grand Rapids: Baker Academic, 2006); Marsden, *The Soul of the American University*; and Conrad Cherry, *Hurrying Toward Zion* (Bloomington: Indiana University Press, 1995).

11. See Harold John Ockenga, "The Secret of America's Greatest Revivalist," sermon 558, preached at Park Street Church in 1937, Ockenga Papers. An earlier and more extended version of my argument can be found in Garth M. Rosell, "A Speckled Bird: Charles G. Finney's Contribution to Higher Education," *Fides et Historia*, Summer 1993, 55–74. For biographical studies of Finney, see Charles E. Hambrick-Stowe, *Charles G. Finney and the Spirit of American Evangelicalism* (Grand Rapids: Eerdmans, 1996); Keith J. Hardman, *Charles Grandison Finney, 1792–1875: Revivalist and Reformer* (Syracuse: Syracuse University Press, 1987); Marianne Perciaccante, *Calling Down Fire* (Albany: State University of New York, 2003); G. Frederick Wright, *Charles Grandison Finney: America's Religious Leader* (Salem, OH: Schmul, 1996); and Lewis A. Drummond, *Charles Grandison Finney and the Birth of Modern Evangelicalism* (London: Hodder and Stoughton, 1983).

12. Finney served as Oberlin's president from 1851 until 1865 and on its faculty from 1835 until 1875. See Robert Samuel Fletcher, *A History of Oberlin College: From Its Foundation Through the Civil War*, 2 vols. (Oberlin, OH: Oberlin College, 1943).

13. Charles G. Finney, *Lectures on Systematic Theology* (Oberlin, OH: James M. Fitch, 1846), v.

went."[14] Then, citing what he called the "wide gulf" between himself and others with regard to educational "views" and "practices," Finney called for fundamental and radical educational reform—reform not only of what was taught but also how, why, and to whom it was taught.[15]

The old system of education, against which Finney was prepared to do battle, had by his day become a recognized and respected part of the American culture. "The old-time American colleges, which dominated the educational scene until after the Civil War," as historians George Marsden and Bradley Longfield have suggested, "retained the outlines of the system of higher education that

Charles Grandison Finney (courtesy of Oberlin College Archives, Oberlin, OH)

had prevailed in the Western world for seven centuries. Higher education simply meant expertise in the classics." While there were exceptions, to be sure, students "spent much of their time reciting classical authors."[16] Finney, along with many of his evangelical colleagues, considered the old system of education to be fundamentally flawed. "It is common," wrote Finney, for graduates "to affirm that their course of studies there did them little or no good, and that they had to *unlearn* what they had there learned, before they could effect much."[17] They were like "David in Saul's armor"—staggering under the weight of an education that Finney described as essentially irrelevant, scattered, impractical, and out of touch with common folk.[18] In contrast to the old system, the Oberlin Collegiate Institute promised an education that would "provide for the *body* and *heart* as well as the *intellect*; for it aims at the best education of the *whole man*."[19] "At Oberlin," as Finney phrased it, "the student can expect to be educated physically, mentally and morally."[20] To

14. William G. McLoughlin, ed., *Lectures on Revivals of Religion by Charles Grandison Finney* (Cambridge, MA: Belknap, 1960), 186–87.

15. Garth M. Rosell and Richard A. G. Dupuis, eds., *The Memoirs of Charles G. Finney* (Grand Rapids: Zondervan, 1989), 89.

16. Marsden and Longfield, *The Secularization of the Academy*, 13.

17. McLoughlin, *Lectures on Revivals of Religion*, 188.

18. Rosell and Dupuis, *The Memoirs of Charles G. Finney*, 85–96, quotation from p. 88.

19. John J. Shipherd's announcement of the opening of the Oberlin Collegiate Institute in the autumn of 1833 was published in the *New York Evangelist*, September 7, 1833; copy in the Oberlin College Archives.

20. *Religious Intelligencer*, August 1, 1835, 130.

help achieve these goals, Oberlin adopted a system which combined rigorous study, regular worship, and manual labor.[21]

Rather than employing the old method of classroom recitation, Finney would put the names of the students in a hat, shake them together, and pick one out at random. The student who was thereby selected would be asked to make his/her oral presentation to the class. This would be followed by a time of lively and intense interaction—as the instructor and other members of the class asked questions, raised objections, and presented alternative interpretations. On occasions, according to student reports, these discussions could continue over several days.[22] After class, students would frequently "swarm" around Finney "like bees," anxious to pursue some issue or other a bit more fully.[23] "It is our custom in this institution," wrote Finney,

> to settle every question, especially in theology, by discussion. I have now for twelve years been going annually over my course of instruction in this manner, and owe not a little to my classes, for I have availed myself to the uttermost of the learning and sagacity and talent of every member of my classes in pushing my investigations. I call on them to discuss the questions which I present for discussion, and take my seat among them and help and guide them according to my ability; and not infrequently, I am happy to say, do I get some useful instruction from them. Thus I sustain the double relation of pupil and teacher.[24]

Finney's method of instruction, as Oberlin President James Fairchild later commented, "was to draw out his pupils in inquiry and discussion, and thus establish in them the power and the habit of independent thought."[25]

In addition to the adoption of manual labor and a new approach to classroom teaching, Finney was convinced that a genuinely "thorough education," as he liked to call it, must be culturally relevant, morally and intellectually rigorous, and available to everyone, including women and African-American students.[26] "Though first and foremost an evangelist," historian Donald Dayton observed, "Finney's work and the way he understood the gospel 'released a mighty impulse toward social reform' that shook the nation and helped destroy slavery."[27] "The time has come, in the providence of God," Finney

21. James H. Fairchild, *Oberlin: The Colony and the College, 1833–1883* (Oberlin, OH: Goodrich, 1883), 186–95.

22. See, for example, George Clark, *Reminiscences of Rev. Charles G. Finney* (Oberlin, OH: Goodrich, 1876), 49–53; and Antoinette Brown Blackwell's reflections in the Oberlin College Archives, General Files, box 12, p. 2.

23. Hiram Mead, "Charles Grandison Finney," *Congregational Quarterly*, January 1877, 11.

24. Hardman, *Charles Grandison Finney*, 357–58.

25. Ibid. Compare Wright, *Charles Grandison Finney*, 154.

26. For a more detailed discussion of each of these principles, see Rosell, "A Speckled Bird," 55–74.

27. Donald W. Dayton, *Discovering an Evangelical Heritage* (New York: Harper & Row, 1976), 15. See Gilbert H. Barnes, *The Anti-Slavery Impulse, 1830–1844* (New York: Harcourt, Brace & World, 1964), 11, for the quotation within the quotation.

argued, when the church must recognize this "abominable abomination" to be "a great national sin." Indeed, the Spirit of God will depart from the church if it turns its back on the two million slaves who "stretch their hands, all shackled and bleeding, and send forth to the church of God the agonizing cry for help." We cannot remain "silent without guilt," he continued, when every "breeze is loaded down with the cries of lamentation, mourning and wo[e]."[28] Oberlin, of course, became a "hotbed of abolitionism."[29] By action of the trustees, in February of 1835, internal administration of the school was placed in the hands of the "new anti-slavery faculty" and a resolution was adopted supporting "the education of people of color." Thereafter, as an *Ohio Observer* report phrased it, Oberlin was "known as the *decided opponent of SLAVERY* as it is practiced upon the colored people of this country."[30]

As the first college in America to open its doors to women and "people of color," the evangelical leaders of Oberlin were simply seeking to apply the teaching of the Bible as they understood it directly to the cultural context in which God had placed them. Faculty and students alike, Finney was convinced, should not be allowed to live their lives in "ivory towers" but rather must be encouraged to move out into the community in active service among common folk. Students who are "shut up in their schools," Finney observed, and "confined to books and shut out from intercourse with the common people or contact with the common mind," will never be able to understand what "common people think." To counteract this dangerous tendency, Finney believed students must be taught both to know their Bibles and to understand their cultures. They must study "human nature" as carefully as if they were seeking to master the principles of mathematics.[31] The "Captain of a fire company, when the city is on fire," Finney liked to say, "does not read to his company an essay, or exhibit fine specimens of rhetoric, when he shouts to them and directs their movements. It is a question of urgency, and he intends that every word shall be understood." Consequently, our students must be taught to abandon "all the fine drapery and furniture of a studied and ornate discourse" and adopt language which is "direct, simple, . . . cogent, . . . powerful," and to the point. Our institutions would be of much greater value than they are "if there was much more about them that was *practical*."[32]

Despite their bold educational initiative, Oberlin College, like virtually all of America's major colleges and universities, tended to adopt more traditional structures and practices as it moved into the twentieth century. While

28. McLoughlin, *Lectures on Revivals of Religion,* 287–89.
29. Fletcher, *A History of Oberlin College,* 1:236–70.
30. *Ohio Observer,* April 9, 1835, as quoted in Fletcher, *A History of Oberlin College,* 1:236.
31. McLoughlin, *Lectures on Revivals of Religion,* 188–89.
32. Rosell and Dupuis, *The Memoirs of Charles G. Finney,* 89–90.

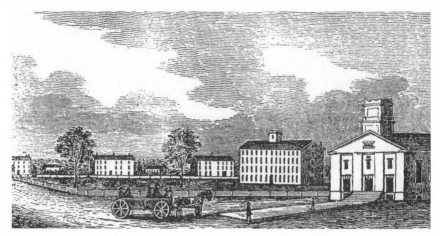

1846 drawing of Oberlin College by Henry Howe (courtesy of Oberlin College Archives, Oberlin, OH)

their rich heritage of independence, community service, and social justice continued to be integral parts of campus life, the growing power of accrediting agencies, increasing influence of the professional guilds, and growing impetus toward academic specialization tended to encourage conformity to recognized standards and procedures. Elite institutions such as Yale, Harvard, and Princeton increasingly became the cultural norms against which other institutions could evaluate their progress. The closer an institution could get to the "gold standard," it was believed, the more respect it could command within the culture and the more outstanding students it could attract from the community.

Finney's vision for a more "thorough education," of course, was not lost. When one examines the more elite institutions, those that have tended to set the cultural standards for higher education, Finney's influence has remained relatively marginal. If, however, one looks to the Bible school movement, storefront night schools, missionary training institutes, and the like—indeed, to the enormous, diverse, under-studied, much maligned, and often invisible wing of American education—the influence of Finney and his evangelical colleagues has been substantial.[33] Here it is, among friends, that Finney's critiques are welcomed and his theories practiced. Here it is, among those who are themselves "outsiders," that the sojourner is received gladly.

These two educational traditions—one that leaned toward the classics and the other that inclined toward the culture, one giving special prominence to theory and the other making sure that adequate attention was given to

33. See Virginia L. Brereton, *Training God's Army: The American Bible School, 1880–1940* (Bloomington: Indiana University Press, 1990); Frank E. Gaebelein, "The Bible College in American Education Today," *School and Society*, May 9, 1959, 223–25; and W. M. Aldrich, "Basic Concepts of Bible College Education," *Bibliotheca Sacra*, July 1962, 244–50.

practice, one maintaining traditional structures and the other more open to innovation—provided a wide range of educational options for evangelical families throughout most of the nineteenth century. The tension between the two, while occasionally producing angry outbursts, for the most part provided evangelicalism with a healthy reminder that theory and practice are both essential parts of an integrated whole. While activist tendencies within evangelicalism have always inclined the movement toward what philosopher William James liked to call "cash value," the great centers of academic research were constant reminders to bright young evangelicals of the importance of the life of the mind.

With the arrival of the bitter controversies between fundamentalists and modernists during the opening decades of the twentieth century, however, increasing numbers of evangelical parents felt that it was necessary to pull their sons and daughters out of what they believed to be dangerously liberal colleges and universities and to send them instead to one or another of the rapidly growing community of Bible schools, Bible colleges, and Christian liberal arts colleges. There are plenty of good reasons to attend a Bible school, a Bible college, or a Christian liberal arts college, to be sure—not least of which is the possibility of securing a first-rate education. Among those reasons, Ockenga was convinced, should not be the fear of losing one's faith. By abandoning America's elite centers of research, evangelicals were tending to also abandon their responsibility to be salt and light within those important cultural centers.

Harold John Ockenga's decision to begin his education at Taylor University, continue his studies at Princeton and Westminster, and complete his work at the University of Pittsburgh—a pattern that was replicated at other educational institutions by Edward John Carnell, Carl F. H. Henry, and a growing number of his evangelical colleagues—is illustrative of a growing hunger among bright young evangelicals to reclaim their educational heritage and to help restore the lost balance between theory and practice. Historian Mark Noll, in his influential study *The Scandal of the Evangelical Mind*, identified the efforts of Ockenga, Carnell, and Henry as "the first and most dramatic story" of an awakening evangelical mind. Billy Graham, he continued, "played a surprisingly large role in promoting the intellectual enlightenment of evangelicalism. . . . Through his cooperation with Ockenga, Henry, and like-minded leaders, Graham provided the evangelical equivalent of an imprimatur for serious intellectual labor. More than any other public figure, Graham protected evangelical scholars from the anti-intellectualism endemic to the movement."[34]

34. Mark A. Noll, *The Scandal of the Evangelical Mind* (Grand Rapids: Eerdmans, 1994), 212–14. See also Mark A. Noll, *Between Faith and Criticism: Evangelicals, Scholarship, and the Bible in America* (San Francisco: Harper & Row, 1986).

Five Initiatives

Five important developments in which Harold John Ockenga was deeply involved during the 1940s and 1950s help illustrate evangelicalism's attempt to move beyond its own intellectual comfort zones and reestablish its credentials within the larger scholarly world: the establishment of the Boston School of the Bible in 1943, the launching of a series of Conferences for the Advancement of Evangelical Scholarship in 1944, the founding of Fuller Theological Seminary in 1947, the establishment of *Christianity Today* in 1956, and the attempt to establish a Christian university that was made between 1954 and 1960.

In an effort to address what they believed to be a growing problem of biblical and theological illiteracy within the church and the community, Park Street Church and Providence Bible Institute decided to join hands in the establishment of what came to be known as the Boston School of the Bible. A six-year curriculum, covering the contents of the entire Bible, the essentials of Christian history and doctrine, personal evangelism, missions, Christian apologetics, and teacher training, was offered on a rotating basis each Tuesday from 7:00 p.m. to 9:20 p.m. for twenty weeks between November and April.[35] Dr. Morton C. Campbell, professor emeritus at the law school of Harvard University, was appointed as dean and treasurer of the new organization. Classes were held at Park Street Church, academic credit was awarded by Providence Bible Institute, and faculty members were drawn from throughout the greater Boston area.[36]

The Boston School of the Bible, like similar initiatives in other communities, seems to have drawn its inspiration more directly from Charles G. Finney's educational model than it did from any of the "gold standard" institutions that had already made Boston one of America's leading educational centers. While Harold John Ockenga and his colleagues sought to encourage the highest possible standards for their new enterprise, they also realized that such efforts, while serving an important purpose, could never hope to touch the elite centers of learning. For such a task, other strategies would need to be employed and other initiatives taken. Among the most important of these, they were convinced, was the launching of a series of scholars conferences designed to identify, empower, and inspire a whole new generation of bright, articulate, theologically orthodox, and thoroughly educated evangelical scholars.

35. Materials and correspondence relating to curricular offerings, listings of instructors, administrative oversight, tuition, promotional efforts, etc. can be found in "University of Life" folder in the Ockenga Papers.

36. Among the teachers were Harold John Ockenga, Howard W. Ferrin, F. Carlton Booth, Charles Seidenspinner, Edgar F. Reibetanz, and Terrelle B. Crum. Crum also served as the evening school director.

Conferences for the Advancement of Evangelical Scholarship

Harold John Ockenga first conceived the idea of holding an annual Conference for the Advancement of Evangelical Scholarship, known more popularly as Scholars Conferences, during the annual meeting of the NAE.[37] "At Columbus in 1944," Ockenga later commented, "I suggested to Mr. John Bolten the getting together of evangelical scholars who would do in apologetics what N.A.E. was doing in ecclesiology. Mr. Bolton agreed to advance the means for such a conference and left the inviting of the scholars and the nature of the conference entirely in my hands."[38]

The first gathering of scholars was held from August 25 to 30, 1944, in the comfortable surroundings of the Mayflower Hotel in Plymouth, Massachusetts. While seventeen scholars were invited to the gathering, only ten were able to attend.[39] Present included Cornelius Van Til (Westminster Theological Seminary), who gave the Friday afternoon paper on "Revelation"; Clarence Bouma (Calvin College), who presented the Saturday morning paper on "Theism"; Clarence Thiessen (Wheaton College), who led a Sunday afternoon discussion on the beach on the topic, "Authority for our Christian Faith"; William Emmet Powers (Eastern Baptist Theological Seminary), who presented the Monday morning paper on the "Atonement"; John Bolten (from Andover, Massachusetts), who provided a Tuesday morning paper on the "Church"; and Stacey Woods (Inter-Varsity Christian Fellowship), who gave the final Wednesday morning paper on "Evangelism."[40]

The gathering was an enormous success. Not only did it provide some very busy evangelical scholars with much-needed rest, fellowship, fresh understanding, and mutual encouragement but it also highlighted "the urgent needs of our evangelical churches for scholarly literature." By way of concrete results from the meetings, the NAE was asked to consider establishing a "book review service to suggest suitable titles to the American Library Association" and "a re-print service for papers and pamphlets in order to encourage the widest

37. For his description of the beginnings, see Harold John Ockenga to Stephen W. Paine, May 6, 1947, Ockenga Papers.

38. Harold John Ockenga to Carl McIntire, September 24, 1945, Ockenga Papers. John Bolten, a wealthy German industrialist who had been forced to leave Germany and "his industrial empire" in 1928 as a result of Adolf Hitler's policies, had emigrated to Boston "where he slowly but steadily rebuilt his fortune." During Billy Graham's Boston Crusade in 1950, Bolten "recommitted his life to Christ" and became a close friend and supporter of both Graham and Ockenga. For a moving description and tribute, see Graham, *Just As I Am*, 168–71. Bolton personally covered the entire $1,405.20 cost of the conference. Travel, lodging, meals, and tips were completely covered for all participants.

39. Invited but unable to attend were William Childs Robinson, Manford Gutzke, Stephen Paine, Walter Maier, Harry Hager, Allan McRae, and William H. Wrighton. Letters of invitation, letters of response, minutes, reports, and financial statements can be found in two folders, labeled "Scholars Conferences," in the Ockenga Papers.

40. Brief descriptions of each paper can be found in "First Meeting of Evangelical Scholars," Mayflower Hotel, Manomet Beach, Massachusetts, August 25–30, 1944, 1, 7, Ockenga Papers.

Delegates at Plymouth Rock during the Conference for the Advancement of Evangelical Scholarship, August 16–23, 1945. From left: Carl F. H. Henry, Harold John Ockenga, T. Leonard Lewis, F. B. Fitzwater, William E. Powers, Clarence Bouma, John Bolten, Stacey Woods, Terrelle B. Crum, Allan McRae, Cornelius Van Til, H. C. Thiessen, Everett Harrison, and Merrill C. Tenney (courtesy of Gordon-Conwell Libraries)

dissemination possible of such needed materials." Furthermore, Cornelius Van Til was encouraged to "undertake, during the coming year, the writing of an apologetic for our common evangelical faith from the philosophical point of view," Clarence Bouma was asked to "undertake during the coming months the preparation of a vigorous, challenging 'spiritual manifesto' showing the complete adequacy of the true Christian view for every area of individual and social life," and Leslie Marston was encouraged "to undertake the preparation of materials for an evaluation of current psychological systems in the light of Christian teaching and a positive presentation of a truly Christian psychology."[41]

The following summer, from August 16 to 23, an even larger group of evangelical scholars gathered once again at the Mayflower Hotel to address the general topic, "Training Ministers for the Post-War World." Of the twenty-four who were invited, fourteen were able to attend: William E. Powers (Eastern Baptist Theological Seminary), Everett Harrison (Dallas Theological Seminary), Allan McRae (Faith Theological Seminary), Merrill C. Tenney (Wheaton College), F. B. Fitzwater (Moody Bible Institute), Terrelle B. Crum (Providence Bible Institute), Clarence Bouma (Calvin Seminary), Stacey Woods (Inter-Varsity Christian Fellowship), Cornelius Van Til (Westminster Theological Seminary), H. C. Thiessen (Wheaton College), Carl F. H. Henry (Northern Baptist Theological Seminary), T. Leonard Lewis (Gordon College), John Bolten (Andover, Massachusetts), and Harold John Ockenga (Park Street Church).[42]

41. Quotations are taken from the report of the "First Meeting of Evangelical Scholars."
42. Those who were invited but unable to attend included Harry Hager, William W. Adams, William A. Mueller, Walter Maier, Theodore Graebner, Howard Tillman Kuist, Manford Gutzke, William Childs Robinson, Leslie Marston, and Clarence Roddy. Correspondence and listings of participants can be found in the Ockenga Papers.

AN EVANGELICAL MANIFESTO

Issued by the Plymouth Conference for the Advancement of Evangelical Scholarship, Plymouth, Mass., August 18

In view of the world-wide catastrophe of two world wars through which humanity has passed in thirty years; and in view of the failure of modern philosophy, both idealistic and naturalistic, to save western culture from disintegration and collapse; and in view of the general ethical irresponsibility growing inevitably out of a man-centered philosophy of life, and the growing moral decadence in family and social life, the increasing stress between capital and labor, the widespread infiltration of modern life by such evils as the liquor traffic, crime and youth delinquency;

Therefore, be it resolved by this Conference for the Advancement of Evangelical Scholarship, that:

(1) We summon men everywhere to repentance for personal, social, national and international irresponsibility and sin which has brought upon men everywhere a divine judgment;

(2) We plead with men to turn to Jesus Christ as the all-sufficient Saviour of men, urging upon them individual commitment to the Christian world-life view which by its dynamic lifted the ancient world above paganism and barbarism, and is the only hope for the modern world.

(3) We call for a repudiation of the man-centered attack on modern problems and for a return to the study of the Holy Scriptures in which God holds forth to man the good tidings of redemption and discloses the only world and life view through which man learns to live in accordance with the will of God, resulting in social, national and international righteousness as the only basis for the preservation of our Christian civilization.

Dr. William Emmett Powers (Eastern Baptist)
Dr. Carl F. H. Henry (Northern Baptist)
Dr. T. Leonard Lewis (Gordon)
Dr. Everett Harrison (Dallas)
Dr. P. B. Fitzwater (Moody)
Dr. Merrill Tenney (Wheaton)
Mr. Stacey B. Woods (Inter-Varsity Fellowship)

Dr. Clarence Bouma (Calvin)
Dr. Cornelius Van Til (Westminster)
Dr. Allen McRae (Faith)
Dr. Henry C. Thiessen (Wheaton)
Prof. Terrelle B. Crum (Providence)
Dr. Harold J. Ockenga (Park St. Church)

Copy of the "Evangelical Manifesto," published in 1945 (courtesy of Gordon-Conwell Libraries)

Throughout their time together, papers were presented on "Exegesis" (Tenney), "Systematics" (Fitzwater), "Theocentric Ethics" (Bouma), "The Christian *Weltanschauung*" (Van Til), and "Practical Theology" (Lewis). Following the presentation of each paper, one member of the group was assigned the task of leading a general discussion of its contents and methodology. "One of the results of the Conference," one report said, "was a renewed and increased awareness of 'the crying need for solid and scholarly books on every phase of the Christian Faith in application to the thought and needs of the present day.'"[43] Another result was the preparation and publication of "An Evangelical Manifesto," signed by the participants, calling for repentance, commitment to Christ, repudiation of a man-centered approach to contemporary problems, and a return to the vigorous study and application of Holy Scripture.[44]

The gatherings of evangelical scholars were not without their controversy. "Ockenga Compromises Faith Seminary's Testimony," an editorial in the *Christian Beacon* proclaimed following the second meeting.[45] At issue, according to Carl McIntire, was whether the Scholars Conferences were being officially sponsored by the NAE. "Faith Seminary was established in 1938 to be an institution of the highest scholarship for the training of Christian

43. Quotation from a report on the proceedings, "This Year at Plymouth Rock," Ockenga Papers.

44. The "Evangelical Manifesto" was published in *United Evangelical Action*, September 15, 1945, 4.

45. Carl McIntire, "Ockenga Compromises Faith Seminary's Testimony," *Christian Beacon*, October 11, 1945, 4.

ministers, with no connection or compromise whatsoever with modernism or with the Federal Council of the Churches of Christ in America," wrote McIntire, who was at that time serving as president of the board of directors for the seminary. "The president of the Faculty is the Rev. Allan A. MacRae, Ph.D. Dr. MacRae is a minister of the Bible Presbyterian Church and has been one of the leading supporters of the American Council's testimony as it has related, first to the Federal Council, and also to the N.A.E."

"Faith Seminary has now been placed in a most embarrassing position," the editorial continued,

> as a result of the activities of Dr. Harold John Ockenga, pastor of the Park Street Church, Boston, and the first president of the National Association of Evangelicals. Dr. Ockenga, though the pastor of a Congregational Church, is a member of the Presbyterian Church, U.S.A., a denomination from which the Bible Presbyterians have broken, and a denomination which vigorously supports the Federal Council, and Dr. Ockenga is a member of the Federal Council.

When MacRae was invited by Ockenga to attend the Conference for the Advancement of Evangelical Scholarship "he was assured by Ockenga that the meeting had no connection whatsoever with the N.A.E. or its testimony." Now, the editorial continued, it is apparent that "the whole evangelical conference was an N.A.E. project."[46]

"Harold, I am surprised that you would pull a trick like this," wrote McIntire in a letter to Ockenga alerting him to the editorial that would soon appear in the *Christian Beacon*. "We love you in the Lord. But this time it is going to be necessary for me to openly—in order to protect the good name of Faith Seminary and to let the world know it is not directly or indirectly connected with the compromise of N.A.E.—involve your good name in the repudiation; and I am sorry."[47] The depth of McIntire's concern was expressed even more clearly in a letter he wrote to Ockenga on September 28, 1945. "I remember the good days that we have had together. On my study desk at home I have the two cathedral book ends that you gave me when Fairy and I made the trip from Collingswood to Point Breeze to have a part in your wedding. They have been a constant reminder to me of you, and especially of our friendship. I am removing them now."[48]

A final gathering of the Conference for the Advancement of Evangelical Scholarship was held from June 23 to 27, 1947, at the New Ocean House in Magnolia, Massachusetts. The major topic for the meeting was "Inspiration and Revelation." In addition to those who had attended one or both of the earlier gatherings, a number of new participants were added, including

46. Ibid.
47. McIntire to Ockenga, September 19, 1945, Ockenga Papers.
48. McIntire to Ockenga, September 28, 1945, Ockenga Papers.

Theodore Graebner (Concordia Seminary), who presented a paper on "The Place of Authority in Christian Theology"; W. Harry Jellema (Indiana University), who made a presentation on "Recent Use of Revelation and Inspiration as Grounded in 19th Century Evolutionary Critical Thought"; Edward John Carnell (Gordon College of Theology and Missions), who presented a paper on "Progressive Revelation as a Solution to the Alleged Moral Difficulties and Contradictions to the Doctrine of Scriptural Infallibility"; Ned B. Stonehouse (Westminster Theological Seminary), who provided a "Historical Survey of the Theories of Inspiration"; R. Laird Harris (Faith Theological Seminary), who made a presentation on "Textual Criticism and Divine Inspiration"; and Arnold C. Schultz (Northern Baptist Theological Seminary), who addressed the question "Does Archaeological Investigation Conserve the Christian View of Revelation and Inspiration?"[49]

While only these three conferences were held, from 1944 to 1947, their impact was enormous.[50] Many of the friendships that were formed—as scholars debated, prayed, broke bread, sang, and laughed together in beautiful surroundings—were to last a lifetime. Even more significant, perhaps, was the concrete affirmation that the conferences provided for a whole generation of evangelical scholars that academic work was critically important and that they did not need to pursue their scholarly endeavors as lone wolves. Indeed, it does not appear to have been a coincidence that the core of the new faculty at Fuller Theological Seminary had also been part of the Massachusetts conversations. "Professor Henry and myself have fellowshipped together as we discussed things theological," wrote Edward John Carnell in his letter applying for a teaching position at Fuller. We have "learned that, by collaboration, we could turn out many lectures, and, perhaps, volumes."[51]

Fuller Theological Seminary

"In the early forties," radio evangelist Charles E. Fuller commented in a letter to Harold John Ockenga and the trustees of Fuller Theological Seminary, "God began laying on my heart the burden of founding a school for training young people for our Lord's service." Combining "high academic standards" with "firm theological convictions," as Fuller described his vision, the new institution would seek to provide the same caliber of training "in the Gospel"

49. A list of the participants, topics, and times of presentation can be found in the Ockenga Papers. No conference was held in 1946 due to a number of logistical difficulties.

50. The vision of those who were involved in the Conferences for the Advancement of Evangelical Scholarship was, in large measure, continued through the establishment of the Evangelical Theological Society. Founded in Cincinnati, Ohio, December 27–28, 1949, the Evangelical Theological Society has continued to encourage serious scholarly work by evangelicals and to provide multiple opportunities for fellowship, academic discussion, and publication.

51. Carnell to Ockenga, September 12, 1947, Ockenga Papers.

as West Point makes available for students in Military Science or Caltech provides for those who wish to study engineering. Students who have been "called of God" should have "the very best of training in order to go out in His service as ministers, missionaries, evangelists [and] teachers." When his plans had become sufficiently mature, as Fuller later described the sequence of events, "I did a rather strange thing. I called a man whom I knew only slightly, to come and counsel with me and that man was Dr. Harold John Ockenga." Ockenga accepted Fuller's invitation and the two men, along with their wives, Audrey and Grace, spent three days together at the Fuller's "little house at Smoke Tree Ranch near Palm Springs" in southern California. "I remember my surprise," Fuller wrote, "when I discovered that he had the same vision as mine for the same need—the need for a Seminary truly orthodox and with a high scholastic standard."[52]

"As we sat outdoors in the bright sunshine," Fuller observed, "I recall telling Dr. Harold the amount of the income from my father's Trust, and he said that would be enough to start the Seminary, though as time passed we would need to look to God to provide much more for future needs."[53] Ockenga then "mentioned the names" of four scholars—Everett Harrison, Wilbur Smith, Carl Henry, and Harold Lindsell—that he believed were "qualified to teach in such a school," and he agreed to contact them to see if they might be interested.[54]

On May 14, 1947, at the offices of the Christian Workers Foundation in Chicago, "a meeting of the faculty of the proposed Fuller Theological Seminary was held." Those who gathered at 9:00 a.m. that Wednesday morning were Charles E. Fuller, Harold John Ockenga, Wilbur M. Smith, Everett Harrison,

52. Fuller to Ockenga and the Trustees of Fuller Theological Seminary, undated six-page letter, probably written in the autumn of 1961 since the letter makes mention "that our beloved school is starting its 15th year so hopefully" at the opening of the letter. The original letter is in the Ockenga Papers. The best study of Fuller Theological Seminary is George M. Marsden, *Reforming Fundamentalism: Fuller Seminary and the New Evangelicalism* (Grand Rapids: Eerdmans, 1987). For studies of Charles E. Fuller and his ministry, see Daniel P. Fuller, *Give the Winds a Mighty Voice: The Story of Charles E. Fuller* (Waco: Word, 1972); Grace Fuller, *Heavenly Sunshine* (Westwood, NJ: Revell, 1956); J. Elwin Wright, *The Old Fashioned Revival Hour and the Broadcasters* (Boston: Fellowship, 1940); and Tona J. Hangen, *Redeeming the Dial: Radio, Religion, and Popular Culture in America* (Chapel Hill: University of North Carolina Press, 2002). Ockenga's comments and the correspondence between Fuller and Ockenga, consisting of hundreds of letters written from 1946 through 1968, can be found in the Ockenga Papers.

53. Henry and Helen Day Fuller, Charles E. Fuller's parents, had a 110–acre orange grove from which they made a comfortable living. Henry, who had been converted under the ministry of evangelist Dwight L. Moody, was deeply interested in missions and Bible study. Not only did Henry and Helen Day Fuller help to support some fifty missionaries and national Christians during their lifetime, often sacrificing their own interests in helping to spread the gospel, but they also established a trust fund to help support those ministries that held the promise of accomplishing "the greatest possible lasting good for the cause of Christ." After Henry Fuller's death in 1926, the trust continued to grow. Its earnings, making about $150,000 each year available for the support of the seminary, helped make the establishment of Fuller Theological Seminary possible. The school is named in Henry Fuller's honor.

54. Fuller to Ockenga and the Trustees of Fuller Theological Seminary.

and Carl F. H. Henry. Since Herbert J. Taylor, in whose offices the meetings were held, was ill, he participated by telephone. Henry was assigned the task of recording minutes of the meeting. "Dr. Ockenga outlined the proposed business for the day," according to the minutes, "and then the group went to its knees in fervent prayer for the wisdom and leading of God." Following the prayer meeting, Fuller described his conversations with Ockenga

Fuller Theological Seminary's founding faculty: Harold John Ockenga, Wilber Smith, Carl F. H. Henry, Harold Lindsell, and Everett Harrison (courtesy of Fuller Theological Seminary Library Archives)

and his surprise "that they agreed so remarkably on the nature of a first-class seminary"—one, they were convinced, that was "so desperately needed, in view of the drift of older evangelical schools to liberalism, and the partial way in which existing conservative schools were dedicating themselves to the task of evangelical scholarship." Fuller also reported that on April 17, 1947, at the NAE annual meetings in Omaha, Fuller, Ockenga, and Smith had met and agreed that Fuller should serve as chairman of the board; that the board of trustees should include Fuller, Herbert J. Taylor, Roy Laurin, and Arnold Grunigen Jr.; that Ockenga should serve as "president in absentia during the school's formative years"; and that "a strong dean" should be appointed "to handle resident problems with faculty concurrence." Furthermore, Fuller reported, the newly established board had authorized Ockenga to invite Wilbur Smith, Carl F. H. Henry, and Everett Harrison to join the faculty and that they had all accepted. Conversations had also been held with Allan MacRae, Charles Woodbridge, Gleason Archer, Terrelle Crum, and Clarence Macartney. While the first round of faculty appointments had been made of necessity by the newly established president and board, those who gathered in Chicago agreed that "no further professors would be hired without the invitation of the whole faculty."

The acquisition of the John Smith Cravens estate, a five-acre parcel on Orange Grove Avenue, appeared to those who had gathered in Chicago as "the first great divine victory of the venture." Valued at $1.5 million, the Fuller Foundation had been able to purchase it for $145,000. "The bankers said they had never seen a deal like it in Southern California." Charles Fuller, who "had summoned his workers in the office of the Old Fashioned Revival Hour

BULLETIN OF
FULLER
THEOLOGICAL SEMINARY

FULLER SEMINARY FACULTY
Top Row: Dr. Ehlert, Dr. Henry, Dr. Archer, Dr. Carnell, Dr. Ladd, Dr. LaSor;
Bottom Row: Dr. Harrison, Dr. Smith, Dr. Lindsell, Dr. Woodbridge, Dr. Roddy.
The twelfth member of the Faculty is Dr. Rebecca R. Price.

| Volume II | October, November, December, 1952 | Number 4 |

Bulletin of Fuller Theological Seminary (October, November, December 1952) including pictures of the Fuller Seminary faculty (courtesy of Fuller Theological Seminary Library Archives)

to prayer," simply concluded that God had intervened. The leaders had hoped to turn the rooms of the estate into offices and classrooms and to build a hotel and multiple units on the property, but the Pasadena Zoning Commission denied their request at its June 1947 meeting. While the Cravens estate could be used for faculty and administrative offices, they determined, it could not be used for classrooms. Until more permanent facilities were built in the early 1950s, seminary classes would have to be held at Lake Avenue Congregational Church.

As is also apparent from the minutes of the Chicago meeting, the new faculty was expected to publish. "In view of faculty salaries and teaching loads," as Carl Henry phrased it in the minutes, much is to be "expected in the way of research and publication. A book approximately every two years from each faculty member was suggested." All honoraria received by the faculty, except during the two months of official vacation, were to be "turned back to the Seminary." Annual student tuition was set at $100 per year. Student lodging would be provided for $100 annually. The cost of meals in the dining hall, if such could be arranged, was set at $7 per week.[55]

What followed the meeting in Chicago, as Ockenga later described it, "were days of labor, travail and of difficulty."[56] Yet, he recalled, "they were also days that gave us a great thrill in the doing of a pioneer work. There was a crusading zeal on the part of each person who was identified with the early days of the

55. Carl F. H. Henry, "Minutes," May 14, 1947. An extensive collection of materials relating to Fuller Theological Seminary, including hundreds of letters, photographs, publications, etc., can be found in the Ockenga Papers.

56. The enormous task of starting an institution from scratch is reflected in the faculty minutes. A set of these minutes, beginning with the Wednesday, September 10, 1947, meeting (titled "Minutes of the First Faculty Meeting") can be found in the Ockenga Papers.

Seminary."[57] "Surely God was leading in those days," reflected Fuller. "When
we met in Chicago, in May, to discuss this challenge and to pray together we
all were <u>deeply</u> impressed with the presence of the Holy Spirit, and no one
there that day could ever forget that meeting." "Do you not see <u>clearly</u> how
God has worked in bringing this school into being, and how He is <u>now</u> working? It thrills my very soul!"[58] While scores of practical concerns demanded
their attention, there can be little question that what most deeply captured the
imagination of the faculty as they began preparing for the opening of Fuller
Theological Seminary in the fall of 1947 was their mutual commitment to the
life of the mind.[59] Evangelicalism can once again become "a vital option,"
wrote Henry in a letter to Ockenga, "only by the corporate effort of a body
of scholars devoted to the task."[60]

These sentiments also lay at the heart of Harold John Ockenga's stirring
address at the seminary's opening convocation held in the Pasadena Civic
Auditorium on October 1, 1947. More than two thousand people gathered on
that historic occasion to help launch the new seminary and to hear what the
new president might say. "We do not intend to allow our Christian heritage
to go because of default," Ockenga declared.

> A revival of Christian thought and life cannot occur in a vacuum. Our minds
> must first be convinced before we commit our lives, our fortunes and our sacred
> honor to any cause. Since in the minds of many people the ground work for the
> Christian view of God, the world, man and the kingdom has been destroyed by
> naturalism and liberalism, it will be the solemn and sacred duty of this faculty
> to attempt the reconstruction of this with scholarly pursuits.[61]

Such a task, Ockenga was certain, would require a commitment to the
highest possible moral and intellectual standards. Every faculty member must
be "an accepted and recognized scholar in his own field" and every student
must be "a graduate of an accepted college." It would be their purpose "to

57. Harold John Ockenga, "Testimonial to Charles E. Fuller," on the occasion of Fuller's death,
Ockenga Papers. "I shall treasure always the hours of fellowship, counsel and prayer which I had with
Dr. Fuller. It was my privilege to live in his home probably 75 weeks during the period of twenty years
in which we were engaged in this activity. I saw the loving, beautiful relationship of Charles and Grace,
and I experienced his love and returned it equally."
58. Fuller to Ockenga and the Trustees of Fuller Theological Seminary.
59. The passion to revitalize evangelical scholarship is reflected in the correspondence between
Carl F. H. Henry and Ockenga (1947–68); Charles E. Fuller and Ockenga (1946–68); Harold Lindsell
and Ockenga (1947–68); Wilbur Smith and Ockenga (1946–64); and Edward John Carnell and Ockenga
(1947–63); in the Ockenga Papers.
60. Henry to Ockenga, April 23, 1947, Ockenga Papers.
61. Harold John Ockenga, "The Challenge to the Christian Culture of the West," 10, Ockenga
Papers. Ockenga later reported that two thousand one hundred had been in attendance, including the
forty students who had been admitted to the seminary's first class, in a letter to Edward John Carnell,
October 7, 1947, Ockenga Papers.

win a standing in the academic world that is second to none," for "God is never satisfied with our second best. He wants the best."[62] The disintegration of Western culture, the decline of morality, and the "threat of persecution and tribulation," presented the Christian church with enormous challenges. "Is it a time to build a theological seminary when the world is on fire?" Ockenga asked those who had gathered. Then, answering his own question, he concluded:

> Yes, this is the fastest way of doing the job before us. We are not going to despair. We are not going to take it sitting down. We are not going to abdicate the leadership in social, educational and civic responsibility. We are not going to say, "Let George do it." By the grace and help of God we are going to build a school and train a student body to redeem the time.[63]

But the winning of academic respectability, as important as the early leaders of Fuller Theological Seminary believed that task to be, was never viewed as an end in itself. Our "emphasis is not on buildings or education," wrote Ockenga, "but on evangelism, getting the gospel out, as Dr. Fuller has been doing."[64] "My earnest hope and prayer," wrote Fuller, is that "this Seminary shall train young men and women to be skilled, efficient, consecrated godly workers for the Church of Jesus Christ which He has purchased with His own blood." While "all the studies offered in this school are important," Fuller observed, they must all

> aim at the one grand end of the knowledge of Holy Scripture and a humble submission to its teaching. Let the authority of Scripture always be given the pre-eminence in these halls of learning, that our graduates may know the riches of the Word of God and how to proclaim these riches to a poor, needy, dying world. To know the Word of God, to live the Word of God, to preach the Word, to teach the Word is the sum of all wisdom, the heart of all Christian service. To this end may this Seminary remain true to the Faith once for all delivered to the saints.[65]

Christianity Today

"About two o'clock one night in 1953," wrote Billy Graham, "an idea raced through my mind, freshly connecting all the things I had seen and pondered about reaching a broader audience. Trying not to disturb Ruth, I slipped out of bed and into my study upstairs to write. A couple of hours later, the

62. Ockenga, "The Challenge to the Christian Culture of the West," 11.
63. Ibid., 14.
64. Harold John Ockenga, "The Need For and Purpose of Fuller Theological Seminary," five pages of handwritten notes for an address in 1950, Ockenga Papers.
65. Fuller to Ockenga and the Trustees of Fuller Theological Seminary.

concept of a new magazine was complete."[66] Within three years, after much prayer and a lot of good old-fashioned hard work, the idea had become a reality and the new magazine, *Christianity Today*, was officially launched.[67] *Christianity Today*, as Billy Graham described its mission, was to serve as "a focal point for the best in evangelical scholarship," support and encourage "a new generation of highly trained scholars who were deeply committed to Christ and His Word," "reaffirm the power of the Word of God to redeem and transform men and women," and help "restore intellectual respectability and spiritual

Original editorial board of *Christianity Today*

impact to evangelical Christianity."[68] In concert with the other educational initiatives, in short, *Christianity Today* was intended to play an important role in the renewal of the evangelical mind.[69]

"I have been giving more thought to the possibilities and potentialities of this magazine than any single thing," Billy Graham wrote in a 1955 letter to J. Howard Pew. Referring to the meetings in Scotland in which he was then engaged, Graham argued that "these campaigns that thrill and excite the clergy for a short period and show them what God can do with old-fashioned theology must be followed through with a periodical that will give them a reason for the hope that is in them." "This is what we must do: we must get the clergy changed."[70]

66. Graham, *Just As I Am*, 286.

67. Correspondence, by-laws, agendas, and minutes of meetings and additional materials relating to the beginning of *Christianity Today* can be found in the Ockenga Papers.

68. Graham, *Just As I Am*, 286. A copy of Graham's typed, seven-page rationale for the establishment of *Christianity Today* can be found in the Ockenga Papers.

69. See "Christianity Today," a twenty-four-page document "prepared as a basis for discussion"; and Carl F. H. Henry to To Whom It May Concern, September 1, 1955, Ockenga Papers.

70. Graham to Pew, April 12, 1955, Ockenga Papers.

Graham suggested immediately forming a board of trustees, consisting of Graham, Nelson Bell, Howard Pew, Paul Rees, Harold Ockenga, Jerry Bevan, Walter Bennett, George Wilson, Maxey Jarman, and Howard Butt. "I also think that I should take the chairmanship at least temporarily," he observed, since "I know each one of you individually and as yet all of you do not know each other well. For the first few months I think it will be necessary for me to give leadership to it." The project was of sufficient importance, Graham concluded, "that I have decided not to take the world tour that I had planned." Rather, "I will come straight back to America and give my time to television, radio and the building of this magazine. I think we should plan publication sometime in February or March of next year."[71]

In the back of everyone's mind, of course, was the *Christian Century*, the influential magazine that had been founded in 1884 as a voice for the liberal wing of the church. "When I was asked early in 1955 if I might be interested in editing a new evangelical magazine that would give the liberally oriented *Christian Century* a run for its biases," wrote Carl F. H. Henry, "I was reminded of a Spring day in 1938" when Wheaton's dean of students asked what was considered to be "Christianity's biggest need." Henry's response, he recalled, was the need for evangelical Christianity to have "a counterpart to *Christian Century*."[72] "*Christianity Today* has its origin in a deepfelt desire to express historical Christianity to the present generation," wrote Henry in the inaugural issue of *Christianity Today*. "Neglected, slighted, misrepresented—evangelical Christianity needs a clear voice, to speak with conviction and love, and to state its true position and its relevance to the world crisis." It was the conviction of those running the magazine, Henry continued, "that the historic evangelical faith is vital for the life of the Church and of the nations." Furthermore, "we believe that the Gospel is still the power of God unto salvation for all who believe; that the basic needs of the social order must meet their solution first in the redemption of the individual; that the Church and the individual Christian *do* have a vital responsibility to be both *salt* and *light* in a decaying and darkening world."[73]

A Christian University

"It meant more to me than I can possibly tell you," wrote John Bolten of his 1954 travels with the Graham team, "that I had the privilege of being with you in Essen, Hamburg, and Berlin, and I want to thank you for going to my old fatherland to preach the Gospel of Jesus Christ." "Ever since those days

71. Ibid.
72. For a more extended version of the story and Henry's discussion of his involvement with *Christianity Today*, see Carl F. H. Henry, *Confessions of a Theologian: An Autobiography* (Waco: Word, 1986), 144–219.
73. Carl F. H. Henry, "Why 'Christianity Today'?" *Christianity Today*, October 15, 1956, 20–23.

together," he continued, "the question of the proposed Christian university in the United States has been before me."[74] Indeed, from the mid-1950s through the end of the decade, the possibility of establishing a Christian university not only generated substantial discussion within evangelical circles but also exposed some deepening divisions.[75] By November 5, 1959, Billy Graham was ready to appoint a committee to explore the possibility of establishing "Crusade University." The committee, whose membership included Graham, David W. Baker, Henderson Belk, Enock C. Dyrness, Carl A. Gundersen, Paul Harvey, Carl F. H. Henry, J. Howard Pew, Charles A. Pitts, and Jacob Stam, gathered at the Statler Hotel in Washington, D.C., on December 29, 1959. "We recognized the need for the establishment of a Christian University to meet needs not now being met by existing institutions," as the committee minutes phrased the rationale for the gathering, and "after a careful consideration of many factors, the Committee recommends that such an institution be established on the East Coast."[76]

The *New York Times*, in its May 5, 1960, issue, carried an article titled "Protestants Map University Here." "Evangelical Protestant laymen are close to deciding whether to start a movement to establish 'a Christian university' in the New York City area," the article reported. "Business men and educators have been meeting in small groups in New York, Philadelphia and Washington for the last two years to discuss the matter and pray about it. A decision on the project is expected this summer." The new institution "would include an undergraduate liberal arts college as well as graduate schools in political and social science, communication, arts, music, theology, and Christian philosophy and education. An opening in September, 1963, has been suggested."[77]

The May 9, 1960, issue of *Christianity Today* carried a strong endorsement of the idea by editor Carl F. H. Henry. To the question "Do We Need a Christian University?" Henry answered with a resounding yes. "We think the *providential moment* is here," he wrote. "The tide of American thought and life makes imperative a Christian university devoted in depth to the biblical revelation of God, of man, and of the world; aggressively challenging pagan and secular theories of reality and history; and supplying a steady stream of

74. Bolten to Graham, November 1, 1960, Ockenga Papers. See also Graham, *Just As I Am*, 243–45.

75. See, for example, Edward John Carnell to Harold John Ockenga, October 12, 1955; John B. Conlan Jr. to Harold John and Audrey Ockenga, January 20, 1957; and Kenneth L. Pike to Carl F. H. Henry, June 2, 1960, Ockenga Papers.

76. "The Minutes of Meeting Concerning CRUSADE UNIVERSITY," Washington, D.C., December 29, 1959, and correspondence relating to these discussions can be found in the Ockenga Papers. Five subcommittees were established: promotion and finance, site, organization and incorporation, academic, and standards and conduct. June 16, 1960, was set for the subcommittees to report back to the full Crusade University Committee.

77. "Protestants Map University Here," *New York Times*, May 5, 1960, Ockenga Papers.

spiritual leadership to all professions and vocations, including diplomacy, business, and communication."[78]

Despite some misgivings, Billy Graham seems to have generally favored the plan. "Dr. Graham has refused to entangle himself with academic responsibilities," Henry reported. However, Graham had "given much encouragement to the plan, though disallowing use of his own name in the naming of an institution. Dr. Graham clearly shares the burden for a Christian university that brings classical distinction to evangelical education," Henry continued, "and has encouraged discussion and planning by interested leaders."[79] Despite strong support from Henry, Ockenga, Carnell, and others, not all of Graham's closest advisors were in favor of the plan. While Bolten was clearly interested in exploring the possibility of establishing "a new Theological Faculty or Seminary in Germany like the Fuller Seminary in [the] USA,"[80] he was clearly troubled about the prospect of establishing a Christian university in America. "Do we imagine if we should be successful and can develop a university of recognized scholarship and academic excellence, that even perhaps might rival Harvard or Princeton," Bolten asked, "that the existence of this university, per se, would change the American educational system?" Furthermore, Bolten continued, where would a first-rate faculty for such an institution be found? "Are you going to siphon them all from Christian colleges" or remove from the secular institutions those few "Christian professors who are shining as light in a dark place, who are the salt in that little piece of earth?" Such a process, Bolten was convinced, "would impoverish" our Christian colleges and would leave our universities bereft of a Christian witness.

"It may be argued," Bolten conceded, "that it is necessary to have Christian colleges to protect our boys and girls from the inroads of secularism, materialism, and unbelief." Yet "there must come a time when a boy becomes a man—when the Christian man stands in the world in the strength of the Lord Jesus Christ." "Are we to perpetuate the philosophy of false separation?" Bolten asked. "We talk about the false separation of the fundamentalist separatists, but is there not a greater degree of error in the separation that constantly insulates and isolates our young people from the world in which God has sent them to be witnesses?" The "most effective means" of helping "the institutions of higher learning," Bolten argued, "is to try to encourage, according to the biblical principle of penetration, Christian men and women to go into these institutions to teach and to stand for the truth, rather than to draw them away from these institutions and to concentrate them in one,

78. Carl F. H. Henry, "Evangelical Advance: Do We Need a Christian University?" *Christianity Today*, May 9, 1960, 3–5. See also Frank E. Gaebelein, "Review of Current Religious Thought," *Christianity Today*, June 20, 1960, 40.

79. Henry, "Evangelical Advance," 4–5.

80. H. Rohrbach to John Bolten, August 22, 1955, Ockenga Papers. Rohrbach was professor of mathematics at the University of Mainz.

single place!" "God has given you the spiritual vision to look at the world as your parish," he reminded Graham. Since this is so, he continued, "why not keep a world-wide vision and now look at the universities of the world again as a potential mission field?" Think of the universities of India, Africa, Asia, Europe, and the Americas, he said. "Are we to turn away from these to give our strength and perhaps spend a hundred million dollars on a hypothetical institution which, to say the very least, is highly questionable, and against which all history with one unanimous voice speaks and witnesses?" "May I end with this one word," Bolten concluded his lengthy letter. "Carl Henry is not the key to this situation. Harold Ockenga is not the key to the situation. You, Billy Graham, are the key! If you are for a Christian university, an attempt will be made; if you are against it, in all probability, the whole idea will collapse. May I ask you, with the Apostle Paul's permission, 'Is this not a more excellent way?'"[81]

The proposal for establishing Crusade University was eventually abandoned, just as John Bolten had hoped. The discussion, however, had exposed yet again a profound uncertainty in the evangelical ranks as to what strategy should be adopted in reclaiming the culture for Christ. Billy Graham, John Bolten, and a host of additional evangelicals had embraced Ockenga's grand vision of infiltrating, penetrating, and transforming the culture for Christ—and had acted upon it—quite simply because they were convinced that it was the most effective way to reach a needy world with the good news of the Gospel.

Christ's commission to the church, as all of the evangelical leaders agreed, was to "go and make disciples of all nations, baptizing them in the name of the Father and of the Son and of the Holy Spirit, and teaching them to obey everything I have commanded you. And surely I am with you always, to the very end of the age" (Matt. 28:19–20, NIV). Indeed, by the end of the 1950s a growing number of evangelicals seemed prepared to spare no expense and withhold no amount of energy in their efforts to do everything humanly possible to see that Christ's great commission was accomplished.

81. John Bolten to Billy Graham, November 1, 1960, Ockenga Papers. For an expression of similar concerns, see John B. Conlan Jr. to Harold John and Audrey Ockenga, January 20, 1957, Ockenga Papers.

9

‡※‡※‡※‡※‡※‡※‡※‡※‡※‡※‡※‡※‡※‡※‡※‡

REACHING THE WORLD

During the nearly three centuries since its beginnings in the Great Awakening, nothing has characterized American evangelicalism quite so clearly as its passionate commitment to spread the Christian gospel around the world. Evangelicals have of course not been alone in their efforts to fulfill the great commission. The nineteenth century is called "The Great Century," to borrow historian Kenneth Scott Latourette's famous description, precisely because so many Christians between 1800 and 1914 were prepared to invest their lives and resources in seeking to accomplish the missionary task. While not all missionaries were evangelicals, almost all evangelicals have been committed to missions.[1]

From eighteenth-century missionaries like David Brainerd, Jonathan Edwards, George Whitefield, Augustus Gottlieb Spangenberg, and the brothers John and Charles Wesley, to the thousands of men and women who committed their lives to the missionary task throughout the following centuries, evangelicals have seen the spread of the gospel as an important part of their agenda. The famous 1806 Haystack Prayer Meeting at Williams College; the

1. Three of the seven volumes in Latourette's *History of the Expansion of Christianity* were devoted to a study of "The Great Century." See Kenneth Scott Latourette, *A History of the Expansion of Christianity* (Grand Rapids: Zondervan, 1970), vol. 4, *The Great Century: Europe and the United States*; vol. 5, *The Great Century: North Africa and Asia*; and vol. 6, *The Great Century: The Americas, Australia, Asia and Africa*.

1812 commissioning of America's first foreign missionaries at Tabernacle Congregational Church in Salem, Massachusetts; the 1886 beginnings of the Student Volunteer Movement at D. L. Moody's Mount Hermon; the 1906 Azusa Street Revival that helped to launch Pentecostalism's amazing spread around the globe; and the 1974 International Congress on World Evangelization in Lausanne, Switzerland, are but a few of the seemingly endless parade of events that illustrate evangelicalism's continuing interest in worldwide evangelization.[2] If we truly love God, Ockenga reminded his Park Street congregation in 1964, "we will keep His commandments and we will subordinate all things unto the ends which He has established, namely that the Gospel shall be preached to every kingdom, tribe, nation and people before the end comes."[3]

A Passion for Missions

There were few topics that seemed to touch Ockenga's heart as deeply as missions. From his earliest years he loved to travel and had developed a lifelong interest in studying the world. Furthermore, he had sensed God's call to missionary service when he was in seminary. Indeed, it was only the persuasive powers of his mentors, Clarence Macartney and Frank Stevenson, that had convinced him that he could strengthen the missionary enterprise more effectively as the pastor of a missionary church than he ever could as an individual missionary. Nevertheless, there seemed to be an unusual tenderness whenever Ockenga spoke about missionary service.[4] "One's own vision of missionary work is a very personal matter," Ockenga reflected in 1960, and the "missionary who was the instrument of God in opening my eyes to the need in the mission field was a fiery Methodist missionary who had almost reached the age of retirement and who testified of the thousands of unoccupied villages in Africa where the Word of God had never been heard." Since hearing that message thirty years ago, he continued, "I cannot hear of the desperate need in the mission field without wanting to go and meet that need. Were it not that the church I serve is sending out scores of missionaries and supporting missionaries in thirty-nine countries of the earth, I should still feel that strong impetus to leave the work in the home field and go where the need is the greatest." "During my first year at Princeton Theological Seminary,"

2. See Ruth A. Tucker, *From Jerusalem to Irian Jaya: A Biographical History of Christian Missions*, 2nd ed. (Grand Rapids: Zondervan, 2004); Patrick Johnstone and Jason Mandryk, eds., *Operation World: When We Pray God Works* (Waynesboro, GA: Paternoster USA, 2001); and Dana L. Robert, *American Women in Mission: A Social History of Their Thought and Practice* (Macon, GA: Mercer University Press, 1996).

3. Harold John Ockenga, "What Twenty-Five Years of Missionary Conferences Have Taught Me," sermon 2540, preached in 1964 at Park Street Church in Boston, Ockenga Papers.

4. For an extended account of how he became interested in missions, see Harold John Ockenga, "Life with a Vision," sermon 2205, preached at Park Street Church in 1960, Ockenga Papers.

Ockenga recalled, "I joined the Student Volunteers, met with them regularly and the second year became president of the group. Three of us students met together regularly to pray for the mission field and finally we came to the conclusion that we were to go as a group to China. That I never reached the field as a missionary did not dim the vision." Indeed, a "comprehension of the need of the mission field and deep responsibility to meet that need has been sustained throughout the years."[5]

Another source for Ockenga's passion for missions was the sudden loss of a close college friend. David Clench, who was known by his Taylor classmates as a person of enormous integrity and personal piety, had gone as a missionary to the Dutch East Indies to oversee a Bible school.[6] Clench and Ocky, as his friend liked to call him, corresponded about the missionary work in which he was engaged, and Ockenga, from time to time, had helped in his support.[7] At the close of the school term, in December of 1933, David and one of his colleagues, C. Russell Deibler, traveled to Shanghai on a brief vacation. While there, Clench was stricken with acute brain fever and meningitis, and within hours he was dead.[8] "Never have I received such tragic news," Ockenga wrote in early February. "It was just time for Dave's Christmas letter to come—the one he always sent in reply to an insignificant remembrance. Instead, came your card." "It hurt, hurt as I cannot tell," he continued.

Some where inside of me something happened—I don't know what. But the hot tears came, and still come. Not that I regret God's Providence, not that I mourn a dear friend, but that an overwhelming white light has shone upon his beautiful life and each of those loving details stands out in such bold relief. His nights spent in prayer at Taylor, his refusal to go on the "Sneak Day" because the funds could be used for missions, his infinite compassion for souls, his musical and poetic nature, his cries of heart loneliness, his utter self-abnegation in the service of a redeeming Christ. Yes, a kind of suffering which we do not understand made him perfect and God took him. His robes are washed white in the blood of the lamb.[9]

David's favorite text, Ockenga continued, was this: "'Except a corn of wheat fall into the ground and die it abideth alone; but if it die it bringeth forth much

5. Ockenga, "Life with a Vision."

6. C. David Clench, from Ninette, Manitoba, Canada, graduated from Taylor in 1927 with a major in history. Written next to his senior class picture in the Taylor yearbook are these words: "Thus, in uncertain radiance, Genius glows And fitful gleams on various mind bestows." See the *Gem* (1927), 44.

7. Clench to Ockenga, March 22, 1930, Ockenga Papers.

8. For accounts of Clench's life and work, see R. A. Jaffray to Harold John Ockenga, January 22, 1934; *Pioneer*, Memorial Number 5, no. 18 (March 1934); "David Clench Dies in China," unidentified article; and a variety of duplicated remembrances circulated to graduates of Taylor; all housed with the Ockenga Papers.

9. Harold John Ockenga to Hazel, February 2, 1934, Ockenga Papers.

fruit.' Certainly, he fulfilled it as did his Lord and Saviour. I remember one night his coming to the room after I had preached in Holiness League on 'I die daily,' that glorious text of Paul. He had expressed the sermon in a poem on the Cross. We prayed," Ockenga continued, and "then he played his violin and we talked long into the night. He knew the Cross. He trusted the satisfaction of Christ and he lived the life of Christ." "Who dare say that this life is all? that David lived in vain? He, in his fevers and sufferings in Borneo, brought forth much fruit. But he is bearing fruit in my heart just now."[10]

Whatever the reasons for Ockenga's interest in missions, there can be no question that it continued to energize him and his ministry throughout his life. In looking back over twenty-five years of missions conferences at Park Street, he reflected on the seven major lessons he had learned: First, "that missions make the church"; second, "that God has a program for His church"; third, "that the local church is the key to world missions"; fourth, "that the individual must have personal contact with the missionaries"; fifth, "that the missionary conference is the most effective means of conveying the missionary challenge"; sixth, "that the faith pledge should be used in missionary giving"; and seventh, "that blessing is connected with obedience."[11]

"The Great Commission," as Ockenga liked to remind his listeners, should engage every believer in "the worldwide evangelistic task." He was convinced, however, that the meaning of Christ's command is far more comprehensive than simply a proclamation of the gospel. Indeed, it must also engage every believer in education, moral reform, and humanitarian action. Furthermore, it must be global in its focus. "We are determined to maintain fidelity of witness and work in Boston, in New England, in the United States, and throughout the world."[12] "It is evident," he concluded, "that the measure of our worship of the Lord Jesus is the measure of our sacrifice."[13]

The World Evangelical Fellowship

Given the deep missionary convictions of leaders such as Ockenga and Graham, whose voice has now been heard in almost every country around the world, it would have been surprising had the evangelical movement of the 1940s and 1950s failed to make world missions a central part of its expanding program. In a sense, of course, evangelicals had never abandoned the task. The mid-twentieth-century spiritual awakening, however, brought new energy, fresh resolve, and hundreds of bright young recruits. Youth for Christ, as we have

10. Ibid.

11. Ockenga, "What Twenty-Five Years of Missionary Conferences Have Taught Me."

12. Harold John Ockenga, "The Foundations of Park Street Church," 16, sermon 2085, preached on February 22, 1959, on the occasion of Park Street Church's 150th Anniversary, Ockenga Papers.

13. Ockenga, "What Twenty-Five Years of Missionary Conferences Have Taught Me."

already seen, was founded in 1945 as Youth for Christ *International*—with a worldwide ministry already in place. Indeed, by the summer of 1948, when delegates from around the world gathered in Beatenberg, Switzerland, Billy Graham had already spent substantial time in the British Isles and Europe and the organization with which he was associated had been regularly holding youth rallies in forty-six countries around the globe. Ockenga, moreover, seems to have been born clutching train, plane, and boat tickets tightly in his hand. Indeed, he had already become a seasoned world traveler by the early 1940s when he became the first president of the NAE, and throughout his life he never seemed to lose his fascination with people and events around the globe.

By 1945, the NAE, with strong encouragement from Ockenga and his colleagues, had helped launch both the Evangelical Foreign Missions Association and World Relief.[14] But since the parent organization "was a *national* association" rather than "*international*," as Arthur H. Matthews has described a problem confronting the NAE's early leaders, it was not able to accept applications for membership from overseas.[15] It appears to have been this problem more than any other that led to the establishment in 1951 of the World Evangelical Fellowship.[16] "The World Evangelical Fellowship," explained Ockenga, "is a projection in the international scale of the same principles which operate the N.A.E. and the Evangelical Alliance in America and Britain.[17] We have twenty-one indigenous associations in twenty-one nations of the earth," he continued with reference to the World Evangelical Fellowship, and "others are in the process of being formed. This is [neither] a Council of Churches nor an organization of individuals, but is an Association of indigenous groups of believers on evangelical lines throughout the world."[18] Convinced that, as an early brochure described the situation, "divisions among evangelical believers" were "destroying our witness," "crippling our ministry," "delaying" missionary deployment, "creating tragic confusion," and "hindering the salvation of the heathen," the

14. The Evangelical Foreign Missions Association was officially established September 19–20, 1945, at the LaSalle Hotel in Chicago, Illinois, with fourteen charter members, to provide a voice for evangelical missions and to encourage cooperative efforts within the membership. Clyde Taylor became its first executive secretary, serving from 1945 until 1974. World Relief served as the humanitarian arm of the NAE. See Arthur H. Matthews, *Standing Up, Standing Together: The Emergence of the National Association of Evangelicals* (Carol Stream, IL: National Association of Evangelicals, 1992), 145–56.

15. Matthews, *Standing Up, Standing Together*, 104.

16. See David M. Howard, *The Dream That Would Not Die: The Birth and Growth of the World Evangelical Fellowship* (Grand Rapids: Baker Academic, 1988); Matthews, *Standing Up, Standing Together*, 103–23; and three files of correspondence and records labeled "N.A.E.: World Evangelical Fellowship," Ockenga Papers.

17. The World Evangelical Fellowship traces its historical roots to the founding in 1846 of The Evangelical Alliance in London. See J. Chambers Long, "Past: The Story; Present: The Opportunities; Future: The Call," in the "World's Evangelical Alliance" folder in the Ockenga Papers. For the American story, see Philip D. Jordan, *The Evangelical Alliance of the United States of America, 1847–1900* (Lewiston, NY: Edwin Mellen, 1983).

18. Harold John Ockenga to Larry Culp, December 7, 1956, Ockenga Papers.

World Evangelical Fellowship called for "cooperative effort" to complete "tasks too long left undone," to meet needs too long unmet and accomplish ministries "too great for any one person or mission to undertake."[19]

Like most new organizations, the World Evangelical Fellowship experienced its share of growing pains as it sought to meet enormous global needs with relatively modest resources. Yet despite financial, organizational, and ideological difficulties, the organization proved to be the "dream that would not die."[20] Based in Singapore since 1987, the World Evangelical Fellowship has continued to provide "both the structure and forum for evangelicals worldwide to join together, defend the faith and cooperate in advancing the gospel."[21] During the 1950s and 1960s, however, the World Evangelical Fellowship—like virtually every American and British mission organization—came face-to-face with an even more difficult challenge. "The hard facts of reality," wrote John Bolten in a letter to the General Secretary of the Fellowship in 1961, were that "there is a new mood in the world, and a very strong resistance to American leadership—rightly or wrongly!" As a result of "the great struggle between the communist world under Russia and the free world under the leadership of the U.S.," he continued, "the smaller nations tend to view both countries with suspicion." Consequently, it was "quite impossible to imagine that sovereign evangelical associations of churches and societies will accept a strong leadership from the United States. Unquestionably, the only way before us is for there to be a free association of national movements which, themselves, are sovereign."[22]

In light of these new realities, American evangelicals should abandon "once and for all" the notion that their "financial contributions in any way give us any right to dictate policy." Many of our Christian brothers and sisters in other countries, he continued, have grown "completely weary" of our "expensive conferences" and our continual "tug-of-war for influence and leadership."[23]

A Global Movement

Such perspectives also hold important implications for the evangelical movement as a whole. Few mid-twentieth-century Christians would have

19. Quotations are taken from the World Evangelical Fellowship brochure "Cooperative Missions . . . is Your Mission," a copy of which is in the Ockenga Papers. See also Harold John Ockenga, "World Evangelical Fellowship," undated sermon outline 952, Ockenga Papers; and Everett L. Cattell, "National Association of Evangelicals and World Evangelical Fellowship," *Christianity Today*, January 29, 1965, 12–14.

20. Howard, *The Dream That Would Not Die*.

21. R. C. Cizik, "World Evangelical Fellowship," in *Dictionary of Christianity in America*, ed. Daniel G. Reid, Robert D. Linder, Bruce L. Shelley, and Harry S. Stout (Downers Grove, IL: InterVarsity, 1990), 1275.

22. John Bolten Sr. to Fred Ferris, September 26, 1961, Ockenga Papers.

23. Ibid.

noticed the enormous changes that were even then beginning to take place as "the center of gravity in the Christian world" continued to move "inexorably southward, to Africa, Asia, and Latin America," to borrow the language of Philip Jenkins.[24] Yet by the end of the last century, as Winston Crawley and others have observed, such a shift was "well under way" and it now "appears irreversible."[25] "The era of Western Christianity has passed within our lifetimes," Jenkins argues, "and the day of Southern Christianity is dawning. The fact of change itself is undeniable: it has happened, and will continue to happen."[26]

While there are some notable exceptions, many of us who study contemporary evangelicalism have remained curiously myopic with regard to the enormous demographic and cultural changes that have taken place within the movement during the past few decades. "The exponential growth of evangelical Christianity in the non-Western world," observed Donald M. Lewis in *Christianity Reborn: The Global Expansion of Evangelicalism in the Twentieth Century*, "has produced a Christianity of amazing cultural diversity but one which is largely hidden from the purview of Western scholars."[27] It is unlikely, of course, that the explosive growth of evangelical Christianity will remain hidden for long. As both Harold John Ockenga and Billy Graham seem to have envisioned many years before, the very nature of the Christian gospel itself would inevitably result in the expansion of the World Christian Movement so as to cover the earth as the waters cover the sea.

It is impossible to know with any certainty what shape and direction the evangelical movement will take in the coming years. Since some of the younger churches, along with many of the more established African-American congregations, seldom use the term "evangelical" at all, it is possible that the movement will gradually fade away. Such a development would hardly be disastrous. After all, Christ's "great commission" was not to make more "evangelicals," to say nothing of creating more evangelical institutions, but rather "to go and make disciples of all nations, baptizing them in the name of the Father and of the Son and of the Holy Spirit, and teaching them to obey everything I have commanded you" (Matt. 28:18–20 NIV). What would be genuinely tragic, however, is if the biblical truth that helped to create and sustain evangelicalism for nearly three centuries were also to fade away. Such a development, as theologian David Wells has suggested, is more than a remote possibility.

24. Philip Jenkins, *The Next Christendom: The Coming of Global Christianity* (New York: Oxford University Press, 2002), 2.

25. Winston Crawley, *World Christianity: 1970–2000* (Pasadena: William Carey Library, 2001), 48–49. For a fuller discussion, see "Some Important New Trends" in chap. 1.

26. Jenkins, *The Next Christendom*, 3.

27. Donald M. Lewis, ed., *Christianity Reborn: The Global Expansion of Evangelicalism in the Twentieth Century* (Grand Rapids: Eerdmans, 2004), 7.

Indeed, there are signs that its "lengthening shadows" are already being cast across "our evangelical world."[28]

The future of evangelicalism, to put it succinctly, depends largely on what answers the worldwide evangelical movement is prepared to give to seven important questions: What is our ultimate authority? What is our primary purpose? What are our most important goals? Where is our ultimate loyalty? What is the foundation of our hope? To what theology do we subscribe? Into what community have we been called?

For most evangelicals, from Jonathan Edwards and George Whitefield to Harold John Ockenga and Billy Graham, the answers to these questions have been absolutely clear and unequivocal: our ultimate authority is the Bible; our primary purpose is to bring glory to God and to serve the common good; our most important goals are worldwide evangelization and the spiritual renewal of the church and the culture; our ultimate loyalty is to the Sovereign and tri-une Lord of the Universe; the foundation of our hope is Christ's spotless life, atoning death on the cross, and glorious resurrection; our theology is "historic orthodoxy," the faith once delivered to the saints (as taught in Scripture and reflected, albeit imperfectly, in the historic creeds and confessions); and the community into which we have been called is the Christian church.

Across the years, as we have seen, these core values provided shape, direction, and motivation for a movement that could never claim an official headquarters, a governing constitution, a statement of faith, or an elected leadership. Yet for nearly three centuries this loose coalition of Christians— held together by a shared focus (the cross), a shared authority (the Bible), a shared experience (conversion), a shared mission (worldwide evangelization), and a shared vision (the spiritual renewal of church and culture)—has chosen to call itself evangelical and to be identified with evangelicalism's programs and purposes. Little wonder that it continues to produce such a wide range of responses—from genuine curiosity to angry criticism, from glowing admiration to smoldering fear, from happy celebration to profound confusion. Since so many movements have taken institutional identities over time, the fact that the evangelical movement should have resisted doing so for nearly three centuries remains a matter of great fascination and considerable consternation.

From its humble beginnings in the Great Awakening, the number of those who identify themselves as evangelical Christians has grown to perhaps as many as half a billion people worldwide.[29] Furthermore, according to

28. David F. Wells, *The Bleeding of the Evangelical Church* (Edinburgh: Banner of Truth, 1995), 1. For a superb analysis of contemporary evangelicalism and its surrounding culture, see David F. Wells, *No Place for Truth* (1993), *God in the Wasteland* (1994), *Losing Our Virtue* (1999), and *Above All Earthly Powers: Christ in a Postmodern World* (2005), all published by Eerdmans in Grand Rapids.

29. Figures are taken from David B. Barrett, Todd M. Johnson, and Peter Crossing, eds., "Missiometrics 2005: A Global Survey of World Mission," *International Bulletin of Missionary Research* 29, no. 1 (January 2005): 27–30. Barrett, Johnson, and Crossing estimate that slightly more than 250

estimates in *The Prospering Parachurch*, there are some one hundred thousand parachurch organizations in North America alone—from Campus Crusade for Christ and World Vision to the Christian Broadcasting Network and the Billy Graham Evangelistic Association. These organizations, many of which are clearly evangelical in their staffing and mission, are engaged in a wide variety of ministries from health care and education to social services and evangelism.[30] The Billy Graham Crusades, conducted in scores of countries around the globe, have now reached "more than 200 million people in person, and millions more have heard him on radio, television, and film."[31] In addition, thousands of evangelical churches, like Park Street Church in Boston, continue their faithful ministries to millions of believers around the world.

Enormous numerical success, of course, has its dangers. Rapid growth, like that which occurred in the Roman Empire under Emperor Constantine, can easily mask a wide range of profound problems within the Christian community from complacency and cultural captivity to spiritual arrogance and moral failure.[32] While its size is impressive, evangelicalism's sins and shortcomings leave little room for pride or arrogant boasting. One cannot help but wonder, in fact, if contemporary evangelicalism's biblical and theological roots are sufficiently strong and planted with sufficient depth to withstand the swirling winds of persecution that often seem to catch the Christian community unexpectedly.

Here is where the study of evangelicalism in the 1930s, 1940s, and 1950s can be of help to the contemporary church. While the movement was far from perfect, it does stand as a continuing reminder of the importance of historic orthodoxy. Activist in style, optimistic in mood, reformist in strategy, Bible-centered in authority, Christ-centered in ministry, mission-centered in outreach, evangelistic in practice, and ecumenical in spirit, the mid-twentieth-century evangelicals sought to spread the Christian gospel to every person around the globe. If we are willing to listen to them carefully, they can also challenge contemporary Christians to root themselves deeply in historic orthodoxy, to live in obedience to the Scriptures, to seek to penetrate the culture for Christ, and to spread the life-giving gospel throughout the world.

---

million people can properly be identified as evangelical and another 588 million can be classified as either Pentecostal, charismatic, or neocharismatic.

30. See Wesley K. Willmer, J. David Schmidt, and Martyn Smith, *The Prospering Parachurch: Enlarging the Boundaries of God's Kingdom* (San Francisco: Jossey-Bass, 1998).

31. *Just As I Am: The Autobiography of Billy Graham* (San Francisco: HarperSanFrancisco, 1997), dust jacket.

32. See Rodney Stark, *The Rise of Christianity: How the Obscure, Marginal Jesus Movement Became the Dominant Religious Force in the Western World in a Few Centuries* (San Francisco: HarperSanFrancisco, 1997); Rodney Stark, *Cities of God* (San Francisco: HarperSanFrancisco, 2006); George Barna, *The Frog in the Kettle* (Ventura, CA: Regal, 1990); and George Barna and Mark Hatch, *Boiling Point: Monitoring Cultural Shifts in the 21st Century* (Ventura, CA: Regal, 2003).

Billy Graham and Audrey and Harold John Ockenga at the Ockengas' Hamilton, MA, home
(courtesy of Park Street Church, Boston)

Two friends, perhaps more than any others, were responsible for giving
shape and direction to the kind of evangelicalism that took root in twentieth-
century America and soon spread throughout the world. Despite their regional,
cultural, and personal differences, Harold John Ockenga and Billy Graham's
friendship and the deep personal regard each had for the other helped forge a
movement that continues to thrive in scores of countries around the world.

Early in 1985, knowing that he was dying of cancer, Ockenga requested that
the elders of Park Street Church gather at his Hamilton, Massachusetts, home
to pray for him and anoint him with oil. He asked his wife Audrey to make sure
that his frail, eighty-pound body was dressed in a suit and tie. When the elders
had gathered around the bed, they began to express to their beloved old pastor,
who had served as the senior minister of Park Street Church from 1936 until 1969,
their deep personal affection and gratitude for the remarkable ministry God had
given him across so many years. "Just think of all the things that God has done
through you," they reminded him. He allowed you to minister to millions of
people, be president of Fuller Theological Seminary and Gordon-Conwell Theological Seminary, be one of the founders of the NAE and the whole evangelical
movement, and be one of the people who helped give Billy Graham his start.

Although Ockenga was too weak to respond, none of the comments seemed
to be bringing him the sense of peace and comfort that the elders hoped they
might be able to convey. Then one of the elders, after all of the others had

Harold John Ockenga, first president of Gordon-Conwell Theological Seminary (courtesy of Gordon-Conwell Libraries)

spoken, leaned forward and quietly commented: "Well, Harold, I suggest that when you see the Master, just say 'God be merciful to me a sinner.'" Upon hearing those words, we are told, tears began to flow down the old pastor's cheeks as the deep comfort of God's promise began its work in his heart.[33]

Soli Deo Gloria

"I have read," wrote Billy Graham at the end of his autobiography, "that Johann Sebastian Bach ended each composition with these words: *Soli Deo Gloria*—'To God alone be the glory.' Those are my words as well, at the end of this project."[34] His old friend, Harold John Ockenga, would have understood perfectly.

33. Gordon Hugenberger, senior minister at Park Street Church, told this touching story at the conclusion of his March 20, 2005, morning sermon, using Luke 19:28–48 as his primary text. He had gotten the story, as he commented during the service, from David McCahon, one of the elders who had visited Harold John Ockenga that day.

34. Graham, *Just As I Am*, 735.

Acknowledgments

Having taught a graduate seminar on historiography for nearly four decades, I am reminded regularly of the enormous debt that is owed to those who have both produced and preserved the evidence from which all historical research and writing must be drawn. Without the thousands of letters, sermons, organizational minutes, pictures, and ephemera in the two remarkable collections of personal papers with which I was privileged to work, the book that you hold in your hands could never have been written.

The Harold John Ockenga Papers, consisting of more than one hundred large archival boxes and currently housed in the Ockenga Institute at Gordon-Conwell Theological Seminary, is a veritable treasure trove of primary documents relating to nearly every aspect of twentieth-century evangelicalism. These materials were supplemented throughout my study by the Mervin E. Rosell Papers, a similarly-sized and incredibly rich collection of materials gathered by my evangelist father, known simply as "Merv" to the thousands who packed the largest auditoriums and stadiums to hear him preach. If this study has the "scent of authenticity to it," as my good friend and colleague, David F. Wells, commented after reading the manuscript, I suspect it is because so much of it is drawn from the primary materials in these two collections. Consequently, throughout the writing I have sought as much as possible to allow the participants to speak for themselves.

Primary documents, of course, neither interpret themselves nor are they always easy to interpret. For this task, the historian must frequently rely on the work of others. The most visible help, reflected in the footnotes, has come from a gifted group of historians—including scholars such as Timothy L. Smith, Lefferts A. Loetscher, George Marsden, Joel Carpenter, Mark Noll, Norris Magnuson, Donald Dayton, Douglas Sweeney, Richard Lovelace, Grant Wacker, Robert Wuthnow, Harold Lindsell, David Bebbington, Sydney E.

Ahlstrom, Leonard Sweet, Bruce Shelley, and Martin Marty—whose books I have used for many years in my graduate seminars and whose scholarship has often provided exactly the right interpretative framework within which to tell the story of twentieth-century evangelicalism. I have been especially grateful throughout this study for the pioneering work of George Marsden and Joel Carpenter. Their studies of the evangelical movement during the 1930s and 1940s not only opened this important era for serious study but they have also provided the foundation on which I have tried to build.

My greatest debts in producing this book, however, rarely show up in the footnotes. Three individuals, in particular, have shaped my thinking in such profound ways that they deserve special mention. Professor Lefferts A. Loetscher, the supervisor for my master of theology thesis at Princeton Theological Seminary, taught me how to do historical research and planted in me a love for the study of Christian history. Professor Timothy L. Smith, the supervisor for my doctor of philosophy thesis and a longtime and treasured friend, provided me with the kind of broad, multidimensional framework for understanding American religious history that undergirds this study. Whatever useful insights a reader might discover in what I have written are probably linked in some fundamental way to the things he taught me many years ago.

But the most formative influence on my understanding of twentieth-century evangelicalism, without any question, was my father. Not only did he introduce me to many of the people, places, and events I have sought to describe in these pages but we also spent many happy hours together poring over old pictures and documents and discussing how each aspect related to the other. Sometimes I would give him books to read and ask him to comment on the authors' interpretations and conclusions. His reflections were always respectful but candid. It was from those conversations that the basic outline for this book began to emerge. Dad's keen mind, irenic spirit, and passion for evangelism opened vistas I could never have seen by myself. It may well be, of course, that some readers might conclude that I have given my father a more prominent place in the story than is warranted. Although I do not believe that this is the case, since there is so much evidence to the contrary, it is a critique with which I am quite content to live.

Throughout the process of research and writing, I have been especially fortunate to have had a number of trusted colleagues, friends, and family members read all or portions of the manuscript and offer a variety of insightful suggestions and needed corrections. Among those who read the entire manuscript—and to whom I owe an enormous debt of gratitude—are George M. Marsden, David F. Wells, Walter and Marge Kaiser, Gwenfair and Kevin Adams, Gordon Hugenberger, John A. Huffman, Robert Dvorak, Muriel Clement, Steve Macchia, Robert Mayer, David Currie, Richard A. G. Dupuis, Leland Eliason, Jennifer Trafton, Joshua Kercsmar, Kerry Skinner, Bethany Sayles Yu, Ruth Brackbill, Mindelynn Young, and (to my great delight) most of the members of my extended family. Others, including Todd Johnson, Allan C. Emery Jr., and Doug Birdsall, were kind enough to read portions of the manuscript and offer their feedback. Still others, including John Adams, Bob Mayer, and David Horn, were at different stages of the project valuable conversation partners in exploring various aspects of the story. John's doctoral thesis, in which he examines the life and ministry of Harold John Ockenga, remains one of the few serious studies of that pivotal figure. I still harbor the hope, as he and I discussed some years ago, of someday collaborating on a full scale biography of Ockenga. My deep gratitude also extends to a number of friends and colleagues, including Stacey Moo, Daryl Olson, Ben Bythewood, Matt Erickson, and Joshua Kercsmar, who helped get the manuscript ready for publication. I am also profoundly indebted to the board of trustees of Gordon-Conwell Theological Seminary, whose generous sabbatical program has made this project possible; to my seminary colleagues, whose support and goodwill has made it such a joy; and to Robert Hosack, Jeremy Wells, Jeremy Cunningham, Karen Steele, and the rest of the superb Baker Academic team for their help throughout the process. To all of these friends and colleagues— and any I might have inadvertently left out—I want to express my deepest appreciation.

Among those who have encouraged me throughout this project, none have been more important than the members of my family. My dear mother, who lived through the events I have described and who represents the very best of the evangelical heritage, has been a constant encouragement. My son and daughter not only read the manuscript but also provided insights on how it might be strengthened. My sister and brother, gifted educators themselves, offered some perceptive suggestions and served as a constant source of inspiration. My new grandson, who proudly carries his great grandfather's name, provides hope that the best of the heritage can continue into the future.

Most important of all, of course, has been my wife. Not only did she read every chapter (often more than once) but we also had many opportunities to discuss them together. Her amazing insights, wise counsel, and unfailing enthusiasm for the project will remain among my most treasured memories. For the past forty-three years, Janie has been the heart of our family, the love of my life, and my dearest friend. It is to her that this volume is dedicated.

BIBLIOGRAPHY

Abraham, William J. *The Coming Great Revival: Recovering the Full Evangelical Tradition*. San Francisco: Harper & Row, 1984.

Adams, John M. "The Making of a Neo-Evangelical Statesman: The Case of Harold John Ockenga." PhD diss., Baylor University, 1994.

Adams, Kevin, and Emyr Jones. *A Diary of Revival*. Nashville: Broadman & Holman, 2004.

Ahlstrom, Sydney E. *An American Reformation: A Documentary History of Unitarian Christianity*. Middletown, CT: Wesleyan University Press, 1985.

———. *A Religious History of the American People*. New Haven: Yale University Press, 1972.

Aldrich, W. M. "Basic Concepts of Bible College Education." *Bibliotheca Sacra*, July 1962, 244–50.

Allan, Tom, ed. *Crusade in Scotland*. London: Pickering & Inglis, 1955.

Allen, Frederick Lewis. *Only Yesterday: An Informal History of the 1920's*. New York: Harper & Row, 1964.

Ammerman, Nancy T. *Bible Believers: Fundamentalists in the Modern World*. New Brunswick, NJ: Rutgers University Press, 1987.

Anderson, Allan. *An Introduction to Pentecostalism: Global Charismatic Christianity*. Cambridge: Cambridge University Press, 2004.

Anderson, Gerald H., and Thomas F. Stansky, eds. *Mission Trends*. No. 3: *Third World Theologies*. New York: Paulist Press, 1976.

Armstrong, John H. *The Coming Evangelical Crisis: Current Challenges to the Authority of Scripture and the Gospel*. Chicago: Moody, 1996.

229

Askew, Thomas A., and Richard V. Pierard. *The American Church Experience: A Concise History*. Grand Rapids: Baker Academic, 2004.

Baker, David D. "The World Council Constituted." *Advance*, October 1948, 22–23.

Balmer, Randall. *Blessed Assurance: A History of Evangelicalism in America*. Boston: Beacon, 1999.

———. *Encyclopedia of Evangelicalism*. Rev. and exp. ed. Waco: Baylor University Press, 2004.

———. *Grant Us Courage*. New York: Oxford University Press, 1996.

———. *Mine Eyes Have Seen the Glory: A Journey into the Evangelical Subculture in America*. New York: Oxford University Press, 1989.

Barna, George. *The Frog in the Kettle*. Ventura, CA: Regal Books, 1990.

Barna, George, and Mark Hatch. *Boiling Point: Monitoring Cultural Shifts in the 21st Century*. Ventura, CA: Regal Books, 2003.

Barnes, Gilbert H. *The Anti-Slavery Impulse, 1830–1844*. New York: Harcourt, Brace & World, 1964.

Barr, James. *Fundamentalism*. Philadelphia: Westminster, 1978.

Barrett, David B., and Todd M. Johnson. *World Christian Trends*. Pasadena: William Carey Library, 2001.

Barrett, David B., Todd M. Johnson, and Peter Crossing, eds. "Missiometrics 2005: A Global Survey of World Mission." *International Bulletin of Missionary Research* 29, no. 1 (January 2005): 27–30.

Barrett, David B., George T. Kurian, and Todd M. Johnson. *World Christian Encyclopedia*. New York: Oxford University Press, 2001.

Bartleman, Frank. *Azusa Street: The Roots of Modern-day Pentecost*. South Plainfield, NJ: Bridge, 1980.

Bass, Clarence B. *Backgrounds to Dispensationalism*. Grand Rapids: Baker Academic, 1978.

Bays, Daniel H., and Grant Wacker, eds. *The Foreign Missionary Enterprise at Home: Explorations in North American Cultural History*. Tuscaloosa: University of Alabama Press, 2003.

Bebbington, David. *Evangelicalism in Modern Britain: A History from the 1730s to the 1980s*. Grand Rapids: Baker Academic, 1992.

Belcher, Joseph. *George Whitefield: A Biography*. New York: American Tract Society, 1857.

Bellah, Robert N., Robert Madsen, William M. Sullivan, Ann Swidler, and Steven M. Tipton. *Habits of the Heart*. New York: Harper & Row, 1985.

Belmonte, Kevin. *Hero for Humanity: A Biography of William Wilberforce*. Colorado Springs: NavPress, 2002.

Bendroth, Margaret Lamberts. *Fundamentalism and Gender, 1875 to the Present*. New Haven: Yale University Press, 1993.

———. *Fundamentalists in the City*. New York: Oxford University Press, 2006.

Bercovitch, Sacvan. *The American Jeremiad*. Madison: University of Wisconsin Press, 1991.

Berger, Peter L. *The Sacred Canopy*. Garden City, NY: Anchor Books, 1969.

Berkouwer, G. C. *The Second Vatican Council and the New Catholicism*. Grand Rapids: Eerdmans, 1965.

Billingsley, Andrew. *Mighty Like a River: The Black Church and Social Reform*. New York: Oxford University Press, 1999.

Bloesch, Donald G. *The Evangelical Renaissance*. Grand Rapids: Eerdmans, 1973.

———. *The Reform of the Church*. Grand Rapids: Eerdmans, 1970.

Blumhofer, Edith L. *The Assemblies of God: A Chapter in the Story of American Pentecostalism*. 2 vols. Springfield, MO: Gospel Publishing House, 1989.

———. *Restoring the Faith: The Assemblies of God, Pentecostalism, and American Culture*. Urbana: University of Illinois Press, 1993.

Blumhofer, Edith L., and Randall Balmer, eds. *Modern Christian Revivals*. Urbana: University of Illinois Press, 1993.

Blumhofer, Edith L., and Joel A. Carpenter. *Twentieth-Century Evangelicalism: A Guide to the Sources*. New York: Garland, 1990.

Boles, John B. *The Great Revival: Beginnings of the Bible Belt*. Lexington: University Press of Kentucky, 1996.

Boyer, Paul. *When Time Shall Be No More: Prophecy Belief in Modern American Culture*. Cambridge, MA: Harvard University Press, 1992.

Bramadat, Paul A. *The Church on the World's Turf*. New York: Oxford University Press, 2000.

Bratt, James D., ed. *Abraham Kuyper: A Centennial Reader*. Grand Rapids: Eerdmans, 1998.

Bremer, Francis J. *John Winthrop: America's Forgotten Founding Father*. New York: Oxford University Press, 2003.

———. *The Puritan Experiment: New England Society from Bradford to Edwards*. Hanover, NH: The University Press of New England, 1995.

Brereton, Virginia L. *Training God's Army: The American Bible School, 1880–1940*. Bloomington: Indiana University Press, 1990.

Bridenbaugh, Carl. *The Colonial Craftsman*. Chicago: University of Chicago Press, 1964.

Brown, Dale W. *Understanding Pietism*. Nappanee, IN: Evangel, 1996.

Bumsted, J. J., ed. *The Great Awakening.* Waltham, MA: Blaisdell, 1970.

Burgess, Stanley M., and Eduard M. van der Maas, eds. *The New International Dictionary of Pentecostal and Charismatic Movements.* Grand Rapids: Zondervan, 2002.

Burnham, George. *Billy Graham: A Mission Accomplished.* New York: Revell, 1955.

Burnham, George, and Lee Fisher. *Billy Graham and the New York Crusade.* Grand Rapids: Zondervan, 1957.

Butler, Jon. *Awash in a Sea of Faith: Christianizing the American People.* Cambridge, MA: Harvard University Press, 1990.

Cairns, Earle E. *An Endless Line of Splendor: Revivals and Their Leaders from the Great Awakening to the Present.* Wheaton: Tyndale House, 1986.

Calhoun, David. *History of Princeton Seminary.* 2 vols. Edinburgh: Banner of Truth, 1996.

Carnell, Edward John. *The Case for Orthodox Theology.* Philadelphia: Westminster, 1959.

———. *Television: Servant or Master?* Grand Rapids: Eerdmans, 1950.

Carpenter, Joel A. *Fundamentalism in American Religion, 1880–1950.* A forty-five volume facsimile series, including *A New Evangelical Coalition: Early Documents of the National Association of Evangelicals; Two Reformers of Fundamentalism: Harold John Ockenga and Carl F. H. Henry;* and *The Youth for Christ Movement.* New York: Garland, 1988.

———. *Revive Us Again: The Reawakening of American Fundamentalism.* New York: Oxford, 1997.

Carson, D. A., and John D. Woodbridge, eds. *God and Culture: Essays in Honor of Carl F. H. Henry.* Grand Rapids: Eerdmans, 1993.

Carwardine, Richard J. *Evangelicals and Politics in Antebellum America.* New Haven: Yale University Press, 1993.

Case, Shirley Jackson. *The Millennial Hope.* Chicago: University of Chicago Press, 1918.

Castronovo, David. *Beyond the Gray Flannel Suit: Books from the 1950s That Made American Culture.* New York: Continuum, 2004.

Cattell, Everett L. "National Association of Evangelicals and World Evangelical Fellowship." *Christianity Today,* January 29, 1965, 12–14.

Cattley, Stephen R., ed. *The Acts and Monuments of John Foxe.* 8 vols. London: Seeley and Burnside, 1841.

Cauthen, Kenneth. *The Impact of American Religious Liberalism.* New York: Harper & Row, 1962.

Charles, J. Daryl. *The Unformed Conscience of Evangelicalism: Recovering the Church's Moral Vision.* Downers Grove, IL: InterVarsity, 2002.

Cherry, Conrad, ed. *God's New Israel: Religious Interpretations of American Destiny.* Englewood Cliffs, NJ: Prentice-Hall, 1971.

———. *Hurrying Toward Zion: Universities, Divinity Schools and American Protestantism.* Bloomington: Indiana University Press, 1995.

Clark, Francis E. *World Wide Endeavor: The Story of the Young People's Society of Christian Endeavor.* Philadelphia: Gillespie, Metzgar and Kelley, 1896.

Clark, George. *Reminiscences of Rev. Charles G. Finney.* Oberlin, OH: Goodrich, 1876.

Clarkson, George. *George Whitefield and Welsh Calvinistic Methodism.* Lewiston, NY: Mellen, 1996.

Clegg, Claude A., III. *The Price of Liberty: African Americans and the Making of Liberia.* Chapel Hill: University of North Carolina Press, 2004.

Coalter, Milton J., John M. Mulder, and Lewis B. Weeks., eds. *The Mainstream Protestant "Decline": The Presbyterian Pattern.* Louisville: Westminster/ John Knox, 1990.

Cole, Stewart G. *The History of Fundamentalism.* Hamden, CT: Archon, 1937.

Coleman, Robert. *The Coming World Revival: Your Part in God's Plan to Reach the World.* Wheaton: Crossway, 1995.

Collins, Kenneth J. *The Evangelical Movement: The Promise of an American Religion.* Grand Rapids: Baker Academic, 2005.

———. *John Wesley: A Theological Journey.* Nashville: Abingdon, 2003.

Colson, Charles, and Richard John Neuhaus, eds. *Evangelicals and Catholics Together.* Dallas: Word, 1995.

Conforti, Joseph. *Jonathan Edwards, Religious Tradition, and American Culture.* Chapel Hill: University of North Carolina Press, 1995.

Congregational Register: Point Breeze Presbyterian Church. Pittsburgh: Arthur Van Senden, 1932.

Conrad, Arcturus Z., ed. *Boston's Awakening.* Boston: The King's Business, 1909.

Corum, Fred T. *Like As of Fire: Newspapers from the Azusa Street World Wide Revival.* Washington, DC: Middle Atlantic Regional Press, 1989.

Costas, Orlando E. *The Church and Its Mission: A Shattering Critique from the Third World.* Wheaton: Tyndale, 1974.

Crawley, Winston. *World Christianity: 1970–2000.* Pasadena: William Carey Library, 2001.

Cromartie, Michael. *A Public Faith: Evangelicals and Civic Engagement.* New York: Rowman and Littlefield, 2003.

Cummins, J. S., ed. *Christianity and Missions, 1450–1800.* Brookfield, VT: Ashgate, 1997.

Davies, Horton. *The Worship of the American Puritans*. Morgan, PA: Soli Deo Gloria, 1999.

Davis, David Brion. *In the Image of God: Religion, Moral Values, and Our Heritage of Slavery*. New Haven: Yale University Press, 2001.

Day, Heather F. *Protestant Theological Education in America: A Bibliography*. Metuchen, NJ: Scarecrow, 1985.

Dayton, Donald W. *Discovering an Evangelical Heritage*. New York: Harper & Row, 1976.

———. *Theological Roots of Pentecostalism*. Peabody, MA: Hendrickson, 1991.

Dayton, Donald W., and Robert K. Johnston, eds. *The Variety of American Evangelicalism*. Downers Grove, IL: InterVarsity, 1991.

DeBerg, Betty A. *Ungodly Women: Gender and the First Wave of American Fundamentalism*. Macon, GA: Mercer University Press, 2000.

Dickens, A. G. *The English Reformation*. Philadelphia: Penn State University Press, 1994.

Dickens, A. G., and John Tonkin. *The Reformation in Historical Thought*. Oxford: Blackwell, 1985.

Dieter, Melvin E. *The Holiness Revival in the Nineteenth Century*. Metuchen, NJ: Scarecrow, 1980.

Doggett, L. L. *History of the Young Men's Christian Association*. London: International Committee of the Young Men's Christian Associations, 1909.

Dollar, George W. *A History of Fundamentalism in America*. Greenville, SC: Bob Jones University Press, 1973.

Drummond, Lewis A. *Charles Grandison Finney and the Birth of Modern Evangelicalism*. London: Hodder and Stoughton, 1983.

Edwards, David L., and John Stott. *Essentials: A Liberal-Evangelical Dialogue*. Downers Grove, IL: InterVarsity, 1988.

Edwards, Jonathan. *A Faithful Narrative of the Surprising Work of God in the Conversion of Many Hundred Souls in Northampton*. In *The Great Awakening*, edited by C. C. Goen, 97–212. New Haven: Yale University Press, 1972.

Ellingsen, Mark. *The Evangelical Movement: Growth, Impact, Controversy, Dialog*. Minneapolis: Augsburg, 1988.

Elliot, Elisabeth. *Through Gates of Splendor*. Carol Stream, IL: Tyndale, 1986.

Elsbree, Oliver W. *The Rise of the Missionary Spirit in America, 1790–1815*. Philadelphia: Porcupine, 1980.

Emerson, Michael, and Christian Smith. *Divided by Faith: Evangelical Religion and the Problem of Race in America*. New York: Oxford University Press, 2000.

England, Edward O. *Hallowed Harringay.* London: Victory, 1955.

Englizian, H. Crosby. *Brimstone Corner: Park Street Church, Boston.* Chicago: Moody, 1968.

Erb, Peter. *Johann Arndt: True Christianity.* New York: Paulist Press, 1979.

Erickson, Millard. *The New Evangelical Theology.* Westwood, NJ: Revell, 1968.

———. *Reclaiming the Center: Confronting Evangelical Accommodation in Postmodern Times.* Wheaton: Crossway, 2004.

Evangelical Action! A Report of the Organization of the National Association of Evangelicals for United Action, Compiled and Edited by the Executive Committee. Boston: United Action Press, 1942.

Evangelical Manifesto: A Strategic Plan for the End of the 20th Century. Wheaton: National Association of Evangelicals, 1995.

Evans, Elizabeth. *The Wright Vision: The Story of the New England Fellowship.* New York: University Press of America, 1991.

Fackre, Gabriel. *The Religious Right and Christian Faith.* Grand Rapids: Eerdmans, 1983.

Fairchild, James H. *Oberlin: The Colony and the College, 1833–1883.* Oberlin, OH: Goodrich, 1883.

Faull, Katherine M. *Moravian Women's Memoirs.* Syracuse: Syracuse University Press, 1997.

Ferm, Robert O. *Cooperative Evangelism: Is Billy Graham Right or Wrong?* Grand Rapids: Zondervan, 1958.

Fernando, Ajith. *Sharing the Truth in Love.* Grand Rapids: Discovery House, 2001.

Fey, H. E., ed. *A History of the Ecumenical Movement.* 2 vols. 4th ed. Geneva: Consul Oecumenique, 1993.

Finke, Robert, and Rodney Stark. *The Churching of America, 1776–1990.* New Brunswick, NJ: Rutgers University Press, 1992.

Finney, Charles Grandison. *Lectures on Revivals of Religion.* Edited by William G. McLoughlin. Cambridge: Belknap, 1960.

———. *Lectures on Systematic Theology.* Oberlin, OH: James M. Fitch, 1846.

Flannery, Austin, ed. *The Basic Sixteen Documents of Vatican Council II: Constitutions, Decrees, Declarations.* Northport, NY: Costello, 1995.

Fletcher, Robert Samuel. *A History of Oberlin College: From Its Foundation Through the Civil War.* 2 vols. Oberlin, OH: Oberlin College, 1943.

Fogel, Robert W. *The Fourth Great Awakening and the Future of Egalitarianism.* Chicago: University of Chicago Press, 2000.

Foster, Frank Hugh. *A Genetic History of the New England Theology.* Chicago: University of Chicago Press, 1907.

Fournier, Keith A. *Evangelical Catholics: A Call for Christian Cooperation to Penetrate the Darkness with the Light of the Gospel*. Nashville: Thomas Nelson, 1990.

Fowler, Robert Booth. *A New Engagement: Evangelical Political Thought, 1966–1976*. Grand Rapids: Eerdmans, 1982.

Frame, Randy. "Modern Evangelicalism Mourns the Loss of One of Its Founding Fathers." *Christianity Today*, March 15, 1985, 34–36.

Frank, Douglas W. *Less Than Conquerors: How Evangelicalism Entered the Twentieth Century*. Grand Rapids: Eerdmans, 1986.

Freston, Paul. *Evangelicals and Politics in Asia, Africa, and Latin America*. Cambridge: Cambridge University Press, 2004.

Fuller, Daniel P. *Give the Winds a Mighty Voice: The Story of Charles E. Fuller*. Waco: Word, 1972.

Fuller, Grace. *Heavenly Sunshine*. Westwood, NJ: Revell, 1956.

Fulop, Timothy E., and Albert J. Raboteau. *African-American Religion*. New York: Routledge, 1996.

Gaebelein, Frank E. "The Bible College in American Education Today." *School and Society*, May 9, 1959, 223–25.

———. "Review of Current Religious Thought." *Christianity Today*, June 20, 1960, 40.

Gallup, George, Jr., and D. Michael Lindsay. *Surveying the Religious Landscape: Trends in U.S. Beliefs*. Harrisburg, PA: Morehouse, 1999.

Garrett, James L., E. Glenn Hinson, and James E. Tull. *Are Southern Baptists "Evangelicals"?* Macon, GA: Mercer University Press, 1983.

Gasper, Louis. *The Fundamentalist Movement, 1930–1956*. Grand Rapids: Baker Academic, 1981.

Gatewood, Willard B., Jr., ed. *Controversy in the Twenties*. Nashville: Vanderbilt University Press, 1969.

Gaustad, Edwin Scott. *The Great Awakening in New England*. New York: Harper & Brothers, 1957.

Geisler, Norman, and Ralph E. MacKenzie. *Roman Catholics and Evangelicals: Agreements and Differences*. Grand Rapids: Baker Academic, 1995.

George, Timothy, ed. *Pilgrims on the Sawdust Trail: Evangelical Ecumenism and the Quest for Christian Identity*. Grand Rapids: Baker Academic, 2004.

———. *Theology of the Reformers*. Nashville: Broadman, 1988.

Gewehr, Wesley M. *The Great Awakening in Virginia*. Durham, NC: Duke University Press, 1930.

Gibson, Scott M. *A. J. Gordon: American Premillennialist*. Lanham, MD: University Press of America, 2001.

Gier, Nicholas F. *God, Reason, and the Evangelicals.* Lanham, MD: University Press of America, 1987.

Gillies, John. *Memoirs of Rev. George Whitefield.* Middletown, CT: Hunt & Noyes, 1838.

Goen, C. C., ed. *Jonathan Edwards: The Great Awakening.* Vol. 4 of *The Works of Jonathan Edwards.* New Haven: Yale University Press, 1972.

Goff, James R., Jr. *Fields White unto Harvest: Charles F. Parham and the Missionary Origins of Pentecostalism.* Fayetteville: University of Arkansas Press, 1988.

Goff, James R., Jr., and Grant Wacker, eds. *Portraits of a Generation: Early Pentecostal Leaders.* Fayetteville: University of Arkansas Press, 2002.

Goodstein, Laurie. "More Religion, but Not the Old-Time Kind." *New York Times,* January 9, 2005, sec. 4, 1 and 4.

Gordon, A. J. "Individual Responsibility Growing Out of Our Perils and Opportunities." In *National Perils and Opportunities: The Discussions of the General Christian Conference of the Evangelical Alliance,* 379–90. New York: Baker & Taylor, 1887.

Graham, Billy. *Angels.* New York: Doubleday, 1975.

———. *Answers to Life's Problems.* Nashville: Thomas Nelson, 1994.

———. *Approaching Hoofbeats.* Nashville: Thomas Nelson, 1984.

———. *Breakfast with Billy Graham.* New York: Random House, 2003.

———. *Calling Youth to Christ.* Grand Rapids: Zondervan, 1947.

———. *The Challenge: Sermons from the Historic New York Crusade.* New York: Pocket Books, 1972.

———. *The Collected Works of Billy Graham.* New York: World, 2001.

———. *Death and the Life After.* Nashville: Thomas Nelson, 1994.

———. *The Enduring Classics of Billy Graham.* Nashville: Thomas Nelson, 2004.

———. "Harold John Ockenga: A Man Who Walked with God." *Christianity Today,* March 15, 1985, 35.

———. *The Holy Spirit.* Nashville: Thomas Nelson, 2000.

———. *Hope for Each Day.* Nashville: Thomas Nelson, 2002.

———. *Hope for the Troubled Heart.* Waco: Word, 1991.

———. *Just As I Am: The Autobiography of Billy Graham.* San Francisco: HarperSanFrancisco, 1997.

———. *Key to Personal Peace.* Nashville: Thomas Nelson, 2003.

———. *Living in God's Love: The New York Crusade.* New York: Putnam, 2005.

———. *Peace With God.* Nashville: Thomas Nelson, 2000.

———. *Revival in Our Time: The Story of the Billy Graham Evangelistic Campaign*. Wheaton: Van Kampen, 1950.

———. *The Secret of Happiness*. Nashville: Thomas Nelson, 1997.

Green, Michael. *Evangelism in the Early Church*. Grand Rapids: Eerdmans, 1970.

Greig, Gary S., and Kevin N. Springer, eds. *The Kingdom and the Power: Are Healing and the Spiritual Gifts Used by Jesus and the Early Church Meant for the Church Today?* Ventura, CA: Regal, 1993.

Grounds, Vernon. *Revolution and the Christian Faith*. Philadelphia: Lippincott, 1971.

Grout, H. M., ed. *The Gospel Invitation: Sermons Related to the Boston Revival of 1877*. Boston: Lockwood, Brooks and Co., 1877.

Gunter, W. Stephen, Scott J. Jones, Ted A. Campbell, Rebekah L. Miles, and Randy L. Maddox. *Wesley and the Quadrilateral: Renewing the Conversation*. Nashville: Abingdon, 1997.

Gurnall, William. *The Christian in Complete Armour*. 3 vols. Edinburgh: Banner of Truth, 2001.

Halberstam, David. *The Fifties*. New York: Villard, 1993.

Hall, David D., ed. *The Antinomian Controversy, 1636–1638: A Documentary History*. Durham, NC: Duke University Press, 1990.

———, ed. *Witch-Hunting in Seventeenth-Century New England: A Documentary History, 1638–1693*. Boston: Northeastern University Press, 1999.

Hall, Douglas. "How to Make Our 'Love in Action' Effective." *Emmanuel Research Review* 3 (June 7, 2004).

Hambrick-Stowe, Charles E. *Charles G. Finney and the Spirit of American Evangelicalism*. Grand Rapids: Eerdmans, 1996.

———. *The Practice of Piety: Puritan Devotional Disciplines in Seventeenth-Century New England*. Chapel Hill: University of North Carolina Press, 1982.

Hamburger, Philip. *Separation of Church and State*. Cambridge, MA: Harvard University Press, 2002.

Handlin, Oscar. *The Uprooted: The Epic Story of the Great Migration That Made the American People*. Toronto: Little, Brown, 1990.

Hangen, Tona J. *Redeeming the Dial: Radio, Religion, and Popular Culture in America*. Chapel Hill: University of North Carolina Press, 2002.

Hardman, Keith J. *Charles Grandison Finney, 1792–1875: Revivalist and Reformer*. Syracuse: Syracuse University Press, 1987.

———. *Seasons of Refreshing: Evangelism and Revivals in America*. Grand Rapids: Baker Books, 1994.

Haroutunian, Joseph. *Piety Versus Moralism: The Passing of the New England Theology*. New York: Harper & Row, 1970.

Harrell, David E., Jr. *Varieties of Southern Evangelicalism*. Macon, GA: Mercer University Press, 1981.

Hart, D. G. *Deconstructing Evangelicalism: Conservative Protestantism in the Age of Billy Graham*. Grand Rapids: Baker Academic, 2004.

———. *Defender of the Faith: J. Gresham Machen and the Crisis of American Protestantism in Modern America*. Baltimore: Johns Hopkins Press, 1994.

———, ed. *Reckoning With the Past: Historical Essays on American Evangelicalism*. Grand Rapids: Baker Academic, 1995.

Hassey, Janette. *No Time for Silence: Evangelical Women in Public Ministry around the Turn of the Century*. Grand Rapids: Zondervan, 1986.

Hatch, Nathan O. *The Democratization of American Christianity*. New Haven: Yale University Press, 1989.

Hauerwas, Stanley, and William H. Willimon. *Resident Aliens*. Nashville: Abingdon, 1989.

Hays, Samuel P. *The Response to Industrialism, 1885–1914*. Chicago: University of Chicago Press, 1968.

Heath, Dwight B., ed. *Mourt's Relation: A Journal of the Pilgrims at Plymouth*. Bedford, MA: Applewood, 1963.

Hefley, James C. *God Goes to High School: An In-Depth Look at an Incredible Phenomenon*. Waco: Word, 1970.

Heimert, Alan, and Andrew Delbanco, eds. *The Puritans in America*. Cambridge, MA: Harvard University Press, 1985.

Heimert, Alan, and Perry Miller, eds. *The Great Awakening: Documents Illustrating the Crisis and Its Consequences*. Indianapolis: Bobbs-Merrill, 1967.

Hendershot, Heather. *Shaking the World for Jesus: Media and Conservative Evangelical Culture*. Chicago: University of Chicago Press, 2004.

Henderson, D. Michael. *John Wesley's Class Meetings: A Model for Making Disciples*. Nappanee, IN: Francis Asbury, 1997.

Henry, Carl F. H. "American Evangelicals in a Turning Time." *Christian Century*, November 5, 1980, 1058–62.

———. *Confessions of a Theologian: An Autobiography*. Waco: Word, 1986.

———. *The Drift of Western Thought*. Grand Rapids: Eerdmans, 1951.

———. "Evangelical Advance: Do We Need a Christian University?" *Christianity Today*, May 9, 1960, 3–5.

———. *Evangelicals at the Brink of Crisis*. Waco: Word, 1967.

————. *Evangelicals in Search of Identity*. Waco: Word, 1976.

————. *A Plea for Evangelical Demonstration*. Grand Rapids: Baker Academic, 1971.

————. *The Uneasy Conscience of Modern Fundamentalism*. Grand Rapids: Eerdmans, 2003.

————. "The Uneasy Conscience Revisited: Current Theological, Ethical and Social Concerns." *Theology, News and Notes*, December 1987, 3–9.

————. "Why 'Christianity Today'?" *Christianity Today*, October 15, 1956, 20–23.

Heyrman, Christine L. *Southern Cross: The Beginnings of the Bible Belt*. New York: Knopf, 1997.

Higginbotham, Evelyn B. *Righteous Discontent: The Women's Movement in the Black Baptist Church, 1880–1920*. Cambridge, MA: Harvard University Press, 1993.

High, Stanley. *Billy Graham*. New York: McGraw-Hill, 1956.

Hill, Patricia R. *The World Their Household: The American Woman's Foreign Mission Movement and Cultural Transformation, 1870–1920*. Ann Arbor: University of Michigan Press, 1985.

Himmelfarb, Gertrude. *The De-Moralization of Society*. New York: Vintage, 1995.

————. *On Looking into the Abyss: Untimely Thoughts on Culture and Society*. New York: Vintage, 1994.

————. *The Roads to Modernity: The British, French, and American Enlightenments*. New York: Knopf, 2004.

Hindmarsh, Bruce. *John Newton and the English Evangelical Tradition*. Grand Rapids: Eerdmans, 2000.

Hofstadter, Richard. *Anti-Intellectualism in American Life*. New York: Vintage, 1962.

Hoge, Dean R. *Division in the Protestant House*. Philadelphia: Westminster, 1976.

Hollenweger, Walter J. *Pentecostalism: Origins and Developments Worldwide*. Peabody, MA: Hendrickson, 1997.

Holmes, Arthur. *All Truth Is God's Truth*. Grand Rapids: Eerdmans, 1977.

————. *Faith Seeks Understanding*. Grand Rapids: Eerdmans, 1971.

Horton, Michael Scott. *Made in America: The Shaping of Modern Evangelical Thought*. Grand Rapids: Baker Academic, 1991.

Howard, David M. *The Dream That Would Not Die: The Birth and Growth of the World Evangelical Fellowship*. Grand Rapids: Baker Academic, 1988.

Howard, Jim. *Student Power in World Evangelism*. Downers Grove, IL: InterVarsity, 1970.

Hunt, Keith, and Gladys Hunt. *For Christ and the University: Story of Inter-Varsity Christian Fellowship in the United States of America, 1940–1990.* Downers Grove, IL: InterVarsity, 1991.

Hunt, Thomas C., and James C. Carper. *Religious Seminaries in America: A Selected Bibliography.* New York: Garland, 1989.

Hunter, James. *American Evangelicalism: Conservative Religion and the Quandary of Modernity.* New Brunswick, NJ: Rutgers University Press, 1983.

———. *Evangelicalism: The Coming Generation.* Chicago: University of Chicago Press, 1987.

Huss, John E. *Robert G. Lee: The Authorized Biography.* Grand Rapids: Zondervan, 1967.

Hutchison, William R. *Between the Times: The Travail of the Protestant Establishment in America, 1900–1960.* New York: Cambridge University Press, 1989.

———. *Errand to the World: American Protestant Thought and Foreign Missions.* Chicago: University of Chicago Press, 1987.

———. *The Modernist Impulse in American Protestantism.* Cambridge, MA: Harvard University Press, 1976.

Hynson, Leon O. *To Reform a Nation: Theological Foundations of Wesley's Ethics.* Grand Rapids: Francis Asbury, 1984.

Jacobsen, Douglas. *Thinking in the Spirit: Theologies of the Early Pentecostal Movement.* Bloomington: Indiana University Press, 2004.

James, Sydney V., Jr., ed. *Three Visitors to Early Plymouth.* Bedford, MA: Applewood, 1997.

Janz, Denis R., ed. *A Reformation Reader: Primary Texts with Introductions.* Minneapolis: Fortress, 1999.

Jenkins, Philip. *God's Continent: Christianity, Islam, and Europe's Religious Crisis.* New York: Oxford University Press, 2007.

———. *The New Faces of Christianity: Believing the Bible in the Global South.* New York: Oxford University Press, 2006.

———. *The Next Christendom: The Coming of Global Christianity.* New York: Oxford University Press, 2002.

Johnson, Jimmie, and Merv Rosell. *Voices of Victory Via Air: Radio Studies.* St. Paul, MN: Northland Publishing House, 1942.

Johnson, Torrey, and Robert Cook. *Reaching Youth for Christ.* Chicago: Moody, 1944.

Johnstone, Patrick, and Jason Mandryk, eds. *Operation World: When We Pray God Works.* Waynesboro, GA: Paternoster USA, 2001.

Jones, Charles E. *Perfectionist Persuasion: The Holiness Movement and American Methodism, 1967–1936.* Metuchen, NJ: Scarecrow, 1974.

Jordan, Philip D. *The Evangelical Alliance of the United States of America, 1847–1900*. Lewiston, NY: Edwin Mellen, 1983.

Juster, Susan, and Lisa MacFarlane, eds. *A Mighty Baptism: Race, Gender, and the Creation of American Protestantism*. Ithaca, NY: Cornell University Press, 1996.

Kaiser, Walter C., Jr. *Revive Us Again: Biblical Insights for Encouraging Spiritual Renewal*. Nashville: Broadman & Holman, 1999.

Kane, Paula. *Separatism and Subculture*. Chapel Hill: University of North Carolina Press, 1994.

Kane, Thomas. *All About Winona: Winona Assembly and Summer School Association: Its History, Methods, and Future*. Winona Lake, IN: Winona Lake Bible Conference, 1904.

Kantzer, Kenneth S., ed. *Evangelical Roots: A Tribute to Wilbur Smith*. Nashville: Thomas Nelson, 1978.

Kantzer, Kenneth S., and Carl F. H. Henry, eds. *Evangelical Affirmations*. Grand Rapids: Zondervan, 1990.

Kelley, Dean. *Why Conservative Churches Are Growing*. New York: Harper & Row, 1972.

Kelly, J. N. D. *Early Christian Creeds*. New York: Longman, 1972.

King, John N., ed. *Voices of the English Reformation*. Philadelphia: University of Pennsylvania Press, 2004.

Kling, David W., and Douglas A. Sweeney. *Jonathan Edwards at Home and Abroad: Historical Memories, Cultural Movements, Global Horizons*. Columbia: University of South Carolina Press, 2003.

Knox, R. A. *Enthusiasm*. Oxford: Oxford University Press, 1958.

Kromminga, John. *All One Body We*. Grand Rapids: Eerdmans, 1970.

Kuyper, Abraham. "Sphere Sovereignty." In *Abraham Kuyper: A Centennial Reader*, edited by James D. Bratt, 461–90. Grand Rapids: Eerdmans, 1998.

Lambert, Frank. *Pedlar in Divinity*. Princeton, NY: Princeton University Press, 1993.

Larsen, Timothy T., et al. *Biographical Dictionary of Evangelicals*. Downers Grove, IL: InterVarsity, 2003.

Larson, Edward J. *Summer for the Gods: The Scopes Trial and America's Continuing Debate over Science and Religion*. Cambridge, MA: Harvard University Press, 1998.

Larson, Mel. *Young Man on Fire: The Story of Torrey Johnson and Youth for Christ*. Chicago: Youth Publications, 1945.

———. *Youth for Christ: Twentieth Century Wonder*. Grand Rapids: Zondervan, 1947.

Latourette, Kenneth Scott. *The Emergence of a World Christian Community.* New Haven: Yale University Press, 1949.

―――. *A History of the Expansion of Christianity.* 7 vols. Grand Rapids: Zondervan, 1970.

Lewis, A. J. *Zinzendorf the Ecumenical Pioneer: A Study in the Moravian Contribution to Christian Mission and Unity.* Philadelphia: Westminster, 1962.

Lewis, Donald M., ed. *Christianity Reborn: The Global Expansion of Evangelicalism in the Twentieth Century.* Grand Rapids: Eerdmans, 2004.

Lightner, Robert. *Neo-Evangelicalism Today.* Schaumburg, IL: Regular Baptist Press, 1978.

Lim, Paul Chang-Ha. *In Pursuit of Purity, Unity, and Liberty: Richard Baxter's Puritan Ecclesiology in Its Seventeenth-Century Context.* Leiden and Boston: Brill, 2004.

Lincoln, C. Eric. *The Black Church Since Frazier.* New York: Schocken Books, 1974.

Lincoln, C. Eric, and Lawrence H. Mamiya. *The Black Church in the African American Experience.* Durham, NC: Duke University Press, 1990.

Lindberg, Carter, ed. *The Pietist Theologians.* Oxford: Blackwell, 2005.

Lindsay, Jay. "Greater Boston in Midst of a Quiet Religious Revival." *Boston Daily Globe.* January 15, 2005.

Lindsell, Harold. *Park Street Prophet: A Life of Harold Ockenga.* Wheaton: Van Kampen, 1951.

Lints, Richard. *The Fabric of Theology: A Prolegomenon to Evangelical Theology.* Grand Rapids: Eerdmans, 1993.

Lippmann, Walter. *A Preface to Morals.* New York: Time-Life Books, 1964.

Lippy, Charles H. *Seasonable Revolutionary: The Mind of Charles Chauncy.* Princeton, NJ: Princeton University Press, 1972.

Lippy, Charles H., and Robert H. Krapohl. *The Evangelicals: A Historical, Thematic, and Biographical Guide.* Westport, CT: Greenwood, 1999.

Loetscher, Lefferts A. *The Broadening Church: A Study of Theological Issues in the Presbyterian Church Since 1869.* Philadelphia: University of Pennsylvania Press, 1954.

―――. *Facing the Enlightenment and Pietism: Archibald Alexander and the Founding of Princeton Theological Seminary.* New York: Greenwood, 1983.

Logan, Ernest E. *The Church That Was Twice Born.* Pittsburgh: Pickwick-Morcraft, 1973.

Long, Kathryn T. *The Revival of 1857–58: Interpreting an American Religious Awakening.* New York: Oxford University Press, 1998.

Longfield, Bradley J. *The Presbyterian Controversy: Fundamentalists, Modernists, and Moderates*. New York: Oxford University Press, 1993.

Lotz, David W., ed. *Altered Landscapes: Christianity in America, 1935–1985*. Grand Rapids: Eerdmans, 1989.

Lovelace, Richard F. *The American Pietism of Cotton Mather: Origins of American Evangelicalism*. Grand Rapids: Christian University Press, 1979.

———. *Dynamics of Spiritual Life*. Downers Grove, IL: InterVarsity, 1979.

Lynn, Robert W. *Big Little School: Two Hundred Years of the Sunday School*. Birmingham, AL: Religious Education Press, 1980.

Macartney, Clarence Edward. *The Making of a Minister: The Autobiography of Clarence E. Macartney*. Edited by J. Clyde Henry. Great Neck, NY: Channel, 1961.

Macchia, Stephen. *Becoming a Healthy Church*. Grand Rapids: Baker Books, 2004.

———. *Becoming a Healthy Disciple*. Grand Rapids: Baker Books, 2004.

MacFarland, Charles S. *Christian Unity in the Making: The First Twenty-Five Years of the Federal Council of the Churches of Christ in America, 1905–1930*. New York: Federal Council of Churches, 1948.

Machen, J. Gresham. *Christianity and Liberalism*. Grand Rapids: Eerdmans, 1923.

MacIntyre, Alasdair. *After Virtue: A Study in Moral Theology*. Notre Dame, IN: University of Notre Dame Press, 1981.

———. *Whose Justice? Which Rationality?* Notre Dame, IN: University of Notre Dame Press, 1988.

Magnuson, Norris A. *Salvation in the Slums: Evangelical Social Work, 1865–1920*. Eugene, OR: Wipf & Stock, 2005.

Magnuson, Norris A., and William G. Travis. *American Evangelicalism: An Annotated Bibliography*. West Cornwall, CT: Locust Hill, 1990.

Marsden, George M. *Evangelicalism and Modern America*. Grand Rapids: Eerdmans, 1984.

———. *Fundamentalism and American Culture: The Shaping of Twentieth-Century Evangelicalism, 1870–1925*. New York: Oxford University Press, 1980.

———. *Jonathan Edwards: A Life*. New Haven: Yale University Press, 2003.

———. *Reforming Fundamentalism: Fuller Seminary and the New Evangelicalism*. Grand Rapids: Eerdmans, 1987.

———. *The Soul of the American University: From Protestant Establishment to Established Nonbelief*. New York: Oxford University Press, 1994.

————. *Understanding Fundamentalism and Evangelicalism*. Grand Rapids: Eerdmans, 1991.

Marsden, George M., and Bradley J. Longfield, eds. *The Secularization of the Academy*. New York: Oxford University Press, 1992.

Martin, Larry. *The Life and Ministry of William J. Seymour*. Joplin, MO: Christian Life Books, 1999.

Martin, Robert P. *A Guide to the Puritans*. Edinburgh: Banner of Truth, 1997.

Martin, William. *A Prophet with Honor: The Billy Graham Story*. New York: William Morrow, 1991.

Marty, Martin E. *Under God, Indivisible, 1941–1960*. Vol. 3 of *Modern American Religion*. Chicago: University of Chicago Press, 1966.

————. *Righteous Empire: The Protestant Experience in America*. New York: Harper, 1970.

Mathews, Donald G. *Religion in the Old South*. Chicago: University of Chicago Press, 1977.

Matthews, Arthur H. *Standing Up, Standing Together: The Emergence of the National Association of Evangelicals*. Carol Stream, IL: National Association of Evangelicals, 1992.

Maxson, Charles H. *The Great Awakening in the Middle Colonies*. Chicago: University of Chicago Press, 1920.

McGee, Gary B., ed. *Initial Evidence*. Peabody, MA: Hendrickson, 1991.

McGrath, Alister E. *Evangelicalism and the Future of Christianity*. Downers Grove, IL: InterVarsity, 1995.

————. *A Passion for Truth*. Downers Grove, IL: InterVarsity, 1999.

————. *Reformation Thought: An Introduction*. 3rd ed. Oxford: Blackwell, 1999.

McIntire, Carl. *Modern Tower of Babel*. Collingswood, NJ: Christian Beacon Press, 1949.

————. "Ockenga Compromises Faith Seminary's Testimony." *The Christian Beacon*, October 11, 1945, 4.

————. *Servants of Apostasy*. Collingswood, NJ: Christian Beacon Press, 1955.

————. *The Testimony of Separation*. Collingswood, NJ: Christian Beacon Press, 1946.

————. *Twentieth-Century Reformation*. Collingswood, NJ: Christian Beacon Press, 1944.

McLoughlin, William G. *The American Evangelicals: 1800–1900*. New York: Harper, 1968.

————. *Billy Graham: Revivalist in a Secular Age*. New York: Ronald, 1960.

————. *Modern Revivalism: Charles Grandison Finney to Billy Graham*. New York: Ronald, 1959.

————. *Revivals, Awakenings, and Reform*. Chicago: University of Chicago Press, 1978.

McManus, Edgar J. *Law and Liberty in Early New England*. Amherst: University of Massachusetts Press, 1993.

Mead, Hiram. "Charles Grandison Finney." *Congregational Quarterly*, January 1877, 11.

Mead, Sidney E. *The Nation with the Soul of a Church*. Macon, GA: Mercer University Press, 1985.

Melton, J. Gordon, Phillip Charles Lucas, and Jon R. Stone. *Prime-Time Religion: An Encyclopedia of Religious Broadcasting*. Phoenix: Oryx, 1997.

Michaelsen, Robert S., and Wade Clark Roof, eds. *Liberal Protestantism: Realities and Possibilities*. New York: Pilgrim, 1986.

Miller, Glenn T. *Piety and Intellect*. Atlanta: Scholars Press, 1990.

Miller, Perry. *Errand into the Wilderness*. Cambridge, MA: Harvard University Press, 1975.

————. *The New England Mind*. Cambridge: Belknap, 1983.

Miller, Perry, and Thomas H. Johnson. *The Puritans: A Sourcebook of Their Writings*. Mineola, NY: Dover, 2001.

Mitchell, Curtis. *Those Who Came Forward: Men and Women Who Responded to the Ministry of Billy Graham*. Philadelphia and New York: Chilton Books, 1966.

Mitchell, Henry H. *Black Preaching*. Philadelphia: Lippincott, 1970.

Mitchell, Rudy. *History of Revivalism in Boston*. Boston: Emmanuel Gospel Center, 2007.

————. "An Introduction to Boston's Quiet Revival." *Emmanuel Research Review* 3 (June 7, 2004).

Moberg, David O. *The Great Reversal: Evangelism and Social Concern*. Rev. ed. Philadelphia and New York: Lippincott, 1977.

Monter, William. *Calvin's Geneva*. New York: Wiley, 1967.

Moore, Martin. *Boston Revival, 1842*. Boston: John Putnam, 1842.

Morgan, Edmund S. *The Puritan Family*. New York: Harper Torchbooks, 1965.

————. *Visible Saints: The History of a Puritan Idea*. Ithaca, NY: Cornell University Press, 1965.

Morison, Samuel Eliot. *Builders of the Bay Colony*. Boston: Northeastern University Press, 1981.

————. *The Intellectual Life of Colonial New England.* Ithaca, NY: Cornell University Press, 1956.

————, ed. *Of Plymouth Plantation, 1620–1647,* by William Bradford. New York: Knopf, 1993.

————. *The Oxford History of the American People.* New York: Oxford University Press, 1972.

Mott, John R. *The World's Student Christian Federation.* New York: Association Press, 1947.

Mouw, Richard J. *The Smell of Sawdust: What Evangelicals Can Learn From Their Fundamentalist Heritage.* Grand Rapids: Zondervan, 2000.

Mouw, Richard J., and Mark A. Noll. *Wonderful Words of Life: Hymns in American Protestant History and Theology.* Grand Rapids: Eerdmans, 2004.

Murch, James DeForest. "As Amsterdam Nears." *United Evangelical Action,* February 15, 1948, 12–13.

————. *Cooperation Without Compromise: A History of the National Association of Evangelicals.* Grand Rapids: Eerdmans, 1956.

Murphy, Larry G., Gordon Melton, and Gary L. Ward, eds. *Encyclopedia of African American Religions.* New York: Garland, 1993.

Murray, Iain H. *Evangelicalism Divided: A Record of Crucial Change in the Years 1950 to 2000.* Edinburgh: Banner of Truth, 2000.

————. *Jonathan Edwards: A New Biography.* Edinburgh: Banner of Truth, 1987.

Nash, Ronald H. *Evangelicals in America: Who They Are, What They Believe.* Nashville: Abingdon, 1987.

————. *The New Evangelicalism.* Grand Rapids: Zondervan, 1963.

Neill, Stephen. *A History of Christian Missions.* 2nd ed. New York: Penguin, 1991.

Nelson, Rudolph. *The Making and Unmaking of an Evangelical Mind: The Case of Edward Carnell.* Cambridge: Cambridge University Press, 1987.

Nichols, Stephen J. *J. Gresham Machen: A Guided Tour of His Life and Thought.* Phillipsburg, NJ: P&R, 2004.

Niebuhr, H. Richard. *Christ and Culture.* Expanded 50th anniversary issue. San Francisco: HarperSanFrancisco, 2001.

————. *The Social Sources of Denominationalism.* Cleveland and New York: Meridian, 1965.

Noll, Mark A. *Between Faith and Criticism: Evangelicals, Scholarship, and the Bible in America.* San Francisco: Harper & Row, 1986.

————. *The Rise of Evangelicalism: The Age of Edwards, Whitefield and the Wesleys.* Downers Grove, IL: InterVarsity, 2003.

―――. *The Scandal of the Evangelical Mind*. Grand Rapids: Eerdmans, 1994.

Noll, Mark A., David W. Bebbington, and George A. Rawlyk, eds. *Evangelicalism: Comparative Studies of Popular Protestantism in North America, the British Isles, and Beyond, 1700–1990*. New York: Oxford University Press, 1994.

Noll, Mark A., and Ronald Thiemann. *Where Shall My Wond'ring Soul Begin? The Landscape of Evangelical Piety and Thought*. Grand Rapids: Eerdmans, 2000.

Northwestern Pilot memorial issue, January 1948 and January 1951.

Norwood, Frederick, and William Warren Sweet. *History of the North Indiana Conference*. Winona Lake, IN: Light and Life, 1957.

Nuttall, Geoffrey F. *Howel Harris, 1714–1773: The Last Enthusiast*. Cardiff: University of Wales Press, 1965.

―――. *Visible Saints: The Congregational Way, 1640–1660*. Oxford: Blackwell, 1957.

Ockenga, Harold John. "Abstract of a Doctor's Dissertation." *University of Pittsburgh Bulletin* 36, no. 4 (January 15, 1940).

―――. "Boston Stirred by Revival." *United Evangelical Action*, January 15, 1950, 2, 4, 15.

―――. "Christ for America." *United Evangelical Action*, May 4, 1943, 3–4, 6.

―――. *The Church God Blesses*. Pasadena and Boston: Fuller Missions Fellowship and Park Street Church Board of Missions, 1959.

―――. *The Church in God: Expository Values in Thessalonians*. New York: Revell, 1956.

―――. *The Comfort of God: Preaching in Second Corinthians*. New York: Revell, 1944.

―――. *Everyone That Believeth: Expository Addresses on St. Paul's Epistle to the Romans*. New York: Revell, 1942.

―――. *Faith in a Troubled World*. Wenham, MA: Gordon College Press, 1972.

―――. *Faithful in Christ Jesus: Preaching in Ephesians*. New York: Revell, 1948.

―――. *The Great Awakening*. Boston: Fellowship Press, 1940.

―――. "The Great Revival." Presented at the W. H. Griffith Thomas Memorial Lectures at Dallas Theological Seminary and published in *Bibliotheca Sacra*, April–June 1947, 223–35.

―――. *Have You Met These Women?* Grand Rapids: Zondervan, 1940.

―――. "The Hope for a Revival." *Bulletin of the National Association of Evangelicals for United Action* 1, no. 2 (September 1, 1942): 1.

————. "Is America's Revival Breaking?" *United Evangelical Action*, July 1, 1950, 3–4, 8, 13–15.

————. "Jesus, the Christian's Example." In *Evangelical Sermons of Our Day*, edited by Andrew W. Blackwood, 323–33. New York: Harper & Brothers, 1959.

————. "The New Evangelicalism." *Park Street Spire*, February 1958, 2–7.

————. *Our Evangelical Faith*. Grand Rapids: Zondervan, 1946.

————. *Our Protestant Heritage*. Grand Rapids: Zondervan, 1938.

————. "Poverty as a Theoretical and Practical Problem of Government in the Writings of Jeremy Bentham and the Marxian Alternative." PhD diss., University of Pittsburgh, 1939.

————. *Power Through Pentecost*. Grand Rapids: Eerdmans, 1959.

————. *Protestant Preaching in Lent*. Grand Rapids: Eerdmans, 1957.

————. "Resurgent Evangelical Leadership." *Christianity Today*, October 10, 1960, 11–15.

————. "The Role of Competition in Marx." MA thesis, University of Pittsburgh, 1934.

————. "The Solution to the Social Question." In *Great Expository Sermons*, edited by Faris D. Whitesell, 163–71. New York: Revell, 1964.

————. *The Spirit of the Living God*. New York: Revell, 1947.

————. *These Religious Affections*. Grand Rapids: Zondervan, 1937.

————. "The Unvoiced Multitudes." In *Evangelical Action! A Report of the Organization of the National Association of Evangelicals for United Action, Compiled and Edited by the Executive Committee*. Boston: United Action Press, 1942. Reprinted in *A New Evangelical Coalition: Early Documents of the National Association of Evangelicals*, edited by Joel A. Carpenter. New York: Garland, 1988, 19–39.

————. *Women Who Made Bible History*. Grand Rapids: Zondervan, 1962.

————. *The Word of the Lord*. Glasgow: Pickering & Inglis, 1951.

Olson, Ann Elizabeth. *A Million for Christ: The Story of Baraca Philathea*. South Hamilton, MA: The Ockenga Institute, 2004.

Orr, J. Edwin. *Campus Aflame: A History of Evangelical Awakenings in Collegiate Communities*. Wheaton: International Awakening Press, 1994.

————. *Good News in Bad Times: Signs of Revival*. Grand Rapids: Zondervan, 1953.

————. *The Light of the Nations: Evangelical Renewal and Advance in the Nineteenth Century*. Grand Rapids: Eerdmans, 1965.

————. "Revival and Social Change." *Fides et Historia*, Spring 1974, 1–12.

———. *The Second Evangelical Awakening in America*. London: Marshall, Morgan & Scott, 1952.

Outler, Albert C., ed. *John Wesley*. New York: Oxford University Press, 1980.

Packer, J. I. "Why I Left." *Christianity Today,* April 5, 1993, 33–36.

Paddon, Eric J. "Modern Mordecai: Billy Graham in the Political Arena, 1948–1980." PhD diss., Ohio University, 1999.

Paine, Stephen W. *"Separation"—Is Separating Evangelicals*. Boston: Fellowship Press, 1951.

Patterson, Bob E. *Makers of the Modern Theological Mind: Carl F. H. Henry*. Waco: Word, 1983.

Pelikan, Jaroslav. *Credo: Historical and Theological Guide to Creeds and Confessions of Faith in the Christian Tradition*. New Haven: Yale University Press, 2003.

———. *Spirit versus Structure: Luther and the Institutions of the Church*. New York: Harper & Row, 1968.

Penning, James M., and Corwin E. Smidt. *Evangelicalism: The Next Generation*. Grand Rapids: Baker Academic, 2002.

Perciaccante, Marianne. *Calling Down Fire*. Albany: State University of New York, 2003.

Pettit, Norman. *The Heart Prepared: Grace and Conversion in Puritan Spiritual Life*. Middletown, CT: Wesleyan University Press, 1989.

Pickering, Ernest D. *The Tragedy of Compromise: The Origin and Impact of the New Evangelicalism*. Greenville, SC: Bob Jones University Press, 1994.

Pierard, Richard V. *The Unequal Yoke: Evangelical Christianity and Political Conservatism*. Philadelphia: Lippincott, 1970.

Poewe, Karla D., ed. *Charismatic Christianity as a Global Culture*. Columbia: University of South Carolina Press, 1994.

Pollack, Norman. *The Populist Response to Industrial America*. New York: W. W. Norton, 1966.

Pollock, John. *Crusades: 20 Years with Billy Graham*. Minneapolis: World Wide Publications, 1969.

Pope, Robert G. *Half-Way Covenant: Church Membership in Puritan New England*. Eugene, OR: Wipf & Stock, 2002.

Postman, Neil. *Amusing Ourselves to Death: Public Discourse in the Age of Show Business*. New York: Penguin, 1985.

———. *Technopoly: The Surrender of Culture to Technology*. New York: Vintage, 1993.

Provenzo, Eugene F., Jr. *Fundamentalism and American Education: The Battle for the Public Schools*. Albany: SUNY Press, 1990.

Quebedeaux, Richard. *The New Charismatics*. New York: Doubleday, 1976.

———. *The Worldly Evangelicals*. San Francisco: Harper & Row, 1978.

———. *The Young Evangelicals*. New York: Harper & Row, 1974.

Raboteau, Albert J. *Canaan Land: A Religious History of African Americans*. New York: Oxford University Press, 2001.

———. *Slave Religion*. New York: Oxford University Press, 1980.

Ramm, Bernard L. *The Evangelical Heritage*. Waco: Word, 1973.

Raschke, Carl. *The Next Reformation: Why Evangelicals Must Embrace Post-modernity*. Grand Rapids: Baker Academic, 2004.

Rawlyk, George A., and Mark A. Noll, eds. *Amazing Grace: Evangelicalism in Australia, Britain, Canada, and the United States*. Grand Rapids: Baker Academic, 1993.

Rice, John R. "God's Power in Scotland." *Sword of the Lord*, May 20, 1955, 1–2.

Riley, William B. *The Perennial Revival*. Philadelphia: Judson, 1933.

Ringenberg, William C. *The Christian College*. 2nd ed. Grand Rapids: Baker Academic, 2006.

———. *Taylor University: The First 125 Years*. Grand Rapids: Eerdmans, 1973.

Robeck, Cecil M., Jr. *The Azusa Street Mission and Revival: The Birth of the Global Pentecostal Movement*. Nashville: Nelson, 2006.

———, ed. *Charismatic Experiences in History*. Peabody, MA: Hendrickson, 1985.

Robert, Dana L. *American Women in Mission: A Social History of Their Thought and Practice*. Macon, GA: Mercer University Press, 1996.

Roberts, Richard Owen. *Revival Literature: An Annotated Bibliography with Biographical and Historical Notices*. Wheaton: Richard Owen Roberts, 1987.

———. *Whitefield in Print*. Wheaton: Richard Owen Roberts, 1988.

Robertson, S. A. "A Description of Pioneer Girls: An International Religious Club Program." PhD diss., Northern Illinois University, 1977.

Rodeheaver, Homer. *Twenty Years with Billy Sunday*. Winona Lake, IN: Rodeheaver Hall-Mack, 1936.

Roe, Earl O., ed. *Dream Big: The Henrietta Mears Story*. Wheaton: Regal, 1991.

Rosell, Garth M. "America's Hour Has Struck." *Christian History & Biography*, Fall 2006, 12–19.

————. "Charles G. Finney: His Place in the Stream of American Evangelical-ism." In *The Evangelical Tradition in America*, edited by Leonard I. Sweet, 131–47. Macon, GA: Mercer University Press, 1997.

————. *Commending the Faith: The Preaching of D. L. Moody*. Peabody, MA: Hendrickson, 1999.

————, ed. *The Evangelical Landscape: Essays on the American Evangelical Tradition*. Grand Rapids: Baker Academic, 1996.

————. "A Godly Heritage." *Contact*, Winter 2007, 26–29.

————. "Grace Under Fire." *Christianity Today*, November 13, 1995, 30–34.

————. "A Speckled Bird: Charles G. Finney's Contribution to Higher Education." *Fides et Historia*, Summer 1993, 55–74.

————, ed. *The Vision Continues: Centennial Papers of Gordon-Conwell Theological Seminary*. South Hamilton, MA: GCTS, 1992.

Rosell, Garth M., and Richard A. G. Dupuis, eds. *The Memoirs of Charles G. Finney: The Complete Restored Text*. Grand Rapids: Zondervan, 1989.

Rosell, Mervin E. *Challenging Youth for Christ*. Grand Rapids: Zondervan, 1945.

————. *Driftwood*. St. Paul: Bruce, 1947.

————. "Remembering Youth for Christ." *Northwestern Pilot*, November 1949, 42–43, 58.

————. "Revival Can Come to Your Town." *Youth for Christ* magazine, special revival issue, October 1950, 51, 76–79.

Rupnow, John. *The Growing of America: 200 Years of U.S. Agriculture*. Atkinson, WI: Johnson Hill, 1975.

Russell, C. Allyn. *Voices of American Fundamentalism*. Philadelphia: Westminster, 1976.

Ryken, Leland. *Worldly Saints: The Puritans as They Really Were*. Grand Rapids: Zondervan, 1990.

Ryrie, Alec. *The Gospel and Henry VIII: Evangelicals in the Early English Reformation*. Cambridge: Cambridge University Press, 2003.

Sandeen, Ernest R. *The Roots of Fundamentalism: British and American Millenarianism, 1800–1930*. Chicago: University of Chicago Press, 1970.

Sanders, Cheryl J. *Saints in Exile: The Holiness-Pentecostal Experience in African American Religion and Culture*. New York: Oxford University Press, 1999.

Sanneh, Lamin. *Abolitionists Abroad: American Blacks and the Making of Modern West Africa*. Cambridge, MA: Harvard University Press, 1999.

————. *Whose Religion Is Christianity? The Gospel Beyond the West*. Grand Rapids: Eerdmans, 2003.

Sattler, Gary R. *God's Glory, Neighbor's Good*. Chicago: Covenant, 1982.

Schaeffer, Edith. *The Tapestry*. Waco: Word, 1981.

Schaeffer, Francis. *The God Who Is There*. Downers Grove, IL: InterVarsity, 1968.

Schaff, Philip, and Henry Wace, eds. *The Seven Ecumenical Councils*. In *A Select Library of Nicene and Post-Nicene Fathers of the Christian Church*. Grand Rapids: Eerdmans, 1971.

Schmidt, Leigh E. *Holy Fairs: Scotland and the Making of American Revivalism*. Grand Rapids: Eerdmans, 2001.

Scott, Kenneth M. *Around the World in Eighty Years*. Franklin, TN: Providence House, 1998.

Selden, William K. *Princeton Theological Seminary: A Narrative History, 1812–1992*. Princeton, NJ: Theological Book Agency, 1992.

Shelley, Bruce. *Evangelicalism in America*. Grand Rapids: Eerdmans, 1967.

———. "The Rise of Evangelical Youth Movements." *Fides et Historia*, January 1986, 47–63.

Shelley, Bruce, and Marshall Shelley. *The Consumer Church*. Downers Grove, IL: InterVarsity, 1992.

Shenk, Wilbert R., ed. *North American Foreign Missions, 1810–1914: Theology, Theory, and Policy*. Grand Rapids: Eerdmans, 2004.

Shibley, Mark A. *Resurgent Evangelicalism in the United States: Mapping Cultural Change Since 1970*. Columbia: University of South Carolina Press, 1996.

Showalter, Nathan D. *The End of a Crusade*. Metuchen, NJ: Scarecrow Press for the ATLA Monograph Series, 1997.

Shuster, Robert D., James Stambaugh, and Ferne Weimer. *Researching Modern Evangelicalism*. New York: Greenwood, 1990.

Sider, Ronald J. *The Scandal of the Evangelical Conscience*. Grand Rapids: Baker Books, 2005.

Sider, Ronald J., and Diane Knippers. *Toward an Evangelical Public Policy*. Grand Rapids: Baker Books, 2005.

Simpson, Alan. *Puritanism in Old and New England*. Chicago: University of Chicago Press, 1955.

Sims, John A. *Missionaries to the Skeptics: Christian Apologists for the Twentieth Century*. Macon, GA: Mercer University Press, 1995.

Sims, Mary W. *The First Twenty-Five Years*. New York: Woman's Press, 1932.

Skinner, Betty Lee. *Daws: A Man Who Trusted God*. Colorado Springs: NavPress, 1993.

Smidt, Corwin E., ed., *Contemporary Evangelical Political Involvement*. Lanham, MD: University Press of America, 1989.

Smith, Christian. *American Evangelicalism: Embattled and Thriving*. Chicago: University of Chicago Press, 1998.

Smith, Oswald. "The Miracle of Youth for Christ in Europe." *Peoples Magazine*, First Quarter, 1949, 10–21.

Smith, Timothy L. "My Rejection of a Cyclical View of 'Great Awakenings.'" *Sociological Analysis* 44 (Summer 1983): 97–102.

———. *Revivalism and Social Reform in Mid-Nineteenth-Century America*. Eugene, OR: Wipf & Stock, 2005.

Smith, Wilbur. *Before I Forget*. Chicago: Moody, 1971.

———. *A Voice for God: The Life of Charles E. Fuller*. Boston: Wilde, 1949.

Snyder, Howard A. *The Divided Flame: Wesleyans and the Charismatic Renewal*. Grand Rapids: Francis Asbury, 1986.

Sobel, Mechal. *Trabelin' On: The Slave Journey to an Afro-Baptist Faith*. Princeton, NJ: Princeton University Press, 1988.

Sparks, Linda. *Institutions of Higher Education: An International Bibliography*. Westport, CT: Greenwood, 1990.

Spener, Philip Jacob. *Pia Desideria*. Philadelphia: Fortress, 1964.

Sproul, R. C. *Getting the Gospel Right: The Tie That Binds Evangelicals Together*. Grand Rapids: Baker Books, 1999.

Stackhouse, John G., Jr. *Canadian Evangelicalism in the Twentieth Century: An Introduction to Its Character*. Toronto: University of Toronto Press, 1993.

———. *Evangelical Ecclesiology: Reality or Illusion?* Grand Rapids: Baker Academic, 2003.

Stanley, Susie C. *Holy Boldness: Women Preachers' Autobiographies and the Sanctified Self*. Nashville: University of Tennessee Press, 2002.

Stark, Rodney. *The Rise of Christianity: How the Obscure, Marginal Jesus Movement Became the Dominant Religious Force in the Western World in a Few Centuries*. San Francisco: HarperSanFrancisco, 1997.

Stein, K. James. *Philipp Jacob Spener: Pietist Patriarch*. Chicago: Covenant, 1982.

Stevick, Daniel. *Beyond Fundamentalism*. Richmond: John Knox, 1964.

Stoeffler, F. Ernest. *Continental Pietism and Early American Christianity*. Grand Rapids: Eerdmans, 1976.

———. *The Rise of Evangelical Pietism*. Leiden: Brill, 1971.

Stokesbury, James L. *A Short History of World War II*. New York: HarperCollins, 2001.

Stone, Jon R. *On the Boundaries of American Evangelicalism: The Postwar Evangelical Coalition*. New York: St. Martin's, 1997.

Stonehouse, Ned B. *J. Gresham Machen: A Biographical Memoir*. Grand Rapids: Eerdmans, 1954.

Stott, John. *Guard the Gospel*. Downers Grove, IL: InterVarsity, 1973.

Stout, Harry S. *The Divine Dramatist*. Grand Rapids: Eerdmans, 1991.

———. *The New England Soul: Preaching and Religious Culture in Colonial New England*. New York: Oxford University Press, 1986.

Strong, Douglas M. *They Walked in the Spirit*. Philadelphia: Westminster, 1997.

Sweeney, Douglas A. *The American Evangelical Story: A History of the Movement*. Grand Rapids: Baker Academic, 2005.

———. *Nathaniel Taylor, New Haven Theology, and the Legacy of Jonathan Edwards*. New York: Oxford University Press, 2003.

Sweet, Leonard I., ed. *The Evangelical Tradition in America*. Macon, GA: Mercer University Press, 1997.

———. "Wise as Serpents, Innocent as Doves: The New Evangelical Historiography." *Journal of the American Academy of Religion* 56 (1988): 397–416.

Sweeting, George. *The Jack Wyrtzen Story*. Grand Rapids: Zondervan, 1960.

Swetland, Kenneth. *Facing Messy Stuff in the Church*. Grand Rapids: Kregel, 2005.

Synan, Vinson. *Century of the Holy Spirit: 100 Years of Pentecostal and Charismatic Renewal, 1901–2001*. Nashville: Thomas Nelson, 2001.

———. *The Holiness-Pentecostal Tradition: Charismatic Movements in the 20th Century*. Grand Rapids: Eerdmans, 1997.

Tennent, Timothy C. *Christianity at the Religious Roundtable*. Grand Rapids: Baker Academic, 2002.

Thorsen, Donald A. D. *The Wesleyan Quadrilateral: Scripture, Tradition, Reason and Experience as a Model of Evangelical Theology*. Grand Rapids: Zondervan, 1990.

Tidball, Derek J. *Who Are the Evangelicals? Tracing the Roots of Today's Movement*. London: Marshall Pickering, 1994.

Tomlinson, Dave. *The Post-Evangelical*. Grand Rapids: Zondervan, 2003.

Tracy, Joseph. *The Great Awakening*. Edinburgh: Banner of Truth, 1997.

Trollinger, William Vance, Jr. *God's Empire: William Bell Riley and Midwestern Fundamentalism*. Madison: University of Wisconsin Press, 1990.

Tucker, Ruth A. *From Jerusalem to Irian Jaya: A Biographical History of Christian Missions*. 2nd ed. Grand Rapids: Zondervan, 2004.

United Evangelical Action, May 4, 1943.

Van Braght, Thieleman J. *The Bloody Theater or Martyrs Mirror*. Scottdale, PA: Herald, 1950.

Van Til, Henry R. *The Calvinistic Concept of Culture*. Foreword by Richard J. Mouw. Grand Rapids: Baker Academic, 2001.

Varhola, Michael J. *Fire and Ice: The Korean War, 1950–1953*. New York: Da Capo, 2000.

Vassady, Bela. *Christ's Church: Evangelical, Catholic, and Reformed*. Grand Rapids: Eerdmans, 1965.

————. *Limping Along: Confessions of a Pilgrim Theologian*. Grand Rapids: Eerdmans, 1985.

Villafane, Eldin, Bruce W. Jackson, Robert A. Evans, and Alice Frazier Evans. *Transforming the City*. Grand Rapids: Eerdmans, 2001.

Wacker, Grant. *Heaven Below: Early Pentecostals and American Culture*. Cambridge, MA: Harvard University Press, 2001.

Walker, Williston. *The Creeds and Platforms of Congregationalism*. New York: Pilgrim, 1991.

Wallace, Charles, Jr., ed. *Susanna Wesley: The Complete Writings*. New York: Oxford University Press, 1997.

Wallis, Jim. *Agenda for Biblical People*. New York: Harper & Row, 1976.

————. *God's Politics: Why the Right Gets It Wrong and the Left Doesn't Get It*. San Francisco: HarperSanFrancisco, 2005.

Walls, Andrew F. *The Missionary Movement in Christian History*. Maryknoll, NY: Orbis, 1996.

Walsh, Arlene M. Sanchez. *Latino Pentecostal Identity: Evangelical Faith, Self, and Society*. New York: Columbia University Press, 2003.

Ward, W. R. *The Protestant Evangelical Awakening*. Cambridge: Cambridge University Press, 1996.

Ware, Norman J. *The Labor Movement in the United States, 1860–1890*. New York: Vintage, 1964.

Warfield, B. B., and William Armstrong, eds. *Centennial Celebration*. Phillipsburg, NJ: P&R, 2001.

Warner, R. Stephen, and Judith G. Wittner, eds. *Gatherings in Diaspora: Religious Communities and the New Immigration*. Philadelphia: Temple University Press, 1998.

Watson, Thomas. *The Doctrine of Repentance*. Edinburgh: Banner of Truth, 1999.

Watt, David Harrington. *A Transforming Faith: Explorations of Twentieth-Century American Evangelicalism*. New Brunswick, NJ: Rutgers University Press, 1991.

Webber, Robert E. *Common Roots: A Call to Evangelical Maturity*. Grand Rapids: Zondervan, 1978.

———. *The Younger Evangelicals: Facing the Challenges of the New World*. Grand Rapids: Baker Books, 2002.

Weber, Timothy P. *Living in the Shadow of the Second Coming: American Premillennialism, 1875–1925*. Chicago: University of Chicago Press, 1987.

———. *On the Road to Armageddon: How Evangelicals Became Israel's Best Friend*. Grand Rapids: Baker Academic, 2004.

Weisberger, Bernard A. *They Gathered at the River: The Story of the Great Revivalists and Their Impact on Religion in America*. Chicago: Quadrangle, 1966.

Wells, David F. *Above All Earthly Powers: Christ in a Postmodern World*. Grand Rapids: Eerdmans, 2005.

———. *The Bleeding of the Evangelical Church*. Edinburgh: Banner of Truth, 1995.

———. *God in the Wasteland*. Grand Rapids: Eerdmans, 1994.

———. *Losing Our Virtue*. Grand Rapids: Eerdmans, 1999.

———. *No Place for Truth*. Grand Rapids: Eerdmans, 1993.

———, ed. *Reformed Theology in America: A History of Its Modern Development*. Grand Rapids: Eerdmans, 1985.

———. *Revolution in Rome*. Downers Grove, IL: InterVarsity, 1972.

Wells, David F., and John Woodbridge. *The Evangelicals*. Grand Rapids: Baker Academic, 1977.

Wells, Robert J., and John R. Rice, eds. *How to Have a Revival*. Wheaton: Sword of the Lord, 1946.

Wesley, John. *A Plain Account of Christian Perfection*. London: Epworth, 1952.

Westminster Alumni Annals 6, no. 1 (January 1936): 8.

White, Ronald C., and C. Howard Hopkins. *Social Gospel: Religion and Reform in a Changing America*. Philadelphia: Temple University Press, 1975.

White, Ronald C., Louis B. Weeks, and Garth M. Rosell, eds. *American Christianity: A Case Approach*. Grand Rapids: Eerdmans, 1986.

Whitefield, George. *George Whitefield's Journals*. Edinburgh: Banner of Truth, 1998.

———. *Letters of George Whitefield: For the Period 1734–1742*. Edinburgh: Banner of Truth, 1976.

Wiebe, Robert H. *The Search for Order, 1877–1920*. New York: Hill and Wang, 1967.

Wigger, John H. *Taking Heaven by Storm: Methodism and the Rise of Popular Christianity in America*. New York: Oxford University Press, 1998.

Wilberforce, William. *A Practical View of Christianity*. Edited by Kevin C. Belmonte with a foreword by Garth M. Rosell and an introduction by Charles Colson. Peabody, MA: Hendrickson, 1996.

Williams, Benjamin W. *The Old South Chapel Prayer Meeting: Its Origin and History; with Interesting Narratives, and Instances of Remarkable Conversions in Answer to Prayer*. Boston: Tilton, 1859.

Willmer, Wesley K., J. David Schmidt, and Martyn Smith. *The Prospering Parachurch: Enlarging the Boundaries of God's Kingdom*. San Francisco: Jossey-Bass, 1998.

Wills, Gary. *Under God: Religion and American Politics*. New York: Simon and Schuster, 1990.

Wills, Gregory A. *Democratic Religion: Freedom, Authority, and Church Discipline in the Southern Baptist South, 1785–1900*. New York: Oxford University Press, 1997.

Wilmore, Gayraud S. *Black Religion and Black Radicalism: An Interpretation of the Religious History of African Americans*. Maryknoll, NY: Orbis, 1998.

Wilson, Grady. *Billy Graham as a Teen-Ager*. Wheaton: Miracle Books, 1957.

Winslow, Edward. *Good Newes from New England*. New Bedford, MA: Applewood, n.d.

Winslow, Ola. *John Eliot: "Apostle to the Indians."* Boston: Houghton Mifflin, 1968.

Wirt, Sherwood. *The Social Conscience of the Evangelical*. New York: Harper & Row, 1968.

Wood, Arthur Skevington. *The Burning Heart: John Wesley, Evangelist*. Grand Rapids: Eerdmans, 1967.

Woodbridge, Charles. *The New Evangelicalism*. Greenville, SC: Bob Jones University Press, 1969.

Woods, C. Stacey. *The Growth of a Work of God*. Downers Grove, IL: InterVarsity, 1978.

Workman, Herbert B. *Persecution in the Early Church*. London: Charles Kelly, 1906.

Wright, Conrad E. *The Beginnings of Unitarianism*. North Haven, CT: Archon, 1976.

Wright, G. Frederick. *Charles Grandison Finney: America's Religious Leader*. Salem, OH: Schmul, 1996.

Wright, J. Elwin. *The Baptism of the Holy Ghost and Its Relation to Speaking in Tongues*. Rumney, NH: First Fruit Harvesters Association, 1922.

———. *The Old Fashioned Revival Hour and the Broadcasters.* Boston: Fellowship Press, 1940.

Wuthnow, Robert. *The Restructuring of American Religion.* Princeton, NJ: Princeton University Press, 1988.

———. *The Struggle for America's Soul: Evangelicals, Liberals, and Secularism.* Grand Rapids: Eerdmans, 1989.

Wyma, Mel. "A World To Reach." *Brown Gold* 49, no. 9 (January–February 1992): 3–5.

Youth for Christ magazine, special revival issue, October 1950, 8–79.

Youth for Christ News-Bulletin 1, no. 3 (August 1950): 1.

Index